UNCTAD/DITE/4(Vol. XI)

United Nations Conference on Trade and Development
Division on Investment, Technology and Enterprise Development

International Investment Instruments: A Compendium

Volume XI

United Nations
New York and Geneva, 2003

Note

UNCTAD serves as the focal point within the United Nations Secretariat for all matters related to foreign direct investment and transnational corporations. In the past, the Programme on Transnational Corporations was carried out by the United Nations Centre on Transnational Corporations (1975-1992) and the Transnational Corporations and Management Division of the United Nations Department of Economic and Social Development (1992-1993). In 1993, the Programme was transferred to the United Nations Conference on Trade and Development. UNCTAD seeks to further the understanding of the nature of transnational corporations and their contribution to development and to create an enabling environment for international investment and enterprise development. UNCTAD's work is carried out through intergovernmental deliberations, technical assistance activities, seminars, workshops and conferences.

The term "country", as used in the boxes added by the UNCTAD secretariat at the beginning of the instruments reproduced in this volume, also refers, as appropriate, to territories or areas; the designations employed and the presentation of the material do not imply the expression of any opinion whatsoever on the part of the Secretariat of the United Nations concerning the legal status of any country, territory, city or area or of its authorities, or concerning the delimitation of its frontiers or boundaries. Moreover, the country or geographical terminology used in the boxes may occasionally depart from standard United Nations practice when this is made necessary by the nomenclature used at the time of negotiation, signature, ratification or accession of a given international instrument.

To preserve the integrity of the texts of the instruments reproduced in this volume, references to the sources of the instruments that are not contained in their original text are identified as "note added by the editor".

The texts of the instruments included in this volume are reproduced as they were written in one of their original languages or as an official translation thereof. When an obvious linguistic mistake has been found, the word "sic" has been added in brackets.

The materials contained in this volume have been reprinted with special permission of the relevant institutions. For those materials under copyright protection, all rights are reserved by the copyright holders.

It should be further noted that this collection of instruments has been prepared for documentation purposes only, and its contents do not engage the responsibility of UNCTAD.

UNCTAD/DITE/4 Vol. XI

UNITED NATIONS
PUBLICATION

Sales No. E.04.II.D.9

ISBN 92-1-112616-9

PREFACE

International Investment Instruments: A Compendium contains a collection of international instruments relating to foreign direct investment (FDI) and transnational corporations (TNCs). The collection is presented in twelve volumes. The first three volumes were published in 1996. *Volumes IV* and *V* were published in 2000 followed by *Volume VI* in 2001. Four volumes -- VII, VIII IX and X were published in 2002 bringing the collection up to date. The present publication comprises *volumes XI* and *XII*.

The collection has been prepared to make the texts of international investment instruments conveniently available to interested policy-makers, scholars and business executives. The need for such a collection has increased in recent years as bilateral, regional, interregional and multilateral instruments dealing with various aspects of FDI have proliferated, and as new investment instruments are being negotiated or discussed at all levels.

While by necessity selective, the *Compendium* seeks to provide a faithful record of the evolution and present status of intergovernmental cooperation concerning FDI and TNCs. Although the emphasis of the collection is on relatively recent documents (the majority of the instruments reproduced date from after 1990), it was deemed useful to include important older instruments as well, with a view towards providing some indications of the historical development of international concerns over FDI in the decades since the end of the Second World War.

The core of this collection consists of legally binding international instruments, mainly multilateral conventions, regional agreements, and bilateral treaties that have entered into force. In addition, a number of "soft law" documents, such as guidelines, declarations and resolutions adopted by intergovernmental bodies, have been included since these instruments also play a role in the elaboration of an international framework for FDI. In an effort to enhance the understanding of the efforts behind the elaboration of this framework, certain draft instruments that never entered into force, or texts of instruments on which the negotiations were not concluded, are also included; prototypes of bilateral investment treaties are reproduced as well. Included also are a number of influential documents prepared by business, consumer and labour organizations, as well as by other non-governmental organizations. It is clear from the foregoing that no implications concerning the legal status or the legal effect of an instrument can be drawn from its inclusion in this collection.

In view of the great diversity of the instruments in this *Compendium* -- in terms of subject matter, approach, legal form and extent of participation of States -- the simplest possible method of presentation was deemed the most appropriate. With regard to previous volumes, the structure and content are indicated in the table of content which is included below (see pp. ix-xxxviii). As far as volumes XI and XII are concerned relevant instruments are distributed as follows:

Volume XI is divided into the following three parts:

- Part One contains additional multilateral instruments.

- Part Two covers additional interregional and regional instruments, including agreements and other texts from regional organizations with an inclusive geographical context.

- Part Three reproduces investment-related provisions in a number of additional free trade, economic integration and cooperation agreements not covered in previous volumes.

Volume XII is divided into the following two parts:

- Part One reproduces investment-related provisions in a number of additional free trade, economic integration and cooperation agreements not covered in previous volumes.

- Part Two contains the texts of a number of additional prototype BITs not covered in previous volumes.

Within each of these subdivisions and in previous volumes, instruments are reproduced in chronological order, except for the sections dedicated to prototype instruments.

The multilateral and regional instruments covered are widely differing in scope and coverage. Some are designed to provide an overall, general framework for FDI and cover many, although rarely all, aspects of investment operations. Most instruments deal with particular aspects and issues concerning FDI. A significant number address core FDI issues, such as the promotion and protection of investment, investment liberalization, dispute settlement and insurance and guarantees. Others cover specific issues, of direct but not exclusive relevance to FDI and TNCs, such as transfer of technology, intellectual property, avoidance of double taxation, competition and the protection of consumers and the environment. A relatively small number of instruments of this last category has been reproduced, since each of these specific issues often constitutes an entire system of legal regulation of its own, whose proper coverage would require an extended exposition of many kinds of instruments and arrangements.[a]

The *Compendium* is meant to be a collection of instruments, not an anthology of relevant provisions. Indeed, to understand a particular instrument, it is normally necessary to take its entire text into consideration. An effort has been made, therefore, to reproduce complete instruments, even though, in a number of cases, reasons of space and relevance have dictated the inclusion of excerpts.

The UNCTAD secretariat has deliberately refrained from adding its own commentary to the texts reproduced in the *Compendium*. The only exception to this rule is the boxes added to each instrument. They provide some basic facts, such as its date of adoption and date of entry into force and, where appropriate, signatory countries. Also, a list of agreements containing investment-related provisions signed by the EFTA countries and by the EC countries with third countries or regional groups are reproduced in the *Compendium*. Moreover, to facilitate the identification of each instrument in the table of contents, additional information has been added, in brackets, next to each title, on the year of its signature and the name of the relevant institution involved.

R Ricupero

Rubens Ricupero
Secretary-General of UNCTAD

Geneva, December 2003

---

[a] For a collection of instruments (or excerpts therefrom) dealing with transfer of technology, see UNCTAD, *Compendium of International Arrangements on Transfer of Technology: Selected Instruments* (Geneva: United Nations), United Nations publication, Sales No. E.01.II.D.28.

ACKNOWLEDGEMENTS

Volumes XI and XII of the *Compendium* were prepared by Abraham Negash under the overall direction of Karl P. Sauvant. Comments and inputs were received from Torbjorn Fredriksson, Sumru Inal, Maryse Robert, Michael D. Urminsky and Dimitri Vlassis. The cooperation of the relevant countries and organizations from which the relevant instruments originate is acknowledged with gratitude.

VOLUME XI

VOLUME XI

PART ONE

MULTILATERAL INSTRUMENTS

PART TWO

REGIONAL AND INTERREGIONAL INSTRUMENTS

PART THREE

BILATERAL INSTRUMENTS

CONTENTS OF OTHER VOLUMES

VOLUME I

MULTILATERAL INSTRUMENTS

VOLUME II

REGIONAL INSTRUMENTS

VOLUME III

REGIONAL INTEGRATION, BILATERAL AND NON-GOVERNMENTAL INSTRUMENTS

ANNEX A.   INVESTMENT-RELATED PROVISIONS IN FREE TRADE AND REGIONAL ECONOMIC INTEGRATION INSTRUMENTS

ANNEX C.   NON-GOVERNMENTAL INSTRUMENTS

VOLUME IV

MULTILATERAL AND REGIONAL INSTRUMENTS

VOLUME V

REGIONAL INTEGRATION, BILATERAL AND NON-GOVERNMENTAL INSTRUMENTS

PART ONE

INVESTMENT-RELATED PROVISIONS IN FREE TRADE AND ECONOMIC INTEGRATION AGREEMENTS

PART TWO

INVESTMENT-RELATED PROVISIONS IN ASSOCIATION AGREEMENTS, BILATERAL AND INTERREGIONAL COOPERATION AGREEMENTS

ANNEX A. INVESTMENT-RELATED PROVISIONS IN FREE TRADE AGREEMENTS SIGNED BETWEEN THE COUNTRIES MEMBERS OF THE EUROPEAN FREE TRADE ASSOCIATION AND THIRD COUNTRIES AND LIST OF AGREEMENTS SIGNED (END-1999)

ANNEX B. INVESTMENT-RELATED PROVISIONS IN ASSOCIATION, PARTNERSHIP AND COOPERATION AGREEMENTS SIGNED BETWEEN THE COUNTRIES MEMBERS OF THE EUROPEAN COMMUNITY AND THIRD COUNTRIESAND LIST OF AGREEMENTS SIGNED (END-1999)

ANNEX C. OTHER BILATERAL INVESTMENT-RELATED AGREEMENTS

PART THREE

PROTOTYPE BILATERAL INVESTMENT TREATIES
AND LIST OF BILATERAL INVESTMENT TREATIES
(MID-1995 — END-1998)

PART FOUR

NON-GOVERNMENTAL INSTRUMENTS

VOLUME VI

PART ONE

MULTILATERAL INSTRUMENTS

PART TWO

INTERREGIONAL AND REGIONAL INSTRUMENTS

PART THREE

INVESTMENT-RELATED PROVISIONS IN FREE TRADE AND ECONOMIC INTEGRATION AGREEMENTS

PART FOUR

INVESTMENT-RELATED PROVISIONS IN ASSOCIATION AGREEMENTS, BILATERAL AND INTERREGIONAL COOPERATION AGREEMENTS

PART FIVE

PROTOTYPE BILATERAL INVESTMENT TREATIES

PART SIX

PROTOTYPE BILATERAL DOUBLE TAXATION TREATIES

VOLUME VII

PART ONE

MULTILATERAL INSTRUMENTS

PART TWO

BILATERAL INSTRUMENTS

PART THREE

PROTOTYPE INSTRUMENTS

VOLUME VIII

PART ONE

INTERREGIONAL AND REGIONAL INSTRUMENTS

PART TWO

BILATERAL INSTRUMENTS

PART THREE

PROTOTYPE INSTRUMENTS

VOLUME IX

PART ONE

INTERREGIONAL AND REGIONAL INSTRUMENTS

PART TWO

BILATERAL INSTRUMENTS

PART THREE

PROTOTYPE INSTRUMENTS

VOLUME X

PART ONE

BILATERAL INSTRUMENTS

PART TWO

PROTOTYPE INSTRUMENTS

VOLUME XII

PART ONE

BILATERAL INSTRUMENTS

PART TWO

PROTOTYPE INSTRUMENTS

PART ONE

MULTILATERAL INSTRUMENTS

INTERNATIONAL LABOUR ORGANIZATION TRIPARTITE DECLARATION OF PRINCIPLES CONCERNING MULTINATIONAL ENTERPRISES AND SOCIAL POLICY[*]

INTERNATIONAL LABOUR ORGANIZATION

> The International Labour Organization Tripartite Declaration of Principles Concerning Multinational Enterprises and Social Policy was adopted by the Governing Body of the International Labour Office at its 204th Session held in Geneva in November 1977 and was amended at its 279th Session held in Geneva on 17 November 2000. The amendment took effect upon its publication in the ILO's Official Bulletin in 2000. The Procedure for the examination of disputes concerning the application of the Tripartite Declaration of Principles concerning Multinational Enterprises and Social Policy by means of interpretation of its provisions was adopted by the Governing Body of the International Labour Organization at its 232nd session in Geneva in March 1986 to replace Part IV of the Procedures adopted by the Governing Body at its 214th session (November 1980). "Addendum II to the Tripartite Declaration of Principles Concerning Multinational Enterprises and Social Policy: References to Conventions and Recommendations in the Tripartite Declaration of Principles Concerning Multinational Enterprises and Social Policy" was adopted by the Governing Body of the International Labour Office at its 277th Session (Geneva, March 2000), replacing the Addendum that was first adopted in November 1987 and amended in November 1995.

The Governing Body of the International Labour Office:

Recalling that the International Labour Organization for many years has been involved with certain social issues related to the activities of multinational enterprises;

Noting in particular that various Industrial Committees, Regional Conferences, and the International Labour Conference since the mid-1960s have requested appropriate action by the Governing Body in the field of multinational enterprises and social policy;

Having been informed of the activities of other international bodies, in particular the UN Commission on Transnational Corporations and the Organization for Economic Cooperation and Development (OECD);

Considering that the ILO, with its unique tripartite structure, its competence, and its long-standing experience in the social field, has an essential role to play in evolving principles for the guidance of governments, workers' and employers' organizations, and multinational enterprises themselves;

Recalling that it convened a Tripartite Meeting of Experts on the Relationship between Multinational Enterprises and Social Policy in 1972, which recommended an ILO programme of

---

[*] *Source*: International Labour Organization (2001). "International Labour Organization Tripartite Declaration of Principles Concerning Multinational Enterprises and Social Policy", (International Labour Office: Geneva) *Official Bulletin*, Vol. LXXXIII, 2000, Series A, No. 3.

research and study, and a Tripartite Advisory Meeting on the Relationship of Multinational Enterprises and Social Policy in 1976 for the purpose of reviewing the ILO programme of research and suggesting appropriate ILO action in the social and labour field;

Bearing in mind the deliberations of the World Employment Conference;

Having thereafter decided to establish a tripartite group to prepare a Draft Tripartite Declaration of Principles covering all of the areas of ILO concern which relate to the social aspects of the activities of multinational enterprises, including employment creation in the developing countries, all the while bearing in mind the recommendations made by the Tripartite Advisory Meeting held in 1976;

Having also decided to reconvene the Tripartite Advisory Meeting to consider the Draft Declaration of Principles as prepared by the tripartite group;

Having considered the Report and the Draft Declaration of Principles submitted to it by the reconvened Tripartite Advisory Meeting;

Hereby approves the following Declaration which may be cited as the Tripartite Declaration of Principles concerning Multinational Enterprises and Social Policy, adopted by the Governing Body of the International Labour Office, and invites governments of States Members of the ILO, the employers' and workers' organizations concerned and the multinational enterprises operating in their territories to observe the principles embodied therein.

1.[**]   Multinational enterprises play an important part in the economies of most countries and in international economic relations. This is of increasing interest to governments as well as to employers and workers and their respective organizations.   Through international direct investment and other means such enterprises can bring substantial benefits to home and host countries by contributing to the more efficient utilization of capital, technology and labour. Within the framework of development policies established by governments, they can also make an important contribution to the promotion of economic and social welfare; to the improvement of living standards and the satisfaction of basic needs; to the creation of employment opportunities, both directly and indirectly; and to the enjoyment of basic human rights, including freedom of association, throughout the world. On the other hand, the advances made by multinational enterprises in organizing their operations beyond the national framework may lead to abuse of concentrations of economic power and to conflicts with national policy objectives and with the interest of the workers. In addition, the complexity of multinational enterprises and the difficulty of clearly perceiving their diverse structures, operations and policies sometimes give rise to concern either in the home or in the host countries, or in both.

2.   The aim of this Tripartite Declaration of Principles is to encourage the positive contribution which multinational enterprises can make to economic and social progress and to minimize and resolve the difficulties to which their various operations may give rise, taking into

---

[**] Paragraphs 1-7, 8, 10, 25, 26, and 52 (formerly paragraph 51) have been the subject of interpretation under the Procedure for the examination of disputes concerning the application of the Tripartite Declaration of Principles concerning Multinational Enterprises and Social Policy. Copies of interpretations are available upon request to the Bureau of Multinational Enterprise Activities, International Labour Office, 4, route des Morillons, CH-1211 Geneva 22, Switzerland, or at http://www.ilo.org.

account the United Nations resolutions advocating the establishment of a New International Economic Order.

3.   This aim will be furthered by appropriate laws and policies, measures and actions adopted by the governments and by cooperation among the governments and the employers' and workers' organizations of all countries.

4.   The principles set out in this Declaration are commended to the governments, the employers' and workers' organizations of home and host countries and to the multinational enterprises themselves.

5.   These principles are intended to guide the governments, the employers' and workers' organizations and the multinational enterprises in taking such measures and actions and adopting such social policies, including those based on the principles laid down in the Constitution and the relevant Conventions and Recommendations of the ILO, as would further social progress.

6.   To serve its purpose this Declaration does not require a precise legal definition of multinational enterprises; this paragraph is designed to facilitate the understanding of the Declaration and not to provide such a definition. Multinational enterprises include enterprises, whether they are of public, mixed or private ownership, which own or control production, distribution, services or other facilities outside the country in which they are based. The degree of autonomy of entities within multinational enterprises in relation to each other varies widely from one such enterprise to another, depending on the nature of the links between such entities and their fields of activity and having regard to the great diversity in the form of ownership, in the size, in the nature and location of the operations of the enterprises concerned. Unless otherwise specified, the term "multinational enterprise" is used in this Declaration to designate the various entities (parent companies or local entities or both or the organization as a whole) according to the distribution of responsibilities among them, in the expectation that they will cooperate and provide assistance to one another as necessary to facilitate observance of the principles laid down in the Declaration.

7.   This Declaration sets out principles in the fields of employment, training, conditions of work and life and industrial relations which governments, employers' and workers' organizations and multinational enterprises are recommended to observe on a voluntary basis; its provisions shall not limit or otherwise affect obligations arising out of ratification of any ILO Convention.

GENERAL POLICIES

8.   All the parties concerned by this Declaration should respect the sovereign rights of States, obey the national laws and regulations, give due consideration to local practices and respect relevant international standards. They should respect the Universal Declaration of Human Rights and the corresponding International Covenants adopted by the General Assembly of the United Nations as well as the Constitution of the International Labour Organization and its principles according to which freedom of expression and association are essential to sustained progress. They should contribute to the realization of the ILO Declaration on Fundamental Principles and Rights and Work and its Follow-up, adopted in 1998. They should also honour commitments which they have freely entered into, in conformity with the national law and accepted international obligations.

9.   Governments which have not yet ratified Conventions Nos. 87, 98, 111, 122, 138 and 182 are urged to do so and in any event to apply, to the greatest extent possible, through their national policies, the principles embodied therein and in Recommendations Nos. 111, 119, 122, 146 and 190[1]. Without prejudice to the obligation of governments to ensure compliance with Conventions they have ratified, in countries in which the Conventions and Recommendations cited in this paragraph are not complied with, all parties should refer to them for guidance in their social policy.

10.   Multinational enterprises should take fully into account established general policy objectives of the countries in which they operate. Their activities should be in harmony with the development priorities and social aims and structure of the country in which they operate. To this effect, consultations should be held between multinational enterprises, the government and, wherever appropriate, the national employers' and workers' organizations concerned.

11.   The principles laid down in this Declaration do not aim at introducing or maintaining inequalities of treatment between multinational and national enterprises. They reflect good practice for all. Multinational and national enterprises, wherever the principles of this Declaration are relevant to both, should be subject to the same expectations in respect of their conduct in general and their social practices in particular.

12.   Governments of home countries should promote good social practice in accordance with this Declaration of Principles, having regard to the social and labour law, regulations and practices in host countries as well as to relevant international standards. Both host and home country governments should be prepared to have consultations with each other, whenever the need arises, on the initiative of either.

EMPLOYMENT

Employment promotion

13.   With a view to stimulating economic growth and development, raising living standards, meeting manpower requirements and overcoming unemployment and underemployment, governments should declare and pursue, as a major goal, an active policy designed to promote full, productive and freely chosen employment.[2]

14.   This is particularly important in the case of host country governments in developing areas of the world where the problems of unemployment and underemployment are at their most serious. In this connection, the general conclusions adopted by the Tripartite World Conference

---

[1] Convention (No. 87) concerning Freedom of Association and Protection of the Right to Organise; Convention (No. 98) concerning the Application of the Principles of the Right to Organise and to Bargain Collectively; Convention (No. 111) concerning Discrimination in Respect of Employment and Occupation; Convention (No. 122) concerning Employment Policy; Convention (No. 138) concerning Minimum Age for Admission to Employment; Convention (No. 182) concerning the Prohibition and Immediate Action for the Elimination of the Worst Forms of Child Labour; Recommendation (No. 111) concerning Discrimination in Respect of Employment and Occupation; Recommendation (No. 119) concerning Termination of Employment at the Initiative of the Employer; Recommendation (No. 122) concerning Employment Policy; Recommendation (No. 146) concerning Minimum Age for Admission to Employment; Recommendation (No. 190) concerning the Prohibition and Immediate Action for the Elimination of the Worst Forms of Child Labour.

[2] Convention (No. 122) and Recommendation (No. 122) concerning Employment Policy.

on Employment, Income Distribution and Social Progress and the International Division of Labour (Geneva, June 1976) should be kept in mind.[3]

15.   Paragraphs 13 and 14 above establish the framework within which due attention should be paid, in both home and host countries, to the employment impact of multinational enterprises.

16.   Multinational enterprises, particularly when operating in developing countries, should endeavour to increase employment opportunities and standards, taking into account the employment policies and objectives of the governments, as well as security of employment and the long-term development of the enterprise.

17.   Before starting operations, multinational enterprises should, wherever appropriate, consult the competent authorities and the national employers' and workers' organizations in order to keep their manpower plans, as far as practicable, in harmony with national social development policies. Such consultation, as in the case of national enterprises, should continue between the multinational enterprises and all parties concerned, including the workers' organizations.

18.   Multinational enterprises should give priority to the employment, occupational development, promotion and advancement of nationals of the host country at all levels in cooperation, as appropriate, with representatives of the workers employed by them or of the organizations of these workers and governmental authorities.

19.   Multinational enterprises, when investing in developing countries, should have regard to the importance of using technologies which generate employment, both directly and indirectly. To the extent permitted by the nature of the process and the conditions prevailing in the economic sector concerned, they should adapt technologies to the needs and characteristics of the host countries. They should also, where possible, take part in the development of appropriate technology in host countries.

20.   To promote employment in developing countries, in the context of an expanding world economy, multinational enterprises, wherever practicable, should give consideration to the conclusion of contracts with national enterprises for the manufacture of parts and equipment, to the use of local raw materials and to the progressive promotion of the local processing of raw materials. Such arrangements should not be used by multinational enterprises to avoid the responsibilities embodied in the principles of this Declaration.

Equality of opportunity and treatment

21.   All governments should pursue policies designed to promote equality of opportunity and treatment in employment, with a view to eliminating any discrimination based on race, colour, sex, religion, political opinion, national extraction or social origin.[4]

22.   Multinational enterprises should be guided by this general principle throughout their operations without prejudice to the measures envisaged in paragraph 18 or to government policies designed to correct historical patterns of discrimination and thereby to extend equality of opportunity and treatment in employment. Multinational enterprises should accordingly make

---

[3] ILO, World Employment Conference, Geneva, 4-17 June 1976.
[4] Convention (No. 111) and Recommendation (No. 111) concerning Discrimination in Respect of Employment and Occupation; Convention (No. 100) and Recommendation (No. 90) concerning Equal Remuneration for Men and Women Workers for Work of Equal Value.

qualifications, skill and experience the basis for the recruitment, placement, training and advancement of their staff at all levels.

23.   Governments should never require or encourage multinational enterprises to discriminate on any of the grounds mentioned in paragraph 21, and continuing guidance from governments, where appropriate, on the avoidance of such discrimination in employment is encouraged.

Security of employment

24.   Governments should carefully study the impact of multinational enterprises on employment in different industrial sectors. Governments, as well as multinational enterprises themselves, in all countries should take suitable measures to deal with the employment and labour market impacts of the operations of multinational enterprises.

25.   Multinational enterprises equally with national enterprises, through active manpower planning, should endeavour to provide stable employment for their employees and should observe freely negotiated obligations concerning employment stability and social security. In view of the flexibility which multinational enterprises may have, they should strive to assume a leading role in promoting security of employment, particularly in countries where the discontinuation of operations is likely to accentuate long-term unemployment.

26.   In considering changes in operations (including those resulting from mergers, take-overs or transfers of production) which would have major employment effects, multinational enterprises should provide reasonable notice of such changes to the appropriate government authorities and representatives of the workers in their employment and their organizations so that the implications may be examined jointly in order to mitigate adverse effects to the greatest possible extent. This is particularly important in the case of the closure of an entity involving collective lay-offs or dismissals.

27.   Arbitrary dismissal procedures should be avoided.[5]

28.   Governments, in cooperation with multinational as well as national enterprises, should provide some form of income protection for workers whose employment has been terminated.[6]

TRAINING

29.   Governments, in cooperation with all the parties concerned, should develop national policies for vocational training and guidance, closely linked with employment.[7] This is the framework within which multinational enterprises should pursue their training policies.

30.   In their operations, multinational enterprises should ensure that relevant training is provided for all levels of their employees in the host country, as appropriate, to meet the needs of the enterprise as well as the development policies of the country. Such training should, to the extent possible, develop generally useful skills and promote career opportunities. This responsibility should be carried out, where appropriate, in cooperation with the authorities of the

---

[5] Recommendation (No. 119) concerning Termination of Employment at the Initiative of the Employer.
[6] ibid.
[7] Convention (No. 142) and Recommendation (No. 150) concerning Vocational Guidance and Vocational Training in the Development of Human Resources.

country, employers' and workers' organizations and the competent local, national or international institutions.

31.   Multinational enterprises operating in developing countries should participate, along with national enterprises, in programmes, including special funds, encouraged by host governments and supported by employers' and workers' organizations. These programmes should have the aim of encouraging skill formation and development as well as providing vocational guidance, and should be jointly administered by the parties which support them. Wherever practicable, multinational enterprises should make the services of skilled resource personnel available to help in training programmes organized by governments as part of a contribution to national development.

32.   Multinational enterprises, with the cooperation of governments and to the extent consistent with the efficient operation of the enterprise, should afford opportunities within the enterprise as a whole to broaden the experience of local management in suitable fields such as industrial relations.

CONDITIONS OF WORK AND LIFE

Wages, benefits and conditions of work

33.   Wages, benefits and conditions of work offered by multinational enterprises should be not less favourable to the workers than those offered by comparable employers in the country concerned.

34.   When multinational enterprises operate in developing countries, where comparable employers may not exist, they should provide the best possible wages, benefits and conditions of work, within the framework of government policies.[8] These should be related to the economic position of the enterprise, but should be at least adequate to satisfy basic needs of the workers and their families. Where they provide workers with basic amenities such as housing, medical care or food, these amenities should be of a good standard.[9]

35.   Governments, especially in developing countries, should endeavour to adopt suitable measures to ensure that lower income groups and less developed areas benefit as much as possible from the activities of multinational enterprises.

Minimum age

36.   Multinational enterprises, as well as national enterprises, should respect the minimum age for admission to employment or work in order to secure the effective abolition of child labour.[10]

---

[8] Recommendation (No. 116) concerning Reduction of Hours of Work.
[9] Convention (No. 110) and Recommendation (No. 110) concerning Conditions of Employment of Plantation Workers; Recommendation (No. 115) concerning Workers' Housing; Recommendation (No. 69) concerning Medical Care; Convention (No. 130) and Recommendation (No. 134) concerning Medical Care and Sickness Benefits.
[10] Convention No. 138, Article 1; Convention No. 182, Article 1.

Safety and health

37.   Governments should ensure that both multinational and national enterprises provide adequate safety and health standards for their employees. Those governments which have not yet ratified the ILO Conventions on Guarding of Machinery (No. 119), Ionising Radiation (No. 115), Benzene (No. 136) and Occupational Cancer (No. 139) are urged nevertheless to apply to the greatest extent possible the principles embodied in these Conventions and in their related Recommendations (Nos. 118, 114, 144 and 147). The codes of practice and guides in the current list of ILO publications on occupational safety and health should also be taken into account.[11]

38.   Multinational enterprises should maintain the highest standards of safety and health, in conformity with national requirements, bearing in mind their relevant experience within the enterprise as a whole, including any knowledge of special hazards. They should also make available to the representatives of the workers in the enterprise, and upon request, to the competent authorities and the workers' and employers' organizations in all countries in which they operate, information on the safety and health standards relevant to their local operations, which they observe in other countries. In particular, they should make known to those concerned any special hazards and related protective measures associated with new products and processes. They, like comparable domestic enterprises, should be expected to play a leading role in the examination of causes of industrial safety and health hazards and in the application of resulting improvements within the enterprise as a whole.

39.   Multinational enterprises should cooperate in the work of international organizations concerned with the preparation and adoption of international safety and health standards.

40.   In accordance with national practice, multinational enterprises should cooperate fully with the competent safety and health authorities, the representatives of the workers and their organizations, and established safety and health organizations. Where appropriate, matters relating to safety and health should be incorporated in agreements with the representatives of the workers and their organizations.

INDUSTRIAL RELATIONS

41.   Multinational enterprises should observe standards of industrial relations not less favourable than those observed by comparable employers in the country concerned.

Freedom of association and the right to organize

42.   Workers employed by multinational enterprises as well as those employed by national enterprises should, without distinction whatsoever, have the right to establish and, subject only to the rules of the organization concerned, to join organizations of their own choosing without previous authorisation.[12]   They should also enjoy adequate protection against acts of anti-union discrimination in respect of their employment.[13]

---

[11] The ILO Conventions and Recommendations referred to are listed in the *Catalogue of ILO Publications on Occupational   Safety   and   Health*,   ed.   1999,   ILO,   Geneva.   See   also <http://www.ilo.org/public/english/protection/safework/publicat/index.htm>.

[12] Convention No. 87, Article 2.

[13] Convention No. 98, Article 1(1).

43.   Organizations representing multinational enterprises or the workers in their employment should enjoy adequate protection against any acts of interference by each other or each other's agents or members in their establishment, functioning or administration.[14]

44.   Where appropriate, in the local circumstances, multinational enterprises should support representative employers' organizations.

45.   Governments, where they do not already do so, are urged to apply the principles of Convention No. 87, Article 5, in view of the importance, in relation to multinational enterprises, of permitting organizations representing such enterprises or the workers in their employment to affiliate with international organizations of employers and workers of their own choosing.

46.   Where governments of host countries offer special incentives to attract foreign investment, these incentives should not include any limitation of the workers' freedom of association or the right to organize and bargain collectively.

47.   Representatives of the workers in multinational enterprises should not be hindered from meeting for consultation and exchange of views among themselves, provided that the functioning of the operations of the enterprise and the normal procedures which govern relationships with representatives of the workers and their organizations are not thereby prejudiced.

48.   Governments should not restrict the entry of representatives of employers' and workers' organizations who come from other countries at the invitation of the local or national organizations concerned for the purpose of consultation on matters of mutual concern, solely on the grounds that they seek entry in that capacity.

Collective bargaining

49.   Workers employed by multinational enterprises should have the right, in accordance with national law and practice, to have representative organizations of their own choosing recognized for the purpose of collective bargaining.

50.   Measures appropriate to national conditions should be taken, where necessary, to encourage and promote the full development and utilization of machinery for voluntary negotiation between employers or employers' organizations and workers' organizations, with a view to the regulation of terms and conditions of employment by means of collective agreements.[15]

51.   Multinational enterprises, as well as national enterprises, should provide workers' representatives with such facilities as may be necessary to assist in the development of effective collective agreements.[16]

52.** Multinational enterprises should enable duly authorized representatives of the workers in their employment in each of the countries in which they operate to conduct negotiations with representatives of management who are authorized to take decisions on the matters under negotiation.

---

[14] Convention No. 98, Article 2(1).
[15] Convention No. 98, Article 4.
[16] Convention (No. 135) concerning Protection and Facilities to be Afforded to Workers' Representatives in the Undertaking.

53.   Multinational enterprises, in the context of bona fide negotiations with the workers' representatives on conditions of employment, or while workers are exercising the right to organize, should not threaten to utilize a capacity to transfer the whole or part of an operating unit from the country concerned in order to influence unfairly those negotiations or to hinder the exercise of the right to organize; nor should they transfer workers from affiliates in foreign countries with a view to undermining bona fide negotiations with the workers' representatives or the workers' exercise of their right to organize.

54.   Collective agreements should include provisions for the settlement of disputes arising over their interpretation and application and for ensuring mutually respected rights and responsibilities.

55.   Multinational enterprises should provide workers' representatives with information required for meaningful negotiations with the entity involved and, where this accords with local law and practices, should also provide information to enable them to obtain a true and fair view of the performance of the entity or, where appropriate, of the enterprise as a whole.[17]

56.   Governments should supply to the representatives of workers' organizations on request, where law and practice so permit, information on the industries in which the enterprise operates, which would help in laying down objective criteria in the collective bargaining process. In this context, multinational as well as national enterprises should respond constructively to requests by governments for relevant information on their operations.

Consultation

57.   In multinational as well as in national enterprises, systems devised by mutual agreement between employers and workers and their representatives should provide, in accordance with national law and practice, for regular consultation on matters of mutual concern. Such consultation should not be a substitute for collective bargaining.[18]

Examination of grievances

58.   Multinational as well as national enterprises should respect the right of the workers whom they employ to have all their grievances processed in a manner consistent with the following provision: any worker who, acting individually or jointly with other workers, considers that he has grounds for a grievance should have the right to submit such grievance without suffering any prejudice whatsoever as a result, and to have such grievance examined pursuant to an appropriate procedure.[19]   This is particularly important whenever the multinational enterprises operate in countries which do not abide by the principles of ILO Conventions pertaining to freedom of association, to the right to organize and bargain collectively and to forced labour.[20]

---

[17] Recommendation (No. 129) concerning Communications between Management and Workers within the Undertaking.

[18] Recommendation (No. 94) concerning Consultation and Co-operation between Employers and Workers at the Level of Undertaking; Recommendation (No. 129) concerning Communications within the Undertaking.

[19] Recommendation (No. 130) concerning the Examination of Grievances within the Undertaking with a View to Their Settlement.

[20] Convention (No. 29) concerning Forced or Compulsory Labour; Convention (No. 105) concerning the Abolition of Forced Labour; Recommendation (No. 35) concerning Indirect Compulsion to Labour.

Settlement of industrial disputes

59.   Multinational as well as national enterprises jointly with the representatives and organizations of the workers whom they employ should seek to establish voluntary conciliation machinery, appropriate to national conditions, which may include provisions for voluntary arbitration, to assist in the prevention and settlement of industrial disputes between employers and workers. The voluntary conciliation machinery should include equal representation of employers and workers.[21]

*

---

[21] Recommendation (No. 92) concerning Voluntary Conciliation and Arbitration.

UNITED NATIONS CONVENTION AGAINST CORRUPTION[*]

UNITED NATIONS GENERAL ASSEMBLY

Resolution 58/4 of the General Assembly of the United Nations -- Convention against Corruption was adopted at its 58th Session held in New York on 31 October 2003.

The General Assembly,

Recalling its resolution 55/61 of 4 December 2000, in which it established an ad hoc committee for the negotiation of an effective international legal instrument against corruption, and requested the Secretary-General to convene an intergovernmental open-ended expert group to examine and prepare draft terms of reference for the negotiation of such an instrument, and its resolution 55/188 of 20 December 2000, in which it invited the intergovernmental open-ended expert group to be convened pursuant to resolution 55/61 to examine the question of illegally transferred funds and the return of such funds to the countries of origin,

Recalling also its resolutions 56/186 of 21 December 2001 and 57/244 of 20 December 2002 on preventing and combating corrupt practices and transfer of funds of illicit origin and returning such funds to the countries of origin,

Recalling further its resolution 56/260 of 31 January 2002, in which it requested the Ad Hoc Committee for the Negotiation of a Convention against Corruption to complete its work by the end of 2003,

Recalling its resolution 57/169 of 18 December 2002, in which it accepted with appreciation the offer made by the Government of Mexico to host a high-level political conference for the purpose of signing the convention, and requested the Secretary-General to schedule the conference for a period of three days before the end of 2003,

Recalling also Economic and Social Council resolution 2001/13 of 24 July 2001, entitled "Strengthening international cooperation in preventing and combating the transfer of funds of illicit origin, derived from acts of corruption, including the laundering of funds, and in returning such funds",

Expressing its appreciation to the Government of Argentina for hosting the informal preparatory meeting of the Ad Hoc Committee for the Negotiation of a Convention against Corruption in Buenos Aires in December 2001,

Recalling the Monterrey Consensus,[2] adopted by the International Conference on Financing for Development, held in Monterrey, Mexico, from 18 to 22 March 2002, in which it was underlined that fighting corruption at all levels was a priority,

---

[*] *Source*: United Nations (2003). "The United Nations Convention against Corruption", A/58/422, available on the Internet (http://www.unodc.org/pdf/crime/convention_corruption/session_7/422e.pdf). [Note added by the editor].

Recalling also the Johannesburg Declaration on Sustainable Development,[3] adopted by the World Summit on Sustainable Development, held in Johannesburg, South Africa, from 26 August to 4 September 2002, in particular its paragraph 19, in which corruption was declared a threat to the sustainable development of people,

Concerned about the seriousness of problems and threats posed by corruption to the stability and security of societies, undermining the institutions and values of democracy, ethical values and justice and jeopardizing sustainable development and the rule of law,

1.   Takes note of the report of the Ad Hoc Committee for the Negotiation of a Convention against Corruption,[4] which carried out its work at the headquarters of the United Nations Office on Drugs and Crime in Vienna, in which the Ad Hoc Committee submitted the final text of the draft United Nations Convention against Corruption to the General Assembly for its consideration and action, and commends the Ad Hoc Committee for its work;

2.   Adopts the United Nations Convention against Corruption annexed to the present resolution, and opens it for signature at the High-level Political Signing Conference to be held in Merida, Mexico, from 9 to 11 December 2003, in accordance with resolution 57/169;

3.   Urges all States and competent regional economic integration organizations to sign and ratify the United Nations Convention against Corruption as soon as possible in order to ensure its rapid entry into force;

4.   Decides that, until the Conference of the States Parties to the Convention established pursuant to the United Nations Convention against Corruption decides otherwise, the account referred to in article 62 of the Convention will be operated within the United Nations Crime Prevention and Criminal Justice Fund, and encourages Member States to begin making adequate voluntary contributions to the above-mentioned account for the provision to developing countries and countries with economies in transition of the technical assistance that they might require to prepare for ratification and implementation of the Convention;

5.   Also decides that the Ad Hoc Committee for the Negotiation of a Convention against Corruption will complete its tasks arising from the negotiation of the United Nations Convention against Corruption by holding a meeting well before the convening of the first session of the Conference of the States Parties to the Convention in order to prepare the draft text of the rules of procedure for the Conference of the States Parties and of other rules described in article 63 of the Convention, which will be submitted to the Conference of the States Parties at its first session for consideration;

6.   Requests the Conference of the States Parties to the Convention to address the criminalization of bribery of officials of public international organizations, including the United Nations, and related issues, taking into account questions of privileges and immunities, as well as of jurisdiction and the role of international organizations, by, *inter alia*, making recommendations regarding appropriate action in that regard;

---

[2] Report of the International Conference on Financing for Development, Monterrey, Mexico, 18-22 March 2002 (United Nations publication, Sales No. E.02.II.A.7), chap. I, resolution 1, annex.
[3] Report of the World Summit on Sustainable Development, Johannesburg, South Africa, 26 August-4 September 2002 (United Nations publication, Sales No. E.03.II.A.1 and corrigendum), chap. I, resolution 1, annex.
[4] A/58/422.

7.   Decides that, in order to raise awareness of corruption and of the role of the Convention in combating and preventing it, 9 December should be designated International Anti-Corruption Day;

8.   Requests the Secretary-General to designate the United Nations Office on Drugs and Crime to serve as the secretariat for and under the direction of the Conference of the States Parties to the Convention;

9.   Also requests the Secretary-General to provide the United Nations Office on Drugs and Crime with the resources necessary to enable it to promote in an effective manner the rapid entry into force of the United Nations Convention against Corruption and to discharge the functions of secretariat of the Conference of the States Parties to the Convention, and to support the Ad Hoc Committee in its work pursuant to paragraph 5 above;

10.   Further requests the Secretary-General to prepare a comprehensive report on the High-level Political Signing Conference to be held in Merida, Mexico, in accordance with resolution 57/169, for submission to the General Assembly at its fifty-ninth session.

Annex

United Nations Convention against Corruption

Preamble

The States Parties to this Convention,

Concerned about the seriousness of problems and threats posed by corruption to the stability and security of societies, undermining the institutions and values of democracy, ethical values and justice and jeopardizing sustainable development and the rule of law,

Concerned also about the links between corruption and other forms of crime, in particular organized crime and economic crime, including money-laundering,

Concerned further about cases of corruption that involve vast quantities of assets, which may constitute a substantial proportion of the resources of States, and that threaten the political stability and sustainable development of those States,

Convinced that corruption is no longer a local matter but a transnational phenomenon that affects all societies and economies, making international cooperation to prevent and control it essential, Convinced also that a comprehensive and multidisciplinary approach is required to prevent and combat corruption effectively,

Convinced further that the availability of technical assistance can play an important role in enhancing the ability of States, including by strengthening capacity and by institution-building, to prevent and combat corruption effectively,

Convinced that the illicit acquisition of personal wealth can be particularly damaging to democratic institutions, national economies and the rule of law,

Determined to prevent, detect and deter in a more effective manner international transfers of illicitly acquired assets and to strengthen international cooperation in asset recovery,

Acknowledging the fundamental principles of due process of law in criminal proceedings and in civil or administrative proceedings to adjudicate property rights,

Bearing in mind that the prevention and eradication of corruption is a responsibility of all States and that they must cooperate with one another, with the support and involvement of individuals and groups outside the public sector, such as civil society, non-governmental organizations and community-based organizations, if their efforts in this area are to be effective,

Bearing also in mind the principles of proper management of public affairs and public property, fairness, responsibility and equality before the law and the need to safeguard integrity and to foster a culture of rejection of corruption,

Commending the work of the Commission on Crime Prevention and Criminal Justice and the United Nations Office on Drugs and Crime in preventing and combating corruption,

Recalling the work carried out by other international and regional organizations in this field, including the activities of the African Union, the Council of Europe, the Customs Cooperation Council (also known as the World Customs Organization), the European Union, the League of Arab States, the Organisation for Economic Cooperation and Development and the Organization of American States,

Taking note with appreciation of multilateral instruments to prevent and combat corruption, including, *inter alia*, the Inter-American Convention against Corruption, adopted by the Organization of American States on 29 March 1996,[5] the Convention on the Fight against Corruption involving Officials of the European Communities or Officials of Member States of the European Union, adopted by the Council of the European Union on 26 May 1997,[6] the Convention on Combating Bribery of Foreign Public Officials in International Business Transactions, adopted by the Organisation for Economic Cooperation and Development on 21 November 1997,[7] the Criminal Law Convention on Corruption, adopted by the Committee of Ministers of the Council of Europe on 27 January 1999,[8] the Civil Law Convention on Corruption, adopted by the Committee of Ministers of the Council of Europe on 4 November 1999,[9] and the African Union Convention on Preventing and Combating Corruption, adopted by the Heads of State and Government of the African Union on 12 July 2003, Welcoming the entry into force on 29 September 2003 of the United Nations Convention against Transnational Organized Crime,[10]

Have agreed as follows:

---

[5] See E/1996/99.
[6] *Official Journal of the European Communities*, C 195, 25 June 1997.
[7] See *Corruption and Integrity Improvement Initiatives in Developing Countries* (United Nations publication, Sales No. E.98.III.B.18).
[8] Council of Europe, European Treaty Series, No. 173.
[9] Ibid., No. 174.
[10] General Assembly resolution 55/25, annex I.

Chapter I

General provisions

Article 1
Statement of purpose

The purposes of this Convention are:

(a)   To promote and strengthen measures to prevent and combat corruption more efficiently and effectively;

(b)   To promote, facilitate and support international cooperation and technical assistance in the prevention of and fight against corruption, including in asset recovery;

(c)   To promote integrity, accountability and proper management of public affairs and public property.

Article 2
Use of terms

For the purposes of this Convention:

(a)   "Public official" shall mean: (i) any person holding a legislative, executive, administrative or judicial office of a State Party, whether appointed or elected, whether permanent or temporary, whether paid or unpaid, irrespective of that person's seniority; (ii) any other person who performs a public function, including for a public agency or public enterprise, or provides a public service, as defined in the domestic law of the State Party and as applied in the pertinent area of law of that State Party; (iii) any other person defined as a "public official" in the domestic law of a State Party. However, for the purpose of some specific measures contained in chapter II of this Convention, "public official" may mean any person who performs a public function or provides a public service as defined in the domestic law of the State Party and as applied in the pertinent area of law of that State Party;

(b)   "Foreign public official" shall mean any person holding a legislative, executive, administrative or judicial office of a foreign country, whether appointed or elected; and any person exercising a public function for a foreign country, including for a public agency or public enterprise;

(c)   "Official of a public international organization" shall mean an international civil servant or any person who is authorized by such an organization to act on behalf of that organization;

(d) "Property" shall mean assets of every kind, whether corporeal or incorporeal, movable or immovable, tangible or intangible, and legal documents or instruments evidencing title to or interest in such assets;

(e)   "Proceeds of crime" shall mean any property derived from or obtained, directly or indirectly, through the commission of an offence;

(f)   "Freezing" or "seizure" shall mean temporarily prohibiting the transfer, conversion, disposition or movement of property or temporarily assuming custody or control of property on the basis of an order issued by a court or other competent authority;

(g)   "Confiscation", which includes forfeiture where applicable, shall mean the permanent deprivation of property by order of a court or other competent authority;

(h)   "Predicate offence" shall mean any offence as a result of which proceeds have been generated that may become the subject of an offence as defined in article 23 of this Convention;

(i)   "Controlled delivery" shall mean the technique of allowing illicit or suspect consignments to pass out of, through or into the territory of one or more States, with the knowledge and under the supervision of their competent authorities, with a view to the investigation of an offence and the identification of persons involved in the commission of the offence.

Article 3
Scope of application

1.   This Convention shall apply, in accordance with its terms, to the prevention, investigation and prosecution of corruption and to the freezing, seizure, confiscation and return of the proceeds of offences established in accordance with this Convention.

2.   For the purposes of implementing this Convention, it shall not be necessary, except as otherwise stated herein, for the offences set forth in it to result in damage or harm to state property.

Article 4
Protection of sovereignty

1.   States Parties shall carry out their obligations under this Convention in a manner consistent with the principles of sovereign equality and territorial integrity of States and that of non-intervention in the domestic affairs of other States.

2.   Nothing in this Convention shall entitle a State Party to undertake in the territory of another State the exercise of jurisdiction and performance of functions that are reserved exclusively for the authorities of that other State by its domestic law.

Chapter II

Preventive measures
Article 5

Preventive anti-corruption policies and practices

1.   Each State Party shall, in accordance with the fundamental principles of its legal system, develop and implement or maintain effective, coordinated anticorruption policies that promote the participation of society and reflect the principles of the rule of law, proper management of public affairs and public property, integrity, transparency and accountability.

2. Each State Party shall endeavour to establish and promote effective practices aimed at the prevention of corruption.

3. Each State Party shall endeavour to periodically evaluate relevant legal instruments and administrative measures with a view to determining their adequacy to prevent and fight corruption.

4. States Parties shall, as appropriate and in accordance with the fundamental principles of their legal system, collaborate with each other and with relevant international and regional organizations in promoting and developing the measures referred to in this article. That collaboration may include participation in international programmes and projects aimed at the prevention of corruption.

Article 6
Preventive anti-corruption body or bodies

1. Each State Party shall, in accordance with the fundamental principles of its legal system, ensure the existence of a body or bodies, as appropriate, that prevent corruption by such means as:

(a) Implementing the policies referred to in article 5 of this Convention and, where appropriate, overseeing and coordinating the implementation of those policies;

(b) Increasing and disseminating knowledge about the prevention of corruption.

2. Each State Party shall grant the body or bodies referred to in paragraph 1 of this article the necessary independence, in accordance with the fundamental principles of its legal system, to enable the body or bodies to carry out its or their functions effectively and free from any undue influence. The necessary material resources and specialized staff, as well as the training that such staff may require to carry out their functions, should be provided.

3. Each State Party shall inform the Secretary-General of the United Nations of the name and address of the authority or authorities that may assist other States Parties in developing and implementing specific measures for the prevention of corruption.

Article 7
Public sector

1. Each State Party shall, where appropriate and in accordance with the fundamental principles of its legal system, endeavour to adopt, maintain and strengthen systems for the recruitment, hiring, retention, promotion and retirement of civil servants and, where appropriate, other non-elected public officials:

(a) That are based on principles of efficiency, transparency and objective criteria such as merit, equity and aptitude;

(b) That include adequate procedures for the selection and training of individuals for public positions considered especially vulnerable to corruption and the rotation, where appropriate, of such individuals to other positions;

(c)   That promote adequate remuneration and equitable pay scales, taking into account the level of economic development of the State Party;

(d)   That promote education and training programmes to enable them to meet the requirements for the correct, honourable and proper performance of public functions and that provide them with specialized and appropriate training to enhance their awareness of the risks of corruption inherent in the performance of their functions. Such programmes may make reference to codes or standards of conduct in applicable areas.

2.   Each State Party shall also consider adopting appropriate legislative and administrative measures, consistent with the objectives of this Convention and in accordance with the fundamental principles of its domestic law, to prescribe criteria concerning candidature for and election to public office.

3.   Each State Party shall also consider taking appropriate legislative and administrative measures, consistent with the objectives of this Convention and in accordance with the fundamental principles of its domestic law, to enhance transparency in the funding of candidatures for elected public office and, where applicable, the funding of political parties.

4.   Each State Party shall, in accordance with the fundamental principles of its domestic law, endeavour to adopt, maintain and strengthen systems that promote transparency and prevent conflicts of interest.

Article 8
Codes of conduct for public officials

1.   In order to fight corruption, each State Party shall promote, *inter alia*, integrity, honesty and responsibility among its public officials, in accordance with the fundamental principles of its legal system.

2.   In particular, each State Party shall endeavour to apply, within its own institutional and legal systems, codes or standards of conduct for the correct, honourable and proper performance of public functions.

3.   For the purposes of implementing the provisions of this article, each State Party shall, where appropriate and in accordance with the fundamental principles of its legal system, take note of the relevant initiatives of regional, interregional and multilateral organizations, such as the International Code of Conduct for Public Officials contained in the annex to General Assembly resolution 51/59 of 12 December 1996.

4.   Each State Party shall also consider, in accordance with the fundamental principles of its domestic law, establishing measures and systems to facilitate the reporting by public officials of acts of corruption to appropriate authorities, when such acts come to their notice in the performance of their functions.

5.   Each State Party shall endeavour, where appropriate and in accordance with the fundamental principles of its domestic law, to establish measures and systems requiring public officials to make declarations to appropriate authorities regarding, *inter alia*, their outside

activities, employment, investments, assets and substantial gifts or benefits from which a conflict of interest may result with respect to their functions as public officials.

6.   Each State Party shall consider taking, in accordance with the fundamental principles of its domestic law, disciplinary or other measures against public officials who violate the codes or standards established in accordance with this article.

Article 9
Public procurement and management of public finances

1.   Each State Party shall, in accordance with the fundamental principles of its legal system, take the necessary steps to establish appropriate systems of procurement, based on transparency, competition and objective criteria in decision-making, that are effective, *inter alia*, in preventing corruption. Such systems, which may take into account appropriate threshold values in their application, shall address, *inter alia*:

(a)   The public distribution of information relating to procurement procedures and contracts, including information on invitations to tender and relevant or pertinent information on the award of contracts, allowing potential tenderers sufficient time to prepare and submit their tenders;

(b)   The establishment, in advance, of conditions for participation, including selection and award criteria and tendering rules, and their publication;

(c)   The use of objective and predetermined criteria for public procurement decisions, in order to facilitate the subsequent verification of the correct application of the rules or procedures;

(d)   An effective system of domestic review, including an effective system of appeal, to ensure legal recourse and remedies in the event that the rules or procedures established pursuant to this paragraph are not followed;

(e)   Where appropriate, measures to regulate matters regarding personnel responsible for procurement, such as declaration of interest in particular public procurements, screening procedures and training requirements.

2.   Each State Party shall, in accordance with the fundamental principles of its legal system, take appropriate measures to promote transparency and accountability in the management of public finances. Such measures shall encompass, *inter alia*:

(a)   Procedures for the adoption of the national budget;
(b)   Timely reporting on revenue and expenditure;
(c)   A system of accounting and auditing standards and related oversight;
(d)   Effective and efficient systems of risk management and internal control; and
(e)   Where appropriate, corrective action in the case of failure to comply with the requirements established in this paragraph.

3.   Each State Party shall take such civil and administrative measures as may be necessary, in accordance with the fundamental principles of its domestic law, to preserve the integrity of

accounting books, records, financial statements or other documents related to public expenditure and revenue and to prevent the falsification of such documents.

Article 10
Public reporting

Taking into account the need to combat corruption, each State Party shall, in accordance with the fundamental principles of its domestic law, take such measures as may be necessary to enhance transparency in its public administration, including with regard to its organization, functioning and decision-making processes, where appropriate. Such measures may include, *inter alia*:

(a) Adopting procedures or regulations allowing members of the general public to obtain, where appropriate, information on the organization, functioning and decision-making processes of its public administration and, with due regard for the protection of privacy and personal data, on decisions and legal acts that concern members of the public;

(b) Simplifying administrative procedures, where appropriate, in order to facilitate public access to the competent decision-making authorities; and (c) Publishing information, which may include periodic reports on the risks of corruption in its public administration.

Article 11
Measures relating to the judiciary and prosecution services

1. Bearing in mind the independence of the judiciary and its crucial role in combating corruption, each State Party shall, in accordance with the fundamental principles of its legal system and without prejudice to judicial independence, take measures to strengthen integrity and to prevent opportunities for corruption among members of the judiciary. Such measures may include rules with respect to the conduct of members of the judiciary.

2. Measures to the same effect as those taken pursuant to paragraph 1 of this article may be introduced and applied within the prosecution service in those States Parties where it does not form part of the judiciary but enjoys independence similar to that of the judicial service.

Article 12
Private sector

1. Each State Party shall take measures, in accordance with the fundamental principles of its domestic law, to prevent corruption involving the private sector, enhance accounting and auditing standards in the private sector and, where appropriate, provide effective, proportionate and dissuasive civil, administrative or criminal penalties for failure to comply with such measures.

2. Measures to achieve these ends may include, *inter alia*:

(a) Promoting cooperation between law enforcement agencies and relevant private entities;

(b)   Promoting the development of standards and procedures designed to safeguard the integrity of relevant private entities, including codes of conduct for the correct, honourable and proper performance of the activities of business and all relevant professions and the prevention of conflicts of interest, and for the promotion of the use of good commercial practices among businesses and in the contractual relations of businesses with the State;

(c)   Promoting transparency among private entities, including, where appropriate, measures regarding the identity of legal and natural persons involved in the establishment and management of corporate entities;

(d)   Preventing the misuse of procedures regulating private entities, including procedures regarding subsidies and licences granted by public authorities for commercial activities;

(e)   Preventing conflicts of interest by imposing restrictions, as appropriate and for a reasonable period of time, on the professional activities of former public officials or on the employment of public officials by the private sector after their resignation or retirement, where such activities or employment relate directly to the functions held or supervised by those public officials during their tenure;

(f)   Ensuring that private enterprises, taking into account their structure and size, have sufficient internal auditing controls to assist in preventing and detecting acts of corruption and that the accounts and required financial statements of such private enterprises are subject to appropriate auditing and certification procedures.

3.   In order to prevent corruption, each State Party shall take such measures as may be necessary, in accordance with its domestic laws and regulations regarding the maintenance of books and records, financial statement disclosures and accounting and auditing standards, to prohibit the following acts carried out for the purpose of committing any of the offences established in accordance with this Convention:

(a) The establishment of off-the-books accounts;
(b) The making of off-the-books or inadequately identified transactions;
(c) The recording of non-existent expenditure;
(d) The entry of liabilities with incorrect identification of their objects;
(e) The use of false documents; and
(f) The intentional destruction of bookkeeping documents earlier than foreseen by the law.

4.   Each State Party shall disallow the tax deductibility of expenses that constitute bribes, the latter being one of the constituent elements of the offences established in accordance with articles 15 and 16 of this Convention and, where appropriate, other expenses incurred in furtherance of corrupt conduct.

Article 13
Participation of society

1.   Each State Party shall take appropriate measures, within its means and in accordance with fundamental principles of its domestic law, to promote the active participation of

individuals and groups outside the public sector, such as civil society, non-governmental organizations and community-based organizations, in the prevention of and the fight against corruption and to raise public awareness regarding the existence, causes and gravity of and the threat posed by corruption.

This participation should be strengthened by such measures as:

(a) Enhancing the transparency of and promoting the contribution of the public to decision-making processes;

(b) Ensuring that the public has effective access to information;

(c) Undertaking public information activities that contribute to non-tolerance of corruption, as well as public education programmes, including school and university curricula;

(d) Respecting, promoting and protecting the freedom to seek, receive, publish and disseminate information concerning corruption. That freedom may be subject to certain restrictions, but these shall only be such as are provided for by law and are necessary:

(i) For respect of the rights or reputations of others;

(ii) For the protection of national security or *ordre public* or of public health or morals.

2. Each State Party shall take appropriate measures to ensure that the relevant anti-corruption bodies referred to in this Convention are known to the public and shall provide access to such bodies, where appropriate, for the reporting, including anonymously, of any incidents that may be considered to constitute an offence established in accordance with this Convention.

Article 14
Measures to prevent money-laundering

1. Each State Party shall:

(a) Institute a comprehensive domestic regulatory and supervisory regime for banks and non-bank financial institutions, including natural or legal persons that provide formal or informal services for the transmission of money or value and, where appropriate, other bodies particularly susceptible to money-laundering, within its competence, in order to deter and detect all forms of money-laundering, which regime shall emphasize requirements for customer and, where appropriate, beneficial owner identification, record-keeping and the reporting of suspicious transactions;

(b) Without prejudice to article 46 of this Convention, ensure that administrative, regulatory, law enforcement and other authorities dedicated to combating money-laundering (including, where appropriate under domestic law, judicial authorities) have the ability to cooperate and exchange information at the national and international levels within the conditions prescribed by its domestic law and, to that end, shall consider the establishment of a financial intelligence unit to serve as a national centre for the collection, analysis and dissemination of information regarding potential money-laundering.

2.   States Parties shall consider implementing feasible measures to detect and monitor the movement of cash and appropriate negotiable instruments across their borders, subject to safeguards to ensure proper use of information and without impeding in any way the movement of legitimate capital. Such measures may include a requirement that individuals and businesses report the cross-border transfer of substantial quantities of cash and appropriate negotiable instruments.

3.   States Parties shall consider implementing appropriate and feasible measures to require financial institutions, including money remitters:

   (a)   To include on forms for the electronic transfer of funds and related messages accurate and meaningful information on the originator;

   (b)   To maintain such information throughout the payment chain; and

   (c)   To apply enhanced scrutiny to transfers of funds that do not contain complete information on the originator.

4.   In establishing a domestic regulatory and supervisory regime under the terms of this article, and without prejudice to any other article of this Convention, States Parties are called upon to use as a guideline the relevant initiatives of regional, interregional and multilateral organizations against money-laundering.

5.   States Parties shall endeavour to develop and promote global, regional, subregional and bilateral cooperation among judicial, law enforcement and financial regulatory authorities in order to combat money-laundering.

Chapter III
Criminalization and law enforcement

Article 15
Bribery of national public officials

Each State Party shall adopt such legislative and other measures as may be necessary to establish as criminal offences, when committed intentionally:

   (a)   The promise, offering or giving, to a public official, directly or indirectly, of an undue advantage, for the official himself or herself or another person or entity, in order that the official act or refrain from acting in the exercise of his or her official duties;

   (b)   The solicitation or acceptance by a public official, directly or indirectly, of an undue advantage, for the official himself or herself or another person or entity, in order that the official act or refrain from acting in the exercise of his or her official duties.

Article 16
Bribery of foreign public officials and officials of public international organizations

1.   Each State Party shall adopt such legislative and other measures as may be necessary to establish as a criminal offence, when committed intentionally, the promise, offering or giving to a foreign public official or an official of a public international organization, directly or indirectly, of an undue advantage, for the official himself or herself or another person or entity, in order that the official act or refrain from acting in the exercise of his or her official duties, in order to obtain or retain business or other undue advantage in relation to the conduct of international business.

2.   Each State Party shall consider adopting such legislative and other measures as may be necessary to establish as a criminal offence, when committed intentionally, the solicitation or acceptance by a foreign public official or an official of a public international organization, directly or indirectly, of an undue advantage, for the official himself or herself or another person or entity, in order that the official act or refrain from acting in the exercise of his or her official duties.

Article 17
Embezzlement, misappropriation or other diversion of property by a public official

Each State Party shall adopt such legislative and other measures as may be necessary to establish as criminal offences, when committed intentionally, the embezzlement, misappropriation or other diversion by a public official for his or her benefit or for the benefit of another person or entity, of any property, public or private funds or securities or any other thing of value entrusted to the public official by virtue of his or her position.

Article 18
Trading in influence

Each State Party shall consider adopting such legislative and other measures as may be necessary to establish as criminal offences, when committed intentionally:

(a)   The promise, offering or giving to a public official or any other person, directly or indirectly, of an undue advantage in order that the public official or the person abuse his or her real or supposed influence with a view to obtaining from an administration or public authority of the State Party an undue advantage for the original instigator of the act or for any other person;

(b)   The solicitation or acceptance by a public official or any other person, directly or indirectly, of an undue advantage for himself or herself or for another person in order that the public official or the person abuse his or her real or supposed influence with a view to obtaining from an administration or public authority of the State Party an undue advantage.

Article 19
Abuse of functions

Each State Party shall consider adopting such legislative and other measures as may be necessary to establish as a criminal offence, when committed intentionally, the abuse of functions or position, that is, the performance of or failure to perform an act, in violation of laws, by a public official in the discharge of his or her functions, for the purpose of obtaining an undue advantage for himself or herself or for another person or entity.

Article 20
Illicit enrichment

Subject to its constitution and the fundamental principles of its legal system, each State Party shall consider adopting such legislative and other measures as may be necessary to establish as a criminal offence, when committed intentionally, illicit enrichment, that is, a significant increase in the assets of a public official that he or she cannot reasonably explain in relation to his or her lawful income.

Article 21
Bribery in the private sector

Each State Party shall consider adopting such legislative and other measures as may be necessary to establish as criminal offences, when committed intentionally in the course of economic, financial or commercial activities:

(a)   The promise, offering or giving, directly or indirectly, of an undue advantage to any person who directs or works, in any capacity, for a private sector entity, for the person himself or herself or for another person, in order that he or she, in breach of his or her duties, act or refrain from acting;

(b)   The solicitation or acceptance, directly or indirectly, of an undue advantage by any person who directs or works, in any capacity, for a private sector entity, for the person himself or herself or for another person, in order that he or she, in breach of his or her duties, act or refrain from acting.

Article 22
Embezzlement of property in the private sector

Each State Party shall consider adopting such legislative and other measures as may be necessary to establish as a criminal offence, when committed intentionally in the course of economic, financial or commercial activities, embezzlement by a person who directs or works, in any capacity, in a private sector entity of any property, private funds or securities or any other thing of value entrusted to him or her by virtue of his or her position.

Article 23
Laundering of proceeds of crime

1.   Each State Party shall adopt, in accordance with fundamental principles of its domestic law, such legislative and other measures as may be necessary to establish as criminal offences, when committed intentionally:

(a)   (i)   The conversion or transfer of property, knowing that such property is the proceeds of crime, for the purpose of concealing or disguising the illicit origin of the property or of helping any person who is involved in the commission of the predicate offence to evade the legal consequences of his or her action;

(ii)   The concealment or disguise of the true nature, source, location, disposition, movement or ownership of or rights with respect to property, knowing that such property is the proceeds of crime;

(b)   Subject to the basic concepts of its legal system:

(i)   The acquisition, possession or use of property, knowing, at the time of receipt, that such property is the proceeds of crime;

(ii)   Participation in, association with or conspiracy to commit, attempts to commit and aiding, abetting, facilitating and counselling the commission of any of the offences established in accordance with this article.

2.   For purposes of implementing or applying paragraph 1 of this article:

(a)   Each State Party shall seek to apply paragraph 1 of this article to the widest range of predicate offences;

(b)   Each State Party shall include as predicate offences at a minimum a comprehensive range of criminal offences established in accordance with this Convention;

(c)   For the purposes of subparagraph (b) above, predicate offences shall include offences committed both within and outside the jurisdiction of the State Party in question. However, offences committed outside the jurisdiction of a State Party shall constitute predicate offences only when the relevant conduct is a criminal offence under the domestic law of the State where it is committed and would be a criminal offence under the domestic law of the State Party implementing or applying this article had it been committed there;

(d)   Each State Party shall furnish copies of its laws that give effect to this article and of any subsequent changes to such laws or a description thereof to the Secretary-General of the United Nations;

(e)   If required by fundamental principles of the domestic law of a State Party, it may be provided that the offences set forth in paragraph 1 of this article do not apply to the persons who committed the predicate offence.

Article 24
Concealment

Without prejudice to the provisions of article 23 of this Convention, each State Party shall consider adopting such legislative and other measures as may be necessary to establish as a criminal offence, when committed intentionally after the commission of any of the offences established in accordance with this Convention without having participated in such offences, the concealment or continued retention of property when the person involved knows that such property is the result of any of the offences established in accordance with this Convention.

Article 25
Obstruction of justice

Each State Party shall adopt such legislative and other measures as may be necessary to establish as criminal offences, when committed intentionally:

(a)   The use of physical force, threats or intimidation or the promise, offering or giving of an undue advantage to induce false testimony or to interfere in the giving of testimony or the production of evidence in a proceeding in relation to the commission of offences established in accordance with this Convention;

(b)   The use of physical force, threats or intimidation to interfere with the exercise of official duties by a justice or law enforcement official in relation to the commission of offences established in accordance with this Convention. Nothing in this subparagraph shall prejudice the right of States Parties to have legislation that protects other categories of public official.

Article 26
Liability of legal persons

1.   Each State Party shall adopt such measures as may be necessary, consistent with its legal principles, to establish the liability of legal persons for participation in the offences established in accordance with this Convention.

2.   Subject to the legal principles of the State Party, the liability of legal persons may be criminal, civil or administrative.

3.   Such liability shall be without prejudice to the criminal liability of the natural persons who have committed the offences.

4.   Each State Party shall, in particular, ensure that legal persons held liable in accordance with this article are subject to effective, proportionate and dissuasive criminal or non-criminal sanctions, including monetary sanctions.

Article 27
Participation and attempt

1.   Each State Party shall adopt such legislative and other measures as may be necessary to establish as a criminal offence, in accordance with its domestic law, participation in any capacity such as an accomplice, assistant or instigator in an offence established in accordance with this Convention.

2.   Each State Party may adopt such legislative and other measures as may be necessary to establish as a criminal offence, in accordance with its domestic law, any attempt to commit an offence established in accordance with this Convention.

3.   Each State Party may adopt such legislative and other measures as may be necessary to establish as a criminal offence, in accordance with its domestic law, the preparation for an offence established in accordance with this Convention.

Article 28
Knowledge, intent and purpose as elements of an offence

Knowledge, intent or purpose required as an element of an offence established in accordance with this Convention may be inferred from objective factual circumstances.

Article 29
Statute of limitations

Each State Party shall, where appropriate, establish under its domestic law a long statute of limitations period in which to commence proceedings for any offence established in accordance with this Convention and establish a longer statute of limitations period or provide for the suspension of the statute of limitations where the alleged offender has evaded the administration of justice.

Article 30
Prosecution, adjudication and sanctions

1.   Each State Party shall make the commission of an offence established in accordance with this Convention liable to sanctions that take into account the gravity of that offence.

2.   Each State Party shall take such measures as may be necessary to establish or maintain, in accordance with its legal system and constitutional principles, an appropriate balance between any immunities or jurisdictional privileges accorded to its public officials for the performance of their functions and the possibility, when necessary, of effectively investigating, prosecuting and adjudicating offences established in accordance with this Convention.

3.   Each State Party shall endeavour to ensure that any discretionary legal powers under its domestic law relating to the prosecution of persons for offences established in accordance with this Convention are exercised to maximize the effectiveness of law enforcement measures in respect of those offences and with due regard to the need to deter the commission of such offences.

4.   In the case of offences established in accordance with this Convention, each State Party shall take appropriate measures, in accordance with its domestic law and with due regard to the rights of the defence, to seek to ensure that conditions imposed in connection with decisions on release pending trial or appeal take into consideration the need to ensure the presence of the defendant at subsequent criminal proceedings.

5.   Each State Party shall take into account the gravity of the offences concerned when considering the eventuality of early release or parole of persons convicted of such offences.

6.   Each State Party, to the extent consistent with the fundamental principles of its legal system, shall consider establishing procedures through which a public official accused of an offence established in accordance with this Convention may, where appropriate, be removed, suspended or reassigned by the appropriate authority, bearing in mind respect for the principle of the presumption of innocence.

7.   Where warranted by the gravity of the offence, each State Party, to the extent consistent with the fundamental principles of its legal system, shall consider establishing procedures for the

disqualification, by court order or any other appropriate means, for a period of time determined by its domestic law, of persons convicted of offences established in accordance with this Convention from:

    (a)   Holding public office; and

    (b)   Holding office in an enterprise owned in whole or in part by the State.

8.   Paragraph 1 of this article shall be without prejudice to the exercise of disciplinary powers by the competent authorities against civil servants.

9.   Nothing contained in this Convention shall affect the principle that the description of the offences established in accordance with this Convention and of the applicable legal defences or other legal principles controlling the lawfulness of conduct is reserved to the domestic law of a State Party and that such offences shall be prosecuted and punished in accordance with that law.

10.   States Parties shall endeavour to promote the reintegration into society of persons convicted of offences established in accordance with this Convention.

Article 31
Freezing, seizure and confiscation

1.   Each State Party shall take, to the greatest extent possible within its domestic legal system, such measures as may be necessary to enable confiscation of:

    (a)   Proceeds of crime derived from offences established in accordance with this Convention or property the value of which corresponds to that of such proceeds;

    (b)   Property, equipment or other instrumentalities used in or destined for use in offences established in accordance with this Convention.

2.   Each State Party shall take such measures as may be necessary to enable the identification, tracing, freezing or seizure of any item referred to in paragraph 1 of this article for the purpose of eventual confiscation.

3.   Each State Party shall adopt, in accordance with its domestic law, such legislative and other measures as may be necessary to regulate the administration by the competent authorities of frozen, seized or confiscated property covered in paragraphs 1 and 2 of this article.

4.   If such proceeds of crime have been transformed or converted, in part or in full, into other property, such property shall be liable to the measures referred to in this article instead of the proceeds.

5.   If such proceeds of crime have been intermingled with property acquired from legitimate sources, such property shall, without prejudice to any powers relating to freezing or seizure, be liable to confiscation up to the assessed value of the intermingled proceeds.

6.   Income or other benefits derived from such proceeds of crime, from property into which such proceeds of crime have been transformed or converted or from property with which such proceeds of crime have been intermingled shall also be liable to the measures referred to in this article, in the same manner and to the same extent as proceeds of crime.

7.   For the purpose of this article and article 55 of this Convention, each State Party shall empower its courts or other competent authorities to order that bank, financial or commercial records be made available or seized. A State Party shall not decline to act under the provisions of this paragraph on the ground of bank secrecy.

8.   States Parties may consider the possibility of requiring that an offender demonstrate the lawful origin of such alleged proceeds of crime or other property liable to confiscation, to the extent that such a requirement is consistent with the fundamental principles of their domestic law and with the nature of judicial and other proceedings.

9.   The provisions of this article shall not be so construed as to prejudice the rights of bona fide third parties.

10.   Nothing contained in this article shall affect the principle that the measures to which it refers shall be defined and implemented in accordance with and subject to the provisions of the domestic law of a State Party.

Article 32
Protection of witnesses, experts and victims

1.   Each State Party shall take appropriate measures in accordance with its domestic legal system and within its means to provide effective protection from potential retaliation or intimidation for witnesses and experts who give testimony concerning offences established in accordance with this Convention and, as appropriate, for their relatives and other persons close to them.

2.   The measures envisaged in paragraph 1 of this article may include, *inter alia*, without prejudice to the rights of the defendant, including the right to due process:

   (a)   Establishing procedures for the physical protection of such persons, such as, to the extent necessary and feasible, relocating them and permitting, where appropriate, non-disclosure or limitations on the disclosure of information concerning the identity and whereabouts of such persons;

   (b)   Providing evidentiary rules to permit witnesses and experts to give testimony in a manner that ensures the safety of such persons, such as permitting testimony to be given through the use of communications technology such as video or other adequate means.

3.   States Parties shall consider entering into agreements or arrangements with other States for the relocation of persons referred to in paragraph 1 of this article.

4.   The provisions of this article shall also apply to victims insofar as they are witnesses.

5.   Each State Party shall, subject to its domestic law, enable the views and concerns of victims to be presented and considered at appropriate stages of criminal proceedings against offenders in a manner not prejudicial to the rights of the defence.

Article 33
Protection of reporting persons

Each State Party shall consider incorporating into its domestic legal system appropriate measures to provide protection against any unjustified treatment for any person who reports in good faith and on reasonable grounds to the competent authorities any facts concerning offences established in accordance with this Convention.

Article 34
Consequences of acts of corruption

With due regard to the rights of third parties acquired in good faith, each State Party shall take measures, in accordance with the fundamental principles of its domestic law, to address consequences of corruption. In this context, States Parties may consider corruption a relevant factor in legal proceedings to annul or rescind a contract, withdraw a concession or other similar instrument or take any other remedial action.

Article 35
Compensation for damage

Each State Party shall take such measures as may be necessary, in accordance with principles of its domestic law, to ensure that entities or persons who have suffered damage as a result of an act of corruption have the right to initiate legal proceedings against those responsible for that damage in order to obtain compensation.

Article 36
Specialized authorities

Each State Party shall, in accordance with the fundamental principles of its legal system, ensure the existence of a body or bodies or persons specialized in combating corruption through law enforcement. Such body or bodies or persons shall be granted the necessary independence, in accordance with the fundamental principles of the legal system of the State Party, to be able to carry out their functions effectively and without any undue influence. Such persons or staff of such body or bodies should have the appropriate training and resources to carry out their tasks.

Article 37
Cooperation with law enforcement authorities

1.   Each State Party shall take appropriate measures to encourage persons who participate or who have participated in the commission of an offence established in accordance with this Convention to supply information useful to competent authorities for investigative and evidentiary purposes and to provide factual, specific help to competent authorities that may contribute to depriving offenders of the proceeds of crime and to recovering such proceeds.

2.   Each State Party shall consider providing for the possibility, in appropriate cases, of mitigating punishment of an accused person who provides substantial cooperation in the investigation or prosecution of an offence established in accordance with this Convention.

3.   Each State Party shall consider providing for the possibility, in accordance with fundamental principles of its domestic law, of granting immunity from prosecution to a person

who provides substantial cooperation in the investigation or prosecution of an offence established in accordance with this Convention.

4.   Protection of such persons shall be, *mutatis mutandis*, as provided for in article 32 of this Convention.

5.   Where a person referred to in paragraph 1 of this article located in one State Party can provide substantial cooperation to the competent authorities of another State Party, the States Parties concerned may consider entering into agreements or arrangements, in accordance with their domestic law, concerning the potential provision by the other State Party of the treatment set forth in paragraphs 2 and 3 of this article.

Article 38
Cooperation between national authorities

Each State Party shall take such measures as may be necessary to encourage, in accordance with its domestic law, cooperation between, on the one hand, its public authorities, as well as its public officials, and, on the other hand, its authorities responsible for investigating and prosecuting criminal offences. Such cooperation may include:

(a)   Informing the latter authorities, on their own initiative, where there are reasonable grounds to believe that any of the offences established in accordance with articles 15, 21 and 23 of this Convention has been committed; or

(b)   Providing, upon request, to the latter authorities all necessary information.

Article 39
Cooperation between national authorities and the private sector

1.   Each State Party shall take such measures as may be necessary to encourage, in accordance with its domestic law, cooperation between national investigating and prosecuting authorities and entities of the private sector, in particular financial institutions, relating to matters involving the commission of offences established in accordance with this Convention.

2.   Each State Party shall consider encouraging its nationals and other persons with a habitual residence in its territory to report to the national investigating and prosecuting authorities the commission of an offence established in accordance with this Convention.

Article 40
Bank secrecy

Each State Party shall ensure that, in the case of domestic criminal investigations of offences established in accordance with this Convention, there are appropriate mechanisms available within its domestic legal system to overcome obstacles that may arise out of the application of bank secrecy laws.

Article 41
Criminal record

Each State Party may adopt such legislative or other measures as may be necessary to take into consideration, under such terms as and for the purpose that it deems appropriate, any previous conviction in another State of an alleged offender for the purpose of using such information in criminal proceedings relating to an offence established in accordance with this Convention.

Article 42
Jurisdiction

1.   Each State Party shall adopt such measures as may be necessary to establish its jurisdiction over the offences established in accordance with this Convention when:

   (a)   The offence is committed in the territory of that State Party; or

   (b)   The offence is committed on board a vessel that is flying the flag of that State Party or an aircraft that is registered under the laws of that State Party at the time that the offence is committed.

2.   Subject to article 4 of this Convention, a State Party may also establish its jurisdiction over any such offence when:

   (a)   The offence is committed against a national of that State Party; or

   (b)   The offence is committed by a national of that State Party or a stateless person who has his or her habitual residence in its territory; or

   (c)   The offence is one of those established in accordance with article 23, paragraph 1 (b) (ii), of this Convention and is committed outside its territory with a view to the commission of an offence established in accordance with article 23, paragraph 1 (a) (i) or (ii) or (b) (i), of this Convention within its territory; or

   (d)   The offence is committed against the State Party.

3.   For the purposes of article 44 of this Convention, each State Party shall take such measures as may be necessary to establish its jurisdiction over the offences established in accordance with this Convention when the alleged offender is present in its territory and it does not extradite such person solely on the ground that he or she is one of its nationals.

4.   Each State Party may also take such measures as may be necessary to establish its jurisdiction over the offences established in accordance with this Convention when the alleged offender is present in its territory and it does not extradite him or her.

5.   If a State Party exercising its jurisdiction under paragraph 1 or 2 of this article has been notified, or has otherwise learned, that any other States Parties are conducting an investigation, prosecution or judicial proceeding in respect of the same conduct, the competent authorities of those States Parties shall, as appropriate, consult one another with a view to coordinating their actions.

6.   Without prejudice to norms of general international law, this Convention shall not exclude the exercise of any criminal jurisdiction established by a State Party in accordance with its domestic law.

Chapter IV
International cooperation

Article 43
International cooperation

1.   States Parties shall cooperate in criminal matters in accordance with articles 44 to 50 of this Convention. Where appropriate and consistent with their domestic legal system, States Parties shall consider assisting each other in investigations of and proceedings in civil and administrative matters relating to corruption.

2.   In matters of international cooperation, whenever dual criminality is considered a requirement, it shall be deemed fulfilled irrespective of whether the laws of the requested State Party place the offence within the same category of offence or denominate the offence by the same terminology as the requesting State Party, if the conduct underlying the offence for which assistance is sought is a criminal offence under the laws of both States Parties.

Article 44
Extradition

1.   This article shall apply to the offences established in accordance with this Convention where the person who is the subject of the request for extradition is present in the territory of the requested State Party, provided that the offence for which extradition is sought is punishable under the domestic law of both the requesting State Party and the requested State Party.

2.   Notwithstanding the provisions of paragraph 1 of this article, a State Party whose law so permits may grant the extradition of a person for any of the offences covered by this Convention that are not punishable under its own domestic law.

3.   If the request for extradition includes several separate offences, at least one of which is extraditable under this article and some of which are not extraditable by reason of their period of imprisonment but are related to offences established in accordance with this Convention, the requested State Party may apply this article also in respect of those offences.

4.   Each of the offences to which this article applies shall be deemed to be included as an extraditable offence in any extradition treaty existing between States Parties. States Parties undertake to include such offences as extraditable offences in every extradition treaty to be concluded between them. A State Party whose law so permits, in case it uses this Convention as the basis for extradition, shall not consider any of the offences established in accordance with this Convention to be a political offence.

5.   If a State Party that makes extradition conditional on the existence of a treaty receives a request for extradition from another State Party with which it has no extradition treaty, it may consider this Convention the legal basis for extradition in respect of any offence to which this article applies.

6.   A State Party that makes extradition conditional on the existence of a treaty shall:

(a)   At the time of deposit of its instrument of ratification, acceptance or approval of or accession to this Convention, inform the Secretary-General of the United Nations whether it will take this Convention as the legal basis for cooperation on extradition with other States Parties to this Convention; and

(b)   If it does not take this Convention as the legal basis for cooperation on extradition, seek, where appropriate, to conclude treaties on extradition with other States Parties to this Convention in order to implement this article.

7.   States Parties that do not make extradition conditional on the existence of a treaty shall recognize offences to which this article applies as extraditable offences between themselves.

8.   Extradition shall be subject to the conditions provided for by the domestic law of the requested State Party or by applicable extradition treaties, including, *inter alia*, conditions in relation to the minimum penalty requirement for extradition and the grounds upon which the requested State Party may refuse extradition.

9.   States Parties shall, subject to their domestic law, endeavour to expedite extradition procedures and to simplify evidentiary requirements relating thereto in respect of any offence to which this article applies.

10.   Subject to the provisions of its domestic law and its extradition treaties, the requested State Party may, upon being satisfied that the circumstances so warrant and are urgent and at the request of the requesting State Party, take a person whose extradition is sought and who is present in its territory into custody or take other appropriate measures to ensure his or her presence at extradition proceedings.

11.   A State Party in whose territory an alleged offender is found, if it does not extradite such person in respect of an offence to which this article applies solely on the ground that he or she is one of its nationals, shall, at the request of the State Party seeking extradition, be obliged to submit the case without undue delay to its competent authorities for the purpose of prosecution. Those authorities shall take their decision and conduct their proceedings in the same manner as in the case of any other offence of a grave nature under the domestic law of that State Party. The States Parties concerned shall cooperate with each other, in particular on procedural and evidentiary aspects, to ensure the efficiency of such prosecution.

12.   Whenever a State Party is permitted under its domestic law to extradite or otherwise surrender one of its nationals only upon the condition that the person will be returned to that State Party to serve the sentence imposed as a result of the trial or proceedings for which the extradition or surrender of the person was sought and that State Party and the State Party seeking the extradition of the person agree with this option and other terms that they may deem appropriate, such conditional extradition or surrender shall be sufficient to discharge the obligation set forth in paragraph 11 of this article.

13.   If extradition, sought for purposes of enforcing a sentence, is refused because the person sought is a national of the requested State Party, the requested State Party shall, if its domestic law so permits and in conformity with the requirements of such law, upon application of the

requesting State Party, consider the enforcement of the sentence imposed under the domestic law of the requesting State Party or the remainder thereof.

14.   Any person regarding whom proceedings are being carried out in connection with any of the offences to which this article applies shall be guaranteed fair treatment at all stages of the proceedings, including enjoyment of all the rights and guarantees provided by the domestic law of the State Party in the territory of which that person is present.

15.   Nothing in this Convention shall be interpreted as imposing an obligation to extradite if the requested State Party has substantial grounds for believing that the request has been made for the purpose of prosecuting or punishing a person on account of that person's sex, race, religion, nationality, ethnic origin or political opinions or that compliance with the request would cause prejudice to that person's position for any one of these reasons.

16.   States Parties may not refuse a request for extradition on the sole ground that the offence is also considered to involve fiscal matters.

17.   Before refusing extradition, the requested State Party shall, where appropriate, consult with the requesting State Party to provide it with ample opportunity to present its opinions and to provide information relevant to its allegation.

18.   States Parties shall seek to conclude bilateral and multilateral agreements or arrangements to carry out or to enhance the effectiveness of extradition.

Article 45
Transfer of sentenced persons

States Parties may consider entering into bilateral or multilateral agreements or arrangements on the transfer to their territory of persons sentenced to imprisonment or other forms of deprivation of liberty for offences established in accordance with this Convention in order that they may complete their sentences there.

Article 46
Mutual legal assistance

1.   States Parties shall afford one another the widest measure of mutual legal assistance in investigations, prosecutions and judicial proceedings in relation to the offences covered by this Convention.

2.   Mutual legal assistance shall be afforded to the fullest extent possible under relevant laws, treaties, agreements and arrangements of the requested State Party with respect to investigations, prosecutions and judicial proceedings in relation to the offences for which a legal person may be held liable in accordance with article 26 of this Convention in the requesting State Party.

3.   Mutual legal assistance to be afforded in accordance with this article may be requested for any of the following purposes:

    (a)   Taking evidence or statements from persons;

    (b)   Effecting service of judicial documents;

(c)   Executing searches and seizures, and freezing;

(d)   Examining objects and sites;

(e)   Providing information, evidentiary items and expert evaluations;

(f)   Providing originals or certified copies of relevant documents and records, including government, bank, financial, corporate or business records;

(g)   Identifying or tracing proceeds of crime, property, instrumentalities or other things for evidentiary purposes;

(h)   Facilitating the voluntary appearance of persons in the requesting State Party;

(i)   Any other type of assistance that is not contrary to the domestic law of the requested State Party;

(j)   Identifying, freezing and tracing proceeds of crime in accordance with the provisions of chapter V of this Convention;

(k)   The recovery of assets, in accordance with the provisions of chapter V of this Convention.

4.   Without prejudice to domestic law, the competent authorities of a State Party may, without prior request, transmit information relating to criminal matters to a competent authority in another State Party where they believe that such information could assist the authority in undertaking or successfully concluding inquiries and criminal proceedings or could result in a request formulated by the latter State Party pursuant to this Convention.

5.   The transmission of information pursuant to paragraph 4 of this article shall be without prejudice to inquiries and criminal proceedings in the State of the competent authorities providing the information. The competent authorities receiving the information shall comply with a request that said information remain confidential, even temporarily, or with restrictions on its use. However, this shall not prevent the receiving State Party from disclosing in its proceedings information that is exculpatory to an accused person. In such a case, the receiving State Party shall notify the transmitting State Party prior to the disclosure and, if so requested, consult with the transmitting State Party. If, in an exceptional case, advance notice is not possible, the receiving State Party shall inform the transmitting State Party of the disclosure without delay.

6.   The provisions of this article shall not affect the obligations under any other treaty, bilateral or multilateral, that governs or will govern, in whole or in part, mutual legal assistance.

7.   Paragraphs 9 to 29 of this article shall apply to requests made pursuant to this article if the States Parties in question are not bound by a treaty of mutual legal assistance. If those States Parties are bound by such a treaty, the corresponding provisions of that treaty shall apply unless the States Parties agree to apply paragraphs 9 to 29 of this article in lieu thereof. States Parties are strongly encouraged to apply those paragraphs if they facilitate cooperation.

8.   States Parties shall not decline to render mutual legal assistance pursuant to this article on the ground of bank secrecy.

9.   (a)   A requested State Party, in responding to a request for assistance pursuant to this article in the absence of dual criminality, shall take into account the purposes of this Convention, as set forth in article 1;

        (b)   States Parties may decline to render assistance pursuant to this article on the ground of absence of dual criminality. However, a requested State Party shall, where consistent with the basic concepts of its legal system, render assistance that does not involve coercive action. Such assistance may be refused when requests involve matters of a de minimis nature or matters for which the cooperation or assistance sought is available under other provisions of this Convention;

(c) Each State Party may consider adopting such measures as may be necessary to enable it to provide a wider scope of assistance pursuant to this article in the absence of dual criminality.

10. A person who is being detained or is serving a sentence in the territory of one State Party whose presence in another State Party is requested for purposes of identification, testimony or otherwise providing assistance in obtaining evidence for investigations, prosecutions or judicial proceedings in relation to offences covered by this Convention may be transferred if the following conditions are met:

(a) The person freely gives his or her informed consent;

(b) The competent authorities of both States Parties agree, subject to such conditions as those States Parties may deem appropriate.

11. For the purposes of paragraph 10 of this article:

(a) The State Party to which the person is transferred shall have the authority and obligation to keep the person transferred in custody, unless otherwise requested or authorized by the State Party from which the person was transferred;

(b) The State Party to which the person is transferred shall without delay implement its obligation to return the person to the custody of the State Party from which the person was transferred as agreed beforehand, or as otherwise agreed, by the competent authorities of both States Parties;

(c) The State Party to which the person is transferred shall not require the State Party from which the person was transferred to initiate extradition proceedings for the return of the person;

(d) The person transferred shall receive credit for service of the sentence being served in the State from which he or she was transferred for time spent in the custody of the State Party to which he or she was transferred.

12. Unless the State Party from which a person is to be transferred in accordance with paragraphs 10 and 11 of this article so agrees, that person, whatever his or her nationality, shall not be prosecuted, detained, punished or subjected to any other restriction of his or her personal liberty in the territory of the State to which that person is transferred in respect of acts, omissions or convictions prior to his or her departure from the territory of the State from which he or she was transferred.

13. Each State Party shall designate a central authority that shall have the responsibility and power to receive requests for mutual legal assistance and either to execute them or to transmit them to the competent authorities for execution. Where a State Party has a special region or territory with a separate system of mutual legal assistance, it may designate a distinct central

authority that shall have the same function for that region or territory. Central authorities shall ensure the speedy and proper execution or transmission of the requests received. Where the central authority transmits the request to a competent authority for execution, it shall encourage the speedy and proper execution of the request by the competent authority. The Secretary-General of the United Nations shall be notified of the central authority designated for this purpose at the time each State Party deposits its instrument of ratification, acceptance or approval of or accession to this Convention. Requests for mutual legal assistance and any communication related thereto shall be transmitted to the central authorities designated by the States Parties. This requirement shall be without prejudice to the right of a State Party to require that such requests and communications be addressed to it through diplomatic channels and, in urgent circumstances, where the States Parties agree, through the International Criminal Police Organization, if possible.

14.   Requests shall be made in writing or, where possible, by any means capable of producing a written record, in a language acceptable to the requested State Party, under conditions allowing that State Party to establish authenticity. The Secretary-General of the United Nations shall be notified of the language or languages acceptable to each State Party at the time it deposits its instrument of ratification, acceptance or approval of or accession to this Convention. In urgent circumstances and where agreed by the States Parties, requests may be made orally but shall be confirmed in writing forthwith.

15.   A request for mutual legal assistance shall contain:

(a)   The identity of the authority making the request;

(b)   The subject matter and nature of the investigation, prosecution or judicial proceeding to which the request relates and the name and functions of the authority conducting the investigation, prosecution or judicial proceeding;

(c)   A summary of the relevant facts, except in relation to requests for the purpose of service of judicial documents;

(d)   A description of the assistance sought and details of any particular procedure that the requesting State Party wishes to be followed;

(e)   Where possible, the identity, location and nationality of any person concerned; and

(f)   The purpose for which the evidence, information or action is sought.

16.   The requested State Party may request additional information when it appears necessary for the execution of the request in accordance with its domestic law or when it can facilitate such execution.

17.   A request shall be executed in accordance with the domestic law of the requested State Party and, to the extent not contrary to the domestic law of the requested State Party and where possible, in accordance with the procedures specified in the request.

18.   Wherever possible and consistent with fundamental principles of domestic law, when an individual is in the territory of a State Party and has to be heard as a witness or expert by the

judicial authorities of another State Party, the first State Party may, at the request of the other, permit the hearing to take place by video conference if it is not possible or desirable for the individual in question to appear in person in the territory of the requesting State Party. States Parties may agree that the hearing shall be conducted by a judicial authority of the requesting State Party and attended by a judicial authority of the requested State Party.

19.   The requesting State Party shall not transmit or use information or evidence furnished by the requested State Party for investigations, prosecutions or judicial proceedings other than those stated in the request without the prior consent of the requested State Party. Nothing in this paragraph shall prevent the requesting State Party from disclosing in its proceedings information or evidence that is exculpatory to an accused person. In the latter case, the requesting State Party shall notify the requested State Party prior to the disclosure and, if so requested, consult with the requested State Party. If, in an exceptional case, advance notice is not possible, the requesting State Party shall inform the requested State Party of the disclosure without delay.

20.   The requesting State Party may require that the requested State Party keep confidential the fact and substance of the request, except to the extent necessary to execute the request. If the requested State Party cannot comply with the requirement of confidentiality, it shall promptly inform the requesting State Party.

21.   Mutual legal assistance may be refused:

(a)   If the request is not made in conformity with the provisions of this article;

(b)   If the requested State Party considers that execution of the request is likely to prejudice its sovereignty, security, *ordre public* or other essential interests; (c) If the authorities of the requested State Party would be prohibited by its domestic law from carrying out the action requested with regard to any similar offence, had it been subject to investigation, prosecution or judicial proceedings under their own jurisdiction;

(d)   If it would be contrary to the legal system of the requested State Party relating to mutual legal assistance for the request to be granted.

22.   States Parties may not refuse a request for mutual legal assistance on the sole ground that the offence is also considered to involve fiscal matters.

23.   Reasons shall be given for any refusal of mutual legal assistance.

24.   The requested State Party shall execute the request for mutual legal assistance as soon as possible and shall take as full account as possible of any deadlines suggested by the requesting State Party and for which reasons are given, preferably in the request. The requesting State Party may make reasonable requests for information on the status and progress of measures taken by the requested State Party to satisfy its request. The requested State Party shall respond to reasonable requests by the requesting State Party on the status, and progress in its handling, of the request. The requesting State Party shall promptly inform the requested State Party when the assistance sought is no longer required.

25.   Mutual legal assistance may be postponed by the requested State Party on the ground that it interferes with an ongoing investigation, prosecution or judicial proceeding.

26. Before refusing a request pursuant to paragraph 21 of this article or postponing its execution pursuant to paragraph 25 of this article, the requested State Party shall consult with the requesting State Party to consider whether assistance may be granted subject to such terms and conditions as it deems necessary. If the requesting State Party accepts assistance subject to those conditions, it shall comply with the conditions.

27. Without prejudice to the application of paragraph 12 of this article, a witness, expert or other person who, at the request of the requesting State Party, consents to give evidence in a proceeding or to assist in an investigation, prosecution or judicial proceeding in the territory of the requesting State Party shall not be prosecuted, detained, punished or subjected to any other restriction of his or her personal liberty in that territory in respect of acts, omissions or convictions prior to his or her departure from the territory of the requested State Party. Such safe conduct shall cease when the witness, expert or other person having had, for a period of fifteen consecutive days or for any period agreed upon by the States Parties from the date on which he or she has been officially informed that his or her presence is no longer required by the judicial authorities, an opportunity of leaving, has nevertheless remained voluntarily in the territory of the requesting State Party or, having left it, has returned of his or her own free will.

28. The ordinary costs of executing a request shall be borne by the requested State Party, unless otherwise agreed by the States Parties concerned. If expenses of a substantial or extraordinary nature are or will be required to fulfil the request, the States Parties shall consult to determine the terms and conditions under which the request will be executed, as well as the manner in which the costs shall be borne.

29. The requested State Party:

   (a) Shall provide to the requesting State Party copies of government records, documents or information in its possession that under its domestic law are available to the general public;

   (b) May, at its discretion, provide to the requesting State Party in whole, in part or subject to such conditions as it deems appropriate, copies of any government records, documents or information in its possession that under its domestic law are not available to the general public.

30. States Parties shall consider, as may be necessary, the possibility of concluding bilateral or multilateral agreements or arrangements that would serve the purposes of, give practical effect to or enhance the provisions of this article.

Article 47
Transfer of criminal proceedings

States Parties shall consider the possibility of transferring to one another proceedings for the prosecution of an offence established in accordance with this Convention in cases where such transfer is considered to be in the interests of the proper administration of justice, in particular in cases where several jurisdictions are involved, with a view to concentrating the prosecution.

Article 48
Law enforcement cooperation

1. States Parties shall cooperate closely with one another, consistent with their respective domestic legal and administrative systems, to enhance the effectiveness of law enforcement action to combat the offences covered by this Convention. States Parties shall, in particular, take effective measures:

(a) To enhance and, where necessary, to establish channels of communication between their competent authorities, agencies and services in order to facilitate the secure and rapid exchange of information concerning all aspects of the offences covered by this Convention, including, if the States Parties concerned deem it appropriate, links with other criminal activities;

(b) To cooperate with other States Parties in conducting inquiries with respect to offences covered by this Convention concerning:

(i) The identity, whereabouts and activities of persons suspected of involvement in such offences or the location of other persons concerned;

(ii) The movement of proceeds of crime or property derived from the commission of such offences;

(iii) The movement of property, equipment or other instrumentalities used or intended for use in the commission of such offences;

(c) To provide, where appropriate, necessary items or quantities of substances for analytical or investigative purposes;

(d) To exchange, where appropriate, information with other States Parties concerning specific means and methods used to commit offences covered by this Convention, including the use of false identities, forged, altered or false documents and other means of concealing activities;

(e) To facilitate effective coordination between their competent authorities, agencies and services and to promote the exchange of personnel and other experts, including, subject to bilateral agreements or arrangements between the States Parties concerned, the posting of liaison officers;

(f) To exchange information and coordinate administrative and other measures taken as appropriate for the purpose of early identification of the offences covered by this Convention.

2. With a view to giving effect to this Convention, States Parties shall consider entering into bilateral or multilateral agreements or arrangements on direct cooperation between their law enforcement agencies and, where such agreements or arrangements already exist, amending them. In the absence of such agreements or arrangements between the States Parties concerned, the States Parties may consider this Convention to be the basis for mutual law enforcement cooperation in respect of the offences covered by this Convention. Whenever appropriate, States

Parties shall make full use of agreements or arrangements, including international or regional organizations, to enhance the cooperation between their law enforcement agencies.

3.   States Parties shall endeavour to cooperate within their means to respond to offences covered by this Convention committed through the use of modern technology.

Article 49
Joint investigations

States Parties shall consider concluding bilateral or multilateral agreements or arrangements whereby, in relation to matters that are the subject of investigations, prosecutions or judicial proceedings in one or more States, the competent authorities concerned may establish joint investigative bodies. In the absence of such agreements or arrangements, joint investigations may be undertaken by agreement on a case-by-case basis. The States Parties involved shall ensure that the sovereignty of the State Party in whose territory such investigation is to take place is fully respected.

Article 50
Special investigative techniques

1.   In order to combat corruption effectively, each State Party shall, to the extent permitted by the basic principles of its domestic legal system and in accordance with the conditions prescribed by its domestic law, take such measures as may be necessary, within its means, to allow for the appropriate use by its competent authorities of controlled delivery and, where it deems appropriate, other special investigative techniques, such as electronic or other forms of surveillance and undercover operations, within its territory, and to allow for the admissibility in court of evidence derived therefrom.

2.   For the purpose of investigating the offences covered by this Convention, States Parties are encouraged to conclude, when necessary, appropriate bilateral or multilateral agreements or arrangements for using such special investigative techniques in the context of cooperation at the international level. Such agreements or arrangements shall be concluded and implemented in full compliance with the principle of sovereign equality of States and shall be carried out strictly in accordance with the terms of those agreements or arrangements.

3.   In the absence of an agreement or arrangement as set forth in paragraph 2 of this article, decisions to use such special investigative techniques at the international level shall be made on a case-by-case basis and may, when necessary, take into consideration financial arrangements and understandings with respect to the exercise of jurisdiction by the States Parties concerned.

4.   Decisions to use controlled delivery at the international level may, with the consent of the States Parties concerned, include methods such as intercepting and allowing the goods or funds to continue intact or be removed or replaced in whole or in part.

Chapter V
Asset recovery

Article 51
General provision

The return of assets pursuant to this chapter is a fundamental principle of this Convention, and States Parties shall afford one another the widest measure of cooperation and assistance in this regard.

Article 52
Prevention and detection of transfers of proceeds of crime

1.   Without prejudice to article 14 of this Convention, each State Party shall take such measures as may be necessary, in accordance with its domestic law, to require financial institutions within its jurisdiction to verify the identity of customers, to take reasonable steps to determine the identity of beneficial owners of funds deposited into high-value accounts and to conduct enhanced scrutiny of accounts sought or maintained by or on behalf of individuals who are, or have been, entrusted with prominent public functions and their family members and close associates. Such enhanced scrutiny shall be reasonably designed to detect suspicious transactions for the purpose of reporting to competent authorities and should not be so construed as to discourage or prohibit financial institutions from doing business with any legitimate customer.

2.   In order to facilitate implementation of the measures provided for in paragraph 1 of this article, each State Party, in accordance with its domestic law and inspired by relevant initiatives of regional, interregional and multilateral organizations against money-laundering, shall:

(a)   Issue advisories regarding the types of natural or legal person to whose accounts financial institutions within its jurisdiction will be expected to apply enhanced scrutiny, the types of accounts and transactions to which to pay particular attention and appropriate account-opening, maintenance and record-keeping measures to take concerning such accounts; and

(b)   Where appropriate, notify financial institutions within its jurisdiction, at the request of another State Party or on its own initiative, of the identity of particular natural or legal persons to whose accounts such institutions will be expected to apply enhanced scrutiny, in addition to those whom the financial institutions may otherwise identify.

3.   In the context of paragraph 2 (a) of this article, each State Party shall implement measures to ensure that its financial institutions maintain adequate records, over an appropriate period of time, of accounts and transactions involving the persons mentioned in paragraph 1 of this article, which should, as a minimum, contain information relating to the identity of the customer as well as, as far as possible, of the beneficial owner.

4.   With the aim of preventing and detecting transfers of proceeds of offences established in accordance with this Convention, each State Party shall implement appropriate and effective measures to prevent, with the help of its regulatory and oversight bodies, the establishment of banks that have no physical presence and that are not affiliated with a regulated financial group. Moreover, States Parties may consider requiring their financial institutions to refuse to enter into

or continue a correspondent banking relationship with such institutions and to guard against establishing relations with foreign financial institutions that permit their accounts to be used by banks that have no physical presence and that are not affiliated with a regulated financial group.

5.   Each State Party shall consider establishing, in accordance with its domestic law, effective financial disclosure systems for appropriate public officials and shall provide for appropriate sanctions for non-compliance. Each State Party shall also consider taking such measures as may be necessary to permit its competent authorities to share that information with the competent authorities in other States Parties when necessary to investigate, claim and recover proceeds of offences established in accordance with this Convention.

6.   Each State Party shall consider taking such measures as may be necessary, in accordance with its domestic law, to require appropriate public officials having an interest in or signature or other authority over a financial account in a foreign country to report that relationship to appropriate authorities and to maintain appropriate records related to such accounts. Such measures shall also provide for appropriate sanctions for non-compliance.

Article 53
Measures for direct recovery of property

Each State Party shall, in accordance with its domestic law:

(a)   Take such measures as may be necessary to permit another State Party to initiate civil action in its courts to establish title to or ownership of property acquired through the commission of an offence established in accordance with this Convention;

(b)   Take such measures as may be necessary to permit its courts to order those who have committed offences established in accordance with this Convention to pay compensation or damages to another State Party that has been harmed by such offences; and

(c)   Take such measures as may be necessary to permit its courts or competent authorities, when having to decide on confiscation, to recognize another State Party's claim as a legitimate owner of property acquired through the commission of an offence established in accordance with this Convention.

Article 54
Mechanisms for recovery of property through international
cooperation in confiscation

1.   Each State Party, in order to provide mutual legal assistance pursuant to article 55 of this Convention with respect to property acquired through or involved in the commission of an offence established in accordance with this Convention, shall, in accordance with its domestic law:

(a)   Take such measures as may be necessary to permit its competent authorities to give effect to an order of confiscation issued by a court of another State Party;

(b)   Take such measures as may be necessary to permit its competent authorities, where they have jurisdiction, to order the confiscation of such property of foreign origin by adjudication of an offence of money-laundering or such other offence as may be within its jurisdiction or by other procedures authorized under its domestic law; and

(c)   Consider taking such measures as may be necessary to allow confiscation of such property without a criminal conviction in cases in which the offender cannot be prosecuted by reason of death, flight or absence or in other appropriate cases.

2.   Each State Party, in order to provide mutual legal assistance upon a request made pursuant to paragraph 2 of article 55 of this Convention, shall, in accordance with its domestic law:

(a)   Take such measures as may be necessary to permit its competent authorities to freeze or seize property upon a freezing or seizure order issued by a court or competent authority of a requesting State Party that provides a reasonable basis for the requested State Party to believe that there are sufficient grounds for taking such actions and that the property would eventually be subject to an order of confiscation for purposes of paragraph 1 (a) of this article;

(b)   Take such measures as may be necessary to permit its competent authorities to freeze or seize property upon a request that provides a reasonable basis for the requested State Party to believe that there are sufficient grounds for taking such actions and that the property would eventually be subject to an order of confiscation for purposes of paragraph 1 (a) of this article; and

(c)   Consider taking additional measures to permit its competent authorities to preserve property for confiscation, such as on the basis of a foreign arrest or criminal charge related to the acquisition of such property.

Article 55
International cooperation for purposes of confiscation

1.   A State Party that has received a request from another State Party having jurisdiction over an offence established in accordance with this Convention for confiscation of proceeds of crime, property, equipment or other instrumentalities referred to in article 31, paragraph 1, of this Convention situated in its territory shall, to the greatest extent possible within its domestic legal system:

(a)   Submit the request to its competent authorities for the purpose of obtaining an order of confiscation and, if such an order is granted, give effect to it; or

(b)   Submit to its competent authorities, with a view to giving effect to it to the extent requested, an order of confiscation issued by a court in the territory of the requesting State Party in accordance with articles 31, paragraph 1, and 54, paragraph 1 (a), of this Convention insofar as it relates to proceeds of crime, property, equipment or other instrumentalities referred to in article 31, paragraph 1, situated in the territory of the requested State Party.

2.   Following a request made by another State Party having jurisdiction over an offence established in accordance with this Convention, the requested State Party shall take measures to identify, trace and freeze or seize proceeds of crime, property, equipment or other

instrumentalities referred to in article 31, paragraph 1, of this Convention for the purpose of eventual confiscation to be ordered either by the requesting State Party or, pursuant to a request under paragraph 1 of this article, by the requested State Party.

3.   The provisions of article 46 of this Convention are applicable, *mutates mutandis*, to this article. In addition to the information specified in article 46, paragraph 15, requests made pursuant to this article shall contain:

(a)   In the case of a request pertaining to paragraph 1 (a) of this article, a description of the property to be confiscated, including, to the extent possible, the location and, where relevant, the estimated value of the property and a statement of the facts relied upon by the requesting State Party sufficient to enable the requested State Party to seek the order under its domestic law;

(b)   In the case of a request pertaining to paragraph 1 (b) of this article, a legally admissible copy of an order of confiscation upon which the request is based issued by the requesting State Party, a statement of the facts and information as to the extent to which execution of the order is requested, a statement specifying the measures taken by the requesting State Party to provide adequate notification to bona fide third parties and to ensure due process and a statement that the confiscation order is final;

(c)   In the case of a request pertaining to paragraph 2 of this article, a statement of the facts relied upon by the requesting State Party and a description of the actions requested and, where available, a legally admissible copy of an order on which the request is based.

4.   The decisions or actions provided for in paragraphs 1 and 2 of this article shall be taken by the requested State Party in accordance with and subject to the provisions of its domestic law and its procedural rules or any bilateral or multilateral agreement or arrangement to which it may be bound in relation to the requesting State Party.

5.   Each State Party shall furnish copies of its laws and regulations that give effect to this article and of any subsequent changes to such laws and regulations or a description thereof to the Secretary-General of the United Nations.

6.   If a State Party elects to make the taking of the measures referred to in paragraphs 1 and 2 of this article conditional on the existence of a relevant treaty, that State Party shall consider this Convention the necessary and sufficient treaty basis.

7.   Cooperation under this article may also be refused or provisional measures lifted if the requested State Party does not receive sufficient and timely evidence or if the property is of a de minimis value.

8.   Before lifting any provisional measure taken pursuant to this article, the requested State Party shall, wherever possible, give the requesting State Party an opportunity to present its reasons in favour of continuing the measure.

9.   The provisions of this article shall not be construed as prejudicing the rights of bona fide third parties.

Article 56
Special cooperation

Without prejudice to its domestic law, each State Party shall endeavour to take measures to permit it to forward, without prejudice to its own investigations, prosecutions or judicial proceedings, information on proceeds of offences established in accordance with this Convention to another State Party without prior request, when it considers that the disclosure of such information might assist the receiving State Party in initiating or carrying out investigations, prosecutions or judicial proceedings or might lead to a request by that State Party under this chapter of the Convention.

Article 57
Return and disposal of assets

1.   Property confiscated by a State Party pursuant to article 31 or 55 of this Convention shall be disposed of, including by return to its prior legitimate owners, pursuant to paragraph 3 of this article, by that State Party in accordance with the provisions of this Convention and its domestic law.

2.   Each State Party shall adopt such legislative and other measures, in accordance with the fundamental principles of its domestic law, as may be necessary to enable its competent authorities to return confiscated property, when acting on the request made by another State Party, in accordance with this Convention, taking into account the rights of bona fde third parties.

3.   In accordance with articles 46 and 55 of this Convention and paragraphs 1 and 2 of this article, the requested State Party shall:

(a)   In the case of embezzlement of public funds or of laundering of embezzled public funds as referred to in articles 17 and 23 of this Convention, when confiscation was executed in accordance with article 55 and on the basis of a final judgement in the requesting State Party, a requirement that can be waived by the requested State Party, return the confiscated property to the requesting State Party;

(b)   In the case of proceeds of any other offence covered by this Convention, when the confiscation was executed in accordance with article 55 of this Convention and on the basis of a final judgement in the requesting State Party, a requirement that can be waived by the requested State Party, return the confiscated property to the requesting State Party, when the requesting State Party reasonably establishes its prior ownership of such confiscated property to the requested State Party or when the requested State Party recognizes damage to the requesting State Party as a basis for returning the confiscated property;

(c)   In all other cases, give priority consideration to returning confiscated property to the requesting State Party, returning such property to its prior legitimate owners or compensating the victims of the crime.

4.   Where appropriate, unless States Parties decide otherwise, the requested State Party may deduct reasonable expenses incurred in investigations, prosecutions or judicial proceedings leading to the return or disposition of confiscated property pursuant to this article.

5.   Where appropriate, States Parties may also give special consideration to concluding agreements or mutually acceptable arrangements, on a case-by-case basis, for the final disposal of confiscated property.

Article 58
Financial intelligence unit

States Parties shall cooperate with one another for the purpose of preventing and combating the transfer of proceeds of offences established in accordance with this Convention and of promoting ways and means of recovering such proceeds and, to that end, shall consider establishing a financial intelligence unit to be responsible for receiving, analysing and disseminating to the competent authorities reports of suspicious financial transactions.

Article 59
Bilateral and multilateral agreements and arrangements

States Parties shall consider concluding bilateral or multilateral agreements or arrangements to enhance the effectiveness of international cooperation undertaken pursuant to this chapter of the Convention.

Chapter VI
Technical assistance and information exchange

Article 60
Training and technical assistance

1.   Each State Party shall, to the extent necessary, initiate, develop or improve specific training programmes for its personnel responsible for preventing and combating corruption. Such training programmes could deal, *inter alia*, with the following areas:

(a)   Effective measures to prevent, detect, investigate, punish and control corruption, including the use of evidence-gathering and investigative methods;

(b)   Building capacity in the development and planning of strategic anticorruption policy;

(c)   Training competent authorities in the preparation of requests for mutual legal assistance that meet the requirements of this Convention;

(d)   Evaluation and strengthening of institutions, public service management and the management of public finances, including public procurement, and the private sector;

(e)   Preventing and combating the transfer of proceeds of offences established in accordance with this Convention and recovering such proceeds;

(f)   Detecting and freezing of the transfer of proceeds of offences established in accordance with this Convention;

(g)   Surveillance of the movement of proceeds of offences established in accordance with this Convention and of the methods used to transfer, conceal or disguise such proceeds;

(h)   Appropriate and efficient legal and administrative mechanisms and methods for facilitating the return of proceeds of offences established in accordance with this Convention;

(i)   Methods used in protecting victims and witnesses who cooperate with judicial authorities; and

(j)   Training in national and international regulations and in languages.

2.   States Parties shall, according to their capacity, consider affording one another the widest measure of technical assistance, especially for the benefit of developing countries, in their respective plans and programmes to combat corruption, including material support and training in the areas referred to in paragraph 1 of this article, and training and assistance and the mutual exchange of relevant experience and specialized knowledge, which will facilitate international cooperation between States Parties in the areas of extradition and mutual legal assistance.

3.   States Parties shall strengthen, to the extent necessary, efforts to maximize operational and training activities in international and regional organizations and in the framework of relevant bilateral and multilateral agreements or arrangements.

4.   States Parties shall consider assisting one another, upon request, in conducting evaluations, studies and research relating to the types, causes, effects and costs of corruption in their respective countries, with a view to developing, with the participation of competent authorities and society, strategies and action plans to combat corruption.

5.   In order to facilitate the recovery of proceeds of offences established in accordance with this Convention, States Parties may cooperate in providing each other with the names of experts who could assist in achieving that objective.

6.   States Parties shall consider using subregional, regional and international conferences and seminars to promote cooperation and technical assistance and to stimulate discussion on problems of mutual concern, including the special problems and needs of developing countries and countries with economies in transition.

7.   States Parties shall consider establishing voluntary mechanisms with a view to contributing financially to the efforts of developing countries and countries with economies in transition to apply this Convention through technical assistance programmes and projects.

8.   Each State Party shall consider making voluntary contributions to the United Nations Office on Drugs and Crime for the purpose of fostering, through the Office, programmes and projects in developing countries with a view to implementing this Convention.

Article 61
Collection, exchange and analysis of information on corruption

1.   Each State Party shall consider analysing, in consultation with experts, trends in corruption in its territory, as well as the circumstances in which corruption offences are committed.

2.   States Parties shall consider developing and sharing with each other and through international and regional organizations statistics, analytical expertise concerning corruption and information with a view to developing, insofar as possible, common definitions, standards and methodologies, as well as information on best practices to prevent and combat corruption.

3.   Each State Party shall consider monitoring its policies and actual measures to combat corruption and making assessments of their effectiveness and efficiency.

Article 62
Other measures: implementation of the Convention through economic development and technical assistance

1.   States Parties shall take measures conducive to the optimal implementation of this Convention to the extent possible, through international cooperation, taking into account the negative effects of corruption on society in general, in particular on sustainable development.

2.   States Parties shall make concrete efforts to the extent possible and in coordination with each other, as well as with international and regional organizations:

(a)   To enhance their cooperation at various levels with developing countries, with a view to strengthening the capacity of the latter to prevent and combat corruption;

(b)   To enhance financial and material assistance to support the efforts of developing countries to prevent and fight corruption effectively and to help them implement this Convention successfully;

(c)   To provide technical assistance to developing countries and countries with economies in transition to assist them in meeting their needs for the implementation of this Convention. To that end, States Parties shall endeavour to make adequate and regular voluntary contributions to an account specifically designated for that purpose in a United Nations funding mechanism. States Parties may also give special consideration, in accordance with their domestic law and the provisions of this Convention, to contributing to that account a percentage of the money or of the corresponding value of proceeds of crime or property confiscated in accordance with the provisions of this Convention;

(d)   To encourage and persuade other States and financial institutions as appropriate to join them in efforts in accordance with this article, in particular by providing more training programmes and modern equipment to developing countries in order to assist them in achieving the objectives of this Convention.

3.   To the extent possible, these measures shall be without prejudice to existing foreign assistance commitments or to other financial cooperation arrangements at the bilateral, regional or international level.

4.   States Parties may conclude bilateral or multilateral agreements or arrangements on material and logistical assistance, taking into consideration the financial arrangements necessary for the means of international cooperation provided for by this Convention to be effective and for the prevention, detection and control of corruption.

Chapter VII
Mechanisms for implementation

Article 63
Conference of the States Parties to the Convention

1.   A Conference of the States Parties to the Convention is hereby established to improve the capacity of and cooperation between States Parties to achieve the objectives set forth in this Convention and to promote and review its implementation.

2.   The Secretary-General of the United Nations shall convene the Conference of the States Parties not later than one year following the entry into force of this Convention. Thereafter, regular meetings of the Conference of the States Parties shall be held in accordance with the rules of procedure adopted by the Conference.

3.   The Conference of the States Parties shall adopt rules of procedure and rules governing the functioning of the activities set forth in this article, including rules concerning the admission and participation of observers, and the payment of expenses incurred in carrying out those activities.

4.   The Conference of the States Parties shall agree upon activities, procedures and methods of work to achieve the objectives set forth in paragraph 1 of this article, including:

(a)   Facilitating activities by States Parties under articles 60 and 62 and chapters II to V of this Convention, including by encouraging the mobilization of voluntary contributions;

(b)   Facilitating the exchange of information among States Parties on patterns and trends in corruption and on successful practices for preventing and combating it and for the return of proceeds of crime, through, *inter alia*, the publication of relevant information as mentioned in this article;

(c)   Cooperating with relevant international and regional organizations and mechanisms and non-governmental organizations;

(d)   Making appropriate use of relevant information produced by other international and regional mechanisms for combating and preventing corruption in order to avoid unnecessary duplication of work;

(e) Reviewing periodically the implementation of this Convention by its States Parties;

(f) Making recommendations to improve this Convention and its implementation;

(g) Taking note of the technical assistance requirements of States Parties with regard to the implementation of this Convention and recommending any action it may deem necessary in that respect.

5. For the purpose of paragraph 4 of this article, the Conference of the States Parties shall acquire the necessary knowledge of the measures taken by States Parties in implementing this Convention and the difficulties encountered by them in doing so through information provided by them and through such supplemental review mechanisms as may be established by the Conference of the States Parties.

6. Each State Party shall provide the Conference of the States Parties with information on its programmes, plans and practices, as well as on legislative and administrative measures to implement this Convention, as required by the Conference of the States Parties. The Conference of the States Parties shall examine the most effective way of receiving and acting upon information, including, *inter alia*, information received from States Parties and from competent international organizations. Inputs received from relevant non-governmental organizations duly accredited in accordance with procedures to be decided upon by the Conference of the States Parties may also be considered.

7. Pursuant to paragraphs 4 to 6 of this article, the Conference of the States Parties shall establish, if it deems it necessary, any appropriate mechanism or body to assist in the effective implementation of the Convention.

Article 64
Secretariat

1. The Secretary-General of the United Nations shall provide the necessary secretariat services to the Conference of the States Parties to the Convention.

2. The secretariat shall:

(a) Assist the Conference of the States Parties in carrying out the activities set forth in article 63 of this Convention and make arrangements and provide the necessary services for the sessions of the Conference of the States Parties;

(b) Upon request, assist States Parties in providing information to the Conference of the States Parties as envisaged in article 63, paragraphs 5 and 6, of this Convention; and

(c) Ensure the necessary coordination with the secretariats of relevant international and regional organizations.

Chapter VIII
Final provisions

Article 65
Implementation of the Convention

1.   Each State Party shall take the necessary measures, including legislative and administrative measures, in accordance with fundamental principles of its domestic law, to ensure the implementation of its obligations under this Convention.

2.   Each State Party may adopt more strict or severe measures than those provided for by this Convention for preventing and combating corruption.

Article 66
Settlement of disputes

1.   States Parties shall endeavour to settle disputes concerning the interpretation or application of this Convention through negotiation.

2.   Any dispute between two or more States Parties concerning the interpretation or application of this Convention that cannot be settled through negotiation within a reasonable time shall, at the request of one of those States Parties, be submitted to arbitration. If, six months after the date of the request for arbitration, those States Parties are unable to agree on the organization of the arbitration, any one of those States Parties may refer the dispute to the International Court of Justice by request in accordance with the Statute of the Court.

3.   Each State Party may, at the time of signature, ratification, acceptance or approval of or accession to this Convention, declare that it does not consider itself bound by paragraph 2 of this article. The other States Parties shall not be bound by paragraph 2 of this article with respect to any State Party that has made such a reservation.

4.   Any State Party that has made a reservation in accordance with paragraph 3 of this article may at any time withdraw that reservation by notification to the Secretary-General of the United Nations.

Article 67
Signature, ratification, acceptance, approval and accession

1.   This Convention shall be open to all States for signature from 9 to 11 December 2003 in Merida, Mexico, and thereafter at United Nations Headquarters in New York until 9 December 2005.

2.   This Convention shall also be open for signature by regional economic integration organizations provided that at least one member State of such organization has signed this Convention in accordance with paragraph 1 of this article.

3.   This Convention is subject to ratification, acceptance or approval.

Instruments of ratification, acceptance or approval shall be deposited with the Secretary-General of the United Nations. A regional economic integration organization may deposit its instrument of ratification, acceptance or approval if at least one of its member States has done likewise. In that instrument of ratification, acceptance or approval, such organization shall declare the extent of its competence with respect to the matters governed by this Convention. Such organization shall also inform the depositary of any relevant modification in the extent of its competence.

4.   This Convention is open for accession by any State or any regional economic integration organization of which at least one member State is a Party to this Convention. Instruments of accession shall be deposited with the Secretary-General of the United Nations. At the time of its accession, a regional economic integration organization shall declare the extent of its competence with respect to matters governed by this Convention. Such organization shall also inform the depositary of any relevant modification in the extent of its competence.

Article 68
Entry into force

1.   This Convention shall enter into force on the ninetieth day after the date of deposit of the thirtieth instrument of ratification, acceptance, approval or accession. For the purpose of this paragraph, any instrument deposited by a regional economic integration organization shall not be counted as additional to those deposited by member States of such organization.

2.   For each State or regional economic integration organization ratifying, accepting, approving or acceding to this Convention after the deposit of the thirtieth instrument of such action, this Convention shall enter into force on the thirtieth day after the date of deposit by such State or organization of the relevant instrument or on the date this Convention enters into force pursuant to paragraph 1 of this article, whichever is later.

Article 69
Amendment

1.   After the expiry of five years from the entry into force of this Convention, a State Party may propose an amendment and transmit it to the Secretary-General of the United Nations, who shall thereupon communicate the proposed amendment to the States Parties and to the Conference of the States Parties to the Convention for the purpose of considering and deciding on the proposal. The Conference of the States Parties shall make every effort to achieve consensus on each amendment. If all efforts at consensus have been exhausted and no agreement has been reached, the amendment shall, as a last resort, require for its adoption a two-thirds majority vote of the States Parties present and voting at the meeting of the Conference of the States Parties.

2.   Regional economic integration organizations, in matters within their competence, shall exercise their right to vote under this article with a number of votes equal to the number of their member States that are Parties to this Convention.

Such organizations shall not exercise their right to vote if their member States exercise theirs and vice versa.

3.   An amendment adopted in accordance with paragraph 1 of this article is subject to ratification, acceptance or approval by States Parties.

4.   An amendment adopted in accordance with paragraph 1 of this article shall enter into force in respect of a State Party ninety days after the date of the deposit with the Secretary-General of the United Nations of an instrument of ratification, acceptance or approval of such amendment.

5.   When an amendment enters into force, it shall be binding on those States Parties which have expressed their consent to be bound by it. Other States Parties shall still be bound by the provisions of this Convention and any earlier amendments that they have ratified, accepted or approved.

Article 70
Denunciation

1.   A State Party may denounce this Convention by written notification to the Secretary-General of the United Nations. Such denunciation shall become effective one year after the date of receipt of the notification by the Secretary-General.

2.   A regional economic integration organization shall cease to be a Party to this Convention when all of its member States have denounced it.

Article 71
Depositary and languages

1.   The Secretary-General of the United Nations is designated depositary of this Convention.

2. The original of this Convention, of which the Arabic, Chinese, English, French, Russian and Spanish texts are equally authentic, shall be deposited with the Secretary-General of the United Nations.

IN WITNESS WHEREOF, the undersigned plenipotentiaries, being duly authorized thereto by their respective Governments, have signed this Convention.

PART TWO

REGIONAL AND INTERREGIONAL INSTRUMENTS

DECISION 40: APPROVAL OF THE AGREEMENT AMONG MEMBER COUNTRIES TO AVOID DOUBLE TAXATION AND OF THE STANDARD AGREEMENT FOR EXECUTING AGREEMENTS ON DOUBLE TAXATION BETWEEN MEMBER COUNTRIES AND OTHER STATES OUTSIDE THE SUBREGION[*]

(ANDEAN COMMUNITY)

DECISION 40: Approval of the agreement among member countries to avoid double taxation and of the standard agreement for executing agreements on double taxation between member countries and other states outside the Subregion was signed in 1971.

The COMMISSION of the CARTAGENA AGREEMENT,

HAVING SEEN: Article 89 of the Agreement of Cartagena and Article 47 of Decision 24 of the Commission,

WHEREAS:

The Commission should, at the proposal of the Board, approve an agreement aimed at avoiding double taxation between Member Countries; and

It should likewise approve a standard agreement for executing agreements on double taxation between Member Countries and other States outside the Subregion;

DECIDES:

Article 1. To approve the Agreement to avoid double taxation among Member Countries which appears in Annex I to this Decision.

Article 2. To approve the Standard Agreement for avoiding double taxation between Member Countries and other States outside the Subregion, which is set out in Annex II to this Decision.

Article 3. The Member Countries shall take the necessary measures before June 30, 1972, to put into effect the Agreement to avoid double taxation among Member Countries so that it may become effective as stipulated in article 21 of that Agreement.

Article 4. If any difficulties or doubts exist as a result of the application of the Agreement to avoid double taxation among Member Countries, that cannot be resolved through the consultation procedure referred to in Article 20 of that Agreement, the respective facts of the case shall be submitted to the Fiscal Policy Council for consideration.

---

[*] *Source*: Organization of American States (1998). "DECISION 40: Approval of the Agreement Among Member Countries to Avoid Double Taxation and of the Standard Agreement for Executing Agreements on Double Taxation between Member Countries and Other States Outside the Subregion", available on the Internet (http://www.sice.oas.org/trade/JUNAC/decisiones/dec040e.asp). [Note added by the editor.]

If the Council's intervention fails to lead to the settlement of the problem, the Member Countries may avail themselves of the procedures established in Chapter II, Section D of the Cartagena Agreement.

For purposes of this article, the Fiscal Policy Council may meet at the request of any Member Country.

Article 5. Such agreements to avoid double taxation as the Member Countries may sign with other States outside the Subregion, shall be guided by the Standard Agreement referred to in Article 2 of this Decision.

Each Member Country shall consult with the others, within the Fiscal Policy Council, before signing those agreements.

Article 6. Member Countries that have signed agreements to avoid double taxation prior to the date of this Decision, shall seek to harmonize the provisions of those agreements with the Standard Agreement.

ANNEX I

AGREEMENT TO AVOID DOUBLE TAXATION
BETWEEN MEMBER COUNTRIES

CHAPTER I
SUBJECT-MATTER OF THE AGREEMENT
AND GENERAL DEFINITIONS

Article 1: Subject-matter of the Agreement

This agreement is applicable to persons residing in any of the Member Countries with regard to their income tax and property taxes. It is applicable mainly and specifically to the following:

In Bolivia, to the income tax created by the law of May 3, 1928 and its subsequent amendments, to the "total income" tax created by Supreme Decree No. 8619 of January 8, 1969, and to the additional income taxes.

In Colombia, to the national income tax and the complementary property and excess profits taxes governed by Law No. 81 of December 22, 1960 and its amendments and addenda contained in Law No. 21 of 1963, Decree No. 1366 of 1967, Law No. 63 of 1968 and Law No. 27 of 1969.

In Chile, to the taxes governed by the Income Tax Law contained in Article 5 of Law No. 15564 of February 14, 1964 and the Property Tax established by Law No. 17073 of December 31, 1968, amended by Law 17416 of March 9, 1971.

In Ecuador, to the general tax on total income and to the proportional and complementary taxes governed by Supreme Decree No. 329 of February 29, 1964 and its subsequent amendments.

In Peru, to the income tax, equity tax and real estate tax governed, respectively, by Titles I, II and III of Supreme Decree No. 287-HC of August 9, 1968, and its amending, complementary and related provisions.

This agreement shall be applicable as well to any changes that may be made in the cited taxes and to any other tax that, because of its tax base, may be essentially and economically analogous to those cited above and that any Member Country may establish after the signing of this agreement.

Article 2: General Definitions

For purposes of this agreement and unless the text states otherwise:

a)   The terms "one of the Member Countries" and "another Member Country" shall be used to designate Bolivia, Colombia, Chile, Ecuador or Peru without distinction.

b)   The terms "territory of one of the Member Countries" and "territory of another Member Country" shall mean the territories of Bolivia, Colombia, Chile, Ecuador or Peru without distinction.

c)   The term "person" shall be used to designate:

1.   An individual or natural person.

2.   A legal entity.

3.   Any other entity or group of persons, whether associated or not, that are subject to the payment of taxes.

d)   An individual shall be considered a resident of the Member Country where his habitual residence is located.

An enterprise is understood to be a resident of the country stated in its articles of incorporation. If such articles of incorporation do not exist or if they do not stipulate a legal residence, the enterprise is considered to be a resident of the place where actual management is located.

If, despite these regulations, it proves impossible to identify the legal residence, the competent authorities of the interested Member Countries shall settle the matter by common agreement.

e)   The term "source of production" refers to the activity, right or good that produces or that could produce an income.

f)   The term "business activities" refers to the activities carried out by an enterprise.

g)   The term "enterprise" denotes an organization consisting or one or more persons that is engaged in gainful activity.

h)   The terms "enterprise of a Member Country" and "enterprise of another Member Country" refer to an enterprise with residence in one Member Country or another.

i)   The term "royalty" refers to any gain, value or sum of money paid for the use or for the privilege of using copyrights, patents, industrial drawings or models, exclusive procedures or formulas, trademarks or other intangible goods of a similar nature.

j)   The term "capital gains" refers to the profit obtained by a person from the transfer of ownership of goods that it does not normally acquire, produce or transfer within its regular line of business.

k)   The term "pension" denotes a periodic payment made in consideration of services rendered or damages sustained; and the term "annuity" refers to a given sum of money paid periodically over the life of the beneficiary or during a set period under gratuitous title or in compensation for a service rendered or one with a cash value.

l)   The term "competent authority" refers to the following:

- In the case of Bolivia, the Finance Minister
- For Colombia, the Minister of the Treasury and Public Credit
- In the case of Chile, the Treasury Minister
- For Ecuador, the Minister of Finance
- In the case of Peru, the Minister of Economy and Finance.

Article 3: Scope of undefined terms

Any term that is not defined in this agreement shall have the meaning given to it in the legislation that is in effect each Member Country.

CHAPTER II
INCOME TAX

Article 4: Tax Jurisdiction

Irrespective of the nationality or residence of the persons, such income of any kind as they may obtain shall be taxable only in the Member Country where the source of production of that income is located, save in the exceptional cases provided for in this agreement.

Article 5: Real estate income

Income of any kind produced by real estate shall be taxable only by the Member Country in which those properties are located.

Article 6: Income from the right to exploit natural resources

Any earnings received from leasing or subleasing, or transferring or granting of the right to exploit or to use in any way the natural resources of one of the Member Countries shall be taxable by that Member Country only.

Article 7: Business earnings

Earnings from business activities shall be taxable only by the Member Country where these were obtained.

An enterprise is considered, among other cases, to perform activities in the territory of a Member Country when it maintains the following in that country:

a)   An office or a management site;

b)   A factory, plant or industrial or assembly workshop;

c)   A construction site;

d)   A site or facility where natural resources are extracted or exploited, such as a mine, oil well, quarry, plantation or fishing vessel;

e)   A sales agency or office;

f)   A procurement agency or office:

g)   A warehouse, storehouse or similar facility for receiving, storing or delivering products;

h)   Any other locale, office or facility whose purpose is to prepare for or help with the activities of the enterprise;

i)   An agent or representative.

In the event that an enterprise carries out activities in two or more Member Countries, each of them may tax the earnings produced in their territory. If the activities are performed through representatives or by using facilities like those cited in the previous paragraph, then the earnings obtained shall be attributed to those persons or facilities as if they were totally independent of the enterprise.

Article 8: Transport company earnings

The earnings obtained by air carriers and overland, ocean, lake or river transport companies shall be subject to taxes only in the Member Country where those enterprises have their legal residence.

Article 9: Royalties from the use of patents, trademarks and technologies

Royalties earned from the use of trademarks, patents, unpatented technical know-how or other intangible goods of a similar nature in the territory of one of the Member Countries shall be taxable only in that Member Country.

Article 10: Interest

Interest earned on loans shall be taxable only in the Member Country where the loan funds were used.

Unless proven otherwise, it is assumed that the loan will be used in the country where the interest is paid.

Article 11: Dividends and equity investments

Dividends and equity investments shall be taxable only by the Member Country where the enterprise that distributes them has its legal residence.

Article 12: Capital gains

Capital gains may be taxed only by the Member Country in whose territory the goods were located at the time of their sale, with the exception of those obtained from the transfer of:

a)   Ships, aircraft, buses and other transport vehicles, which shall be taxable only by the Member Country in which they were registered at the moment of their transfer, and

b)   Bonds, stock and other securities, which shall be taxable only by the Member Country where they were issued.

Article 13: Income from personal services

Payments, fees, salaries, wages, earnings and similar compensation received in return for services provided by employees, professionals, technicians or for personal services in general shall be taxable only in the territory where those services were rendered, with the exception of salaries, wages, pay and similar earnings received by:

a)   Persons that provide services to a Member Country in the exercise of duly accredited official functions, which may be taxed only by that country, although the services may be rendered in the territory of another Member Country.

b)   Crews of ships, airplanes, buses and other vehicles that provide international transport, which shall be taxed only by the Member Country where the employer has its residence.

Article 14: Companies Providing Professional Services and Technical Assistance

The income earned by companies that provide professional services and technical assistance shall be taxable only in the Member Country in whose territory those services are rendered.

Article 15: Pensions and annuities

Pensions, annuities and other similar periodic income shall be taxable only by the Member Country in whose territory the source of production is located.

The source shall be considered to be located in the territory of the country where the contract that produced the periodic income was signed and, if no contract exists, in the country from which that income is paid.

Article 16: Public entertainment activities

Income from the exercise of artistic and public entertainment activities shall be taxable only in the Member Country in whose territory the activity was performed, irrespective of the length of time spent in the territory in question by the persons performing those activities.

CHAPTER III
PROPERTY TAXES

Article 17: Property taxes

The assets of individuals or enterprises located in the territory of a Member Country shall be taxable only by that country.

Article 18: Situation of transport vehicles, leans and securities

For purposes of the previous article, the following is understood:

a)   Aircraft, ships, buses and other transport vehicles and the movable property used in their operation are located in the Member Country where their ownership is registered; and

b)   Loans, shares and other securities are located in the Member Country where the debtor or the issuing enterprise, as the case may be, has its residence.

CHAPTER IV
GENERAL PROVISIONS

Article 19: Tax treatment applicable to persons residing in other Member Countries

None of the Member Countries shall give less favorable treatment to persons residing in other Member Countries than that which they apply to persons residing in their own territory with regard to the taxes that are the subject-matter of this agreement.

Article 20: Consultations and information

The competent authorities of the Member Countries shall hold consultations with each other and shall exchange the information that is necessary to resolve by mutual agreement any problem or doubt that may result from the implementation of this agreement and to establish the administrative controls needed to avoid fraud and tax evasion.

The information that is exchanged pursuant to the stipulation of the previous paragraph shall be considered confidential and may not be transmitted to any person other than the authorities responsible for the administration of the taxes that are the subject-matter of this agreement.

For purposes of this article, the competent authorities of the Member Countries may communicate with each other directly.

Article 21: Duration

The Member Countries shall deposit with the Secretariat of the Board of the Cartagena Agreement the instruments that put this agreement into effect.

This agreement shall become effective:

a)   For individuals in regard to the income they receive or earned starting on the January 1st following the date of deposit of the cited instruments, by all Member Countries.

b)   For legal entities, in regard to the income received or earned during the first accounting period starting after the referred date of deposit.

c)   For the tax on tax, starting on the January 1st following the cited date of deposit.

ANNEX II

STANDARD AGREEMENT TO AVOID DOUBLE TAXATION BETWEEN MEMBER COUNTRIES AND OTHER STATES OUTSIDE THE SUBREGION

TITLE OF THE AGREEMENT

Agreement between (State A) and (State B) to avoid double taxation with regard to income tax, capital tax and net worth or corporation tax.

PREAMBLE

(It shall be drawn up in accordance with the procedures and rules and regulations in effect in the Contracting States.)

CHAPTER I
SUBJECT-MATTER OF THE AGREEMENT AND GENERAL DEFINITIONS

Article 1: Subject-matter of the Agreement

The taxes that are the subject-matter of this agreement are:

In (State A) _____.

In (State B) _____.

This agreement shall be applicable as well to any changes that may be made in the cited taxes and to any other tax that, because of its tax base, is essential and economically analogous to those cited above and that any Member Country may establish after the signing of this agreement.

Article 2: General Definitions

For purposes of this agreement and unless the text states otherwise:

a)   The terms "one of the Contracting States" and "another Contracting State" shall be used to designate (State A) or (State B) without distinction.

b)   The terms "territory of one of the Member States" and "territory of another Contracting State" shall mean the territories of (State A) or (State B) without distinction.

c)   The term "person" shall be used to designate:

   1.   An individual or natural person.

   2.   A corporate body or juridical person.

   3.   Any other entity or group of persons, whether associated or not, that is subject to the payment of taxes.

d)   An individual shall be considered a resident of the Contracting State where his habitual residence is located.

An enterprise is understood to be a resident of the State indicated in its articles of incorporation. If such articles of incorporation do not exist or if they do not stipulate a legal residence, the enterprise is considered to be a resident of the place where its effective administration is located.

If, despite these regulations, it proves impossible to identify the legal residence, the competent authorities of the Contracting States shall settle the matter by common agreement.

e)   The term "source of production" refers to the activity, right or good that produces or that could produce an income.

f)   The term "business activities" refers to the activities carried out by enterprises.

g)   The term "enterprise" denotes an organization consisting or one or more persons that is engaged in gainful activity.

h)   The terms "enterprise of a Contracting State" and "an enterprise of another Contracting State" refer to an enterprise residing in one Contracting State or another.

i)   The term "royalty" refers to any gain, value or sum of money paid for the use or for the privilege of using copyrights, patents, industrial drawings or models, exclusive procedures or formulas, trademarks or other intangible goods or goods of a similar nature.

j)   The term "capital gains" refers to the profit obtained by a person from transfer of the ownership of goods that it does not normally acquire, produce or transfer within its regular line of business.

k)   The term "pension" denotes a periodic payment made in consideration of services rendered or damages sustained; and the term "annuity" refers to a given sum of money paid periodically over the life of the beneficiary or during a set period under gratuitous title or in compensation for a service rendered or one with a cash value.

l)   The term "competent authority" denotes in the case of (State A) _____ and in the case of (State B) _____.

Article 3: Scope of undefined terms

Any term that is not defined in this agreement shall have the meaning given to it in the effective legislation of each Contracting State.

CHAPTER II
INCOME TAX

Article 4: Tax Jurisdiction

Irrespective of the nationality or residence of the persons, such income of any kind as they may obtain shall be taxable only in the Contracting State where the source of production of that income is located, save in the exceptional cases provided for in this agreement.

Article 5: Real estate income

Income of any kind produced by real estate shall be taxable only by the Contracting State in which those goods are located.

Article 6: Income from the right to exploit natural resources

Any earnings received from leasing or subleasing, or transferring or granting the right to exploit or to use in any way the natural resources of one of the Contracting States shall be taxable by that Contracting State only.

Article 7: Business earnings

Earnings from business activities shall be taxable only by the Contracting State where these were obtained.

An enterprise is considered, among other cases, to perform activities in the territory of a Contracting State when it maintains the following in that State:

a)   An office or a business management site;

b)   A factory, plant or industrial or assembly workshop;

c)   A construction site being worked;

d)   A site or facility where natural resources are extracted or worked, such as a mine, oil well, quarry, plantation or fishing vessel;

e)   A sales agency or office;

f)   A procurement agency or office:

g)   A warehouse, storehouse or similar facility for receiving, storing or delivering products;

h)   Any other locale, office or facility whose purpose is to prepare for or help with the activities of the enterprise;

i)   An agent or representative.

In the event that an enterprise carries out activities in both Contracting States, each of them may tax the earnings produced in their territory. If the activities are performed through representatives or by using facilities like those cited in the previous paragraph, then the earnings obtained shall be attributed to those persons or facilities as if they were totally independent of the enterprise.

Article 8: Transport company earnings

The earnings obtained by air carriers and overland, ocean, lake or river transport companies shall be subject to taxes only in the Contracting State where those enterprises have their legal residence.

Article 8: Alternative

The earnings obtained by air carriers and overland, sea, lake and river transport companies from their operations in any of the Contracting States shall be taxable in that Contracting State.

Article 9: Royalties from the use of patents, trademarks and technologies

Royalties earned from the use of trademarks, patents, unpatented technical know-how or other intangible goods of a similar nature in the territory of one of the Contracting States shall be taxable only in that Contracting State.

Article 10: Interest

Interest earned on loans shall be taxable only in the Contracting State where the loan funds were used.

Unless proven otherwise, it is assumed that the loan shall be used in the Contracting State where the interest is paid.

Article 11: Dividends and equity investments

Dividends and equity investments shall be taxable only by the Contracting State where the enterprise distributing them has its legal residence.

Article 12: Capital gains

Capital gains may be taxed only by the Contracting State in whose territory the goods were located at the time of their sale, with the exception of those obtained from the transfer of:

a)   Ships, aircraft, buses and other transport vehicles, which shall be taxable only by the Contracting State in which they were registered at the moment of the transfer, and

b)   Bonds, stock and other securities, which shall be taxable only by the Member Country where they were issued.

Article 13: Income from personal services

Payments, fees, salaries, wages, earnings and similar compensation received in return for services provided by employees, professionals, technicians or for personal services in general shall be taxable only in the territory where those services were rendered, with the exception of salaries, wages, pay and similar earnings received by:

a)   Persons that provide services to a Contracting State in the exercise of duly accredited official functions, which shall be taxable only by that State, although the services may be rendered in the territory of another Contracting State.

b)   Crews of ships, airplanes, buses and other vehicles that provide international transport, which shall be taxable only by the Contracting State where the employer has its residence.

Article 14: Professional Service and Technical Assistance Companies

The income earned by professional service and technical assistance companies shall be taxable only in the Contracting State in whose territory those services are rendered.

Article 15: Pensions and annuities

Pensions, annuities and other similar periodic income shall be taxable only by the Contracting State in whose territory the source of production is located.

The sources shall be considered to be situated in the territory of the State where the contract was signed that produced the periodic income and, if no contract exists, in the State from which that income is paid.

Article 16: Public entertainment activities

Income from the exercise of artistic and public entertainment activities shall be taxable only in the Contracting State in whose territory the activity was performed, irrespective of the length of time spent in the territory in question by the persons performing those activities.

CHAPTER III
NET WORTH AND CORPORATION TAX

Article 17: Net worth and Corporation tax

The individual or business assets located in the territory of one of the Contracting States shall be taxable only by that State.

Article 18: Situation of transport vehicles, credits and bearer securities

For purposes of the previous article, the following is understood:

a)   Aircraft, ships, buses and other transport vehicles and the movable property used in their operation are located in the Contracting State where their ownership is registered; and

b)   Credits, shares and other bearer securities are situated in the Contracting State where the debtor or the issuing enterprise, as the case may be, has its residence.

CHAPTER IV
GENERAL PROVISIONS

Article 19: Consultations and information

The competent authorities of the Contracting States shall hold consultations with each other and shall exchange the information that is necessary to resolve by mutual agreement any problem or doubt that may result from the implementation of this agreement and to establish the administrative controls needed to avoid fraud and tax evasion.

The information that is exchanged pursuant to the stipulation of the previous paragraph shall be considered confidential and may not be transmitted to any person other than the authorities responsible for the administration of the taxes covered by this agreement.

For purposes of this article, the competent authorities of the Contracting States may communicate with each other directly.

Article 20: Ratification

This agreement shall be ratified by the governments of the Contracting States in keeping with their respective constitutional and legal requirements.

The instruments of ratification shall be exchanged in _____ as soon as possible.

Once the instruments of ratification of this agreement have been exchanged, it shall become operative and shall be implemented:

a)   With regard to the income received by individuals, starting on the January 1st of the calendar year following that of ratification.

b)   With regard to the income received by juridical persons, during the fiscal year starting after the ratification of this agreement.

c)   With regard to the other taxes, those that must be paid in the calendar year following that of ratification.

Article 21: Duration

This agreement shall remain in effect indefinitely, but either of the contracting governments, from January 1st through June 30th of any calendar year, may notify the other contracting government in writing, denouncing the agreement and it shall cease to be operative:

a)   With regard to the income received by individuals, from January 1st of the calendar year following that of the notification.

b)   With regard to the income received by juridical persons, after the close of the fiscal year which began in the calendar year when notification was given of the denunciation of the agreement.

c)   With regard to the other taxes, starting on January 1st of the calendar year following that in which notification was given of the denunciation of the agreement.

*

AGREEMENT ON CUSTOMS UNION AND SINGLE ECONOMIC AREA BETWEEN THE KYRGYZ REPUBLIC, THE RUSSIAN FEDERATION, THE REPUBLIC OF BELARUS, THE REPUBLIC OF KAZAKHSTAN AND THE REPUBLIC OF TAJIKISTAN[*]
[Revision]
[Exerpts]

> The agreement on customs union and single economic area between the Kyrgyz Republic, the Russian Federation, the Republic of Belarus, the Republic of Kazakhstan and the Republic of Tajikistan was signed on 26 February 1999.

Signatory states to this Agreement hereinafter referred to as the Parties;

….

Acknowledging that the removal of existing barriers and restrictions requires coordinated actions, the harmonized development of market relationships of the states and creation of equal conditions and opportunities for business entities;

Hereby agreed as follows:

CHAPTER IV
Creation of a Single Economic Area

SECTION 4
Common Economic Policy and Development of an Infrastructure

Article 25

The parties shall agree upon main directions and stages of structural reform of member states' economy ensuring efficient utilization of industrial potential, formation of a favorable investment climate, support of highly efficient manufactures, carrying out a coordinated anti-monopoly, tax and financial policy and also creation of conditions for fair competition within the framework of the Single Economic Area.

SECTION 5
Common Market of Services

Article 37

1.   Member states shall aspire to provide to each other national regime of services market access on a mutual basis.

---

[*]   *Source*: World Trade Organization (2000). "Agreement on Customs Union and Single Economic Area between the Kyrgyz Republic, the Russian Federation, the Republic of Belarus, the Republic of Kazakhstan and the Republic of Tajikistan"; World Trade Organization, WT/REG71/5/Rev., 17 December 2000; also available on the Internet (http://www.wto.org). [Note added by the editor.]

2.   The Parties shall remove existing limitations of services market access gradually within the framework of Single Economic Area for legal entities and individuals of the member states of this Agreement.

3.   With these purposes the Parties shall accept a program of trade in services development within the framework of the Single Economic Area and they shall follow universally acknowledged international regulations and rules.

SECTION 7
Movement of Capital

Article 46

The Parties shall continue successive liberalization of foreign exchange policy with towards abrogation of other countries' currencies usage limitations in current operations, introduction of a unified exchange rate of national currency on the current operations of payment balance, access of banks – non residents to the domestic currency markets, abrogation of limitations on import and export of national currency by authorized banks and shall access Article 8 of International Monetary Fund Charter, while implementing agreements on mutual convertibility of national currencies. In order to implement measures on ensuring interaction of domestic currency and financial systems and upon finalizing these measures the Parties shall sign relevant Protocols.

Article 47

The Parties shall implement provisions of agreements on double taxation removal and prevention of evasion income and capital taxes payment.

Article 48

The Parties shall agree mechanism of establishment of national currencies' exchange rates.

Article 49

The Parties shall form member states payment system in order to serve payments on commodity circulation in domestic and enterprise spheres, non trade operations, transport, telecommunication and other services, and also on governmental, banking and commercial credits, currency exchange operations.

Article 50

Each of the Parties has right to apply temporary safeguard measures in the field of capital movement with immediate notification of other Parties to the Agreement, if the existing capital movement causes disturbances in functioning of domestic capital market.

Article 51

The Parties shall aspire to increase level of liberalization of capital movement as the member states' economic situation improves.

*

PART THREE

BILATERAL INSTRUMENTS

ACUERDO DE COMPLEMENTACIÓN ECONÓMICA ENTRE EL GOBIERNO DE LA REPÚBLICA DE BOLIVIA Y EL GOBIERNO DE LA REPÚBLICA DE CHILE (ACE N° 22)*
[excerpts]

The agreement on economic cooperation between the Government of the Republic of Bolivia and the Government of the Republic of Chile (ACE NO 22) was signed on 6 April 1993. It entered into force on 7 July 1993.

El Gobierno de la República de Bolivia y el Gobierno de la República de Chile,

CONSIDERANDO:

...

La trascendencia que para el desarrollo económico de los países signatarios tiene una adecuada cooperación en las áreas productivas de bienes y servicios.

La conveniencia de lograr una participación más activa de los agentes económicos de los países signatarios, mediante la existencia de reglas claras y predecibles para el desarrollo del comercio y la inversión.

CONVIENEN:

Capítulo I
Objetivos del Acuerdo

Artículo 1.
El presente Acuerdo tiene como objetivos:

a.   Sentar las bases para una creciente y progresiva integración de las economías de los países signatarios;

b.   Facilitar, ampliar y diversificar el intercambio comercial de bienes y servicios entre los países signatarios, fomentar y estimular actividades productivas localizadas en sus territorios y facilitar las inversiones de cada país signatario en el territorio del otro;

c.   Crear condiciones para lograr un avance armónico y equilibrado en el comercio bilateral;

d.   Servir de marco jurídico e institucional para el desarrollo de una más amplia cooperación económica en aquellas áreas que sean de mutuo interés; y

* *Source*: Organization of American States (1993). "Acuerdo de Complementación Económica entre el Gobierno de la República de Bolivia y el Gobierno de la República de Chile (ACE NO 22)", available on the Internet (http://www.sice.oas.org/Trade/chibol/chibol1.asp). [Note added by the editor.]

e.   Establecer mecanismos para promover una activa participación de los agentes económicos privados en los esfuerzos para lograr la ampliación y profundización de las relaciones económicas entre los países signatarios y conseguir la progresiva integración de sus economías.

Capítulo II
Programa de liberación

Artículo 2.

Los países signatarios acuerdan otorgarse preferencias arancelarias según el siguiente esquema:

- Chile otorga a Bolivia concesiones arancelarias sin reciprocidad para importaciones originarias de ese país, cuya clasificación, tratamiento y condiciones se encuentran especificados en el Anexo I * del presente Acuerdo.

- Los países signatarios acuerdan liberar de gravámenes las importaciones de los productos incluidos en los Anexos II y III del presente Acuerdo.

- En el Anexo IV se incluyen los productos beneficiados con preferencias arancelarias en el Acuerdo de Alcance Parcial suscrito entre Chile y Bolivia en el marco de la ALADI, y que, en el presente Acuerdo no han sido sujetas a profundización en su preferencia arancelaria en favor de ninguno de los dos países, quedando vigente el margen preferencial existente.

- Los países signatarios podrán, de común acuerdo y previa negociación, incorporar nuevos productos a los Anexos II y III, así como, profundizar las preferencias arancelarias incluídas en el Anexo IV del presente Acuerdo.

Capítulo V
Prácticas desleales de comercio y condiciones de competencia

Artículo 10.

Los países signatarios condenan el "dumping" y toda práctica desleal de comercio, así como el otorgamiento de subvenciones a la exportación y otros subsidios internos de efecto equivalente.

Artículo 11.

En caso de presentarse en el comercio recíproco situaciones de "dumping" o distorsiones en la competencia como consecuencia de la aplicación de subvenciones a las exportaciones y otros subsidios de efecto equivalente, tanto de productos amparados en los beneficios del Programa de Liberalización del presente Acuerdo como de productos que no están amparados en tales beneficios, el país signatario afectado aplicará las medidas correctivas previstas en su legislación interna. Al respecto, los países signatarios se comprometen a seguir los criterios y procedimientos que se estipulan en el ámbito del Acuerdo General sobre Aranceles Aduaneros y Comercio (GATT), a la fecha de suscripción del presente Acuerdo.

Capítulo VIII
Inversiones

Artículo 14.

A fin de estimular la circulación de capitales entre los dos países y la localización de inversiones procedentes de uno u otro en sus respectivos territorios, los países signatarios adoptarán, entre otros, los siguientes criterios en la aplicación de sus correspondientes legislaciones internas:

Los capitales procedentes de cualesquiera de los países signatarios gozarán en el territorio del otro país signatario de un tratamiento no menos favorable que aquel que se concede a los capitales provenientes de cualquier otro país, y

Los capitales procedentes de cualesquiera de los países signatarios gozarán en el territorio del otro país signatario de un tratamiento no menos favorable que aquel que se concede a los capitales nacionales.

Los mencionados criterios se aplicarán sin perjuicio de la plena vigencia, en lo que sea pertinente, de las disposiciones de carácter constitucional o legal sobre la materia que rijan en los países signatarios.

Capítulo IX
Complementación energética

Artículo 15.

Los países signatarios llevarán a cabo acciones orientadas a promover estudios y proyectos de complementación energética en las áreas eléctrica, geotérmica y de hidrocarburos. Dichas acciones se llevarán a efecto a través de los organismos nacionales competentes y, en particular, mediante la Comisión Técnica instituída por el Acta de Intenciones, suscrita en Río de Janeiro del 12 de noviembre de 1990, por el Ministro de Energía e Hidrocarburos de Bolivia y el Ministro Vicepresidente de la Comisión Nacional de Energía de Chile.

Artículo 16.

Sobre la base de las orientaciones acordadas en el Acta de Entendimiento suscrita en la ciudad de La Paz el 20 de junio de 1991, por el Ministro de Energía e Hidrocarburos de Bolivia y el Ministro Presidente de la Comisión Nacional de Energía de Chile, los países signatarios llevarán a cabo las acciones pertinentes para promover la ejecución de proyectos específicos de integración energética. De igual manera, los países signatarios procurarán que, en el futuro, se concreten entendimientos para la compra y venta de gas natural de origen boliviano, cuando se presenten las condiciones de disponibilidad de reservas bolivianas de gas natural, cuya producción correspondiente no esté comprometida y cuando se presenten las condiciones de factibilidad técnica y económica conveniente.

Artículo 17.

Las acciones de compra de gas boliviano, financiamiento y construcción del gasoducto podrán ser ejecutadas por empresas o consorcios privados bolivianos, chilenos, de terceros países e instituciones financieras internacionales, de acuerdo a la legislación vigente en cada país signatario.

Artículo 18.

Los países signatarios, tomando en consideración los trabajos que realice la Comisión Técnica a la que se refiere el Artículo 15, examinarán las conveniencias y la necesidad de negociar y suscribir, oportunamente, los instrumentos jurídicos adicionales que sean necesarios para regular la ejecución de los proyectos de integración energética y, en particular, aquellos proyectos basados en la utilización de gas natural de origen boliviano.

Capítulo X
Cooperación económica

Artículo 19.

Los países signatarios promoverán la cooperación en materias tales como:

a.   Regímenes normativos y sistemas de control en materia de sanidad animal y vegetal;

b.   Normas técnicas y bromatológicas;

c.   Normas en materia de seguridad y salud pública;

d.   Desarrollo de la actividad turística con el ánimo de que la misma contribuya al mejor conocimiento recíproco de los valores históricos y culturales de los países signatarios;

e.   Desarrollar acciones en las áreas de la información y promoción del comercio;

f.   Acciones destinadas a promover un crecinete intercambio de tecnología, particularmente en los sectores agropecuario, agroindustrial, industrial, minero y comunicaciones;

g.   Regímenes normativos y sistemas de control en materia de preservación del medio ambiente; y

h.   Regímenes sobre Propiedad Intelectual e Industrial.

Para llevar a cabo acciones específicas de cooperación en estas materias, los organismos competentes en las áreas respectivas de cada país signatario prodrán concertar convenios dentro del marco de sus atribuciones. La Comisión Administradora del Acuerdo promoverá la concreción de estas acciones y se mantendrá informada de los avances que se logren en las acciones que se acuerden.

Capítulo XI
Comisión Administradora del Acuerdo

Artículo 20.

La administración del presente Acuerdo estará a cargo de una Comisión integrada por Representantes Gubernamentales de Alto Nivel de los países signatarios.

La Comisión Administradora se reunirá en sesiones ordinarias, una vez al año, en el lugar y fecha que sean determinados de mutuo acuerdo y en sesiones extraordinarias, cuando los países signatarios, previas consultas, así lo convengan.

Las delegaciones de los países signatarios a las reuniones de la Comisión estarán presididas por el funcionario de Alto Nivel que cada uno de los respectivos Gobiernos designe y podrán estar integradas por otros delegados y asesores que éstos resuelvan acreditar.

Dicha Comisión deberá ser constituida dentro de los 90 días de suscrito el Acuerdo y en su primera sesión establecerá su propio reglamento.

Artículo 21.

La Comisión Administradora tentrá las siguientes competencias, atribuciones y funciones:

a.   Velar por el cumplimiento de las disposiciones del presente Acuerdo;

b.   Evaluar, periódicamente, los resultados de la aplicación del presente Acuerdo, negociar y acordar las medidas que estime más convenientes para el logro de los objetivos del mismo;

c.   Examinar y evaluar, periódicamente, los resultados en el comercio bilateral de la aplicación del Programa de Liberalización establecido en el presente Acuerdo y promover las consultas y negociaciones para la adopción de medidas destinadas a su perfeccionamiento;

d.   Acordar, con arreglo a las normas contenidas en el Capítulo II la inclusión de nuevos productos a los Anexos II, III y IV del mismo;

e.   Mantener actualizada la nomenclatura arancelaria adoptada para la clasificación de los productos incorporados en los Anexos I, II, III, y IV, del presente Acuerdo;

f.   Promover las consultas y negociaciones y acordar las medidas que sean pertinentes en todo lo relativo a la aplicación de las normas del presente Acuerdo sobre requisitos específicos de origen, cláusulas de salvaguardia y prácticas desleales de comercio y condiciones de competencia;

g.   Promover las consultas y negociaciones con objeto de estimular la cooperación económica entre los países signatarios, con arreglo a las normas contenidas en el Capítulo X del presente Acuerdo, y coordinar las actividades que desarrollen, en forma conjunta, los organismos nacionales competentes;

h.   Ejercer las funciones que le conciernen dentro de los procedimientos sobre Solución de Controversias, según lo estipulado en las normas contenidas en el Capítulo XIII del presente Acuerdo;

i.   Solicitar el asesoramiento y la opinión del Comité Asesor Empresarial y considerar los informes, recomendaciones, iniciativas y propuestas que sean elevadas por éste, particularmente en lo que respecta a la inclusión de nuevos productos a los Anexos II, III y IV;

j.   Aprobar, emendar o sustituir su propio Reglamento;

k.   Proponer a los Gobiernos de los países signatarios la ampliación, enmienda o sustitución del presente Acuerdo; y

l.   Ejercer las demás facultades y cumplir las demás funciones que le son atribuídas por el presente Acuerdo.

Artículo 22.

Los Acuerdos que resulten del ejercicio de las competencias y funciones atribuídas a la Comisión Administradora y que versen sobre materias específicas no reguladas en detalle por las normas del presente Acuerdo, se formalizarán mediante Protocolos Adicionales a éste y se entenderán amparados en el marco jurídico establecido por el mismo.

Artículo 23.

Los vínculos institucionales de los países signatarios con la Comisión Administradora estarán a cargo del Organismo Nacional Competente que cada uno de ellos designe.

Dicho Organismo cumplirá, asimismo, la función de mantener las comunicaciones y los vínculos entre los Gobiernos de los países signatarios en todo lo relativo a la aplicación del presente Acuerdo.

Capítulo XII
Comité Asesor Empresarial

Artículo 24.

A fin de promover y estimular una más activa participación de los sectores empresariales en las tareas referentes a la aplicación del presente Acuerdo, institúyese el Comité Asesor Empresarial que estará integrado por representantes de las organizaciones empresariales de cúpulas de los países signatarios.

El Comité, que tendrá el carácter de órgano asesor, estará destinado a coadyuvar, en lo pertinente, al cumplimiento de las funciones de la Comisión Administradora y a facilitar, de esa manera, la consecución de los objetivos enunciados en el presente Acuerdo.

Artículo 25.

El Comité Asesor Empresarial tendrá las siguientes competencias, atribuciones y funciones:

a.   Prestar asesoramiento a la Comisión Administradora en todas las materias comprendidas por el presente Acuerdo y en aquellas áreas que, a su juicio, contribuyan a ampliar y profundizar las relaciones económicas entre los países signatarios y en particular, la cooperación empresarial;

b.   Promover iniciativas a la Comisión Administradora sobre acciones a ser emprendidas para la aplicación de los mecanismos y el mejor cumplimiento de los objetivos previstos en el presente Acuerdo, especialmente en materias cooperación económica bilateral, así como en materia de tratamiento a las inversiones, circulación de capitales e inversiones conjuntas;

c.   Proponer a la Comisión Administradora la incorporación de nuevos productos a los Anexos del presente Acuerdo;

d.   Examinar, dentro del ámbito de su competencia, los resultados derivados de la aplicación de los mecanismos del presente Acuerdo;

e.   Promover entendimientos o acuerdos operativos de cooperación recíproca entre las organizaciones empresariales, de los países signatarios;

f.   Adoptar, enmendar y sustituir las normas destinadas a regular su funcionamiento y actividades; y

g.   Realizar otras actividades o tareas que le sean expresamente solicitadas por la Comisión Administradora o que, de común acuerdo, convengan las delegaciones de las organizaciones empresariales de los países signatarios.

Capítulo XIII
Solución de controversias

Artículo 26.

Para la solución de controversias que pudieran presentarse con motivo de la interpretación de las disposiciones contenidas en el presente Acuerdo, así como de su aplicación o incumplimiento o de cualquier otra naturaleza distinta de las previstas en el Capítulo V, los países signatarios se someterán al procedimiento que se indica en los artículos siguientes.

Artículo 27.

El país signatario que entienda que está afectado por una situación de aplicación no ajustada a derecho o basada en una interpretación que no comparte o por una situación de incumplimiento de las normas del presente Acuerdo, hará conocer al otro país signatario, a través del Organismo Nacional Competente a que se refiere el Artículo 23, sus observaciones al respecto, las cuales deberán ser respondidas por este último en un plazo no mayor a 15 días.

En caso de que el país signatario requerido no responda en el plazo indicado o que su respuesta no satisfaga al país signatario afectado, se dará curso, en forma inmediata, a un procedimiento de negociación directa a través de los Organismos Nacionales Competentes a que se refiere el Artículo 23 o en el seno de la Comisión Administradora según elija el país signatario afectado.

En este segundo caso, la Comisión será convocada para reunirse en un plazo no mayor a 20 días después de conocida la solicitud del país signatario afectado.

Para el mejor cumplimiento de su cometido, la Comisión Administradora podrá solicitar a especialistas individuales u organismos especializados independientes opiniones técnicas, que serán tomadas en consideración como elementos de juicio adicionales.

Artículo 28.

Si en las negociaciones directas a través de los Organismos Nacionales Competentes o en el seno de la Comisión Administradora no se lograse, en un plazo de 30 días prorrogable de mutuo acuerdo, una solución mutuamente satisfactoria para la controversia planteada, ésta será sometida a la consideración y fallo de una Comisión Arbitral integrada por tres expertos de reconocida idoneidad, dos de ellos designados por cada uno de los países signatarios y un tercer árbitro que la presidirá. Este no podrá ser nacional de los países signatarios y deberá ser designado por el Secretario General de la ALADI, de entre los nombres incluídos en una lista de expertos que la Comisión Administradora elaborará anualmente para estos efectos.

La Comisión Arbitral deberá estar constituída e iniciar sus tareas en un plazo no mayor a 20 días después de la designación de sus integrantes.

Artículo 29.

La Comisión Arbitral ajustará su actuación a las disposiciones del Reglamento sobre Procedimiento de Arbitraje a ser adoptado por la Comisión Administradora del Acuerdo, dentro de un plazo no mayor a 90 días de la fecha de su constitución.

Emitirá su fallo a través de una Resolución, la cual deberá ser adoptada en un plazo no mayor a 60 días a partir de la fecha de su constitución.

Artículo 30.

Sin perjuicio de la facultad de sus miembros de decidir en conciencia sobre la controversia sometida a su consideración, la Comisión Arbitral apreciará las situaciones y hechos sujetos a su examen a la luz de las normas del presente Acuerdo y del Tratado de Montevideo 1980, así como de otras normas y principios de Derecho Internacional que sean pertinentes.

Artículo 31.

La Resolución de la Comisión Arbitral deberá contener el pronunciamiento de ésta sobre si la situación sometida a su consideración configura un incumplimiento o una interpretación no ajustada a derecho y sobre las medidas a ser adoptadas por el país requerido para rectificar esta situación.

De igual manera, deberá determinar aquellas medidas que el país afectado podrá adoptar para el caso en que el país requerido incumpla la misma.

Artículo 32.

La Resolución de la Comisión Arbitral será inapelable y dará lugar, únicamente, a un recurso de aclaración.

Será plenamente obligatoria para los países signatarios a partir de su notificación.

Su incumplimiento por parte del país requerido podrá dar lugar a la suspensión transitoria de la aplicación por parte del país afectado de algunas o todas las disposiciones del presente Acuerdo, así como configurar, en caso de persistir dicho incumplimiento, causal de denuncia de éste.

Cuarto Protocolo Adicional

La República de Bolivia y la República de Chile en adelante "Las Partes Contratantes":

Deseando intensificar la cooperación económica en beneficio de ambos Estados:

Con la intención de crear y de mantener condiciones favorables para las inversiones de inversionistas de una Parte Contratante en el territorio de la otra Parte Contratante que impliquen transferencias de capitales.

Reconociendo la necesidad de promover y de proteger las inversiones extranjeras con miras a favorecer la prosperidad económica de ambos Estados.

Conscientes de la necesidad de establecer un marco jurídico adecuado que regule y garantice la promoción y protección recíproca de las inversiones entre ambos países;

Acuerdan lo siguiente:

Artículo 1
Definiciones

Para los efectos del presente Acuerdo:

1.   El término "inversionista" designa, para cada una de las Partes Contratantes a los siguientes sujetos que hayan efectuado inversiones en el territorio de la otra Parte Contratante conforme al presente Acuerdo:

  a)   Las personas naturales que, de acuerdo con la legislación de una Parte Contratante, sean consideradas nacionales de la misma;

  b)   Las personas jurídicas debidamente constituidas según la legislación de una Parte Contratante, que tengan su sede, así como sus actividades económicas sustanciales, en el territorio de dicha Parte Contratante;

  c)   Las personas jurídicas constituidas conforme a la legislación de cualquier país, que fueren efectivamente controladas por los inversionistas señalados en los literales a) y b) anteriores.

2.   El término "inversión" se refiere a toda clase de bienes o derechos relacionados con una inversión siempre que ésta se haya efectuado de conformidad con las leyes y reglamentos de la Parte Contratante en cuyo territorio se realizó la inversión y comprenderá, en particular, aunque no exclusivamente a:

  a)   Los bienes muebles e inmuebles, así como todos los demás derechos reales;

  b)   Las acciones, cuotas societarias y cualquier otro tipo de participación en sociedades;

  c)   Los derechos de crédito o cualquier otra prestación que tenga valor económico;

  d)   Los derechos de propiedad intelectual, incluidos los derechos de autor y de propiedad industrial;

  e)   Las concesiones comerciales otorgadas por ley o en virtud de un contrato, incluidas concesiones para explorar, cultivar, extraer, explotar e industrializar recursos naturales.

3.   El término "territorio" comprende todo el espacio sujeto a la soberanía y jurisdicción de cada Parte Contratante, conforme a sus respectivas legislaciones y al derecho internacional.

Artículo II
Ámbito de Aplicación

El presente Acuerdo se aplicará a las inversiones efectuadas antes y después de la entrada en vigencia del Acuerdo, por inversionistas de una Parte Contratante, conforme a las disposiciones legales de la otra Parte Contratante, en el territorio de esta última. Sin embargo, no se aplicará a divergencias o controversias que hubieran surgido con anterioridad a su entrada en vigencia.

Artículo III
Promoción y Protección de las Inversiones

1.   Cada Parte Contratante, con sujeción a su política general en el campo de las inversiones extranjeras, incentivará en su territorio las inversiones de inversionistas de la otra Parte Contratante y autorizará dichas inversiones de conformidad con su legislación.

2.   Cada Parte Contratante protegerá dentro de su territorio las inversiones efectuadas de conformidad con sus leyes y reglamentos, por los inversionistas de la otra Parte Contratante y no obstaculizará la libre administración, mantenimiento, uso, usufructo, extensión, transferencia, venta y liquidación de dichas inversiones a través de medidas injustificadas o discriminatorias.

Artículo IV
Tratamiento de las Inversiones

1.   Cada Parte Contratante deberá garantizar un tratamiento justo y equitativo dentro de su territorio a las inversiones de los inversionistas de la otra Parte Contratante y asegurará que el ejercicio de los derechos reconocidos en el presente Acuerdo no será obstaculizado.

2.   Cada Parte Contratante otorgará a las inversiones de los inversionistas de la otra Parte Contratante, efectuadas en su territorio, un trato no menos favorable que aquél otorgado a las inversiones de sus propios inversionistas o a inversionistas de un tercer país, si este último tratamiento fuere más favorable.

3.   En caso que una Parte Contratante otorgare ventajas especiales a los inversionistas de cualquier tercer estado en virtud de un convenio relativo a la creación de un área de libre comercio, una unión aduanera, un mercado común, una unión económica o cualquier otra forma de organización económica regional o en virtud de un acuerdo relacionado en su totalidad o principalmente con materias tributarias, dicha parte no estará obligada a conceder las referidas ventajas a los inversionistas de la otra Parte Contratante.

Artículo V
Libre Transferencia

1.   Cada Parte Contratante autorizará, sin demora, a los inversionistas de la otra Parte Contratante para que realicen la transferencia de los fondos relacionados con las inversiones en moneda de libre convertibilidad, en particular, aunque no exclusivamente:

a)   Los intereses, dividendos, utilidades y otros beneficios;

b)   Las amortizaciones de créditos externos relacionadas con una inversión;

c)   El producto de la venta o liquidación total o parcial de una inversión o cuando corresponda el capital invertido;

d)   Los pagos producto del arreglo de una controversia y las compensaciones de conformidad con el Artículo VI.

2.   Las transferencias se realizarán conforme al tipo de cambio vigente en el mercado a la fecha de la transferencia, de acuerdo a la ley de la Parte Contratante que haya admitido la inversión.

Artículo VI
Expropiación y Compensación

1.   Ninguna de las Partes Contratantes adoptará medidas que priven, directa o indirectamente, a un inversionista de la otra Parte Contratante, de su inversión a menos que se cumplan los siguientes requisitos:

   a)   Las medidas se adopten por causa de utilidad pública o interés nacional y de conformidad con la ley;

   b)   Las medidas no sean discriminatorias;

   c)   Las medidas vayan acompañadas de disposiciones para el pago de una compensación inmediata, suficiente y efectiva.

2.   La compensación se basará en el valor de mercado de las inversiones afectadas en una fecha inmediatamente anterior a aquella en que la medida llegue a conocimiento público.

Cuando resulte difícil determinar dicho valor, la compensación podrá ser fijada de acuerdo con los principios de avaluación generalmente reconocidos como equitativos, teniendo en cuenta el capital invertido, su depreciación, el capital repatriado hasta esa fecha, el valor de reposición y otros factores relevantes. Ante cualquier atraso en el pago de la compensación se acumularán intereses a una tasa comercial establecida sobre la base del valor de mercado, a contar de la fecha de expropiación o pérdida hasta la fecha de pago.

3.   De la legalidad de la nacionalización, expropiación o de cualquiera otra medida que tenga un efecto equivalente y del monto de la compensación, se podrá reclamar en procedimiento judicial ordinario.

4.   Los inversionistas de cada Parte Contratante cuyas inversiones en el territorio de la otra Parte Contratante sufrieren pérdidas debido a una guerra o cualquier otro conflicto armado; a un estado de emergencia nacional; disturbios civiles u otros acontecimientos similares en el territorio de la otra Parte Contratante, deberán recibir de esta última, por concepto de reparación, indemnización, compensación u otro arreglo, un tratamiento no menos favorable que el que concede esta Parte Contratante a los inversionistas nacionales o de cualquier tercer estado.

Artículo VII
Subrogación

1.   Cuando una Parte Contratante o un organismo autorizado por ella hubiere otorgado un contrato de seguro o alguna otra garantía financiera contra riesgos no comerciales, con respecto a alguna inversión de uno de sus inversionistas, en el territorio de la otra Parte Contratante, ésta última deberá reconocer los derechos de la primera Parte Contratante de subrogarse en los derechos del inversionista, cuando hubiere efectuado un pago en virtud de dicho contrato o garantía.

2.   Cuando una Parte Contratante haya pagado a su inversionista y en tal virtud haya asumido sus derechos y prestaciones, dicho inversionista no podrá reclamar tales derechos y prestaciones a la otra Parte Contratante, salvo autorización expresa de la primera Parte Contratante.

Artículo VIII
Consultas

Las Partes Contratantes se consultarán sobre cualquier materia relacionada con la aplicación o interpretación de este Acuerdo.

Artículo IX
Solución de Controversias entre las Partes Contratantes

1.   Las diferencias que surgieren entre las Partes Contratantes relativas a la interpretación y aplicación del presente Acuerdo, deberán ser resueltas, en la medida de lo posible, por medio de negociaciones directas.

2.   En caso que ambas Partes Contratantes no pudieran llegar a un acuerdo dentro del plazo de seis meses a contar de la fecha de la notificación de la controversia, ésta será remitida, a petición de cualquiera de las Partes Contratantes, a un tribunal arbitral compuesto por tres miembros. Cada Parte Contratante deberá designar a un árbitro y esos dos árbitros deberán designar a un Presidente, que deberá ser nacional de un tercer estado.

3.   Si una de las Partes Contratantes no hubiere designado a su árbitro y no hubiere aceptado la invitación de la otra Parte Contratante para realizar la designación dentro del plazo de dos meses contados desde la fecha de notificación de la solicitud de arbitraje, el árbitro será designado, a petición de dicha Parte Contratante, por el Presidente de la Corte Internacional de Justicia.

4.   Si los dos árbitros no pudieren llegar a un acuerdo en cuanto a la elección del Presidente dentro de dos meses luego de su designación, éste será designado, a, a petición de cualquiera de las Partes Contratantes, por el Presidente de la Corte Internacional de Justicia.

5.   Si, en los casos especificados en los párrafos tres y cuatro de este Artículo, el Presidente de la Corte Internacional de Justicia se viere impedido de desempeñar dicha función o si fuere nacional de alguna de las Partes Contratantes, el Vicepresidente deberá realizar la designación, y si este último se viere impedido de hacerlo o fuere nacional de alguna de las Partes Contratantes, el Juez de la Corte que lo siguiere en antigüedad y que no fuere nacional de ninguna de las Partes Contratantes deberá realizar la designación.

6.   El Presidente del tribunal deberá ser nacional de un estado con el cual ambas Partes Contratantes mantengan relaciones diplomáticas.

7.   El tribunal arbitral deberá adoptar su decisión mediante mayoría de votos. En todos los demás aspectos, el procedimiento del tribunal arbitral será determinado por el propio tribunal.

8.   La decisión arbitral será definitiva y obligará a las Partes Contratantes.

9.   Cada Parte Contratante deberá solventar los gastos del miembro designado por dicha Parte Contratante, así como los gastos de su representación en los procedimientos del arbitraje; los gastos del Presidente así como cualesquiera otros costos serán solventados en partes iguales por las dos Partes Contratantes.

Artículo X
Solución de Controversias entre una Parte Contratante y
un Inversionista de la otra Parte Contratante

1.	Las controversias que surjan en el ámbito de este Acuerdo, entre una de las Partes Contratantes y un inversionista de la otra Parte Contratante que haya realizado inversiones en el territorio de la primera, serán, en la medida de lo posible, solucionadas por medio de consultas amistosas.

2.	Si mediante dichas consultas no se llegare a una solución dentro del plazo de seis meses a contar de la fecha de solicitud de arreglo, el inversionista podrá remitir la controversia:

a)	Al tribunal competente de la Parte Contratante en cuyo territorio se efectuó la inversión; o

b)	A arbitraje internacional del Centro Internacional de Arreglo de Diferencias Relativas a Inversiones (CIADI), creado por la Convención para el Arreglo de Diferencias Relativas a Inversiones entre Estados y Nacionales de otros Estados, firmada en Washington el 18 de marzo de 1965.

3.	Una vez que el inversionista haya remitido la controversia al tribunal competente de la Parte Contratante en cuyo territorio se hubiere efectuado la inversión o al tribunal arbitral, la elección de uno u otro procedimiento será definitiva.

4.	Para los efectos de este Artículo, cualquier persona jurídica que se hubiere constituido de conformidad con la legislación de una de las Partes Contratantes y cuyas acciones, previo al surgimiento de la controversia, se encontraren mayoritariamente en poder de inversionistas de la otra Parte Contratante, será tratada, conforme al Artículo 25 2) b) de la referida Convención de Washington, como una persona jurídica de la otra Parte Contratante.

5.	La decisión arbitral será definitiva y obligará a ambas partes. Cada Parte Contratante la ejecutará de conformidad con su legislación.

6.	Las Partes Contratantes se abstendrán de tratar por medio de canales diplomáticos, asuntos relacionados con controversias sometidas a proceso judicial o a arbitraje internacional, de conformidad a lo dispuesto en este Artículo, hasta que los procesos correspondientes estén concluidos, salvo en el caso en que la otra parte en la controversia no haya dado cumplimiento a la sentencia judicial o a la decisión del tribunal arbitral, en los términos establecidos en la respectiva sentencia o decisión.

Artículo XI
Disposiciones Finales

1.	Las Partes Contratantes se notificarán entre sí, cuando las exigencias constitucionales para la entrada en vigencia del presente Acuerdo se hayan cumplido. El Acuerdo entrará en vigencia treinta días después de la fecha de la última notificación.

2.	Este Acuerdo permanecerá en vigor por un período de quince años y se prolongará después por tiempo indefinido. Transcurridos los quince años, cada Parte Contratante podrá denunciar el Acuerdo en cualquier momento, con un preaviso de un año y comunicado por la vía diplomática.

3.   Con respecto a las inversiones efectuadas con anterioridad a la fecha en que se hiciere efectivo el aviso de terminación de este Acuerdo, sus disposiciones permanecerán en vigor por un período adicional de quince años a contar de dicha fecha.

4.   El presente Acuerdo será aplicable independientemente de que existan o no relaciones diplomáticas entre ambas Partes Contratantes.

Hecho en la ciudad de La Paz, a los veintidós días del mes de setiembre de 1994.

PROTOCOLO

Al firmar el Acuerdo para la Promoción y Protección Recíproca de las Inversiones, la República de Bolivia y la República de Chile, convienen las siguientes disposiciones, que constituyen parte integrante del Acuerdo referido:

Ad, Artículo I 1, c)

Las Partes Contratantes en cuyo territorio se realicen las inversiones podrán exigir prueba del control efectivo por parte de los inversionistas de la otra Parte Contratante. Los siguientes hechos, entre otros, se aceptarán como prueba de dicho control:

1.   Una participación sustancial directa o indirecta en el capital de la persona jurídica que permita el manejo real, por ejemplo, una participación directa o indirecta superior a un 50% del capital o participación accionaria mayoritaria;

2.   El control directo o indirecto de los derechos de votación que permitan:

    a)   El ejercicio de la facultad de decidir sobre la administración y operaciones; o

    b)   El ejercicio de la facultad de decidir sobre la composición del directorio o de cualquier cuerpo administrativo.

Ad. Artículo II

Este Acuerdo no se aplicará a una persona jurídica organizada en virtud de las leyes de un tercer país, dentro del significado del Artículo I 1, c), cuando se hayan invocado las disposiciones de un acuerdo de protección de inversiones con ese país o ese tercer país invoque la protección diplomática mediante una petición formal con respecto a la misma materia.

Ad. Artículo V

1.   Las transferencias correspondientes a inversiones realizadas de acuerdo con el Programa Chileno para la Conversión de la Deuda Externa, se regirán por las normas especiales que dicho programa establece.

2.   El capital invertido podrá ser transferido sólo después de un año contado desde su ingreso al territorio de la Parte Contratante, salvo que la legislación de ésta contemple un tratamiento más favorable.

3.   Una transferencia se considerará realizada "sin demora" cuando se haya efectuado dentro del plazo normalmente necesario para el cumplimiento de las formalidades de transferencia. El

plazo, que en ningún caso podrá exceder de treinta días, comenzará a correr en el momento de entrega de la correspondiente solicitud, debidamente presentada.

Suscrito en la ciudad de La Paz, el 22 de setiembre de mil novecientos noventa y cuatro, en dos ejemplares en idioma español, siendo ambos textos igualmente auténticos.

Quinto Protocolo Adicional

El Instituto Nacional de Promoción de Exportaciones de la República de Bolivia, denominado en éste más adelante como INPEX y la Dirección General de Relaciones Económicas Internacionales del Ministerio de Relaciones Exteriores de la República de Chile denominada en éste más adelante como DIRECON y

Por cuanto INPEX y DIRECON consideran que el fomento y la promoción del comercio es esencial para el desarrollo efectivo de las relaciones comerciales de las Repúblicas de Chile y Bolivia y constituye uno de los objetivos de cooperación económica, comprendidos en el Artículo 19 del Acuerdo de Complementación Económica Nº 22 y

Considerando además que el referido Artículo 19 faculta a los organismos competentes de las áreas respectivas de cada país signatario para concertar convenios dentro del marco de sus atribuciones para llevar a cabo acciones específicas de cooperación,

Por el presente, se conviene mutuamente en lo siguiente:

Artículo 1
INPEX y DIRECON se comprometen a identificar áreas de cooperación mutua, a intercambiar información comercial y divulgar, en los centros de negocios de ambos países, información sobre los bienes y servicios de la República de Chile y Bolivia, con el objeto de incrementar el comercio entre los dos países.

Artículo 2
INPEX y DIRECON concertarán programas de asistencia técnica y adoptarán las medidas que se requieran en favor del desarrollo conjunto de ambas instituciones, según las necesidades de cada Servicio.

Artículo 3
INPEX y DIRECON se notificarán y ayudarán mutuamente en la realización de exposiciones comerciales y seminarios sobre productos y servicios de los dos países.

Artículo 4
INPEX y DIRECON deberán promover el intercambio de visitas de delegaciones comerciales, y la cooperación y asistencia se extenderá a los delegados patrocinados por ambas partes.

Artículo 5
INPEX y DIRECON deberán reunirse con regularidad para analizar el progreso y desarrollo de los esfuerzos conjuntos dirigidos a la expansión del comercio.

Artículo 6

INPEX y DIRECON deberán tomar todas aquellas otras medidas que fueren necesarias y factibles para fomentar la cooperación en el campo de la promoción del comercio entre los dos países.

Artículo 7

INPEX y DIRECON concertarán un plan de trabajo para la implementación del presente Convenio que detalle las acciones concretas a desarrollar, sus fechas de ejecución y la asignación de sus recursos y sus variables de evaluación, a ser definido en un plazo de noventa días.

Ambas partes se reservan el derecho a determinar sus propias asignaciones de presupuesto con el objeto de implementar cualesquiera programas en virtud del presente Convenio.

Este Convenio será válido hasta que las partes acordaren lo contrario por escrito.

El presente Convenio se ha extendido en originales, en idioma español.

El presente Convenio se suscribe en la ciudad de La Paz, el 21 de setiembre de 1994.

*

FREE TRADE AREA AGREEMENT BETWEEN TURKEY AND ISRAEL[*]
[excerpts]

The free trade area agreement between Turkey and Israel was signed on 14 March 1996. It entered into force on 1 May 1997.

CHAPTER IV

RIGHT OF ESTABLISHMENT AND SUPPLY OF SERVICES

ARTICLE 20

1.   The Parties agree to widen the scope of the Agreement to cover the right of establishment of firms of one Party in the territory of the other Party and the liberalization of the provisions of services by one Party's firms to consumers of services in the other Party.

2.   The Joint Committee shall make the necessary recommendations for the implementation of the objective described in paragraph 1.

In making such recommendations, the Joint Committee shall take account of past experience of implementation of the reciprocal most-favoured-nation treatment and of the obligations of each Party under the General Agreement on Trade in Services, hereinafter referred to as the 'GATS', particularly those in Article V of the latter.

3.   The Joint Committee shall make a first assessment of the achievement of this objective no later than three years after the Agreement enters into force.

ARTICLE 21

1.   At the outset, each Party reaffirms its obligations under the GATS, particularly the obligation to grant reciprocal most-favoured-nation treatment in the services sectors covered by that obligation.

In accordance with the GATS, this treatment shall not apply to:

   a)   advantages accorded by either Party under the terms of an agreement of the type defined in Article V of the GATS nor to measures taken on the basis of such an agreement.

   b)   other advantages granted in accordance with the list of most-favoured-nation exemptions annexed by either Party to the GATS.

---

[*] *Source*: The Government of Turkey and the Government of Israel (1996). "Free Trade Area Agreement between Turkey and Israel", available on the Internet (http://www.foreigntrade.gov.tr/ab/ingilizce/STA/israil/israel.htm). [Note added by the editor.]

CHAPTER V

GENERAL, INSTITUTIONAL AND FINAL PROVISIONS

ARTICLE 22
Intellectual, Industrial and Commercial Property

1.   Pursuant to the provisions of this Article and of Annex IX, the Parties shall grant and ensure adequate and effective protection of intellectual, industrial and commercial property rights in accordance with the highest international standards, including effective means of enforcing such rights.

2.   The implementation of this Article and of Annex IX shall be regularly reviewed by the Parties. If problems in the area of intellectual, industrial and commercial property affecting trading conditions were to occur, urgent consultation within the Joint Committee shall be undertaken, at the request of either Party, with a view to reaching mutually satisfactory solutions.

ARTICLE 23
Payments

1.   Payments in freely convertible currencies relating to commercial transactions between the Parties and the transfer of such payments to the territory of the State Party to this Agreement, where the creditor resides shall be free from any restrictions.

2.   The Parties shall refrain from any exchange or administrative restrictions on the grant, repayment or acceptance of short-term and medium-term credits covering commercial transactions in which a resident participates.

3.   Any measures concerning current payments connected with the movement of goods shall be in conformity with the conditions laid down under Article VIII of the Statutes of the International Monetary Fund.

ARTICLE 24
Public Procurement

1.   The Parties to this Agreement consider the effective liberalization of their respective public procurement markets an integral objective of this Agreement.

2.   The Joint Committee will review progress in this area annually.

ARTICLE 25
Competition

1.   The following are incompatible with the proper functioning of the Agreement, insofar as they may affect trade between Turkey and Israel:

   i)   all agreements between undertakings, decisions by associations of undertakings and concerted practices between undertakings which have as their object or effect the prevention, restriction or distortion of competition;

ii)   abuse by one or more undertakings of a dominant position in the territories of Turkey or Israel as a whole or in substantial part thereof;

iii)   any state aid which distorts or threatens to distort competition by favouring certain undertakings or the production of certain goods.

2.   The Joint Committee shall, within three years of the entry into force of the Agreement, adopt by decision the necessary rules for the implementation of paragraph 1.

Until these rules are adopted, the provisions of the Agreement on interpretation and application of Articles VI, XVI and XXIII of the GATT shall be applied as the rules for the implementation of paragraph 1 (iii).

3.   Each Party shall ensure transparency in the area of state aid, inter alia by reporting annually to the other Party on the total amount and the distribution of the aid given and by providing, upon request, information on aid schemes. Upon request by one Party, the other Party shall provide information on particular individual cases of state aid.

4.   With regard to agricultural products referred to in Chapter II, paragraph 1 (iii) does not apply.

5.   If Turkey or Israel consider that a particular practice is incompatible with the terms of the first paragraph and:

- is not adequately dealt with under the implementing rules referred to in paragraph 2, or

- in the absence of such rules, and if such practice causes or threatens to cause serious prejudice to the interest of the other Party or material injury to its domestic industry, including its services industry,

it may take appropriate measures after consultation within the Joint Committee or after thirty working days following referral for such consultation.

With reference to practices incompatible with paragraph 1 (iii), such appropriate measures, when the GATT is applicable to them, may only be adopted in accordance with the procedures and under the conditions laid down by the GATT or by any other relevant instrument negotiated under its auspices and applicable to the Parties.

6.   Notwithstanding any provision to the contrary adopted in accordance with paragraph 2, the Parties shall exchange information taking into account the limitations imposed by the requirements of professional and business secrecy.

ARTICLE 34
Protocols and Annexes

Protocol A and Protocol B, and Annexes I to IX of this Agreement and Joint Declearations related to provisions and implementation of this Agreement shall form an integral part of the Agreement. The Joint Committee may decide to amend the Protocols and Annexes.

ARTICLE 26
Balance of Payments Difficulties

When Turkey or Israel is in a serious balance of payment difficulty, or under threat thereof, Turkey or Israel, as the case may be, may in accordance with the conditions laid down within the framework of GATT and with Article VIII of the Articles of Agreement of the International Monetary Fund, adopt restrictive measures, which shall be of limited duration and may not go beyond what is necessary to remedy the balance of payments situation. Turkey or Israel, as the case may be, shall inform the other Party forthwith and present to the other Party, as soon as possible, a time schedule of their removal.

ARTICLE 27
Establishment of the Joint Committee

1.   A Joint Committee is hereby established in which each Party shall be represented. The Joint Committee shall be responsible for the administration of this Agreement and shall ensure its proper implementation.

2.   For the purpose of the proper implementation of this Agreement, the Parties shall exchange information and, at the request of either Party, shall hold consultations within the Joint Committee. The Joint Committee shall keep under review the possibility of further removal of the obstacles to trade between Turkey and Israel.

3.   The Joint Committee may, in accordance with the provisions of paragraph 3 of Article 28, take decisions in the cases provided for in this Agreement. On other matters the Joint Committee may make recommendations.

ARTICLE 28
Procedures of the Joint Committee

1.   For the proper implementation of this Agreement, the Joint Committee shall meet at an appropriate level whenever necessary but at least once a year. Either Party to this Agreement may request a meeting to be held.

2.   The Joint Committee shall act by common agreement.

3.   If a representative of a Party in the Joint Committee has accepted a decision subject to the fulfilment of constitutional requirements the decision shall enter into force, if no later date is contained therein, on the date of the receipt of written notification as to the fulfillment of such requirements.

4.   The Joint Committee shall adopt its rules of procedure which shall, inter alia, contain provisions for convening meetings and for the designation of the Chairman and his term of office.

5.   The Joint Committee may decide to set up such sub-committees and working parties as it considers necessary to assist it in accomplishing its tasks.

ANNEX IX

Intellectual, Industrial and Commercial Property Rights
referred to in Article 22

1.   By the end of the third year after the entry into force of the Agreement Israel shall accede to the following multilateral conventions on intellectual, industrial and commercial property rights to which Turkey shall accede or is Party.

- Bern Convention for the Protection of Literary and Artistic Works (Paris Act, 1971);

- Protocol relating to the Madrid Agreement concerning the International Registration of Marks (Madrid, 1989)

2.   Turkey shall also accede to the following multilateral conventions by the end of the third year after the entry into force of the Agreement to which Israel shall accede or is Party.

- Protocol relating to the Madrid Agreement concerning the International Registration of Marks (Madrid, 1989)

- Budapest Treaty on the International Recognition of the Deposit of Microorganisms for the Purposes of Patent Procedure (1977, modified in 1980).

- International Convention for the Protection of New Varieties of Plants (UPOV) (Geneva Act, 1991).

3.   The Joint Committee may recommend that the Parties accede to other multilateral conventions in this field.

4.   Israel shall ratify, by the end of the second year after the entry into force of the Agreement, the International Convention for the Protection of Performers, Producers of Phonograms and Broadcasting Organizations (Rome, 1961).

5.   The Parties confirm the importance they attach to the obligations arising from following multilateral conventions:

- Paris Convention for the Protection of Industrial Property (Stockholm Act. 1967, and amended in 1979);

- International Convention for the Protection of New Varieties of Plants (UPOV) (Geneva Act, 1991);

- Patent Cooperation Treaty (Washington, 1970, amended in 1979 and modified in 1984);

- Budapest Treaty on the International Recognition of the Deposit of Microorganisms for the Purposes of Patent Procedure (1977, modified in 1980).

*

FREE TRADE AGREEMENT BETWEEN TURKEY AND LITHUANIA*
[excerpts]

The free trade agreement between Turkey and Lithuania was signed on 2 June 1997. It entered in to force on 1 March 1998.

CHAPTER III

RIGHT OF ESTABLISHMENT AND SUPPLY OF SERVICES

ARTICLE 13

1.   The Parties shall seek to widen the scope of the Agreement to cover the right of establishment of firms of one Party in the territory of another Party and the liberalization of the provision of services by one Party's firms to consumers of services in the other.

2.   The Parties will discuss this cooperation in the Joint Committee with the aim of developing and deepening their relations under this Article.

CHAPTER IV

ARTICLE 25
Rules of Competition Concerning Undertakings, Public Aid

1.   The following are incompatible with the proper functioning of this Agreement, in so far as they affect trade between Turkey and Lithuania:

   a.   all agreements between undertakings, decisions by associations of undertakings and concerted practices between undertakings which have as their object or effect the prevention, restriction or distortion of competition;

   b.   abuse by one or more undertakings of a dominant position in the territories of Turkey or of Lithuania as a whole or in a substantial part thereof;

   c.   any public aid which distorts or threatens to distort competition by favoring certain undertakings or the production of certain goods.

2.   Each Party shall ensure transparency in the area of public aid inter alia by reporting annually to the other Party on the total amount and the distribution of the aid given and by providing, upon request, information on aid schemes. Upon request by one Party, the other Party shall provide information on particular individual cases of public aid.

---

* *Source*: The Government of Turkey and the Government of Lithuania (1997). "Free Trade Agreement between Turkey and Lithuania", available on the Internet (http://www.foreigntrade.gov.tr/ab/ingilizce/STA/litvanya/litvanya .htm). [Note added by the editor.]

3.   If Lithuania or Turkey considers that a particular practice is incompatible with the terms of the first paragraph of this Article, and:

    a.   is not adequately dealt with under the implementing rules referred to in paragraph 4 of the Record of Understanding, or

    b.   in the absence of such rules, and if such practice causes or threatens to cause serious prejudice to the interest of the other Party or material injury to its domestic industry, including its services industry,

it may take appropriate measures after consultation within the Joint Committee or after thirty working days following referral for such consultation.

4.   In the case of practices incompatible with paragraph 1.c) of this Article, such appropriate measures may, where the WTO/GATT 1994 applies thereto, only be adopted in conformity with the procedures and under the conditions laid down by the WTO/GATT 1994 and any other relevant instrument negotiated under its auspices which are applicable between the Parties.

5.   Notwithstanding any provisions to the contrary adopted in conformity with paragraph 4 of the Record of Understanding, the Parties shall exchange information taking into account the limitations imposed by the requirements of professional and business secrecy.

ARTICLE 26
Balance of Payments Difficulties

Where either Party is in a serious balance of payment difficulties or under threat thereof, Turkey and Lithuania as the case may be, may in accordance with the conditions laid down within the framework of WTO/GATT 1994 and with Article VIII of the Articles of Agreement of International Monetary Fund, adopt restrictive measures, which shall be of limited duration and may not go beyond what is necessary to remedy the balance of payment situation. Either Party, as the case may be, shall inform the other Party forthwith and present to the other Party, as soon as possible, of a time schedule of their removal.

ARTICLE 27
Protection of Intellectual Property

1.   The Parties shall grant and ensure protection of intellectual property rights on a non-discriminatory basis, including measures for the grant and enforcement of such rights. The protection shall be gradually improved on a level corresponding to the substantive standards of the multilateral agreements specified in Annex VI by 1 January 2001 at the latest.

2.   For the purpose of this Agreement "intellectual property protection" includes in particular protection of copyright, neighboring rights, trade marks, geographical indications, industrial designs, patents, topographies of integrated circuits, as well as undisclosed information (know-how).

3.   The Parties to this Agreement may conclude further agreements exceeding the requirements of this Agreement in conformity with TRIPS Agreement.

4.   The Parties shall co-operate in matters of intellectual property. They shall hold, upon request of a Party, expert consultations on these matters, in particular on activities relating to the existing or to future international conventions on harmonisation, administration and enforcement of intellectual property and on activities in international organizations, such as the World Trade Organization, WIPO, as well as on relations of Parties with third countries in matters concerning intellectual property.

ARTICLE 28
Public Procurement

1.   The Parties consider the opening up of the award of public contracts on the basis of non-discrimination and reciprocity, to be a desirable objective.

2.   As of the entry into force of this Agreement, both Parties shall grant each other's companies access to contract award procedures a treatment no less favorable than that accorded to companies of any other country.

3.   The Joint Committee, acting in accordance with Articles 30 and 31, shall periodically examine the practical modalities for the implementation of paragraphs 1 and 2 above. The Joint Committee shall lay down the necessary scope, timetable and rules as soon as possible, taking into account the solutions agreed upon within the WTO/ GATT 1994.

ARTICLE 29
Establishment of the Joint Committee

1.   A Joint Committee is hereby established in which each Party shall be represented. The Joint Committee shall be responsible for the administration of this Agreement and shall ensure its proper implementation.

2.   For the purpose of the proper implementation of this Agreement, the Parties shall exchange information and, at the request of any Party, shall hold consultations within the Joint Committee. The Joint Committee shall keep under review the possibility of further removal of the obstacles to trade between the Parties

3.   The Joint Committee may, in accordance with the provisions of paragraph 3 of Article 30, take decisions in the cases provided for in this Agreement. On other matters the Joint Committee may make recommendations.

ARTICLE 30
Procedures of the Joint Committee

1.   For the proper implementation of this Agreement, the Joint Committee shall meet at an appropriate level whenever necessary upon request but at least once a year. Either Party may request a meeting to be held.

2.   The Joint Committee shall act by common agreement.

3.   If a representative in the Joint Committee of a Party to this Agreement has accepted a decision subject to the fulfillment of constitutional requirements the decision shall enter into force, if no later date is contained therein, on the day the lifting of the reservation is notified.

4.   The Joint Committee shall adopt its rules of procedure which shall, inter alia, contain provisions for convening meetings and for the designation of the Chairman and his/her term of office.

5.   The Joint Committee may decide to set up such sub-committees and working parties as it considers necessary to assist it in accomplishing its tasks.

ARTICLE 35
Protocols and Annexes

Protocols 1, 2 and 3 and Annexes I to VI to this Agreement shall form an integral part thereof. The Joint Committee may decide to amend the Protocols and Annexes.

ANNEX VI (referred to in Article 27)

1.   Paragraph 1 of Article 27 concerns the following multilateral conventions:

- WTO Agreement on Trade Related Aspects of Intellectual Property Rights (TRIPS Agreement)

- International Convention for the Protection of Performers, Producers of Phonograms and Broadcasting Organisations (Rome, 1961);

- Nice Agreement concerning the International Classification of Goods and Services for the purposes of the Registration of Marks (Geneva, 1977 and amended in 1979);

- Protocol relating with Madrid Agreement concerning the International Registration of Marks (Madrid, 1989)

- Budapest Treaty of 28 April 1977 on the International Recognition of the Deposit of Micro-organisms for the Purposes of Patent Procedure;

- International Convention for the Protection of New Varieties of Plants (UPOV) (Geneva Act, 1991)

The Joint Committee may decide that the paragraph 1 of Article 27 shall apply to other multilateral conventions.

2.   The Parties confirm the importance they attach to the obligations arising from the following multilateral conventions:

- Bern Convention for the Protection of Literary and Artistic Works (Paris Act, 1971);

- Paris Convention for the Protection of Industrial Property (Stockholm Act 1967 amended 1979);

- Patent Co-operation Treaty (Washington 1970 amended in 1979 and modified in 1984).

FREE TRADE AGREEMENT BETWEEN TURKEY AND ROMANIA[*]
[excerpts]

The free trade agreement between Turkey and Romania was signed 29 April 1997. It entered in to force on 1 February 1998.

CHAPTER III

SERVICES AND INVESTMENT

ARTICLE 17

1.   The Parties recognize the growing importance of certain areas, such as services and investments. In their efforts to gradually develop and broaden their co-operation, in particular in the context of European integration, they will co-operate with the aim of achieving gradual liberalization and mutual opening of markets for investments and trade in services, taking into account relevant WTO provisions.

2.   Turkey and Romania will discuss in the Joint Committee this coopertion with the aim to develop and deepen their relations under the Agreement.

ARTICLE 24
Rules of Competition Concerning Undertakings

1.   The following are incompatible with the proper functioning of this Agreement in so far as they may affect trade between the Parties:

   a.   all agreements between undertakings, decisions by associations of undertakings and concerted practices between undertakings which have as their object or effect the prevention, restriction or distortion of competition;

   b.   abuse by one or more undertakings of a dominant position in the territories of the Parties as a whole or in a substantial part thereof;

   c.   any public aid which distorts or threatens to distort competition by favoring certain undertakings or the production of certain goods.

2.   Any practices contrary to this Article shall be assessed on the basis of criteria arising from the application of the rules of Articles 85, 86 and 92 of the Treaty establishing the European Economic Community.

3.   The Joint Committee shall, within three years of the entry into force of this Agreement adopt the necessary rules for the implementation of paragraph 1 and 2.

---

[*]   *Source*: The Government of Turkey and the Government of Romania (1997). "Free Trade Agreement between Turkey and Romania", WT/REG59/1, 18 May 1998; available on the Internet (http://www.foreigntrade.gov.tr/ab/ingilizce/STA/romanya/romanya.htm). [Note added by the editor.]

4.   a)   For the purpose of applying the provisions of paragraph 1, point (c), the Parties recognize that during the first five years after the entry into force of the Agreement, any public aid granted by Romania shall be assessed taking into account the fact that Romania shall be regarded as an area identical to those areas of Turkey described in Article 92 (3) (a) of the Treaty establishing the European Economic Community. The Joint Committee shall taking into account the economic situation of Romania, decide whether that period should be extended by further periods of five years.

b)   Each Party shall ensure transparency in the area of public aid, inter alia by reporting annually to the other Party on the total amount and the distribution of the aid given and by providing, upon request, information on aid schemes. Upon request by one Party, the other Party shall provide information on particular individual cases of public aid.

5.   With regard to agricultural products referred to in Chapter II, paragraph 1(c) of this Article does not apply.

6.   If Turkey or Romania considers that a particular practice is incompatible with the terms of paragraph 1, and:

-is not adequately dealt with under the implementing rules referred to in paragraph 2, or

- in the absence of such rules, and if such practice causes or threatens to cause serious prejudice to the interest of the other Party or material injury to its domestic industry, it may take appropriate measures after consultation within the Joint Committee or after 30 working days following referral for such consultation.

In the case of practices incompatible with paragraph 1(c) of this Article, such appropriate measures may, where WTO/GATT 94 applies thereto, only be adopted in conformity with the procedures and under the conditions laid down by WTO/GATT 94 and any other relevant instrument negotiated under its auspices which are applicable between the Parties.

7.   Notwithstanding any provisions to the contrary adopted in conformity with paragraph 2, the Parties shall exchange information taking into account the limitations imposed by the requirements of professional and business secrecy.

ARTICLE 25
Public Procurement

1.   The Parties consider the liberalization of their respective public procurement markets an objective of this Agreement.

2.   The Joint Committee will review progress in this area annually

ARTICLE 26
Intellectual, Industrial and Commercial Property

1.   Pursuant to the provisions of this Article, the Parties shall grant and ensure adequate and effective protection of intellectual, industrial and commercial property rights by the end of 1998 in accordance with the highest international standards and multilateral conventions referred to in Annex IX, including effective means of enforcing such rights.

2.   The Parties to this Agreement shall take all necessary measures to enforce these rights against trade distortion, infringement, and particularly against counterfeiting and piracy.

3.   The Joint Committee shall keep the implementation of intellectual property rights under review. At the request of one of the Parties to this Agreement consultations will take place in the Joint Committee on any matter concerning intellectual property rights.

4.   Upon entry into force of the Agreement treatment no less favourable than that granted to any third country under any bilateral agreement shall be granted by both Parties.

ARTICLE 33
Balance of Payments Difficulties

1.   The Parties shall endeavor to avoid the imposition of restrictive measures including measures relating to imports for balance of payments purposes. In the event of their introduction, the Party having introduced the same shall present to the other Party a time schedule for their removal.

2.   Where Turkey or Romania is in serious balance of payments difficulties, or under imminent threat thereof, Turkey or Romania, as the case may be, may, in accordance with the conditions established under the General Agreement on Tariffs and Trade and with Article VIII of the Articles of International Monetary Fund, adopt restrictive measures, including measures relating to imports, which shall be of limited duration and may not go beyond what is necessary to remedy the balance of payments situation. Turkey or Romania, as the case may be shall inform the other Party forthwith.

3.   Any restrictive measures shall not apply to transfers related to investments and in particular to the repatriation of amounts invested or reinvested and of any kind of revenues stemming therefrom.

ARTICLE 35
Establishment of the Joint Committee

1.   A Joint Committee is hereby established in which each Party shall be represented. The Joint Committee shall be responsible for the administration of this Agreement and shall ensure its proper implementation.

2.   For the purpose of the proper implementation of this Agreement, the Parties shall exchange information and, at the request of any Party, shall hold consultations within the Joint Committee. The Joint Committee shall keep under review the possibility of further removal of the obstacles to trade between the Parties.

3.   The Joint Committee may take decisions in the cases provided for in this Agreement. On other matters the Joint Committee may make recommendations.

ARTICLE 36
Procedures of the Joint Committee

1.   For the proper implementation of this Agreement, the Joint Committee shall meet at an appropriate level whenever necessary but at least once a year. Each Party may request a meeting to be held.

2.   The Joint Committee shall act by common agreement.

3.   If a representative in the Joint Committee of a Party has accepted a decision subject to the fulfillment of constitutional requirements, the decision shall enter into force, if no later date is contained therein, on the day the lifting of the reservation is notified.

4.   For the purpose of this Agreement, the Joint Committee shall adopt its rules of procedure which shall, inter alia, contain provisions for convening meetings and for the designation of the Chairman and his term of office.

5.   The Joint Committee may decide to set up such subcommittees and working groups as it considers necessary to assist it in accomplishing its tasks.

ARTICLE 38
Annexes and Protocols

1.   The Annexes, Protocols and Joint Declarations to this Agreement are an integral part of this Agreement

2.   The Joint Committee may decide to modify or amend the Annexes and Protocols.

ANNEX IX

Protection of Intellectual Property Referred to in Article 26

1.   By the end of the fifth year after the entry into force of the Agreement the Parties shall accede, as it will be the case, the following multilateral conventions on intellectual, industrial and commercial property rights:

-   Munich Convention on Granting European Patents of 5 October 1973;

-   Budapest Treaty on the International Agreement concerning the International Registration for the Purposes of Patent Procedure (1977, modified in 1980);

-   Protocol relating to the Madrid Agreement concerning the International Registration of Marks (Madrid, 1989);

-   Bern Convention for the Protection of Literary and Artistic Works (Paris Act, 1979);

- International Convention for the Protection of Performers, Producers of Phonograms and Broadcasting Organizations (Rome, 1961);

2.   The Joint Committee may recommend that the parties accede other multilateral conventions in this field.

3.   The Parties confirm the importance they attach to the obligations arising from the following multilateral conventions;

- Paris Convention for the Protection of Industrial Property (Stockholm Act 1967 amended 1979);

- Madrid Agreement concerning the International Registration of Marks (Stockholm Act 1967, amended 1979);

- Patent Cooperation Treaty (Washington 1970 amended in 1979 and modified in 1984).

*

FREE TRADE AREA AGREEMENT BETWEEN THE REPUBLIC OF TURKEY AND THE REPUBLIC OF ESTONIA[*]
[excerpts]

The free trade area agreement between the Republic of Turkey and the Republic of Estonia was signed on 3 June 1997. It entered into force on 1 July 1998.

CHAPTER III

GENERAL PROVISIONS

ARTICLE 12
Services and Investment

1.   The Parties to this Agreement recognize the growing importance of certain areas, such as services and investments. In their efforts to gradually develop and broaden their co-operation, in particular in the context of the European integration, they will co-operate with the aim of achieving a progressive liberalization and further opening of their markets mutually for investments and trade in services, taking into account relevant provisions of the General Agreement on Trade in Services.

2.   The Parties will discuss in the Joint Committee the possibilities to extend their trade relations to the fields of foreign direct investment and trade in services.

ARTICLE 23
Payments

1.   Payments in freely convertible currencies relating to trade in goods and services between the Parties and the transfer of such payments to the territory of the Party to this Agreement, where the creditor resides, shall be free from any restrictions.

2.   The Parties shall refrain from any exchange control or administrative restrictions other than existing in the current legislation of the Parties on the grant, repayment or acceptance of short and medium-term credits to trade transactions in which a resident of a Party participates.

3.   Notwithstanding the provisions of paragraph 2, any measure concerning current payments connected with the movement of goods shall be in conformity with the conditions laid down under Article VIII of the Articles of the Agreement of the International Monetary Fund.

---

[*] *Source*: The Government of Turkey and the Government of Estonia (1997). "Free Trade Area Agreement between the Republic of Turkey and the Republic of Estonia", available on the Internet (http://www.foreigntrade.gov.tr/ab/ingilizce/STA/estonya/estonya.htm). [Note added by the editor.]

ARTICLE 24
Rules of Competition Concerning Undertakings, Public Aid

1.   The following are incompatible with the proper functioning of this Agreement, in so far as they affect trade between Turkey and Estonia:

   a.   all agreements between undertakings, decisions by associations of undertakings and concerted practices between undertakings which have as their object or effect the prevention, restriction or distortion of competition;

   b.   abuse by one or more undertakings of a dominant position in the territories of Turkey or of Estonia as a whole or in a substantial part thereof;

   c.   any public aid which distorts or threatens to distort competition by favoring certain undertakings or the production of certain goods.

2.   Each Party shall ensure transparency in the area of public aid inter alia by reporting annually to the other Party on the total amount and the distribution of the aid given and by providing, upon request, information on aid schemes. Upon request by one Party, the other Party shall provide information on particular individual cases of public aid.

3.   For the purpose of applying the provisions of paragraph 1 of this Article, the Parties will take the measures in conformity with the procedures and under the conditions laid down in their respective Agreements with the European Communities. In case of any change in those procedures and/or conditions these changes will be applicable between the Parties.

4.   If Turkey or Estonia considers that a particular practice is incompatible with the terms of the paragraph 1 of this Article, and:

   a.   is not adequately dealt with under the implementing rules referred to in paragraph 3 of this Article, or

   b.   in the absence of such rules, and if such practice causes or threatens to cause serious prejudice to the interest of the other Party or material injury to its domestic industry, including its services industry,

   it may take appropriate measures after consultation within the Joint Committee or after thirty working days following referral for such consultation.

5.   In the case of practices incompatible with paragraph 1.c) of this Article, such appropriate measures may, where the WTO/GATT 1994 applies thereto, only be adopted in conformity with the procedures and under the conditions laid down by the WTO/GATT 1994 and any other relevant instrument negotiated under its auspices which are applicable between the Parties.

6.   Notwithstanding any provisions to the contrary adopted in conformity with paragraph 3 of this Article, the Parties shall exchange information taking into account the limitations imposed by the requirements of professional and business secrecy.

ARTICLE 25
Balance of Payments Difficulties

1.   The Parties shall endeavor to avoid the imposition of restrictive measures including measures relating to imports for balance of payments purposes.

2.   Where either Party is in serious balance of payment difficulties or under threat thereof, Turkey and Estonia as the case may be, may, in accordance with the conditions laid down within the framework of GATT and with Article VIII of the Articles of Agreement of International Monetary Fund, adopt restrictive measures, which shall be of limited duration and may not go beyond what is necessary to remedy the balance of payment situation. Either Party, as the case may be, shall inform the other Party forthwith and present to the other Party, as soon as possible, of a time schedule of their removal.

ARTICLE 26
Protection of Intellectual, Industrial and Commercial Property Rights

1.   The Parties shall grant and ensure adequate and effective protection of intellectual property rights on a non-discriminatory basis, including measures for granting and enforcing such rights.

2.   The Parties shall take all necessary measures to enforce these rights against infringement, and particularly against counterfeiting and piracy.

3.   In fulfillment of their commitment under international agreements and legislation in the field of intellectual property rights, the Parties shall not grant less favorable treatment to nationals of each other than that accorded to nationals of any other State.

4.   The Parties shall co-operate in matters of intellectual property. They shall hold, upon request of any Party, expert consultations on these matters, in particular, on activities relating to the existing or to future international conventions on harmonization, administration and enforcement of intellectual property and on activities in international organizations, such as the World Trade Organization and the World Intellectual Property Organization, as well as relations of the Parties with any third country on matters concerning intellectual property.

ARTICLE 27
Public Procurement

1.   The Parties consider the liberalization of their respective public procurement markets as an objective of this Agreement.

2.   The Parties shall progressively adjust their respective regulations concerning public procurement with a view to grant suppliers of the other Parties, at the latest by December 31, 2000, access to contract award procedures on their respective public procurement markets according to the provisions of the Agreement on Government Procurement in Annex IV to the Agreement establishing the World Trade Organization.

3.   The Joint Committee shall examine developments related to the achievement of the objectives of this Article and may recommend practical modalities of implementing the

provisions of paragraph 2 of this Article, so as to ensure free access, transparency and full balance of rights and obligations.

4.   During the examination, referred to in paragraph 3 of this Article, the Joint Committee may consider, especially in the light of international regulations in this area, the possibility of extending the coverage and/or the degree of the market opening provided for in paragraph 2.

5.   The Parties shall endeavor to accede to the relevant Agreements negotiated under the auspices of the General Agreement on Tariffs and Trade 1994 and the Agreement establishing the World Trade Organization.

ARTICLE 28
Establishment of the Joint Committee

1.   A Joint Committee is hereby established in which each Party shall be represented. The Joint Committee shall be responsible for the administration of this Agreement and shall ensure its proper implementation.

2.   For the purpose of the proper implementation of this Agreement, the Parties shall exchange information and, at the request of any Party, shall hold consultations within the Joint Committee. The Joint Committee shall keep under review the possibility of further removal of the obstacles to trade between the Parties.

3.   The Joint Committee may, in accordance with the provisions of paragraph 3 of Article 29, take decisions in the cases provided for in this Agreement. On other matters the Joint Committee may make recommendations.

ARTICLE 29
Procedures of the Joint Committee

1.   For the proper implementation of this Agreement, the Joint Committee shall meet at an appropriate level whenever necessary upon request but at least once a year. Either Party may request a meeting to be held.

2.   The Joint Committee shall act by common agreement.

3.   If a representative in the Joint Committee of a Party to this Agreement has accepted a decision subject to the fulfillment of constitutional requirements, the decision shall enter into force, if no later date is contained therein, on the day the lifting of the reservation notified.

4.   The Joint Committee shall adopt its rules of procedure which shall, inter alia, contain provisions for convening meetings and for the designation of the Chairman and his/her term of office.

5.   The Joint Committee may decide to set up such sub-committees and working parties as it considers necessary to assist it in accomplishing its tasks.

*

ACUERDO ENTRE EL GOBIERNO DE LOS ESTADOS UNIDOS DE AMÉRICA Y LOS GOBIERNOS DE COSTA RICA, EL SALVADOR, GUATEMALA, HONDURAS, NICARAGUA Y LA REPÚBLICA DOMINICANA CONCERNIENTE A UN CONSEJO REGIONAL CENTROAMERICANO-ESTADOUNIDENSE DE COMERCIO E INVERSIÓN*

The agreement between the Government of the United States of America and the Governments of Costa Rica, the Dominican Republic, El Salvador, Guatemala, Honduras and Nicaragua concerning a Central America- United States Regional Council of Trade and Investment was signed in March 1998.

El Gobierno de los Estados Unidos de América y los Gobiernos de Costa Rica, El Salvador, Guatemala, Honduras, Nicaragua y la República Dominicana (que en adelante se llamarán las Partes):

1. Deseando promover el espíritu de la Cumbre de San José celebrada en San José, Costa Rica, el 8 de mayo de 1997;

2. Subrayando la importancia de las economías de libre mercado y de las iniciativas del sector privado cono fuentes (de prosperidad, y reafirmando el objetivo de promover reuniones empresariales y otras actividades complementarias que amplían las relaciones de comercio e inversión entre los sectores privados de nuestro países.

3. Reconociendo los avances en la liberalización económica logrados por las Partes;

4. Deseando colaborar conjunta y expeditivamente, en forma congruente con los acuerdos de la Organización Mundial del Comercio (OMC) y del proceso del Área de Libre Comercio de las Américas (ALCA), para identificar los pasos, incluidos los acuerdos comerciales bilaterales, multilaterales y recíprocos, que intensificarían las relaciones económicas entre nuestras naciones;

5. Reconociendo la importancia del comercio y la inversión para las economías de las Partes;

6. Tomando en cuenta los compromisos de todas las Partes para implementar las obligaciones asumidas y ejercer los derechos acordados en la OMC;

7. Reconociendo y procurando aprovechar los esfuerzos hechos por las Partes para liberalizar sus economías;

---

* *Source*: Secretaria de Integracción Económic Centroamericana (1998). "Acuerdo entre el Gobierno de los Estados Unidos de América y los Gobiernos de Costa Rica, El Salvador, Guatemala, Honduras, Nicaragua y la República Dominicana Concerniente a un Consejo Regional Centroamericano-Estadounidense de Comercio e Inversión", available on the Internet (http://www.sieca.org.gt/publico/OACUERDOS/ACUERDO_USA-COM_E_INVER.htm). [Note added by the editor.]

8.   Reconociendo la importancia de promover un ambiente abierto y previsible para el comercio y la inversión internacional;

9.   Reconociendo los beneficios para cada una de las Partes resultantes de un aumento en el comercio y la inversión internacional y reconociendo, asimismo, los efectos perjudiciales del proteccionismo y de las medidas que distorsionan o restringen el flujo de las inversiones internacionales;

10.   Reconociendo que la inversión directa extranjera confiere beneficios a cada una de las Partes;

11.   Reconociendo la importancia de proporcionar una protección adecuada y el cumplimiento eficaz de los derechos de propiedad intelectual y tomando en cuenta los derechos y las obligaciones asumidos en el marco del Acuerdo sobre Aspectos de los Derechos de Propiedad Intelectual Relacionados con el Comercio (ADPICS).

12.   Reconociendo la contribución al bienestar económico de todas las Partes que proporcionan la observancia y promoción de los derechos fundamentales de los trabajadores, según figuran en la Constitución y las Convenciones de la Organización Internacional del Trabajo y en otros convenios pertinentes;

13.   Reconociendo los avances logrados por las Partes en los aspectos de protección ambiental y desarrollo sostenible, y la relevancia que éstos revisten en relación con la aplicación de los acuerdos que rigen el comercio y la inversión.

14.   Reconociendo que es deseable que los problemas del comercio y la inversión entre las Partes se resuelvan por acuerdo mutuo con la mayor prontitud posible;

15.   Teniendo en cuenta la Declaración de San José en cuanto a que es necesario avanzar hacia una relación comercial que ofrezca a las Partes condiciones de mutuo beneficio, manteniendo los mercados abiertos al comercio y la inversión asegurando la participación de toda la población en los beneficios del crecimiento económico y preservando la estabilidad macroeconómica y financiera; y

16.   Considerando que en la Cumbre de San José nuestros dirigentes decidieron dar instrucciones a los Ministros de Comercio para establecer un Consejo Regional Centroamericano-Estadounidense de Comercio e Inversión con el mandato de hacer recomendaciones específicas. En apoyo a esos objetivos, nuestros dirigentes convinieron en continuar sus esfuerzos para concertar tratados bilaterales de comercio e inversión y acuerdos sobre derechos de propiedad intelectual, así como otros acuerdos para promover el comercio con los Estados Unidos. Convinieron, asimismo, bajo los auspicios de la OMC, en tratar de liberalizar los sectores de finanzas, telecomunicaciones y tecnología de la información.

Con este fin, los Estados Unidos y las Partes convienen en lo siguiente:

Artículo Primero

Establecer entre el Gobierno de los Estados Unidos y los Gobiernos de Costa Rica, El Salvador, Guatemala, Honduras, Nicaragua y la República Dominicana, un Consejo de Comercio e Inversión a Nivel Ministerial (en adelante llamado "el Consejo"). El Consejo será de carácter exclusivamente multilateral y funcionará en forma complementaria a los Consejos de Comercio e Inversión bilaterales ya existentes.

Artículo Segundo

El Consejo estará integrado por representantes de las Partes a nivel Ministerial. En el caso de los países miembros del Mercado Común Centroamericano y la República Dominicana, se integrará con los Ministros responsables de las negociaciones comerciales y en el caso de los Estados Unidos, con el Representante de Comercio de los Estados Unidos. Estas representaciones no serán delegables.

Artículo Tercero

1.   El Consejo tendrá los siguientes objetivos:

Cumplir lo dispuesto en la Declaración de San José del 8 mayo de 1997, sobre la Promoción de la Prosperidad por medio de la integración económica en el libre comercio y la inversión

Para esos fines el Consejo deberá:

i)   Identificar en forma conjunta y expedita pasos y acciones específicas compatibles con los acuerdos de la OMC y al proceso del ALCA, incluyendo acuerdos bilaterales, multilaterales y regionales de comercio basados en la reciprocidad, que intensifiquen la integración y consoliden las relaciones económicas que, (finalmente, eliminarán las barreras al comercio entre los países miembros del Consejo.

ii)   Identificar los mecanismos que faciliten y promuevan las corrientes de comercio e inversión.

iii)   Intensificar los esfuerzos emprendidos para concluir los tratados de inversión y de derechos de propiedad intelectual, tomando en cuenta los esfuerzos realizados y los resultados obtenidos en esta materia en el marco de la OMC y el ALCA.

iv)   Analizar la posibilidad, en el marco de la OMC, de promover la liberalización de bienes y servicios de importancia al comercio entre los países miembros del Consejo.

2.   Efectuar consultas entre ambas Partes en materia de comercio e inversión, con el propósito de:

i.   Cumplir con los compromisos y objetivos establecidos en esos campos en la Declaración de Principios y el Plan de Acción del la Cumbre de las Américas, celebrada en Miami en diciembre de 1994;

ii.   Coordinar esfuerzos en foros tales como la OMC y las Reuniones Ministeriales de Comercio a niveles hemisférico, regional y subregional.

3.   Mantener entre ambas Partes un sistema fluido de información en materia de comercio e inversión que permita valorar periódicamente la evolución de dichas relaciones.

4.   Examinar en forma oportuna y expedita, así como congruente con la naturaleza multilateral, la jerarquía y el mandato del Consejo, cualquier asunto de mutuo interés que, previa consulta, las Partes decidan estudiar.

Artículo Cuarto

1.   El Consejo se reunirá por los menos una vez al año y cuando lo convengan las Partes.

2.   Las Partes podrán consultar, de conformidad con sus mecanismos internos, al sector privado de sus respectivos países sobre cuestiones relacionadas con la labor del Consejo.

Artículo Quinto

El Consejo comenzará su labor mediante el establecimiento de un Comité Ejecutivo a nivel viceministerial para preparar un Plan de Trabajo sobre las cuestiones de comercio e inversión de interés para las Partes. Las Partes procurarán elaborar dicho Plan de Trabajo en el plazo de noventa días a partir de la firma de presente Acuerdo.

Artículo Sexto

Este Acuerdo no perjudica los derechos y las obligaciones preexistentes de cada una de las Partes a tenor de:

1.   El ordenamiento interno.

2.   La OMC y sus códigos, junto con sus convenios, entendimientos y otros instrumentos, de los cuales sean signatarias las Partes; y

3.   Los acuerdos regionales u otros instrumentos internacionales de los cuales sean

signatarias las Partes.

Artículo Séptimo

Este Acuerdo surtirá efecto a partir de la fecha de su firma por las Partes y permanecerá en vigor a menos que sea denunciado por consentimiento mutuo. Cualquier país podrá retirarse del Acuerdo previa notificación por escrito a los demás países con seis meses de antelación.

EN FE DE LO CUAL, los suscritos, habiendo sido autorizados debidamente por sus gobiernos respectivos, han firmado el presente Acuerdo.

HECHO en San José, Costa Rica el vigésimo día del mes de marzo de 1998, en siete ejemplares en los idiomas español e inglés, siendo cada uno igualmente auténtico.

*

AGREEMENT BETWEEN THE GOVERNMENT OF THE UNITED STATES OF AMERICA AND THE GOVERNMENTS OF BOLIVIA, COLOMBIA, ECUADOR, PERU AND VENEZUELA, MEMBER COUNTRIES OF THE ANDEAN COMMUNITY, CONCERNING THE ESTABLISHMENT OF A TRADE AND INVESTMENT COUNCIL*

The agreement between the Government of the United States of America and the Governments of Bolivia, Colombia, Ecuador, Peru and Venezuela, Member Countries of the Andean Community, concerning the establishment of a trade and investment council was signed on 30 October 1998.

The Government of the United States of America, as one Party, and the Governments of Bolivia, Colombia, Ecuador, Peru and Venezuela, Member States of the Andean Community as the other Party:

1) Wishing to strengthen the ties of friendship and the spirit of cooperation existing between the Parties;

2) Highlighting the importance of trade and investment to the economies of the Parties;

3) Underscoring the importance of a stable and transparent environment for international trade and investment;

4) Recognizing that it is desirable that trade and investment problems between the Parties should be resolved by mutual agreement as expeditiously as possible;

5) Desiring to work together, in a manner that is consistent with the Marrakesh Agreement establishing the World Trade Organization ("WTO Agreement") and is complementary to the process for the creation of the Free Trade Area of the Americas (FTAA), to identify the steps that would intensify the economic relationships between the Parties;

6) Recognizing the importance of providing adequate and effective protection and enforcement of intellectual property rights, and taking into account the Parties commitments to the protection of intellectual property rights in conventions and agreements to which they are parties;

7) Desiring to ensure that trade liberalization and environmental policies are mutually supportive in furtherance of sustainable development, while avoiding disguised restrictions on trade, in accordance with the WTO and other international obligations;

8) Recognizing the significance to the economic welfare of all Parties provided by working toward observance and promotion of the internationally recognized rights of workers; and

---

* *Source*: The Government of the United States (1998). "Agreement Between the Government of the United States of America and the Governments of Bolivia, Colombia, Ecuador, Peru and Venezuela, Member Countries of the Andean Community, Concerning the Establishment of a Trade and Investment Council", available on the Internet (http://www.comunidadandina.org/documentos/actas/acu30-10-98.htm). [Note added by the editor.]

9)   Considering that the establishment of a trade and investment council between the Parties would result in mutual benefits.

To this end, the Parties agree as follows:

ARTICLE ONE

To establish between the Government of the United States of America and the Governments of Bolivia, Colombia, Ecuador, Peru and Venezuela, Member States of the Andean Community, a Trade and Investment Council (hereinafter called "the Council").

The Council shall be multilateral in nature and shall operate in a manner that is complementary to the existing bilateral Trade and Investment Councils.

ARTICLE TWO

The Council shall have the following objectives:

1)   Promote a dialogue concerning the exchange of goods and services and the flows of investment between the Parties;

2)   Identify and propose the adoption of mechanisms that facilitate trade and investment;

3)   Promote measures to improve the effectiveness of the Andean Trade Preference Act (ATPA);

4)   Identify and work toward the elimination of restrictions on trade and investment, consistent with the WTO Agreement and complementary to the negotiation of the Free Trade Area of the Americas (FTAA), including through bilateral, multilateral, and regional trade agreements;

5)   Exchange and review information on our trade and investment relations in order to conduct periodic evaluations of the evolution of said relations;

6)   Coordinate efforts in multilateral and regional fora and bodies, such as the FTAA and the WTO;

7)   Encourage the organization of business meetings and other complementary activities that broaden trade and investment relations between our respective countries;

8)   Consult as appropriate, in a timely and expeditious manner, on any matter of mutual interest to the Parties.

ARTICLE THREE

The Council shall be composed of ministerial-level representatives of both Parties. In the case of the United States, it shall be composed of the United States Trade Representative, and in the case of Bolivia, Colombia, Ecuador, Peru and Venezuela, of the Heads of Delegation to the Commission of the Andean Community.

To support their participation in the Council, the Member States of the Andean Community may be assisted by the General Secretariat of the Andean Community.

ARTICLE FOUR

The Council shall meet at least once every two years and occasionally whenever the Parties so agree.

ARTICLE FIVE

The Council shall have the support of an Executive Committee at the senior official level composed of representatives of the Government of the United States, as one Party, and of representatives of the Governments of Bolivia, Colombia, Ecuador, Peru and Venezuela, as the other Party. This Committee shall prepare a Work Plan on matters of trade and investment of interest to the Parties and shall carry out the tasks assigned to it by the Council.

To support their participation in the Executive Committee, the Member States of the Andean Community may be assisted by the General Secretariat of the Andean Community.

ARTICLE SIX

The Parties may, in accordance with their internal mechanisms, consult the private sector and other relevant groups of their respective countries on matters related to the work of the Council.

ARTICLE SEVEN

This Agreement is without prejudice to the rights and obligations under the Parties domestic laws and procedures and under international agreements including:

1)   The WTO Agreement;

2)   Regional agreements and other international instruments to which the Parties are signatories; and

3)   The bilateral agreements in matters of trade and investment signed between the United States and the Member States of the Andean Community.

ARTICLE EIGHT

This Agreement shall enter into force on the date of its signature and shall remain in force unless terminated by mutual consent of the Parties or by either Party upon six months written notice to the other Party.

TRANSITIONAL PROVISION

The Executive Committee shall prepare a Work Plan, as referenced in Article Five, within 90 days from the signing of this Agreement.

IN WITNESS WHEREOF, the undersigned, being duly authorized by their respective governments, have signed this Agreement.

Signed at Washington, D.C., in twelve copies, in English and Spanish versions, each being equally valid, on the thirtieth of October of 1998.

*

AGREEMENT BETWEEN THE GOVERNMENT OF THE UNITED STATES OF AMERICA AND THE GOVERNMENT OF THE PEOPLE'S DEMOCRATIC REPUBLIC OF ALGERIA CONCERNING THE DEVELOPMENT OF TRADE AND INVESTMENT RELATIONS*

The agreement between the Government of the United States of America and the Government of The People's Democratic Republic of Algeria concerning the development of trade and investment relations was signed on 13 July 2001.

PREAMBLE

The Government of the United States of America and the Government of the People's Democratic Republic of Algeria individually a "Party" and collectively the "Parties":

1.   Desiring to enhance the bonds of friendship and the spirit of cooperation between the two countries;

2.   Desiring to develop further trade and investment between the two countries;

3.   Recognizing the importance of fostering an open and predictable environment for international trade and investment;

4.   Recognizing the benefits to each Party resulting from increased international trade and investment, and that trade-distorting investment measures and protectionism would deprive the Parties of such benefits;

5.   Recognizing the essential role of private investment, both domestic and foreign, in furthering growth, creating jobs, expanding international trade, improving technology, and enhancing economic development;

6.   Recognizing that foreign direct investment confers positive benefits on each Party;

7.   Acknowledging among others: the Agreement establishing the United States-Algerian Joint Commission for economic, technical and technological cooperation, signed April 17, 1985; the Investment Incentive Agreement, signed June 22, 1990; the Agricultural Commodities Agreement, signed February 23, 1966; and the Memorandum of Understanding Concerning Cooperation and Trade in the Field of Agriculture;

8.   Noting that this present Agreement is in no way prejudicial to the rights and obligations of the two Parties arising from the bilateral and international agreements in effect that are binding with respect to each Party;

---

*   *Source*: The Government of the United States (2001). "Agreement between the Government of the United States of America and the Government of The People's Democratic Republic of Algeria Concerning the Development of Trade and Investment Relations", available also on the Internet (http://www.ustr.gov/regions/eu-med/middleeast/tifa.PDF). [Note added by the editor.]

9.   Recognizing the increased importance of services in their economies and in their bilateral and international relations;

10.   Taking into account the need to eliminate non-tariff barriers in order to facilitate greater access to the markets of both countries;

11.   Recognizing the importance of providing adequate and effective protection and enforcement of intellectual property rights and of membership in and adherence to intellectual property rights conventions;

12.   Recognizing the importance to both Parties of promoting internationally recognized workers' rights;

13.   Desiring to work towards trade and environmental protection policies that are mutually supportive in furtherance of sustainable development; and

14.   Considering that it would be in their mutual interest to establish a bilateral mechanism between the Parties for encouraging the liberalization of trade and investment by consulting on bilateral trade and investment issues;

To this end, the Parties agreed as follows:

ARTICLE ONE

The Parties affirm their desire to promote an attractive investment climate and expand trade in products and services consistent with the terms of this Agreement. They shall take appropriate measures to encourage and facilitate the exchange of goods and services and to secure favorable conditions for long-term development and diversification of trade between their respective nationals and companies.

ARTICLE TWO

The Parties shall establish a United States-Algeria Council on Trade and Investment (the "Council"), which shall be composed of representatives of both Parties. The United States of America side will be chaired by the Office of the U.S. Trade Representative (USTR), and the Algeria side will be chaired by the Ministry of Commerce. Each Chair may be assisted by officials of other government entities as circumstances require. Consultations will be held annually, unless otherwise agreed by the Parties. The Parties shall arrange, by mutual agreement, a date for these consultations to be held.

ARTICLE THREE

The objectives of the Council are to hold consultations on specific trade and investment matters of interest to the Parties; to identify agreements appropriate for negotiation; and to identify and work toward the removal of impediments to trade and investment flows.

ARTICLE FOUR

1.   For the purpose of further developing bilateral trade and fostering a steady increase in the exchange of products and services and promoting investment in the two countries, the Parties shall consider whether the conclusion of further trade related agreements would be desirable.

2.   The Parties will consider in their discussions their special respective needs for and levels of development, financing and trade.

ARTICLE FIVE

1.   Either Party may raise for consultations any trade or investment matter between the Parties. Requests for consultations shall be accompanied by a written explanation of the subject to be discussed, and consultations shall be held within 30 days of the request, unless the requesting Party agrees to a later date.

2.   This Agreement shall be without prejudice to the rights of either Party under its domestic law or under any international agreements to which either country is a party.

ARTICLE SIX

Each Party shall notify the other Party of the completion of its respective requirements for the entry into force of this Agreement, which shall take effect on the date of receipt of the last notification.

ARTICLE SEVEN

This Agreement shall remain in force unless terminated by mutual consent of the Parties or by either Party, subject to six months written notice. In the event that the two parties decide by mutual consent to amend this agreement, such amendment may be done by an exchange of letters.

IN WITNESS WHEREOF, the undersigned, being duly authorized by their respective governments, have signed this Agreement.

*

AGREEMENT BETWEEN THE GOVERNMENT OF THE UNITED STATES OF AMERICA AND THE GOVERNMENT OF THE KINGDOM OF BAHRAIN CONCERNING THE DEVELOPMENT OF TRADE AND INVESTMENT RELATIONS*

The agreement between the Government of the United States of America and the Government of The Kingdom of Bahrain concerning the development of trade and investment relations was signed on 18 June 2002. It entered into force on the date of signature.

The Government of the United States of America and the Government of the Kingdom of Bahrain (individually a "Party" and collectively the "Parties"):

1)   Desiring to enhance the bonds of friendship and spirit of cooperation between the two countries;

2)   Recognizing the importance of fostering an open and predictable enviromnent for international trade and investment and economic cooperation;

3)   Acknowledging the membership of the two countries in the World Trade Organization (WTO) and noting that this Agreement is without prejudice to each Party's rights and obligations under the agreements, understandings, and other instruments related to or concluded under the auspices of the WTO;

4)   Recognizing the benefits to each Party resulting from increased international trade and investment, and that trade-distorting investment measures and protectionist trade barriers would deprive the Parties of such benefits;

5)   Recognizing the desirability of resolving trade and investment problems as expeditiously as possible;

6)   Recognizing that foreign direct investment confers net positive benefits on each Party;

7)   Recognizing the essential role of private investment, both domestic and foreign, in furthering growth, creating jobs, expanding trade, improving technology and enhancing economic development;

8)   Desiring to encourage and facilitate private sector contacts between the two countries;

9)   Acknowledging the Treaty Between the Government of the United States of America and the Government of the State of Bahrain Concerning the Encouragement and Reciprocal Protection of Investment ("the Bilateral Investment Treaty"), signed September 29, 1999 and

---

* *Source*: The Government of the United States (2002). "Agreement between the Government of the United States of America and the Government of The Kingdom of Bahrain Concerning the Development of Trade and Investment Relations", available also on the Internet (http://www.ustr.gov/regions/eu-med/middleeast/2002bahrainTIFA.PDF). [Note added by the editor.]

entered into force on May 30, 2001; and the Visa Arrangement Between the Government of Bahrain and the (Government of the United States Concerning Textiles and Textile Products, effected by exchange of notes dated January 28, 1991 and September 9, 1991;

10)   Recognizing the increased importance of services in their economies and in their bilateral relations;

11)   Taking into account the need to eliminate non-tariff barriers in order to facilitate greater access to the markets of both countries and the mutual benefits thereof;

12)   Recognizing the importance of providing adequate and effective protection and enforcement of intellectual property rights and of membership in and adherence to intellectual property rights conventions;

13)   Recognizing the significance to the Parties' economic welfare of working toward the observance and promotion of internationally recognized core labor standards;

14)   Recognizing the Parties' desire to ensure that trade and environmental policies are mutually supportive in furtherance of sustainable development; and

15)   Considering that it would be in their mutual interest to establish a bilateral mechanism between the Parties for encouraging the liberalization of trade and investment between them.

To this end, the Parties agree as follows:

ARTICLE ONE

The Parties affirm their desire to promote an attractive investment climate and expand trade in products and services consistent with the terms of this Agreement. They will take appropriate measures to encourage and facilitate the exchange of goods and services and to secure favorable conditions for long-term development and diversification of trade between the two countries.

ARTICLE TWO

The Parties shall establish a United States-Bahrain Council on Trade and Investment ("theCouncil"), which shall be composed of representatives of both Parties. The Bahrain side will be chaired by the Ministry of Finance and National Economy, and the U.S. side will be chaired by the Office of the U.S. Trade Representative ("USTR"). Both Parties may be assisted by officials of other government entities as circumstances require. The Council will meet at least once a year and at such times as agreed by the two Parties.

ARTICLE TWO

The objectives of the Council are as follows:

1.   To monitor trade and investment relations, to identify opportunities for expanding trade and investment, and to identify issues appropriate for negotiation.

2.   To hold consultations on specific trade matters, and those investment matters not arising under the Bilateral Investment Treaty, of interest to the Parties.

3.   To identify and work toward the removal of impediments to trade and investment flows.

4.   To seek the advice of the private sector in their respective countries on matters related to the work of the Council where the Parties deem it appropriate.

ARTICLE FOUR

For the purpose of further developing bilateral trade and providing for a steady increase in the exchange of products and services, the Parties shall consider whether further agreernetits relating to trade, taxation, intellectual property, investment, vocational training, labor, environmental issues, and other matters agreed upon by the Parties would be desirable.

ARTICLE FIVE

Either Party may raise for consultation any trade matters, and those investment matters not arising under the Bilateral Investment Treaty, between the Parties. Requests for consultation shall be accompanied by a written explanation of the subject to be discussed and consultation shall be held within 30 days of the request, unless the requesting Party agrees to a later date. Each party shall endeavor to provide for an opportunity for consultations before taking actions that could affect adversely the trade or investment interests of the other Party.

ARTICLE SIX

This Agreement is without prejudice to the rights and obligations of either Party under its domestic law or under any other agreement to which either country is a party,

ARTICLE SEVEN

This Agreement is effective from the date of its signature by both Parties.

ARTICLE EIGHT

This Agreement shall remain in effect unless terminated by mutual consent of the Parties or by either Party upon six months written notice to the other Party.

IN WITNESS WHEREOF, the undersigned, being duly authorized by their respective governments, have signed this Agreement.

*

AGREEMENT BETWEEN THE GOVERNMENT OF THE UNITED STATES OF AMERICA AND THE WEST AFRICAN ECONOMIC AND MONETARY UNION CONCERNING THE DEVELOPMENT OF TRADE AND INVESTMENT RELATIONS[*]

The agreement Between the Government of the United States of America and the West African Economic and Monetary Union concerning the development of trade and investment relations was signed on 24 April 2002. It entered into force on the date of signature.

The West African Economic and Monetary Union (WAEMU) and the Government of the United States of America, hereinafter referred to as "the Parties,"

1. Desiring to enhance the friendship and spirit of cooperation between them;

2. Highlighting the importance of trade and investment to their economies;

3. Recognizing the need for a stable and transparent environment for international trade and investment;

4. Desiring to develop further their trade and economic relationships;

5. Underscoring the importance of the market economy and private sector initiatives as sources of prosperity, and reaffirming the goal of promoting business relations among their nationals and other activities capable of expanding trade and investment relations between their respective private sectors;

6. Taking into account the participation of the United States of America and the member States of WAEMU in the multilateral trade system of the World Trade Organization (WTO) and noting further that this Agreement shall be without prejudice to the rights and obligations of the Parties under the terms of the Marrakech Agreement establishing the World Trade Organization, or under agreements, understandings, and other instruments relating to it or concluded under the aegis thereof;

7. Recognizing that issues related to their trade and investment must be addressed by mutual agreement;

8. Recognizing both the benefits to the Parties derived from international trade and investment and the fact that any obstacles to such trade and investment would deprive the Parties of these benefits;

---

[*] *Source*: The Government of the United States (2002). "Agreement Between the Government of the United States of America and the West African Economic and Monetary Union Concerning the Development of Trade and Investment Relations", available on the Internet (http://www.ustr.gov/regions/africa/finalenglishwaemu.htm). [Note added by the editor.]

9.   Recognizing the essential role of private investment, both domestic and foreign, in furthering growth, creating jobs, expanding trade, improving technology, and enhancing economic development;

10.   Recognizing that foreign direct investment confers benefits on each Party;

11.   Recognizing the increased importance of services in their economies and in their bilateral relations;

12.   Taking into account the need to eliminate non-tariff barriers in order to facilitate greater access to the markets of both Parties;

13.   Recognizing the importance of adequate and effective protection of intellectual property rights;

14.   Recognizing the importance for the economic prosperity of the Parties of embarking on a path of compliance with, and promotion of, fundamental, internationally-recognized labor standards;

15.   Desiring to ensure the necessary relationship between trade liberalization and general environmental protection policies, in furtherance of sustainable development; and

16.   Considering that it would be in the mutual interest of the Parties to establish a mechanism between them for encouraging the liberalization of trade and investment;

Have reached the following Agreement:

Chapter One: Definitions

Article One:

For the purposes of this Agreement, the following definitions shall apply:

"Council" means the Council on Trade and Investment, established in Chapter III of this Agreement;

"Commission" means the Commission of WAEMU;

"WTO" means the World Trade Organization;

"WAEMU" means the West African Economic and Monetary Union, consisting of its member States, which are, currently: the Republic of Benin; Burkina Faso, the Republic of Côte d'Ivoire; the Republic of Guinea-Bissau; the Republic of Mali; the Republic of Niger; the Republic of Senegal; and the Togolese Republic.

"USTR" means the United States Trade Representative.

Chapter II: Agreement Objectives

Article Two:

The Parties affirm their desire to expand trade between them in products and services consistent with the terms of this Agreement.

They undertake to adopt appropriate measures to encourage and facilitate trade in goods and services, and to secure favorable conditions for long-term investment, development, and diversification of trade among their respective nationals and companies.

Chapter III: Council on Trade and Investment

Article Three:

The Parties agree to establish a Council on Trade and Investment, comprising their representatives. WAEMU shall be represented by the Commission, assisted, as necessary, by outside resource persons. The Government of the United States of America shall be represented by the Office of the United States Trade Representative (USTR), assisted by officials of other government agencies, as necessary.

Article Four:

The Council shall meet at such times and in such places as agreed by the Parties.

Article Five:

The role of the Council shall be to consult on specific trade- and investment-related issues of special interest to the Parties. The Council shall also be responsible for identifying and working towards the removal of impediments to trade and investment, and to coordinate, as necessary, the Parties' efforts in fora dealing with subjects of mutual interest, such as the WTO.

Article Six:

Each Party may raise for consultation in the Council any bilateral trade or investment matter. Requests for consultation shall be accompanied by a written explanation of the subject to be discussed. Council consultations shall be held within no more than six months of the date on which the request is submitted, unless the Parties decide otherwise.

Article Seven:

With regard to matters concerning the jurisdiction of the Council, each Party may request, whenever it deems it useful to do so, the views of civil society in the areas of business, labor, consumer affairs, environmental protection, and education.

Chapter IV: Final Disposition

Article Eight:

For the purposes of further developing their trade and investment, and with a view to achieving a steady increase in the pace of trade in products and services, the Parties may conclude further agreements, particularly in the areas of commerce, taxation, intellectual property, labor, and investment. This Agreement shall be without prejudice to the rights of either Party under its domestic law, its regulations, or any other international legal instrument to which either is a party.

Article Nine:

The Parties agree to enter negotiations for the purpose of examining, as appropriate, the necessary adjustments to this Agreement should there be new WAEMU members. If the consultations held in application of the preceding subparagraph are conclusive, the Parties agree to extend the application of the provisions of this Agreement to any State that becomes a member of WAEMU. Should the abovementioned consultations fail, the Parties may choose to terminate this Agreement without regard to the time periods specified in Article 11 below.

Article Ten:

Any dispute concerning the interpretation and application of this Agreement shall be settled through diplomatic channels or by any other means of settlement agreed upon by the Parties.

Article Eleven:

This Agreement shall enter into force on the date of its signature. It may be amended by mutual agreement. It may be terminated either by mutual consent or when one of the Parties terminates it, without prejudice to the continuation of any activities under way. Termination shall take effect six months following written notification of the other Party through diplomatic channels.

IN WITNESS WHEREOF, the undersigned, being duly authorized for such purpose, have signed this Agreement below.

*

TRADE AND INVESTMENT FRAMEWORK AGREEMENT BETWEEN THE UNITED STATES OF AMERICA AND THE DEMOCRATIC SOCIALIST REPUBLIC OF SRI LANKA *

The trade and investment framework agreement between the United States of America and the Democratic Socialist Republic of Sri Lanka was signed on 25 July 2002. It entered into force on the date of signature.

The Government of the United States and the Government of the Democratic Socialist Republic of Sri Lanka (individually a "Party" and collectively the "Parties"):

Desiring to strengthen further the bonds of friendship and spirit of cooperation that have existed between the United States and the Democratic Socialist Republic of Sri Lanka for over fifty years;

Desiring to foster an open and predictable environment for international trade and investment and economic cooperation;

Recognizing the benefits to each Party resulting from increased international trade and investment;

Reaffirming their membership in and strong support for the World Trade Organization (WTO);

Desiring that this Framework Agreement reinforce the multilateral trading system by strengthening efforts to complete successfully the Doha Development Agenda;

Recognizing the benefits of eliminating non-tariff barriers as a means to facilitate greater access to the markets of both countries;

Recognizing that foreign investment confers net positive benefits on each Party;

Recognizing the essential role of private investment, both domestic and foreign, in furthering growth, creating jobs, expanding trade, improving technology and enhancing economic development;

Desiring to encourage and facilitate private sector contacts between the two countries;

Recognizing that the effective protection and enforcement of intellectual property rights encourages technological innovation and investment;

Recognizing the increased importance of services in their economies and in their bilateral and international relations;

---

* *Source*: The Government of the United States and the Government of Sri Lanka (2002). "Trade and Investment Framework Agreement between the United States of America and the Democratic Socialist Republic of Sri Lanka", available on the Internet (http://www.ustr.gov/regions/africa/srilankaTIFA.PDF). [Note added by the editor.]

Reaffirming our commitment in the Doha Declaration that expansion of trade and investment and the promotion of sustainable development and protection of the environment can and must be mutually supportive;

Reiterating our commitment reaffirmed in the Doha Declaration to uphold internationally recognized core labor standards;

Acknowledging the Treaty Between the Government of the United States of America and the Government of Sri Lanka Concerning the Encouragement and Reciprocal Protection of Investment ("the Bilateral Investment Treaty") of 1991; the Bilateral Agreement for the Protection of Intellectual Property Rights of 1991; and the Bilateral Air Services Agreement of 2002; and

Stressing that the liberalization of trade and investment promotes economic growth and development and considering that it would be in their interest to establish a bilateral framework to further promote trade and investment between them.

To this end, the Parties agree as follows.

ARTICLE ONE

The Parties affirm their desire to expand trade in products and services consistent with the terms of this Agreement. They shall take appropriate measures to encourage and facilitate in a mutually beneficial way the exchange of goods and services and to secure favorable conditions for long-term development and diversification of trade between their respective nationals and companies.

ARTICLE TWO

In accordance with their prevailing laws and regulations, the Parties agree to establish a Joint Council on Trade and Investment.

The Joint Council will be composed of representatives of both Parties. All meetings of the Joint Council will be jointly chaired by the United States Trade Representative (USTR) on behalf of the United States of America and by the Minister of Commerce and Consumer Affairs on behalf of the Democratic Socialist Republic of Sri Lanka. The chairs may delegate their authority to their respective senior officials to conduct a meeting of the Joint Council. Both Parties may be assisted by officials from other government agencies as circumstances require.

ARTICLE THREE

The Parties plan to coordinate, as appropriate, their efforts to advance the Doha Development Agenda. Such coordination should occur in the Joint Council, and in the various bodies of the WTO.

ARTICLE FOUR

The Parties agree to initiate consultations on areas of cooperation that may be agreed by the Joint Council to liberalize trade and/or investment.

ARTICLE FIVE

The Joint Council shall be responsible for:

(1)   convening regular meetings of the Parties regarding the terms of this Agreement.

(2)   monitoring the Parties' bilateral trade and investment relations and identifying opportunities to expand trade and investment; and

(3)   organizing consultations on specific trade matters and those investment issues not arising under the Bilateral Investment Treaty.

ARTICLE SIX

The Joint Council may establish ad hoc working groups that may meet concurrently or separately to facilitate its work.

ARTICLE SEVEN

The Joint Council may meet at the request of either Party on a mutually convenient date and at an agreed location to consider any trade matter or investment issue not arising under the Bilateral Investment Treaty between them.

ARTICLE EIGHT

This Agreement shall be without prejudice to preexisting rights and obligations of the United States of America and the Democratic Socialist Republic of Sri Lanka under their respective domestic laws, the WTO, or under any other binding agreements to which either Party is a signatory.

ARTICLE NINE

This Agreement may be added to or amended at any time by mutual consent of the Parties.

ARTICLE TEN

This Agreement is effective from the date of signature by both Parties and shall remain in effect unless terminated by mutual consent of the Parties or by either Party upon six months written notice to the other Party.

IN WITNESS WHEREOF, the undersigned, being duly authorized by their respective governments, have signed this Agreement.

*

TRADE AND INVESTMENT FRAMEWORK AGREEMENT BETWEEN THE GOVERNMENT OF THE UNITED STATES OF AMERICA AND THE GOVERNMENT OF BRUNEI DARUSSALAM[*]

> The trade and investment framework agreement between the Government of the United States of America and the Government of Brunei Darussalam was signed on 12 December 2002.

The Government of the United States of America and the Government of His Majesty the Sultan and Yang Di-Pertuan of Brunei Darussalam, individually a "Party" and collectively the "Parties";

Desiring to strengthen further the bonds of friendship and the spirit of cooperation that has existed between the Parties since the signing of the 1850 Treaty of Peace, Friendship, Commerce, and Navigation;

Reaffirming their membership in and strong support for the World Trade Organization (WTO) and desiring that this Framework Agreement reinforce the multilateral trading system;

Desiring to promote further the trade and investment existing between the two countries;

Recognizing that the liberalization of trade and investment promotes economic growth and development;

Recognizing the importance of fostering an open and predictable environment for international trade and investment;

Recognizing the essential role of investment, both domestic and foreign, in furthering growth, creating jobs, expanding trade, improving technology and enhancing economic development;

Encouraging membership in and adherence to intellectual property rights (IPR) conventions, and recognizing that the effective protection and enforcement of IPR encourages technological innovation and investment;

Reaffirming their commitment in the Doha Declaration that expansion of trade and investment and the promotion of sustainable development and protection of the environment can and must be mutually supportive;

Recognizing the importance of providing adequate and effective protection and enforcement of worker rights in accordance with each nation's own labor laws and of the observance of internationally accepted core labor standards;

---

[*] *Source*: The Government of Brunei Darussalam and the Government of the United States (2002). "Trade and Investment Framework Agreement Between the Government of the United States of America and the Government of Brunei Darussalam", available on the Internet (http://www.ustr.gov/regions/eu-med/middleeast/2002-12-16-brunei-tifa.pdf). [Note added by the editor.]

Desiring to encourage and facilitate private sector contacts between the two countries;

Recognizing the contribution of the Memorandum of Understanding Between the Government of the United States of America and the Governments of ASEAN member countries, signed at Washington D.C. on 21 December 1990, to increase the flows of trade and investment between ASEAN countries and the United States of America; and

Recognizing APEC's contribution to trade and investment liberalization and facilitation and to economic and technical cooperation.

To this end, the parties agree as follows:

ARTICLE ONE

The Parties agree to cooperate, coordinate, and consider ways, as appropriate, to enhance and liberalize trade and investment between the two countries at the bilateral, regional and multilateral levels; including, as appropriate, their efforts to advance the Doha Development Agenda. Such cooperation and coordination should occur in the Joint Council created by this Framework Agreement, and in the various bodies of the WTO.

ARTICLE TWO

The Parties shall undertake the work program, set out in the Annex, as follows:

1.   the Parties agree to initiate consultations on the areas of cooperation covered in Part 1 of the Annex and to proceed with the implementation of the work program; and

2.   at the appropriate time, the United States Trade Representative and the Minister of Industry and Primary Resources of the Government of His Majesty the Sultan and Yang Di-Pertuan of Brunei Darussalam may decide to proceed to Part 2 of the Annex.

ARTICLE THREE

In accordance with their respective prevailing laws and regulations, the Parties agree to establish a Joint Council on Trade and Investment.

ARTICLE FOUR

The Joint Council:

1.   shall be composed of representatives of both Parties. All meetings of the Joint Council shall be jointly chaired by the United States Trade Representative (USTR) on behalf of the Government of the United States of America and by the Minister of Industry and Primary Resources on behalf of the Government of His Majesty the Sultan and Yang Di-Pertuan of Brunei Darussalam. The chairs may delegate their authority to their respective senior officials to conduct a meeting of the Joint Council. The USTR and the Minister of Industry and Primary Resources will be assisted by officials from other government agencies, as necessary; and

2.   may establish ad hoc working groups that may meet concurrently or separately to facilitate its work.

ARTICLE FIVE

The Joint Council will meet at least once a year and at such times agreed by both Parties to:

1.   oversee the implementation of this agreement;

2.   review the bilateral trade and investment relationship and identify opportunities to expand and liberalize trade and investment;

3.   undertake the work program outlined in the Annex and periodic reviews of progress;

4.   organize consultations on specific trade or investment issues; and

5.   resolve amicably any issues that might arise from implementing the provisions of this agreement.

ARTICLE SIX

This Agreement is without prejudice to the domestic laws and regulations of either Party or the rights and obligations of either Party under any other international agreement to which it is a party.

ARTICLE SEVEN

This Agreement may be amended at any time by written mutual consent of the Parties.

ARTICLE EIGHT

This Agreement is effective from the date of signature by both Parties and shall remain in effect unless terminated by written mutual consent of the Parties or by either Party upon six (6) months written notice to the other Party.

IN WITNESS WHEREOF, the undersigned, being duly authorized by their respective governments, have signed this Agreement, authentic in the English language.

DONE at Washington, D.C. this 16th day of December 2002.

Annex
WORK PROGRAM

Part 1

The Parties agree to initiate consultations on the following areas:

(1) Facilitation and liberalization of trade and investment, including non-tariff barriers;
(2) Promotion and protection of investment;
(3) Protection of intellectual property;
(4) Regulatory issues affecting trade and investment policies;
(5) Information and Communications Technology;

(6) Biotechnology;
(7) Tourism;
(8) Trade and Capacity Building;
(9) Enhancing the participation of SMEs in trade and investment;
(10) WTO/APEC/WCO coordination; and
(11) Other areas of economic cooperation to be mutually agreed upon.

Part 2

The Parties agree to examine the most effective means of reducing trade and investment barriers between them, including consultations on the elements of a possible free trade agreement.

UNITED STATES - SINGAPORE FREE TRADE AGREEMENT*
[excerpts]

The United States - Singapore free trade agreement was signed on 6 May 2003.

CHAPTER 8: CROSS-BORDER TRADE IN SERVICES

ARTICLE 8.1: DEFINITIONS

For purposes of this Chapter:

1.   central level of government means

    (a)   for the United States, the federal level of government; and

    (b)   for Singapore, the national level of government;

2.   cross-border trade in services or cross-border supply of services means the supply of a service

    (a)   from the territory of one Party into the territory of the other Party;

    (b)   in the territory of one Party by a person of that Party to a person of the other Party; or

    (c)   by a national of a Party in the territory of the other Party;

    but does not include the supply of a service in the territory of a Party by an investor of the other Party or a covered investment as defined in Article 15.1 (Definitions);

3.   enterprise means an entity constituted or organized under applicable law, whether or not for profit, and whether privately or governmentally owned or controlled, including a corporation, trust, partnership, sole proprietorship, joint venture, association, or similar organization and a branch of an enterprise;

4.   enterprise of a Party means an enterprise organized or constituted under the laws of a Party and a branch located in the territory of a Party and carrying out business activities there;

5.   local level of government means, for Singapore, entities with sub-national legislative or executive powers under domestic law, including Town Councils and Community Development Councils;

---

* *Source*: Organization of American States (OAS) (2003). "United States - Singapore Free Trade Agreement", available on the Internet (http://www.sice.oas.org/Trade/USA-Singapore/USASingind_e.asp). [Note added by the editor.]

6.   professional services means services, the provision of which requires specialized post-secondary education, or equivalent training or experience, and for which the right to practice is granted or restricted by a Party, but does not include services provided by trades-persons or vessel and aircraft crew members;

7.   regional level of government means, for the United States, a state of the United States, the District of Columbia, or Puerto Rico; for Singapore, "regional level of government" is not applicable, as Singapore has no government at the regional level;

8.   service supplier means a person of a Party that seeks to supply or supplies a service;[8-1] and

9.   specialty air services means any non-transportation air services, such as aerial fire-fighting, sightseeing, spraying, surveying, mapping, photography, parachute jumping, glider towing and helicopter-lift for logging and construction, and other airborne agricultural, industrial, and inspection services.

ARTICLE 8.2: SCOPE AND COVERAGE

1.   (a)   This Chapter applies to measures by a Party affecting cross-border trade in services by service suppliers of the other Party.

(b)   Measures covered by subparagraph (a) include measures affecting:

(i)   the production, distribution, marketing, sale and delivery of a service;

(ii)   the purchase or use of, or payment for, a service;

(iii)   the access to and use of distribution, transport, or telecommunications networks and services in connection with the supply of a service; and

(iv)   the provision of a bond or other form of financial security as a condition for the supply of a service.

(c)   For purposes of this Chapter, measures by a Party means measures taken by:

(i)   central, regional or local governments and authorities; and

(ii)   non-governmental bodies in the exercise of powers delegated by central, regional or local governments or authorities.

2.   Articles 8.5, 8.8 and 8.12 also apply to measures by a Party affecting the supply of a service in its territory by an investor of the other Party or a covered investment as defined in Article 15.1 (Definitions).[8-2]

[8-1] The Parties understand that seeks to supply or supplies a service has the same meaning as supplies a service as used in GATS Article XXVIII(g). The Parties understand that for purposes of Articles 8.3, 8.4, and 8.5 of this Agreement, service suppliers has the same meaning as services and service suppliers as used in GATS Articles II, XVI, and XVII.

[8-2] The Parties understand that nothing in this Chapter, including this paragraph, is subject to investor-state dispute settlement pursuant to Section C of Chapter 15 (Investor-State Dispute Settlement).

3.   This Chapter does not apply to:

   (a)   financial services as defined in Article 10.20 (Definitions), except that paragraph 2 shall apply where the service is supplied by an investor or investment of the other Party that is not an investor or an investment in a financial institution (as defined in Article 10.20.4) in the Party's territory;

   (b)   government procurement;

   (c)   air services, including domestic and international air transportation services, whether scheduled or non-scheduled, and related services in support of air services, other than:

        (i)   aircraft repair and maintenance services during which an aircraft is withdrawn from service; and

        (ii) specialty air services; or

   (d)   subsidies or grants provided by a Party, including government-supported loans, guarantees and insurance.

4.   This Chapter does not impose any obligation on a Party with respect to a national of the other Party seeking access to its employment market, or employed on a permanent basis in its territory, and does not confer any right on that national with respect to that access or employment.

5.   (a)   This Chapter does not apply to services supplied in the exercise of governmental authority within the territory of each respective Party.

   (b)   For purposes of this Chapter, a service supplied in the exercise of governmental authority means any service which is supplied neither on a commercial basis, nor in competition with one or more service suppliers.

ARTICLE 8.3: NATIONAL TREATMENT

1.   Each Party shall accord to service suppliers of the other Party treatment no less favorable than that it accords, in like circumstances, to its own service suppliers.

2.   The treatment to be accorded by a Party under paragraph 1 means, with respect to a regional level of government, treatment no less favorable than the most favorable treatment accorded, in like circumstances, by that regional level of government to service suppliers of the Party of which it forms a part.

ARTICLE 8.4: MOST-FAVORED-NATION TREATMENT

Each Party shall accord to service suppliers of the other Party treatment no less favorable than that it accords, in like circumstances, to service suppliers of a non-Party.

ARTICLE 8.5: MARKET ACCESS

A Party shall not adopt or maintain, either on the basis of a regional subdivision or on the basis of its entire territory, measures that:

(a)   limit

   (i)   the number of service suppliers whether in the form of numerical quotas, monopolies, exclusive service suppliers or the requirement of an economic needs test;

   (ii)   the total value of service transactions or assets in the form of numerical quotas or the requirement of an economic needs test;

   (iii)   the total number of service operations or the total quantity of services output expressed in terms of designated numerical units in the form of quotas or the requirement of an economic needs test;[8-3]

   (iv)   the total number of natural persons that may be employed in a particular service sector or that a service supplier may employ and who are necessary for, and directly related to, the supply of a specific service in the form of numerical quotas or the requirement of an economic needs test; and

(b)   restrict or require specific types of legal entity or joint venture through which a service supplier may supply a service.

ARTICLE 8.6: LOCAL PRESENCE

A Party shall not require a service supplier of the other Party to establish or maintain a representative office or any form of enterprise, or to be resident, in its territory as a condition for the cross-border supply of a service.

ARTICLE 8.7: NON-CONFORMING MEASURES

1.   Articles 8.3, 8.4, 8.5, and 8.6 do not apply to:

   (a)   any existing non-conforming measure that is maintained by a Party at

      (i)   the central level of government, as set out by that Party in its Schedule to Annex 8A;

      (ii)   a regional level of government, as set out by that Party in its Schedule to Annex 8A; and

      (iii)   a local government level of government;

   (b)   the continuation or prompt renewal of any non-conforming measure referred to in subparagraph (a); or

---

[8-3] This paragraph does not cover measures of a Party which limit inputs for the supply of services.

(c)   an amendment to any non-conforming measure referred to in subparagraph (a) to the extent that the amendment does not decrease the conformity of the measure, as it existed immediately before the amendment, with Articles 8.3, 8.4, 8.5, and 8.6.

2.   Articles 8.3, 8.4, 8.5, and 8.6 do not apply to any measure that a Party adopts or maintains with respect to sectors, sub-sectors or activities as set out in its Schedule to Annex 8B.

ARTICLE 8.8: DOMESTIC REGULATION

1.   Where a Party requires authorization for the supply of a service, the Party's competent authorities shall, within a reasonable period of time after the submission of an application considered complete under domestic laws and regulations, inform the applicant of the decision concerning the application. At the request of the applicant, the competent authorities of the party shall provide, without undue delay, information concerning the status of the application. This obligation shall not apply to authorization requirements that are within the scope of Article 8.7.2.

2.   With a view to ensuring that measures relating to qualification requirements and procedures, technical standards and licensing requirements do not constitute unnecessary barriers to trade in services, each Party shall endeavor to ensure, as appropriate for individual sectors, that such measures are:

(a)   based on objective and transparent criteria, such as competence and the ability to supply the service;

(b)   not more burdensome than necessary to ensure the quality of the service; and

(c)   in the case of licensing procedures, not in themselves a restriction on the supply of the service.

3.   If the results of the negotiations related to Article VI:4 of GATS (or the results of any similar negotiations undertaken in other multilateral fora in which both Parties participate) enter into effect, this Article shall be amended, as appropriate, after consultations between the Parties, to bring those results into effect under this Agreement. The Parties agree to coordinate on such negotiations, as appropriate.

ARTICLE 8.9: RECOGNITION

1.   For the purposes of the fulfillment, in whole or in part, of its standards or criteria for the authorization, licensing or certification of services suppliers, and subject to the requirements of paragraph 4, a Party may recognize the education or experience obtained, requirements met, or licenses or certifications granted in a particular country, including the other Party and non-Parties. Such recognition, which may be achieved through harmonization or otherwise, may be based upon an agreement or arrangement with the country concerned or may be accorded autonomously.

2.   Where a Party recognizes, autonomously or by agreement or arrangement, the education or experience obtained, requirements met or licenses or certifications granted in the territory of a non-Party, nothing in Article 8.4 shall be construed to require the Party to accord such

recognition to the education or experience obtained, requirements met or licenses or certifications granted in the territory of the other Party.

3.   A Party that is a party to an agreement or arrangement of the type referred to in paragraph 1, whether existing or future, shall afford adequate opportunity for the other Party, if the other Party is interested, to negotiate its accession to such an agreement or arrangement or to negotiate comparable ones with it. Where a Party accords recognition autonomously, it shall afford adequate opportunity for the other Party to demonstrate that education, experience, licenses, or certifications obtained or requirements met in that other Party's territory should be recognized.

4.   A Party shall not accord recognition in a manner which would constitute a means of discrimination between countries in the application of its standards or criteria for the authorization, licensing or certification of services suppliers, or a disguised restriction on trade in services.

5.   Annex 8C applies to measures by a Party relating to the licensing or certification of professional service suppliers as set out in the provisions of that Annex.

ARTICLE 8.10: TRANSFERS AND PAYMENTS

1.   Each Party shall permit all transfers and payments relating to the cross-border supply of services to be made freely and without delay into and out of its territory.[8-4] Such transfers and payments include:

   (a)   payments for services;

   (b)   funds taken abroad to consume a service;

   (c)   interest, royalty payments, management fees, licensing fees, and technical assistance and other fees;

   (d)   payments made under a contract; and

   (e)   inflows of funds necessary to perform a service.

2.   Each Party shall permit such transfers and payments relating to the cross-border supply of services to be made in a freely usable currency at the market rate of exchange prevailing on the date of transfer.

3.   Notwithstanding paragraphs 1 and 2, a Party may prevent a transfer or payment through the equitable, non-discriminatory and good faith application of its laws relating to:

   (a)   bankruptcy, insolvency or the protection of the rights of creditors;

   (b)   issuing, trading or dealing in securities, futures, options, or derivatives;

[8-4] The Parties understand that this Article does not extend to Singapore's requirements in relation to the Central Provident Fund regarding the withdrawal of monies from individual accounts.

(c)   financial reporting or record keeping of transfers when necessary to assist law enforcement or financial regulatory authorities;

(d)   criminal or penal offenses; or

(e)   ensuring compliance with orders or judgments in judicial or administrative proceedings.

ARTICLE 8.11: DENIAL OF BENEFITS

A Party may deny the benefits of this Chapter to a service supplier of the other Party if:

(a)   the service is being supplied by an enterprise owned or controlled by nationals of a non-Party and the denying Party:

(i)   does not maintain diplomatic relations with the non-Party; or

(ii)   adopts or maintains measures with respect to the non-Party that prohibit transactions with the enterprise or that would be violated or circumvented if the benefits of this Chapter were accorded to the enterprise; or

(b)   the service is being supplied by an enterprise that has no substantial business activities in the territory of the other Party and it is owned or controlled by persons of a non-Party or the denying Party.

ARTICLE 8.12: TRANSPARENCY IN DEVELOPMENT AND APPLICATION OF REGULATIONS

In addition to the obligations in Chapter 19 (Transparency):

(a)   Each Party shall maintain or establish appropriate mechanisms for responding to inquiries from interested persons regarding regulations[8-5] relating to the subject matter of this Chapter and their requirements.

(b)   If a Party does not provide advance notice and comment pursuant to Article 19.3, it shall, to the extent possible, provide by publicly available means the reasons therefor.

(c)   At the time it adopts final regulations relating to the subject matter of this Chapter, each Party shall, to the extent possible, including upon request, address by publicly available means substantive comments received from interested persons with respect to the proposed regulations.

(d)   To the extent possible, each Party shall allow reasonable time between publication of final regulations and their effective date.

[8-5] The Parties understand that "regulation" includes regulations establishing or applying to licensing authorization or criteria.

ARTICLE 8.13: IMPLEMENTATION

The Parties will meet annually, or as otherwise agreed, on issues related to implementation of this Chapter and any issues of mutual interest.

ANNEX 8A

1. A Party's Schedule to this Annex sets out, pursuant to Articles 8.7.1 and 15.12.1 (Non-Conforming Measures), a Party's existing measures that are not subject to some or all of the obligations imposed by:

   (a) Article 8.3 (National Treatment) or 15.4.1 (National Treatment and Most-Favored-Nation Treatment);

   (b) Article 8.4 (Most-Favored-Nation Treatment) or 15.4.3 (National Treatment and Most-Favored-Nation Treatment);

   (c) Article 8.5 (Market Access);

   (d) Article 8.6 (Local Presence);

   (e) Article 15.8 (Performance Requirements); or

   (f) Article 15.9 (Senior Management and Boards of Directors).

2. Each Schedule entry sets out the following elements:

   (a) sector refers to the sector for which the entry is made;

   (b) sub-sector, for Singapore, refers to the subsector for which the entry is made;

   (c) industry classification refers, for Singapore, where applicable, to the activity covered by the non-conforming measure, according to the provisional CPC codes as used in the Provisional Central Product Classification (Statistical Papers Series M No. 77, Department of International Economic and Social Affairs, Statistical Office of the United Nations, New York, 1991);

   (d) obligations concerned specifies the obligation(s) referred to in paragraph 1 that, pursuant to Article 8.7.1(a) (Non-Conforming Measures) or 15.12.1(a) (Non-Conforming Measures), as the case may be, do not apply to the listed measure(s);

   (e) level of government indicates the level of government maintaining the listed measure(s);

   (f) measures identifies the laws, regulations or other measures for which the entry is made. A measure cited in the measures element:

      (i) means the measure as amended, continued or renewed as of the date of entry into force of this Agreement, and

(ii)   includes any subordinate measure adopted or maintained under the authority of and consistent with the measure;

(g)   description, for Singapore, sets out the non-conforming aspects of the measure for which the entry is made; and description, for the United States, provides a general, non-binding, description of the measures; and

(h)   phase-out sets out commitments, if any, for liberalization after the date of entry into force of this Agreement.

3.   In accordance with Article 8.7.1(a) (Non-Conforming Measures) and 15.12.1(a) (Non-Conforming Measures), the articles of this Agreement specified in the "obligations concerned" element of an entry do not apply to the law, regulation or other measure identified in the "measures" or "description" element of that entry.

4.   Where a Party maintains a measure that requires that a service provider be a citizen, permanent resident, or resident of its territory as a condition to the provision of a service in its territory, a Schedule entry for that measure taken in the Schedule to Annex 8A or 8B with respect to Articles 8.3, 8.4 or 8.6 shall operate as a Schedule entry with respect to Articles 15.4 (National Treatment and Most-Favored-Nation Treatment) or 15.8 (Performance Requirements) to the extent of that measure.

ANNEX 8B

1.   A Party's Schedule to this Annex sets out, pursuant to Articles 8.7.2 (Non-Conforming Measures) and 15.12.2 (Non-Conforming Measures), the specific sectors, sub-sectors or activities for which that Party may maintain existing, or adopt new or more restrictive, measures that do not conform with obligations imposed by:

(a)   Article 8.3 (National Treatment) or 15.4.1 (National Treatment and Most-Favored- Nation Treatment);

(b)   Article 8.4 (Most-Favored-Nation Treatment) or 15.4.3 (National Treatment and Most-Favored-Nation Treatment);

(c)   Article 8.5 (Market Access);

(d)   Article 8.6 (Local Presence);

(e)   Article 15.8 (Performance Requirements); or

(f)   Article 15.9 (Senior Management and Boards of Directors).

2.   Each Schedule entry sets out the following elements:

(a)   sector refers to the sector for which the entry is made;

(b)   sub-sector, for Singapore, refers to the subsector for which the entry is made;

(c)   industry classification refers, for Singapore, where applicable, to the activity covered by the non-conforming measure, according to the provisional CPC codes as used in the Provisional Central Product Classification (Statistical Papers Series M No. 77, Department of International Economic and Social Affairs, Statistical Office of the United Nations, New York, 1991);

(d)   obligations concerned specifies the obligation(s) referred to in paragraph 1 that, pursuant to Articles 8.7.2 (Non-Conforming Measures) and Article 15.12.2 (Non-Conforming Measures), do not apply to the sectors, sub-sectors or activities listed in the entry;

(e)   description sets out the scope of the sector, sub-sector or activities covered by the entry; and

(f)   existing measures identifies, for transparency purposes, existing measures that apply to the sector, sub-sector or activities covered by the entry.

3.   In accordance with Articles 8.7.2 (Non-Conforming Measures) and 15.12.2 (Non-Conforming Measures), the articles of this Agreement specified in the "obligations concerned" element of an entry do not apply to the sectors, sub-sectors and activities identified in the description element of that entry.

ANNEX 8C
PROFESSIONAL SERVICES

DEVELOPMENT OF PROFESSIONAL STANDARDS

1.   The Parties shall encourage the relevant bodies in their respective territories to develop mutually acceptable standards and criteria for licensing and certification of professional service providers and to provide recommendations on mutual recognition to the Joint Committee.

2.   The standards and criteria referred to in paragraph 1 may be developed with regard to the following matters:

(a)   education - accreditation of schools or academic programs;

(b)   examinations - qualifying examinations for licensing, including alternative methods of assessment such as oral examinations and interviews;

(c)   experience - length and nature of experience required for licensing;

(d)   conduct and ethics - standards of professional conduct and the nature of disciplinary action for non-conformity with those standards;

(e)   professional development and re-certification - continuing education and ongoing requirements to maintain professional certification;

(f)   scope of practice - extent of, or limitations on, permissible activities;

    (g)   local knowledge - requirements for knowledge of such matters as local laws, regulations, language, geography or climate; and

    (h)   consumer protection - alternatives to residency requirements, including bonding, professional liability insurance and client restitution funds, to provide for the protection of consumers.

3.   On receipt of a recommendation referred to in paragraph 1, the Joint Committee shall review the recommendation within a reasonable time to determine whether it is consistent with this Agreement. Based on the Joint Committee's review, each Party shall encourage its respective competent authorities, where appropriate, to implement the recommendation within a mutually agreed time.

TEMPORARY LICENSING

4.   Where the Parties agree, each Party shall encourage the relevant bodies in its territory to develop procedures for the temporary licensing of professional service providers of another Party.

REVIEW

5.   The Joint Committee shall, at least once every three years, review the implementation of this Section.

CHAPTER 9: TELECOMMUNICATIONS

ARTICLE 9.1: SCOPE AND COVERAGE

1.   This Chapter applies to measures affecting trade in telecommunications services.

2.   This Chapter does not apply to any measure adopted or maintained by a Party relating to cable or broadcast distribution of radio or television programming.[9-1]

3.   Nothing in this Chapter shall be construed to:

    (a)   require a Party (or require a Party to compel any enterprise) to establish, construct, acquire, lease, operate, or provide telecommunications transport networks or telecommunications services where such networks or services are not offered to the public generally; or

    (b)   require a Party to compel any enterprise engaged in the cable or broadcast distribution of radio or television programming to make available its cable or broadcast facilities as a public telecommunications transport network, unless a Party specifically designates such facilities as such.

[9-1] For greater certainty, Singapore's obligations under this Chapter shall not apply to measures adopted or maintained relating to broadcasting services as defined in Singapore's Schedule to Annex 8B.

ARTICLE 9.2: ACCESS TO AND USE OF PUBLIC TELECOMMUNICATIONS TRANSPORT NETWORKS AND SERVICES[9-2]

1.   Each Party shall ensure that enterprises of the other Party have access to and use of any public telecommunications transport network and service, including leased circuits, offered in its territory or across its borders on reasonable, non-discriminatory (including with respect to timeliness), and transparent terms and conditions, including as set out in paragraphs 2 through 4.

2.   Each Party shall ensure that such enterprises are permitted to:

(a)   purchase or lease, and attach terminal or other equipment that interfaces with the public telecommunications network;

(b)   provide services to individual or multiple end-users over any leased or owned circuit(s);

(c)   connect leased or owned circuits with public telecommunications transport networks and services in the territory, or across the borders, of that Party, or with circuits leased or owned by another enterprise;

(d)   perform switching, signaling, processing, and conversion functions; and

(e)   use operating protocols of their choice.

3.   Each Party shall ensure that enterprises of the other Party may use public telecommunications transport networks and services for the movement of information in its territory or across its borders and for access to information contained in data bases or otherwise stored in machine-readable form in the territory of either Party.

4.   Notwithstanding paragraph 3, a Party may take such measures as are necessary to

(a)   ensure the security and confidentiality of messages; or

(b)   protect the privacy of customer proprietary network information; subject to the requirement that such measures are not applied in a manner that would constitute a means of arbitrary or unjustifiable discrimination or a disguised restriction on trade in services.

ARTICLE 9.3: INTERCONNECTION WITH SUPPLIERS OF PUBLIC TELECOMMUNICATIONS SERVICES

1.   Each Party shall ensure that suppliers of public telecommunications services in its territory provide, directly or indirectly, interconnection with the facilities and equipment of suppliers of public telecommunications services of the other Party.

2.   In carrying out paragraph 1, each Party shall ensure that suppliers of public telecommunications services in its territory take reasonable steps to protect the confidentiality of

---

[9-2] This Article does not apply to access to unbundled network elements, including access to leased circuits as an unbundled network element, which is addressed in Article 9.4.3.

proprietary information of, or relating to, suppliers and end-users of public telecommunications services and only use such information for the purpose of providing public telecommunications services.

ARTICLE 9.4: CONDUCT OF MAJOR SUPPLIERS[9-3][9-4]

Treatment by Major Suppliers

1.   Each Party shall ensure that any major supplier in its territory accords suppliers of public telecommunications services of the other Party treatment no less favorable than such major supplier accords to itself, its subsidiaries, its affiliates, or any non-affiliated service supplier regarding:

(a)   the availability, provisioning, rates, or quality of like public telecommunications services; and

(b)   the availability of technical interfaces necessary for interconnection. A Party shall assess such treatment on the basis of whether such suppliers of public telecommunications services, subsidiaries, affiliates, and non-affiliated service suppliers are in like circumstances.

Competitive Safeguards

2.   (a)   Each Party shall maintain appropriate measures for the purpose of preventing suppliers of public telecommunications services who, alone or together, are a major supplier in its territory from engaging in or continuing anti-competitive practices.

(b)   For purposes of subparagraph (a), anti-competitive practices include:

(i)   engaging in anti-competitive cross-subsidization;

(ii)   using information obtained from competitors with anti-competitive results; and

(iii)   not making available, on a timely basis, to suppliers of public telecommunications services, technical information about essential facilities and commercially relevant information that is necessary for them to provide public telecommunications services.

Unbundling of Network Elements

3.   (a)   Recognizing that both Parties currently provide for access to unbundled network elements, each Party shall provide its telecommunications regulatory body the

---

[9-3] For the purpose of the United States' obligations, Article 9.4 does not apply to rural telephone companies, as defined in section 3(37) of the Communications Act of 1934, as amended by the Telecommunications Act of 1996, unless a state regulatory authority orders otherwise. Moreover, a state regulatory authority may exempt a rural local exchange carrier, as defined in section 251(f)(2) of the Communications Act of 1934, as amended by the Telecommunications Act of 1996, from the obligations contained in Article 9.4.

[9-4] Article 9.4 does not apply to suppliers of commercial mobile services.

authority to require that major suppliers in its territory provide suppliers of public telecommunications services of the other Party access to network elements on an unbundled basis at terms, conditions, and cost-oriented rates, that are reasonable, non-discriminatory (including with respect to timeliness), and transparent for the supply of public telecommunications services.

(b)   Which network elements will be required to be made available in the territory of a Party, and which suppliers may obtain such elements, shall be determined in accordance with national law and regulation.

(c)   In determining the network elements to be made available, a Party's telecommunications regulatory body shall consider, at a minimum, in accordance with national law and regulation:

    (i)   whether access to such network elements as are proprietary in nature are necessary; and whether the failure to provide access to such network elements would impair the ability of suppliers of public telecommunications services of the other Party to provide the services it seeks to offer; or

    (ii)   whether the network elements can be replicated or obtained from other sources at reasonable rates, such that the unavailability of these network elements from the major supplier will not impair the ability of other suppliers of public telecommunications services to provide a competing service; or

    (iii)   whether the network elements are technically or operationally required for the provision of a competing service; or

    (iv)   other factors as established in national law;

    as that body construes these factors.

Co-Location

4.   (a)   Each Party shall ensure that major suppliers in its territory provide to suppliers of public telecommunications services of the other Party physical co-location, at premises owned or controlled by the major supplier, of equipment necessary for interconnection or access to unbundled network elements on terms and conditions, and at cost-oriented rates, that are reasonable, non-discriminatory (including with respect to timeliness), and transparent.

(b)   Where physical co-location is not practical for technical reasons or because of space limitations, each Party shall ensure that major suppliers in its territory provide or facilitate virtual co-location on terms and conditions, and at cost-oriented rates, that are reasonable, non-discriminatory (including with respect to timeliness), and transparent.

(c)   Each Party may determine, in accordance with national law and regulation, which premises in its territory shall be subject to subparagraphs (a) and (b)

Resale

5.   Each Party shall ensure that major suppliers in its territory:

(a)   offer for resale, at reasonable[9-5] rates, to suppliers of public telecommunications services of the other Party, public telecommunications services that such major supplier provides at retail to end-users; and

(b)   do not impose unreasonable or discriminatory conditions or limitations on the resale of such public telecommunications services.[9-6]

Poles, Ducts, and Conduits

6.   (a)   Each Party shall ensure that major suppliers in its territory provide access to poles, ducts, and conduits, owned or controlled by such major suppliers to suppliers of public telecommunications services of the other Party, under terms, conditions, and cost-oriented[9-7] rates, that are reasonable, non-discriminatory (including with respect to timeliness), and transparent.

(b)   Nothing shall prevent a Party from determining, under its domestic law and regulation, which particular structures owned or controlled by the major suppliers in its territory, are required to be made available in accordance with paragraph (a) provided that this is based on a determination that such structures cannot feasibly be economically or technically substituted in order to provide a competing service.

Number Portability

7.   Each Party shall ensure that major suppliers in its territory provide number portability to the extent technically feasible, on a timely basis and on reasonable terms and conditions.

Interconnection

8.   (a)   General Terms and Conditions Each Party shall ensure that any major supplier in its territory provides interconnection for the facilities and equipment of suppliers of public telecommunications services of the other Party:

(i)   at any technically feasible point in the major supplier's network;

(ii)   under non-discriminatory terms, conditions (including technical standards and specifications), and rates;

[9-5] In the United States, a wholesale rate set pursuant to domestic law and regulation shall be considered to be reasonable for purposes of subparagraph (a). In Singapore, wholesale rates are not required by the telecommunications regulatory body and therefore are not factored into a determination of what is considered to be reasonable for the purposes of subparagraph (a).

[9-6] In the United States, a reseller that obtains at wholesale rates a telecommunications service that is available at retail only to a category of subscribers may be prohibited from offering such service to a different category of subscribers. In Singapore, where national law and regulation provides for this, resellers that obtain public telecommunications services available at retail only to a category of subscribers at particular rates may be prohibited from offering such service to a different category of subscribers at that particular rate.

[9-7] In the United States, this obligation may not apply to those states that regulate such rates as a matter of state law.

(iii)   of a quality no less favorable than that provided by such major supplier for its own like services or for like services of non-affiliated suppliers of public telecommunications services or for its subsidiaries or other affiliates;

(iv)   in a timely fashion, on terms, conditions, (including technical standards and specifications), and cost-oriented rates, that are transparent, reasonable, having regard to economic feasibility, and sufficiently unbundled so that the supplier need not pay for network components or facilities that it does not require for the service to be provided; and

(v)   upon request, at points in addition to the network termination points offered to the majority of suppliers of public telecommunications services, subject to charges that reflect the cost of construction of necessary additional facilities.[9-8]

(b)   Options for Interconnecting with Major Suppliers Each Party shall ensure that suppliers of public telecommunications services of the other Party may interconnect their facilities and equipment with those of major suppliers in its territory pursuant to at least one of the following options:

(i)   a reference interconnection offer or another standard interconnection offer containing the rates, terms, and conditions that the major supplier offers generally to suppliers of public telecommunications services; or

(ii)   the terms and conditions of an existing interconnection agreement or through negotiation of a new interconnection agreement.

(c)   Public Availability of Interconnection Offers Each Party shall require each major supplier in its territory to make publicly available either a reference interconnection offer or another standard interconnection offer containing the rates, terms, and conditions that the major supplier offers generally to suppliers of public telecommunications services.

(d)   Public Availability of the Procedures for Interconnection Negotiations Each Party shall make publicly available the applicable procedures for interconnection negotiations with major suppliers in its territory.

(e)   Public Availability of Interconnection Agreements Concluded with Major Suppliers

(i)   Each Party shall require major suppliers in its territory to file all interconnection agreements to which they are party with its telecommunications regulatory body.

(ii)   Each Party shall make available for inspection to suppliers of public telecommunications services which are seeking interconnection, interconnection agreements in force between a major supplier in its

---

[9-8] These costs may include the cost of physical or virtual co-location referenced in Article 9.4.4.

territory and any other supplier of public telecommunications services in such territory, including interconnection agreements concluded between a major supplier and its affiliates and subsidiaries.

(f)   Resolution of Interconnection Disputes Each Party shall ensure that suppliers of public telecommunications services of the other Party, that have requested interconnection with a major supplier in the Party's territory have recourse to a telecommunications regulatory body to resolve disputes regarding the terms, conditions, and rates for interconnection within a reasonable and publicly available period of time.

Provisioning and Pricing of Leased Circuits Services[9-9]

9.   (a)   Each Party shall ensure that major suppliers of leased circuits services in its territory provide enterprises of the other Party leased circuits services that are public telecommunications services, on terms and conditions under pricing structures, and at rates that are reasonable, non-discriminatory (including with respect to timeliness), and transparent.

(b)   Each Party may determine whether rates for leased circuits services in its territory are reasonable by taking into account the rates of like leased circuits services in comparable markets in other countries.

ARTICLE 9.5: SUBMARINE CABLE LANDING STATIONS

1.   Where under national law and regulation, a Party has authorized a supplier of public telecommunications services in its territory to operate a submarine cable system (including the landing facilities and services) as a public telecommunications service, that Party shall ensure that such supplier provides that public telecommunications service[9-10] to suppliers of public telecommunications services of the other Party on reasonable terms, conditions, and rates that are no less favorable than such supplier offers to any other supplier of public telecommunications services in like circumstances.

2.   Where submarine cable landing facilities and services cannot be economically or technically substituted, and a major supplier of public international telecommunication services that controls such cable landing facilities and services has the ability to materially affect the price and supply for those facilities and services for the provision of public telecommunications services in a Party's territory, the Party shall ensure that such major supplier:

(a)   permits suppliers of public telecommunications services of the other Party to:

(i)   use the major supplier's cross-connect links in the submarine cable landing station to connect their equipment to backhaul links and submarine cable capacity of any supplier of telecommunications; and

(ii)   co-locate their transmission and routing equipment used for accessing submarine cable capacity and backhaul links at the submarine cable

---

[9-9] The obligation under this article is not an obligation to provide leased circuits as an unbundled network element, which is addressed in Article 9.4.3.

[9-10] This shall include any submarine cable landing facilities included as part of that authorization.

landing station at terms, conditions, and cost-oriented rates, that are reasonable and non-discriminatory; and

(b)   provides suppliers of telecommunications of the other Party submarine cable capacity, backhaul links, and cross-connect links in the submarine cable landing station at terms, conditions, and rates that are reasonable and non-discriminatory.

ARTICLE 9.6: INDEPENDENT REGULATION AND PRIVATIZATION

1.   Each Party shall ensure that its telecommunications regulatory body is separate from, and not accountable to, any supplier of public telecommunications services. To this end, each Party shall ensure that its telecommunications regulatory body does not hold any financial interest or maintain an operating role in such a supplier.

2.   Each Party shall ensure that the decisions of, and procedures used by its telecommunications regulatory body are impartial with respect to all interested persons. To this end, each Party shall ensure that any financial interest that it holds in a supplier of public telecommunications services does not influence the decisions of and procedures of its telecommunications regulatory body.

3.   Where a Party has an ownership interest in a supplier of public telecommunications services, it shall notify the other Party of any intention to eliminate such interest as soon as feasible.

ARTICLE 9.7: UNIVERSAL SERVICE

Each Party shall administer any universal service obligation that it maintains in a transparent, non-discriminatory, and competitively neutral manner and shall ensure that its universal service obligation is not more burdensome than necessary for the kind of universal service that it has defined.

ARTICLE 9.8: LICENSING PROCESS

1.   When a Party requires a supplier of public telecommunications services to have a license, the Party shall make publicly available:

(a)   all the licensing criteria and procedures it applies;

(b)   the period of time normally required to reach a decision concerning an application for a license; and

(c)   the terms and conditions of all licenses it has issued.

2.   Each Party shall ensure that an applicant receives, upon request, the reasons for the denial of a license.

ARTICLE 9.9: ALLOCATION AND USE OF SCARCE RESOURCES[9-11]

1.   Each Party shall administer its procedures for the allocation and use of scarce resources, including frequencies, numbers, and rights of way, in an objective, timely, transparent, and non-discriminatory fashion.

2.   Each Party shall make publicly available the current state of allocated frequency bands but shall not be required to provide detailed identification of frequencies assigned or allocated by each government for specific government uses.

ARTICLE 9.10: ENFORCEMENT

Each Party shall ensure that its telecommunications regulatory body maintains appropriate procedures and authority to enforce domestic measures relating to the obligations under Articles 9.2 through 9.5. Such procedures and authority shall include the ability to impose effective sanctions, which may include financial penalties, injunctive relief (on an interim or final basis), or modification, suspension, and revocation of licenses.

ARTICLE 9.11: RESOLUTION OF DOMESTIC TELECOMMUNICATIONS DISPUTES

Further to Articles 19.5 (Administrative Proceedings) and 19.6 (Review and Appeal), each Party shall ensure the following:

Recourse to Telecommunications Regulatory Bodies

1.   Each Party shall ensure that enterprises of the other Party have recourse (within a reasonable period of time) to a telecommunications regulatory body or other relevant body to resolve disputes arising under domestic measures addressing a matter set out in Articles 9.2 through 9.5.

Reconsideration

2.   Each Party shall ensure that any enterprise aggrieved or whose interests are adversely affected by a determination or decision of the telecommunications regulatory body may petition that body for reconsideration of that determination or decision. Neither Party may permit such a petition to constitute grounds for non-compliance with such determination or decision of the telecommunications regulatory body unless an appropriate authority stays such determination or decision.

Judicial Review

3.   Each Party shall ensure that any enterprise aggrieved by a determination or decision of the telecommunications regulatory body may obtain judicial review of such determination or decision by an impartial and independent judicial authority.

[9-11] The Parties understand that decisions on allocating and assigning spectrum, and frequency management are not measures that are per se inconsistent with Article 8.5 (Market Access) and Article 15.8 (Performance Requirements). Accordingly, each Party retains the right to exercise its spectrum and frequency management policies, which may affect the number of suppliers of public telecommunications services, provided that this is done in a manner that is consistent with the provisions of this Agreement. The Parties also retain the right to allocate frequency bands taking into account existing and future needs.

ARTICLE 9.12: TRANSPARENCY

Further to Chapter 19 (Transparency), each Party shall ensure that:

1.   rulemakings, including the basis for such rulemakings, of its telecommunications regulatory body and end-user tariffs filed with its telecommunications regulatory body are promptly published or otherwise made available to all interested persons;

2.   interested persons are provided with adequate advance public notice of and the opportunity to comment on any rulemaking proposed by the telecommunications regulatory body;

3.   its measures relating to public telecommunications services are made publicly available, including:

   (a)   tariffs and other terms and conditions of service;

   (b)   specifications of technical interfaces;

   (c)   conditions applying to attachment of terminal or other equipment to the public telecommunications transport network; and

   (d)   notification, permit, registration, or licensing requirements, if any; and

4.   information on bodies responsible for preparing, amending, and adopting standards-related measures is made publicly available.

ARTICLE 9.13: FLEXIBILITY IN THE CHOICE OF TECHNOLOGIES

A Party shall endeavor not to prevent suppliers of public telecommunications services from having the flexibility to choose the technologies that they use to supply their services, including commercial mobile services, subject to the ability of each Party to take measures to ensure that end-users of different networks are able to communicate with each other.

ARTICLE 9.14: FORBEARANCE AND MINIMAL REGULATORY ENVIRONMENT

The Parties recognize the importance of relying on market forces to achieve wide choice and efficient supply of telecommunications services. To this end, each Party may forbear from applying regulation to a telecommunications service that such Party classifies, under its laws and regulations, as a public telecommunications service upon a determination by its telecommunications regulatory body that:

(a)   enforcement of such regulation is not necessary to prevent unreasonable or discriminatory practices;

(b)   enforcement of such regulation is not necessary for the protection of consumers; and

(c)   forbearance is consistent with the public interest, including promoting and enhancing competition among suppliers of public telecommunications services.

ARTICLE 9.15: RELATIONSHIP TO OTHER CHAPTERS

In the event of any inconsistency between this Chapter and another Chapter, this Chapter shall prevail to the extent of such inconsistency.

ARTICLE 9.16: DEFINITIONS

For purposes of this Chapter:

1.   backhaul links means end-to-end transmission links from a submarine cable landing station to another primary point of access to the Party's public telecommunications transport network;

2.   physical co-location means physical access to and control over space in order to install, maintain, or repair equipment used to provide public telecommunications services;

3.   cost-oriented means based on cost, and may include a reasonable profit, and may involve different cost methodologies for different facilities or services;

4.   commercial mobile services means public telecommunications services supplied through mobile wireless means;

5.   cross-connect links means the links in a submarine cable landing station used to connect submarine cable capacity to the transmission, switching and routing equipment of different suppliers of public telecommunications services co-located in that submarine cable landing station;

6.   customer proprietary network information means information made available to the supplier of public telecommunications services by the end-user solely by virtue of the end-user-telecommunications service supplier relationship. This includes information regarding the end-user's calling patterns (including the quantity, technical configuration, type, destination, location, and amount of use of the service) and other information that appears on or may pertain to an end-user's telephone bill;

7.   end-user means a final consumer of or subscriber to a public telecommunications service, including a service supplier but excluding a supplier of public telecommunications services;

8.   enterprise means an entity constituted or organized under applicable law, whether or not for profit, and whether privately or government owned or controlled. Forms that an enterprise may take include a corporation, trust, partnership, sole proprietorship, branch, joint venture, association, or similar organization;

9.   essential facilities means facilities of a public telecommunications transport network or service that:

   (a)   are exclusively or predominantly provided by a single or limited number of suppliers; and

   (b)   cannot feasibly be economically or technically substituted in order to provide a service;

10.   interconnection means linking with suppliers providing public telecommunications transport networks or services in order to allow the users of one supplier to communicate with users of another supplier and to access services provided by another supplier;

11.   leased circuits means telecommunications facilities between two or more designated points which are set aside for the dedicated use of or availability to a particular customer or other users of the customer's choosing;

12.   major supplier means a supplier of public telecommunications services that has the ability to materially affect the terms of participation (having regard to price and supply) in the relevant market for public telecommunications services as a result of:

      (a)   control over essential facilities; or

      (b)   use of its position in the market;

13.   network element means a facility or equipment used in the provision of a public telecommunications service, including features, functions, and capabilities that are provided by means of such facility or equipment;

14.   non-discriminatory means treatment no less favorable than that accorded to any other user of like public telecommunications transport networks or services in like circumstances;

15.   number portability means the ability of end-users of public telecommunications services to retain, at the same location, existing telephone numbers without impairment of quality, reliability, or convenience when switching between like suppliers of public telecommunications services;

16.   person means either a natural person or an enterprise;

17.   public telecommunications transport network means telecommunications infrastructure which a Party requires to provide public telecommunications services between defined network termination points;

18.   public telecommunications service means any telecommunications service (which a Party may define to include certain facilities used to deliver these telecommunications services) that a Party requires, explicitly or in effect, to be offered to the public generally. Such services may include inter alia, telephone and data transmission typically involving customer-supplied information between two or more points without any end-to-end change in the form or content of the customer's information;[9-12]

19.   reference interconnection offer means an interconnection offer extended by a major supplier and filed with or approved by a telecommunications regulatory body that is sufficiently detailed to enable a supplier of public telecommunications services that is willing to accept its rates, terms, and conditions to obtain interconnection without having to engage in negotiations with the major supplier concerned;

[9-12] Because the United States does not classify services described in 47 U.S.C. § 153(20) as public telecommunications services, these services are not considered public telecommunications services for the purposes of this Agreement. This does not prejudice either Party's positions in the WTO on the scope and definition of these services.

20.   service supplier means any person that supplies a service;

21.   submarine cable landing station means the premises and buildings where international submarine cables arrive and terminate and are connected to backhaul links;

22.   supplier of public telecommunications services means any provider of public telecommunications services, including those who provide such services to other suppliers of public telecommunications services;[9-13]

23.   telecommunications means the transmission and reception of signals by any electromagnetic means;[9-14]

24.   telecommunications regulatory body means a national body responsible for the regulation of telecommunications; and

25.   user means an end-user or a supplier of public telecommunications services.

CHAPTER 10: FINANCIAL SERVICES

ARTICLE 10.1: SCOPE AND COVERAGE

1.   This Chapter applies to measures adopted or maintained by a Party relating to:

(a)   financial institutions of the other Party;

(b)   investors of the other Party, and investments of such investors, in financial institutions in the Party's territory; and

(c)   cross-border trade in financial services.

2.   Chapters 8 (Cross-Border Trade in Services) and 15 (Investment) apply to measures described in paragraph 1 only to the extent that such Chapters or Articles of such Chapters are incorporated into this Chapter.

(a)   Articles 8.11 (Denial of Benefits), 15.6 (Expropriation),[10-1] 15.7 (Transfers), 15.10 (Investment and Environment), 15.11 (Denial of Benefits), and 15.13 (Special Formalities and Information Requirements) are hereby incorporated into and made a part of this Chapter.

[9-13] (a)   For purposes of Singapore's obligations in Articles 9.3, 9.4.1, 9.4.5, 9.4.8, and 9.13, the phrase supplier of public telecommunications services means a facilities-based licensee or services-based licensee that uses switching or routing equipment, in accordance with the Singapore Code of Practice for Competition in the Provision of Telecommunications Services, 2000.

(b)   For purposes of Singapore's obligations in Articles 9.4.3, 9.4.4, 9.4.6 and 9.5, the phrase supplier of public telecommunications services means a facilities-based licensee in accordance with the Singapore Code of Practice for Competition in the Provision of Telecommunications Services, 2000.

[9-14] Including by photonic means.

[10-1] For greater certainty, the letters referred to in Article 15.26 (Status of Letter Exchanges), to the extent relevant, are applicable to Article 15.6 (Expropriation) as incorporated into this Chapter.

(b)   Section C of Chapter 15 (Investor-State Dispute Settlement) is hereby incorporated into and made a part of this Chapter solely for claims that a Party has breached Articles 15.6 (Expropriation), 15.7 (Transfers), 15.11 (Denial of Benefits), and 15.13 (Special Formalities and Information Requirements), as incorporated into this Chapter.

(c)   Article 8.10 (Transfers and Payments), is incorporated into and made a part of this Chapter to the extent that cross-border trade in financial services is subject to obligations pursuant to Article 10.5.

3.   This Chapter does not apply to measures adopted or maintained by a Party relating to:

(a)   activities or services forming part of a public retirement plan or statutory system of social security; or

(b)   activities or services conducted for the account or with the guarantee or using the financial resources of the Party, including its public entities, except that this Chapter shall apply if a Party allows any of the activities or services referred to in subparagraphs (a) or (b) to be conducted by its financial institutions in competition with a public entity or a financial institution.

4.   This Chapter does not apply to laws, regulations or requirements governing the procurement by government agencies of financial services purchased for governmental purposes and not with a view to commercial resale or use in the supply of services for commercial sale.

ARTICLE 10.2: NATIONAL TREATMENT

1.   Each Party shall accord to investors of the other Party treatment no less favorable than that it accords to its own investors, in like circumstances, with respect to the establishment, acquisition, expansion, management, conduct, operation, and sale or other disposition of financial institutions and investments in financial institutions in its territory.

2.   Each Party shall accord to financial institutions of the other Party and to investments of investors of the other Party in financial institutions treatment no less favorable than that it accords to its own financial institutions, and to investments of its own investors in financial institutions, in like circumstances, with respect to the establishment, acquisition, expansion, management, conduct, operation, and sale or other disposition of financial institutions and investments.

3.   For purposes of the national treatment obligations in Article 10.5.1, a Party shall accord to cross-border financial service suppliers of the other Party treatment no less favorable than that it accords to its own financial service suppliers, in like circumstances, with respect to the supply of the relevant service.

ARTICLE 10.3: MOST-FAVORED-NATION TREATMENT

1.   Each Party shall accord to investors of the other Party, financial institutions of the other Party, investments of investors in financial institutions, and cross-border financial service suppliers of the other Party treatment no less favorable than that it accords to the investors,

financial institutions, investments of investors in financial institutions and cross-border financial service suppliers of a non-Party, in like circumstances.

2.   A Party may recognize prudential measures of the other Party or of a non-Party in the application of measures covered by this Chapter. Such recognition may be:

(a)   accorded unilaterally;

(b)   achieved through harmonization or other means; or

(c)   based upon an agreement or arrangement with the non-Party.

3.   A Party according recognition of prudential measures under paragraph 2 shall provide adequate opportunity to the other Party to demonstrate that circumstances exist in which there are or would be equivalent regulation, oversight, implementation of regulation, and, if appropriate, procedures concerning the sharing of information between the Parties.

4.   Where a Party accords recognition of prudential measures under paragraph 2(c) and the circumstances set out in paragraph 3 exist, the Party shall provide adequate opportunity to the other Party to negotiate accession to the agreement or arrangement, or to negotiate a comparable agreement or arrangement.

ARTICLE 10.4: MARKET ACCESS FOR FINANCIAL INSTITUTIONS

A Party shall not adopt or maintain, with respect to financial institutions of the other Party,[10-2] either on the basis of a regional subdivision or on the basis of its entire territory, measures that:

(a)   impose limitations on

(i)   the number of financial institutions whether in the form of numerical quotas, monopolies, exclusive service suppliers or the requirements of an economic needs test;

(ii)   the total value of financial service transactions or assets in the form of numerical quotas or the requirement of an economic needs test;

(iii)   the total number of financial service operations or the total quantity of financial services output expressed in terms of designated numerical units in the form of quotas or the requirement of an economic needs test; or

(iv)   the total number of natural persons that may be employed in a particular financial service sector or that a financial institution may employ and who are necessary for, and directly related to, the supply of a specific financial service in the form of a numerical quota or the requirement of an economic needs test; or

---

[10-2] For purposes of this Article, the term "financial institutions of the other Party" includes financial institutions that are located within the territory of the other Party and controlled by persons of the other Party that seek to establish financial institutions within the territory of the Party.

(b) restrict or require specific types of legal entity or joint venture through which a financial institution may supply a service.

ARTICLE 10.5: CROSS-BORDER TRADE IN FINANCIAL SERVICES

1. Each Party shall permit, under terms and conditions that accord national treatment, cross-border financial service suppliers of the other Party to supply the services it has specified in Annex 10A.

2. Each Party shall permit persons located in its territory, and its nationals wherever located, to purchase financial services from cross-border financial service suppliers of the other Party located in the territory of the other Party. This obligation does not require a Party to permit such suppliers to do business or solicit in its territory. Each Party may define "doing business" and "solicitation" for purposes of this obligation, as long as such definitions are not inconsistent with paragraph 1.

ARTICLE 10.6: NEW FINANCIAL SERVICES

Each Party shall permit a financial institution of the other Party to supply any new financial service that the first Party would permit its own financial institutions, in like circumstances, to supply without additional legislative action by the first Party. Notwithstanding Article 10.4(b), a Party may determine the institutional and juridical form through which the new financial service may be supplied and may require authorization for the supply of the service. Where a Party requires such authorization of the new financial service, a decision shall be made within a reasonable time and the authorization may only be refused for prudential reasons.[10-3]

ARTICLE 10.7: TREATMENT OF CERTAIN INFORMATION

Nothing in this Chapter requires a Party to furnish or allow access to:

(a) information related to the financial affairs and accounts of individual customers of financial institutions or cross-border financial service suppliers; or

(b) any confidential information, the disclosure of which would impede law enforcement or otherwise be contrary to the public interest or prejudice legitimate commercial interests of particular enterprises.

ARTICLE 10.8: SENIOR MANAGEMENT AND BOARDS OF DIRECTORS

1. A Party may not require financial institutions of the other Party[10-4] to engage individuals of any particular nationality as senior managerial or other essential personnel.

[10-3] The Parties understand that nothing in Article 10.6 prevents a financial institution of a Party from applying to the other Party to consider authorizing the supply of a financial service that is supplied in neither Party's territory. Such application shall be subject to the law of the Party to which the application is made and, for greater certainty, shall not be subject to the obligations of Article 10.6.

[10-4] For purposes of this Article, the term "financial institutions of the other Party" includes financial institutions that are located within the territory of the other Party and controlled by persons of the other Party that seek to establish financial institutions within the territory of the Party.

2.   A Party may not require that more than a simple majority of the board of directors of a financial institution of the other Party be composed of nationals of the Party, persons residing in the territory of the Party, or a combination thereof.

ARTICLE 10.9: NON-CONFORMING MEASURES

1.   Articles 10.2 through 10.5 and 10.8 do not apply to:

    (a)   any existing non-conforming measure that is maintained by a Party at

        (i)   the central level of government, and set out by that Party in its Schedule to Annex 10B,

        (ii)   a regional level of government, and set out by that Party in its Schedule to Annex 10B, or

        (iii)   a local level of government;

    (b)   the continuation or prompt renewal of any non-conforming measure referred to in subparagraph (a); or

    (c)   an amendment to any non-conforming measure referred to in subparagraph (a) to the extent that the amendment does not decrease the conformity of the measure, as it existed immediately before the amendment, with Articles 10.2 through 10.4 and 10.8.

2.   Annex 10C sets out certain specific commitments by each Party.

3.   A non-conforming measure set out in a Party's Schedule to Annex 8A or 8B as a measure to which Article 8.3 (National Treatment), 8.4 (Most-Favored-Nation Treatment), 8.5 (Market Access), or 15.4 (National Treatment and Most-Favored-Nation Treatment) does not apply shall be treated as a non-conforming measure described in paragraph 1(a) to which Article 10.2, 10.3, or 10.4, as the case may be, does not apply, to the extent that the measure, sector, sub-sector or activity set out in the schedule of non-conforming measures is covered by this Chapter.

ARTICLE 10.10: EXCEPTIONS

1.   Notwithstanding any other provision of this Chapter or Chapters 9 (Telecommunications), 14 (Electronic Commerce), or 15 (Investment), including specifically Article 9.15 (Relationship to Other Chapters), and in addition Article 8.2.2 (Scope and Coverage) with respect to the supply of financial services in the territory of a Party by an investor of the other Party or a covered investment, a Party shall not be prevented from adopting or maintaining measures for prudential reasons,[10-5] including for the protection of investors, depositors, policy holders or persons to whom a fiduciary duty is owed by a financial institution or cross-border financial service supplier, or to ensure the integrity and stability of the financial system. Where such measures do not conform with the provisions of this Agreement referred to

---

[10-5] It is understood that the term "prudential reasons" includes the maintenance of the safety, soundness, integrity or financial responsibility of individual financial institutions or cross-border financial service suppliers.

in this paragraph, they shall not be used as a means of avoiding the Party's commitments or obligations under such provisions.

2.   Nothing in this Chapter or Chapters 9 (Telecommunications), 14 (Electronic Commerce), or 15 (Investment), including specifically Article 9.15 (Relationship to Other Chapters), and in addition Article 8.2.2 (Scope and Coverage) with respect to the supply of financial services in the territory of a Party by an investor of the other Party or a covered investment, applies to non-discriminatory measures of general application taken by any public entity in pursuit of monetary and related credit policies or exchange rate policies. This paragraph shall not affect a Party's obligations under Article 8.10 (Transfers and Payments), Article15.7 (Transfers), or Article 15.8 (Performance Requirements).

3.   Notwithstanding Articles 8.10 (Transfers and Payments) and 15.7 (Transfers), as incorporated into this Chapter, a Party may prevent or limit transfers by a financial institution or cross-border financial service supplier to, or for the benefit of, an affiliate of or person related to such institution or supplier, through the equitable, non-discriminatory and good faith application of measures relating to maintenance of the safety, soundness, integrity or financial responsibility of financial institutions or cross-border financial service suppliers. This paragraph does not prejudice any other provision of this Agreement that permits a Party to restrict transfers.

4.   For greater certainty, nothing in this Chapter shall be construed to prevent the adoption or enforcement by a Party of measures necessary to secure compliance with laws or regulations that are not inconsistent with this Chapter including those relating to the prevention of deceptive and fraudulent practices or to deal with the effects of a default on financial services contracts, subject to the requirement that such measures are not applied in a manner which would constitute a means of arbitrary or unjustifiable discrimination between countries where like conditions prevail, or a disguised restriction on investment in financial institutions or cross-border trade in financial services.

ARTICLE 10.11: TRANSPARENCY

1.   The Parties recognize that transparent regulations and policies governing the activities of financial institutions and cross-border financial service suppliers are important in facilitating the ability of financial institutions located outside the territory of the Party, financial institutions of the other Party, and cross-border financial service suppliers to gain access to and operate in each other's markets. Each Party commits to promote regulatory transparency in financial services. Accordingly, the Financial Services Committee established under Article 10.16 shall consult with the goal of promoting objective and transparent regulatory processes in each Party, taking into account (1) the work undertaken by the Parties in the General Agreement on Trade in Services and the Parties' work in other fora relating to trade in financial services and (2) the.101 importance for regulatory transparency of identifiable policy objectives and clear and consistently applied regulatory processes that are communicated or otherwise made available to the public.

2.   In lieu of Article 19.3.2 (Publication), each Party shall, to the extent practicable,

        (a)   publish in advance any regulations of general application relating to the subject matter of this Chapter that it proposes to adopt; and

(b)   provide interested persons and the other Party a reasonable opportunity to comment on such proposed regulations.

3.   Each Party's regulatory authorities shall make available to interested persons their requirements, including any documentation required, for completing applications relating to the supply of financial services.

4.   On the request of an applicant, the regulatory authority shall inform the applicant of the status of its application. If such authority requires additional information from the applicant, it shall notify the applicant without undue delay.

5.   A regulatory authority shall make an administrative decision on a completed application of an investor in a financial institution, a financial institution or a cross-border financial service supplier of the other Party relating to the supply of a financial service within 120 days, and shall promptly notify the applicant of the decision. An application shall not be considered complete until all relevant hearings are held and all necessary information is received. Where it is not practicable for a decision to be made within 120 days, the regulatory authority shall notify the applicant without undue delay and shall endeavor to make the decision within a reasonable time thereafter.

6.   Each Party shall maintain or establish appropriate mechanisms that will respond to inquiries from interested persons regarding measures of general application covered by this Chapter.

7.   Each Party shall ensure that the rules of general application adopted or maintained by self-regulatory organizations of the Party are promptly published or otherwise made available in such a manner as to enable interested persons to become acquainted with them.

8.   To the extent practicable, each Party should allow reasonable time between publication of final regulations and their effective date.

9.   At the time it adopts final regulations, a Party should, to the extent practicable, address in writing substantive comments received from interested persons with respect to the proposed regulations.

ARTICLE 10.12: SELF-REGULATORY ORGANIZATIONS

Where a Party requires a financial institution or a cross-border financial service supplier of the other Party to be a member of, participate in, or have access to, a self-regulatory organization to provide a financial service in or into the territory of that Party, the Party shall ensure observance of the obligations of Articles 10.2 and 10.3 by such self-regulatory organization.

ARTICLE 10.13: PAYMENT AND CLEARING SYSTEMS

Under terms and conditions that accord national treatment, each Party shall grant to financial institutions of the other Party established in its territory access to payment and clearing systems operated by public entities, and to official funding and refinancing facilities available in the normal course of ordinary business. This paragraph is not intended to confer access to the Party's lender of last resort facilities.

ARTICLE 10.14: DOMESTIC REGULATION

Except with respect to non-conforming measures listed in its schedule to Annex 10B, each Party shall ensure that all measures of general application to which this Chapter applies are administered in a reasonable, objective and impartial manner.

ARTICLE 10.15: EXPEDITED AVAILABILITY OF INSURANCE SERVICES

The Parties recognize the importance of maintaining and developing regulatory procedures to expedite the offering of insurance services by licensed suppliers. The Parties recognize the importance of consulting, as necessary, regarding any such initiatives.

ARTICLE 10.16: FINANCIAL SERVICES COMMITTEE

1.   The Parties hereby establish a Financial Services Committee. The principal representative of each Party shall be an official of the Party's authority responsible for financial services set out in Annex 10D.

2.   The Committee shall:

(a)   supervise the implementation of this Chapter and its further elaboration;

(b)   consider issues regarding financial services that are referred to it by a Party; and

(c)   participate in the dispute settlement procedures in accordance with Article 10.18.

3.   The Committee shall meet annually, or as otherwise agreed, to assess the functioning of this Agreement as it applies to financial services. The Committee shall inform the Joint Committee established under Article 20.1 (Joint Committee) of the results of each meeting.

ARTICLE 10.17: CONSULTATIONS

1.   A Party may request consultations with the other Party regarding any matter arising under this Agreement that affects financial services. The other Party shall give sympathetic consideration to the request. The Parties shall report the results of their consultations to the Financial Services Committee.

2.   Consultations under this Article shall include officials of the authorities specified in Annex 10D.

ARTICLE 10.18: DISPUTE SETTLEMENT

1.   Article 20.4 (Additional Dispute Settlement Procedures) applies as modified by this Article to the settlement of disputes arising under this Chapter.

2.   When a Party claims that a dispute arises under this Chapter, Article 20.4.4(a) (Additional Dispute Settlement Procedures) shall apply, except that:

(a)   where the Parties so agree, the panel shall be composed entirely of panelists meeting the qualifications in paragraph 3;

(b)   in any other case,

(i)   each Party may select panelists meeting the qualifications set out in paragraph 3 or Article 20.4.4(c) (Additional Dispute Settlement Procedures), and

(ii)   if the Party complained against invokes Article 10.10 (Exceptions), the chair of the panel shall meet the qualifications set out in paragraph 3, unless the Parties agree otherwise.

3.   Financial services panelists shall:

(a)   have expertise or experience in financial services law or practice, which may include the regulation of financial institutions;

(b)   be chosen strictly on the basis of objectivity, reliability and sound judgment; and

(c)   meet the qualifications set out in Article 20.4.4(b)(ii) and 20.4.4(b)(iii) (Additional Dispute Settlement Procedures).

4.   Notwithstanding Article 20.6 (Non-Implementation), where a Panel finds a measure to be inconsistent with this Agreement and the measure under dispute affects:

(a)   only the financial services sector, the complaining Party may suspend benefits only in the financial services sector;.104

(b)   the financial services sector and any other sector, the complaining Party may suspend benefits in the financial services sector that have an effect equivalent to the effect of the measure in the Party's financial services sector; or (c) only a sector other than the financial services sector, the complaining Party may not suspend benefits in the financial services sector.

ARTICLE 10.19: INVESTMENT DISPUTES IN FINANCIAL SERVICES

1.   Where an investor of a Party submits a claim under Section C of Chapter 15 (Investor-State Dispute Settlement) against the other Party and the respondent invokes Article 10.10, on request of the respondent, the tribunal shall refer the matter in writing to the Financial Services Committee for a decision. The tribunal may not proceed pending receipt of a decision or report under this Article.

2.   In a referral pursuant to paragraph 1, the Financial Services Committee shall decide the issue of whether and to what extent Article 10.10 is a valid defense to the claim of the investor. The Committee shall transmit a copy of its decision to the tribunal and to the Joint Committee. The decision shall be binding on the tribunal.

3.   Where the Financial Services Committee has not decided the issue within 60 days of the receipt of the referral under paragraph 1, the respondent or the Party of the claimant may request the establishment of a panel under Article 20.4.4 (Additional Dispute Settlement Procedures). The panel shall be constituted in accordance with Article 10.18. The panel shall transmit its final report to the Committee and to the tribunal. The report shall be binding on the tribunal.

4.   Where no request for the establishment of a panel pursuant to paragraph 3 has been made within 10 days of the expiration of the 60-day period referred to in paragraph 3, a tribunal may proceed to decide the matter.

5.   For purposes of this Article, tribunal means a tribunal established pursuant to Section C of Chapter 15 (Investor-State Dispute Settlement).

ARTICLE 10.20: DEFINITIONS

For purposes of this Chapter:

1.   central level means

    (a)   for the United States, the federal level, and

    (b)   for Singapore, the national level;

2.   cross-border financial service supplier of a Party means a person of a Party that is engaged in the business of supplying a financial service within the territory of the Party and that seeks to supply or supplies financial services through the cross-border supply of such services;

3.   cross-border supply of a financial service or cross-border trade in financial services means the supply of a financial service:

    (a)   from the territory of one Party into the territory of the other Party,

    (b)   in the territory of one Party by a person of that Party to a person of the other Party, or

    (c)   by a national of one Party in the territory of the other Party, but does not include the supply of a financial service in the territory of one Party by an investor of the other Party, or investments of such investors, in financial institutions in the Party's territory.

4.   financial institution means any financial intermediary or other institution, that is authorized to do business and regulated or supervised as a financial institution under the law of the Party in whose territory it is located;

5.   financial institution of the other Party means a financial institution, including a branch, located in the territory of a Party that is controlled by persons of the other Party;

6.   financial service means any service of a financial nature. Financial services include all insurance and insurance-related services, and all banking and other financial services (excluding insurance), as well as services incidental or auxiliary to a service of a financial nature. Financial services include the following activities:

Insurance and insurance-related services

    (a)   Direct insurance (including co-insurance):

       (i)   life

       (ii)   non-life

(b)   Reinsurance and retrocession;

(c)   Insurance intermediation, such as brokerage and agency;

(d)   Service auxiliary to insurance, such as consultancy, actuarial, risk assessment and claim settlement services.

Banking and other financial services (excluding insurance)

(e)   Acceptance of deposits and other repayable funds from the public;

(f)   Lending of all types, including consumer credit, mortgage credit, factoring and financing of commercial transactions;

(g)   Financial leasing;

(h)   All payment and money transmission services, including credit, charge and debit cards, travelers checks and bankers drafts;

(i)   Guarantees and commitments;

(j)   Trading for own account or for account of customers, whether on an exchange, in an over-the-counter market or otherwise, the following:

       (i)   money market instruments (including checks, bills, certificates of deposits);

       (ii)   foreign exchange;

       (iii)   derivative products including, but not limited to, futures and options;

       (iv)   exchange rate and interest rate instruments, including products such as swaps, forward rate agreements;

       (v)   transferable securities;

       (vi)   other negotiable instruments and financial assets, including bullion;

(k)   Participation in issues of all kinds of securities, including underwriting and placement as agent (whether publicly or privately) and supply of services related to such issues;

(l)   Money broking;

(m)   Asset management, such as cash or portfolio management, all forms of collective investment management, pension fund management, custodial, depository and trust services;

(n)   Settlement and clearing services for financial assets, including securities, derivative products, and other negotiable instruments;

(o)   Provision and transfer of financial information, and financial data processing and related software by suppliers of other financial services;

(p)   Advisory, intermediation and other auxiliary financial services on all the activities listed in subparagraphs (e) through (o), including credit reference and analysis, investment and portfolio research and advice, advice on acquisitions and on corporate restructuring and strategy.

7.   financial service supplier of a Party means a person of a Party that is engaged in the business of supplying a financial service within the territory of that Party;

8.   investment means "investment" as defined in Article 15.1.13 (Definitions), except that, with respect to "loans" and "debt instruments" referred to in that Article:

(a)   a loan to or debt instrument issued by a financial institution is an investment only where it is treated as regulatory capital by the Party in whose territory the institution is located; and

(b)   a loan granted by or debt instrument owned by a financial institution, other than a loan to or debt instrument of a financial institution referred to in subparagraph (a), is not an investment.

For greater certainty, a loan granted by or debt instrument owned by a cross-border financial service supplier, other than a loan to or debt instrument issued by a financial institution, is an investment if such loan or debt instrument meets the criteria for investments set out in Article 15.1.13 (Definitions).

9.   investor of a Party means a Party or state enterprise thereof, or a person of that Party, that attempts to make, is making, or has made an investment in the territory of the other Party; provided, however, that a natural person who is a dual national shall be deemed to be exclusively a national of the State of his/her dominant and effective nationality;

10.   new financial service means, for purposes of Article 10.6, a financial service not supplied in the territory of the first Party that is supplied within the territory of the other Party, and includes any new form of delivery of a financial service or the sale of a financial product that is not sold in the first Party's territory.

11.   person of a Party means "person of a Party" as defined in Article 1.2 (General Definitions) and, for greater certainty, does not include a branch of an institution of a non-party;

12.   public entity means a central bank or monetary authority of a Party, or any financial institution owned or controlled by a Party that is principally engaged in carrying out governmental functions or activities for governmental purposes, not including an entity

principally engaged in supplying financial services on commercial terms; for greater certainty, a public entity[10-6] shall not be considered a designated monopoly or a government enterprise for purposes of Chapter 12 (Anticompetitive Business Conduct, Designated Monopolies and Government Enterprises);

13.   regional level means

(a)   for the United States, the 50 states, the District of Columbia and Puerto Rico, and

(b)   Singapore has no government at the regional level; for Singapore, "local government level" means entities with sub-national legislative or executive powers under domestic law, including Town Councils and Community Development Councils.

14.   self-regulatory organization means any non-governmental body, including any securities or futures exchange or market, clearing agency, other organization or association, that exercises regulatory or supervisory authority over financial service suppliers or financial institutions, by statute or delegation from central, regional or local governments or authorities; for greater certainty, a self-regulatory organization shall not be considered a designated monopoly for purposes of Chapter 12 (Anticompetitive Business Conduct, Designated Monopolies and Government Enterprises).

ANNEX 10A

APPLICATION OF ARTICLE 10.5

UNITED STATES

Insurance and insurance-related services

1.   For the United States, Article 10.5 applies to the cross-border supply of or trade in financial services as defined in subparagraph (a) of the definition of cross-border supply of financial services in Article 10.20 with respect to

(a)   insurance of risks relating to:

(i)   maritime shipping and commercial aviation and space launching and freight (including satellites), with such insurance to cover any or all of the following: the goods being transported, the vehicle transporting the goods and any liability arising therefrom; and

(ii)   goods in international transit;

(b)   reinsurance and retrocession, services auxiliary to insurance as referred to in subparagraph (d) of the definition of financial service, and insurance

---

[10-6] The Federal Deposit Insurance Corporation of the United States and any entity that administers a deposit insurance scheme in Singapore shall be deemed to be within the definition of public entity for purposes of Chapter 12 (Anticompetitive Business Conduct, Government Monopolies, and Government Enterprises).

intermediation such as brokerage and agency as referred to in subparagraph (c) of the definition of financial service.

2.   For the United States, Article 10.5 applies to the cross-border supply of or trade in financial services as defined in paragraph (c) of the definition of cross-border supply of financial services in Article 10.20 with respect to insurance services.

Banking and other financial services (excluding insurance)

3.   For the United States, Article 10.5 applies with respect to the provision and transfer of financial information and financial data processing and related software as referred to in subparagraph (o) of the definition of financial service, and advisory and other auxiliary services, excluding intermediation, relating to banking and other financial services as referred to in subparagraph (p) of the definition of financial service.

SINGAPORE

Insurance and insurance-related services

1.   For Singapore, Article 10.5 applies to the cross-border supply of or trade in financial services as defined in sub paragraph (a) of the definition of cross-border supply of a financial service or cross-border trade in financial services in Article 10.20 with respect to:

   (a)   reinsurance and retrocession;

   (b)   services auxiliary to insurance comprising actuarial, loss adjustors, average adjustors and consultancy services;

   (c)   insurance of "MAT" risks comprising

      (i)   maritime shipping and commercial aviation and space launching and freight (including satellites), with such insurance to cover any or all of the following: the goods being transported, the vehicle transporting the goods and any liability arising therefrom; and

      (ii)   goods in international transit;

   (d)   reinsurance intermediation by brokerages; and

   (e)   MAT intermediation by brokerages.

2.   For Singapore, Article 10.5 applies to the cross-border supply of or trade in financial services as defined in subparagraph (c) of the definition of cross-border supply of a financial service or cross-border trade in financial services in Article 10.20 with respect to services auxiliary to insurance comprising actuarial, loss adjustors, average adjustors and consultancy services.

Banking and other financial services (excluding insurance)

3.   For Singapore, Article 10.5 applies with respect to

(a)   financial leasing, provided that access to customer information of banks in Singapore is limited to financial institutions licensed in Singapore;

(b)   provision and transfer of financial information;

(c)   provision of financial data processing and related software;

(d)   trading in money market instruments, foreign exchange, exchange rate and interest rate instruments with financial institutions in Singapore;

(e)   corporate finance advisory services, offered:

    (i)   to a related corporation or accredited investors only, provided that clients do not engage in public offerings of securities on the basis of such advice, and that such advice is not disclosed to clients' shareholders who are not accredited investors or to the public; or

    (ii)   through a related corporation that is holding (or exempted from holding) a capital markets services license to advise on corporate finance under the Securities and Futures Act (Cap. 289); and.111

(f)   advisory and other auxiliary services, excluding intermediation and services described in subparagraph (e), relating to banking and other financial services referred to in subparagraph (p) in the definition of "financial service" in Article 10.20 to the extent that such services are permitted in the future by Singapore.

ANNEX 10B

INTRODUCTORY NOTE FOR THE SCHEDULE OF SINGAPORE TO ANNEX 10B

1.   The Schedule of Singapore to Annex 10B sets out:

(a)   in Section A, the headnotes that limit or clarify the commitments of Singapore with respect to the obligations described in subparagraphs (i) – (v) of paragraph (b), and

(b)   in Section B, pursuant to Article 10.9 (Non-Conforming Measures), the existing measures of Singapore that are not subject to some or all of the obligations imposed by:

    (i)   Article 10.2 (National Treatment);

    (ii)   Article 10.3 (Most-Favored-Nation Treatment);

    (iii)   Article 10.4 (Market Access for Financial Institutions);

    (iv)   Article 10.5 (Cross-Border Trade);

    (v)   Article 10.8 (Senior Management and Boards of Directors).

2.   Each entry in Section B as described in paragraph 1(b) sets out the following elements:

(a)   Type of reservation sets out the obligations referred to in paragraph 1(b) with respect to which the entry is made;

(b)   Level of government indicates the level of government maintaining the listed measure(s);

(c)   Measure identifies the laws, regulations or other measures for which the entry is made. A measure cited in the measure element:

(i)   means the measure as amended, continued or renewed as of the date of entry into force of this Agreement;

(ii)   includes any subordinate measure adopted or maintained under the authority of and consistent with the measure;

(d)   Description sets out the non-conforming aspects of the entry.

3.   In accordance with Article 10.9.1(a), the articles of this Agreement referred to by their titles in the Type of reservation element of an entry do not apply to the law, regulation or other measures identified in the Measures element or described in the Description element of that entry.

4.   Both Parties agree that references in the Schedule of a Party to the Annex to any enterprise or entity apply as well to any successor enterprise or entity, which shall be entitled to benefit from any listing of a non-conforming measure with respect to that enterprise or entity.

INTRODUCTORY NOTE FOR THE UNITED STATES SCHEDULE TO ANNEX 10B

Relating to Banking and Other Non-Insurance Financial Services

1.   The Schedule of the United States to Annex 10B with respect to banking and other non-insurance financial services sets out:

(a)   in Section A, the headnotes that limit or clarify the commitments of the United States with respect to the obligations described in subparagraphs (i)-(iv) of paragraph (b), and

(b)   in Section B, pursuant to Article 10.9 (Non-Conforming Measures), the existing measures of the United States that are not subject to some or all of the obligations imposed by:

(i)   Article 10.2 (National Treatment);

(ii)   Article 10.3 (Most-Favored-Nation Treatment);

(iii)   Article 10.4 (Market Access for Financial Institutions); or

(iv)   Article 10.8 (Senior Management and Boards of Directors).

2.   Each entry in Section B as described in paragraph 1(b) sets out the following elements:

(a)   Description of Non-Conforming Measures sets out the non-conforming aspects of the entry and the subsector, financial institution, or activities covered by the entry;

(b)   Measures identifies the laws, regulations or other measures for which the entry is made. A measure cited in the Measures element:

(i)   means the measure as amended, continued or renewed as of the date of entry into force of this Agreement, and

(ii)   includes any subordinate measure adopted or maintained under the authority of and consistent with the measure;

(c)   Obligations Concerned indicates the obligations referred to in paragraph 1(b) with respect to which the entry is made.

Relating to Insurance:

3.   The Schedule of the United States to Annex 10B with respect to insurance sets out:

(a)   headnotes that limit or clarify the commitments of the United States with respect to the obligations described in subparagraphs (i)-(v) of paragraph (b), and.115

(b)   pursuant to Article 10.9 (Non-Conforming Measures), a schedule of existing measures of the United States that do not conform to some or all of the obligations imposed by:

(i)   Article 10.2 (National Treatment);

(ii)   Article 10.3 (Most-Favored-Nation Treatment);

(iii)   Article 10.4 (Market Access for Financial Enterprises);

(iv)   Article 10.5 (Cross-Border Trade); or

(v)   Article 10.8 (Senior Management and Boards of Directors).

4.   Each entry in the schedule of non-conforming measures described in paragraph 3(b) sets out the following elements:

(a)   Obligations Concerned specified the obligations(s) referred to in paragraph 1(b) that, pursuant to Article 10.9, do not apply to the listed measure(s);

(b)   Level of Government indicates the level of government maintaining the listed measures(s);

(c) Measures identifies the laws, regulations or other measures for which the entry is made. A measure cited in the Measures element:

(i) means the measure as amended, continued or renewed as of the date of entry into force of this Agreement, and

(ii) includes any subordinate measure adopted or maintained under the authority of and consistent with the measure;

(d) Description provides a general, nonbinding description of the Measures.

Common Provisions

5. In accordance with Article 10.9.1 (a), the articles of this Agreement specified in the Obligations Concerned element of an entry do not apply to the law, regulation or other measure identified in the Measures element or in the Description of Non-Conforming Measures element of that entry.

6. Where the United States maintains a measure that requires that a service supplier be a citizen, permanent resident or resident of its territory as a condition to the provision of a service in its territory, a listing for that measure taken in Annex 10B with respect to Articles 10.2, 10.3, 10.4, or 10.5 shall operate as a reservation with respect to Articles 15.4 (National Treatment and Most-Favored-Nation Treatment) and 15.8 (Performance Requirements), or to the extent of that measure.

7. Both Parties agree that references in the Schedule of a Party to Annex 10B to any enterprise or entity apply as well to any successor enterprise or entity, which shall be entitled to benefit from any listing of a non-conforming measure with respect to that enterprise or entity.

ANNEX 10C

SPECIFIC COMMITMENTS

SINGAPORE

Related to Article 10.1 (Scope and Coverage)

1. This Chapter shall apply to the following services to the extent they are covered by the obligations of this Chapter through application of the exception in Article 10.1.3:

- Sale and distribution services for government debt.

Related to Article 10.4 (Market Access)

2. Notwithstanding item 1 of the non-conforming measures related to banking listed in Singapore's Schedule to Annex 10B, Singapore shall approve, by the date of entry into force of this Agreement, one new full bank license and two additional customer service locations for a financial institution of the United States.

Related to Article 10.5 (Cross Border Trade)

3.   No later than January 1, 2006, the Parties shall consult on further liberalization by Singapore of cross-border trade in the services described in paragraph 3(f) of Singapore's Schedule to Annex 10A.

Related to Article 10.15 (Expedited Availability of Insurance Services)

4.   Singapore shall not require product filing or approval for insurance products other than for life insurance products, Central Provident Fund-related products and investment-linked products. Where product filing or approval is required, Singapore shall allow the introduction of the product, which Singapore shall deem to be approved unless the product is disapproved within a reasonable time, endeavoring to do so within 30 days. Singapore shall not maintain limitations on the number or frequency of product introductions. This specific commitment does not apply where a financial institution of the United States seeks to supply a new financial service pursuant to Article 10.6 (New Financial Services).

Related to Article 10.17 (Consultations)

5.   No later than January 1, 2007, and every three years thereafter, the Parties shall consult concerning any existing limitations on acquisitions of control by United States financial institutions of Singapore-incorporated banks that are controlled by persons of Singapore.

Related to Portfolio Management

6.   (a)   Singapore shall allow, in a manner consistent with Article 10.1, a financial institution (other than a trust company or insurance company), organized outside its territory, to provide investment advice and portfolio management services, excluding (1) custodial services, (2) trustee services, and (3) execution services that are not related to managing a collective investment scheme, to the manager of a collective investment scheme, where the manager is

        (i)   located in the territory of Singapore, and

        (ii)   related to the financial institution.

    (b)   For purposes of this paragraph,

        (i)   collective investment scheme has the meaning given to it under Section 2 of the Securities and Futures Act (Cap. 289); and

        (ii)   related means a related corporation as defined under Section 6 of the Companies Act (Cap. 50).

7.   Singapore shall accord most-favored-nation treatment to financial institutions of the United States in the award of asset management mandates by the Government of Singapore Investment Corporation.

Related to Credit and Charge Cards

8.   Singapore shall consider applications for access to automated teller machine networks operated by local banks in the territory of Singapore for credit and charge cards of non-bank issuers that are controlled by persons of the United States.

UNITED STATES

Related to Article 10.1 (Scope and Coverage)

1.   For the United States, this chapter shall apply to the following services to the extent they are covered by the obligations of this chapter through application of the exception in Article 10.1.3:

    (a)   fiscal agency or depository services,

    (b)   liquidation and management services for regulated financial institutions; and

    (c)   sale and distribution services for government debt.

Related to Article 10.15 (Expedited Availability of Insurance Services)

2.   Recognizing the principles of federalism under the U.S. Constitution, the history of state regulation of insurance in the United States, and the McCarran-Ferguson Act, the United States welcomes the efforts of the National Association of Insurance Commissioners ("NAIC") relating to the availability of insurance services as expressed in the NAIC's "Statement of Intent: The Future of Insurance Regulation.", including the initiatives on speed-to-market intentions and regulatory re-engineering (under Part II of the Statement of Intent). This specific commitment does not apply where a financial institution of Singapore seeks to supply a new financial service pursuant to Article 10.6.

Related to Portfolio Management

3.   (a)   The United States shall allow, in a manner consistent with Article 10.1, a financial institution (other than a trust company or insurance company), organized outside its territory, to provide investment advice and portfolio management services, excluding (1) custodial services, (2) trustee services, and (3) execution services that are not related to managing a collective investment scheme, to a collective investment scheme located in the territory of the United States.

        (b)   For purposes of this paragraph, collective investment scheme means an investment company registered with the Securities and Exchange Commission under the Investment Company Act of 1940..120

ANNEX 10D

THE FINANCIAL SERVICES COMMITTEE

1.   On request by either Party, the Financial Services Committee shall consider any matter relating to:

(a)   the transfer of information in electronic or other form, into and out of a Party's territory, by a financial institution for data processing where such processing is required in the ordinary course of business;

(b)   the protection of the privacy of individuals in relation to the processing and dissemination of personal data and the protection of confidentiality of individual records and accounts.

Authorities Responsible for Financial Services

2.   The authority of each Party responsible for financial services is:

(a)   for Singapore, the Monetary Authority of Singapore;

(b)   for the United States, the Department of the Treasury for banking and other financial services and the Office of the United States Trade Representative, in coordination with the Department of Commerce and other agencies, for insurance services.

CHAPTER 11: TEMPORARY ENTRY OF BUSINESS PERSONS

ARTICLE 11.1: DEFINITIONS

For purposes of this Chapter:

business person means a national of a Party who is engaged in trade in goods, the provision of services or the conduct of investment activities;

immigration measure means any law, regulation, or procedure affecting the entry and sojourn of aliens, including the issuance of immigration documents authorizing employment to an alien; and

temporary entry means entry into the territory of a Party by a business person of the other Party without the intent to establish permanent residence.

ARTICLE 11.2: GENERAL PRINCIPLES

1.   This Chapter reflects the preferential trading relationship between the Parties, the Parties' mutual desire to facilitate temporary entry on a comparable basis and of establishing transparent criteria and procedures for temporary entry, and the need to ensure border security and to protect the domestic labor force and permanent employment in their respective territories.

2.   This Chapter shall not apply to measures regarding citizenship, permanent residence, or employment on a permanent basis.

ARTICLE 11.3: GENERAL OBLIGATIONS

1.   Each Party shall apply its measures relating to the provisions of this Chapter in accordance with Article 11.2 and, in particular, shall apply expeditiously those measures so as to avoid unduly impairing or delaying trade in goods or services or conduct of investment activities under this Agreement.

2.   For greater certainty, nothing in this Chapter shall prevent a Party from applying measures to regulate the entry of natural persons into, or their temporary stay in, its territory, including those measures necessary to protect the integrity of, and to ensure the orderly movement of natural persons across its borders, provided that such measures are not applied in such a manner as to unduly impair or delay trade in goods or services or conduct of investment activities under this Agreement. The sole fact of requiring a visa, or other document authorizing employment to a business person, for natural persons shall not be regarded as unduly impairing or delaying trade in goods or services or conduct of investment activities under this Agreement.

ARTICLE 11.4: GRANT OF TEMPORARY ENTRY

1.   Each Party shall grant temporary entry to business persons listed in Annex 11A who are otherwise qualified for entry under applicable measures relating to public health and safety and national security, in accordance with this Chapter.

2.   A Party may refuse to issue an immigration document authorizing employment to a business person where the temporary entry of that person might affect adversely:

   (a)   the settlement of any labor dispute that is in progress at the place or intended place of employment; or

   (b)   the employment of any person who is involved in such dispute.

3.   When a Party refuses pursuant to paragraph 2 to issue an immigration document authorizing employment, it shall:

   (a)   take measures to allow the business person to be informed in writing; and

   (b)   promptly notify the other Party in writing of the reasons for the refusal.

4.   Each Party shall set any fees for processing applications for temporary entry of business persons in a manner consistent with Article 11.3.1.

ARTICLE 11.5: REGULATORY TRANSPARENCY

1.   Each Party shall maintain or establish contact points or other mechanisms to respond to inquiries from interested persons regarding regulations affecting the temporary entry of business persons.

2.   If a Party receives comments regarding a proposed regulation from interested persons, it should publish a concise statement addressing those comments at the time that it adopts the final regulations.

3.   To the extent possible, each Party shall allow reasonable time between publication of final regulations affecting the temporary entry of business persons and their effective date.

4.   Each Party shall, within a reasonable period of time after an application requesting temporary entry is considered complete under its domestic laws and regulations, inform the applicant of the decision concerning the application. At the request of the applicant, the Party shall provide, without undue delay, information concerning the status of the application.

5.   Prior to the entry into force of this Agreement, the Parties shall exchange information on current procedures relating to the processing of applications for temporary entry, including processing goals that apply to business persons of the other Party. Each Party shall endeavor to achieve these goals and make available upon request to the other Party, in accordance with its domestic law, data respecting the attainment of these processing goals.

6.   For purposes of this Article, regulation means a measure of general application other than a law, and includes a measure that establishes or applies to licensing authorization or criteria.

ARTICLE 11.6: PROVISION OF INFORMATION

Further to Article 19.3 (Publication), each Party shall:

(a)   provide to the other Party such materials as will enable it to become acquainted with its measures relating to this Chapter; and

(b)   no later than six months after the date of entry into force of this Agreement, prepare, publish, and make available in its own territory, and in the territory of the other Party, explanatory material in a consolidated document regarding the requirements for temporary entry under this Chapter in such a manner as will enable business persons of the other Party to become acquainted with them.

ARTICLE 11.7: TEMPORARY ENTRY COORDINATORS

1.   Each Party shall establish a Temporary Entry Coordinator, which shall include officials responsible for immigration measures.

2.   The Temporary Entry Coordinators of the Parties shall:

(a)   establish their own schedule of meetings;

(b)   exchange information on measures that affect the temporary entry of business persons under this Chapter;

(c)   consider the development of measures to facilitate the temporary entry of business persons on a comparable basis;

(d)   consider the implementation and administration of this Chapter; and

(e)   make available, upon request, to the other Party in accordance with its domestic law, data respecting the granting of temporary entry under this Chapter to business persons of the other Party who have been issued immigration documents.

ARTICLE 11.8: DISPUTE SETTLEMENT

1.   A Party may not initiate proceedings under Article 20.4 (Additional Dispute Settlement Procedures) regarding a refusal to grant temporary entry under this Chapter or a particular case arising under Article 11.3.1 unless:

(a)   the matter involves a pattern of practice; and

(b)   the business person has exhausted the available administrative remedies regarding the particular matter.

2.   The remedies referred to in paragraph (1)(b) shall be deemed to be exhausted if a final determination in the matter has not been issued by the competent authority within one year of the institution of an administrative proceeding, and the failure to issue a determination is not attributable to delay caused by the business person.

ARTICLE 11.9: RELATION TO OTHER CHAPTERS

Except for this Chapter, Chapters 1 (Establishment of a Free Trade Area and Definitions), 20 (Administration and Dispute Settlement), and 21 (General Provisions), and Articles 19.2 (Contact Points), 19.3 (Publication), 19.4 (Notification and Provision of Information), and 19.5 (Administrative Proceedings) of Chapter 19 (Transparency), no provision of this Agreement shall impose any obligation on a Party regarding its immigration measures.

ANNEX 11A

SECTION I: BUSINESS VISITORS

1.   Each Party shall grant temporary entry for up to 90 days to a business person seeking to engage in a business activity set out in Appendix 11A.1, without requiring that person to obtain an employment authorization, provided that the business person otherwise complies with immigration measures applicable to temporary entry, and on presentation of:

(a)   proof of nationality of a Party;

(b)   documentation demonstrating that the business person will be so engaged and describing the purpose of entry; and

(c)   evidence demonstrating that the proposed business activity is international in scope and that the business person is not seeking to enter the local labor market.

2.   Each Party may provide that a business person satisfy the requirements of paragraph 1 by demonstrating that:

(a)   the primary source of remuneration for the proposed business activity is outside the territory of the Party granting temporary entry; and

(b)   the business person's principal place of business and the actual place of accrual of profits, at least predominantly, remain outside such territory.

3.   A Party shall normally accept an oral declaration as to the principal place of business and the actual place of accrual of profits. Where the Party requires further proof, it shall normally consider a letter from the employer attesting to these matters as sufficient proof.

4.   Neither Party may:

(a)   as a condition for temporary entry under paragraph 1, require prior approval procedures, petitions, labor certification tests, or other procedures of similar effect; or

(b)   impose or maintain any numerical restriction relating to temporary entry under paragraph 1.

SECTION II: TRADERS AND INVESTORS

1.   Each Party shall grant temporary entry and provide confirming documentation to a business person seeking to:

(a)   carry on substantial trade in goods or services principally between the territory of the Party of which the business person is a national and the territory of the other Party into which entry is sought, or

(b)   establish, develop, administer, or provide advice or key technical services to the operation of an investment to which the business person or the business person's enterprise has committed, or is in the process of committing, a substantial amount of capital, in a capacity that is supervisory, executive, or involves essential skills, provided that the business person otherwise complies with immigration measures applicable to temporary entry.

2.   Neither Party may:

(a)   as a condition for temporary entry under paragraph 1, require labor certification tests or other procedures of similar effect; or

(b)   impose or maintain any numerical restriction relating to temporary entry under paragraph 1.

SECTION III: INTRA-COMPANY TRANSFEREES

1.   Each Party shall grant temporary entry and provide confirming documentation to a business person employed by an enterprise who seeks to render services to that enterprise or a subsidiary or affiliate thereof, in a capacity that is managerial, executive, or involves specialized knowledge, provided that the business person otherwise complies with existing immigration measures applicable to temporary entry. A Party may require the business person to have been

employed continuously by the enterprise for one year within the three-year period immediately preceding the date of the application for admission. The Parties understand that, as used in this paragraph, "a business person employed by an enterprise who seeks to render services to that enterprise or a subsidiary or affiliate thereof, in a capacity that is managerial, executive or involves special knowledge" has the same meaning as "managers, executives and specialists" as defined in relation to intra-corporate transferees in a Party's Schedule of Specific Commitments to the GATS.

2.   A Party shall not:

(a)   as a condition for temporary entry under paragraph 1, require labor certification tests or other procedures of similar effect; or

(b)   impose or maintain any numerical restriction relating to temporary entry under paragraph 1.

SECTION IV: PROFESSIONALS

1.   Each Party shall grant temporary entry and provide confirming documentation to a business person seeking to engage in a business activity as a professional, or to perform training functions related to a particular profession, including conducting seminars, if the business person otherwise complies with immigration measures applicable to temporary entry, on presentation of:

(a)   proof of nationality of a Party;

(b)   documentation demonstrating that the business person will be so engaged and describing the purpose of entry; and

(c)   documentation demonstrating the attainment of the relevant minimum educational requirements or alternative credentials.

2.   For purposes of this Chapter, professional means a national of a Party who is engaged in a specialty occupation requiring:

(a)   theoretical and practical application of a body of specialized knowledge; and

(b)   attainment of a post-secondary degree in the specialty requiring four or more years of study (or the equivalent of such a degree) as a minimum for entry into the occupation. Such degrees include the Bachelor's Degree, Master's Degree, and the Doctoral Degree conferred by institutions in the United States and Singapore.

3.   Notwithstanding paragraph 2, each Party shall grant temporary entry to business persons seeking to engage in a business activity as a professional in one of the professions listed in Appendix 11A.2, provided that the business person possesses the credentials specified and otherwise complies with the requirements in paragraph 1 of this Section.

4.   To assist in the implementation of this Chapter, the Parties shall exchange illustrative lists of professions that meet the definition of professional by the date of entry into force of this

Agreement. The Parties shall also exchange information on post-secondary education, in order to facilitate the evaluation of applications for temporary entry.

5.   A Party shall not:

(a)   as a condition for temporary entry under paragraph 1, require prior approval procedures, petitions, labor certification tests, or other procedures of similar effect; or

(b)   impose or maintain any numerical restriction relating to temporary entry under paragraph 1.

6.   Notwithstanding paragraph 5(a), a Party may require a business person seeking temporary entry under this Section to comply with procedures applicable to temporary entry of professionals, such as an attestation of compliance with the Party's labor and immigration laws or a requirement that the business person meet certain salary criteria.

7.   Notwithstanding paragraphs 1 and 5, a Party may establish an annual numerical limit, which shall be set out in Appendix 11A.3, regarding temporary entry of business persons of the other Party seeking to engage in business activities as a professional.

8.   A Party establishing a numerical limit pursuant to paragraph 7, unless the Parties agree otherwise, may, in consultation with the other Party, grant temporary entry under paragraph 1 to a business person who practices in a profession where accreditation, licensing, and certification requirements are mutually recognized by the Parties.

9.   Nothing in paragraph 7 or 8 shall be construed to limit the ability of a business person to seek temporary entry under a Party's applicable immigration measures relating to the entry of professionals other than those adopted or maintained pursuant to paragraph 1.

APPENDIX 11A.1
BUSINESS VISITORS

Definitions

For purposes of this Appendix, territory of the other Party means the territory of the Party other than the territory of the Party into which temporary entry is sought.

The Parties agree that the business visitors referred to below are not seeking to establish a direct employer-employee relationship in the territory of the Party into which temporary entry is sought.

Research and Design

- Technical, scientific, and statistical researchers conducting independent research or research for an enterprise located in the territory of the other Party.

Growth, Manufacture, and Production

- Purchasing and production management personnel conducting commercial transactions for an enterprise located in the territory of the other Party.

Marketing

- Market researchers and analysts conducting independent research or analysis or research or analysis for an enterprise located in the territory of the other Party.

- Trade fair and promotional personnel attending a trade convention.

Sales

- Sales representatives and agents negotiating contracts for, but not delivering or providing, goods or services for an enterprise located in the territory of the other Party that do not involve direct transactions with the general public.

- Buyers purchasing for an enterprise located in the territory of the other Party.

Distribution

- With respect to temporary entry into the United States, Singaporean customs brokers performing brokerage duties relating to the export of goods from the territory of the United States to or through the territory of Singapore. With respect to temporary entry into the territory of Singapore, United States customs brokers performing brokerage duties relating to the export of goods from the territory of Singapore to or through the territory of the United States.

- Customs brokers providing consulting services regarding the facilitation of the import or export of goods.

After-sales Service

- Installers, repair and maintenance personnel, and supervisors, possessing highly specialized knowledge essential to a seller's contractual obligation, performing services or training workers to perform services, pursuant to a warranty or other directly-related service contract included as part of the sale of commercial or industrial equipment or machinery, including computer software, purchased from an enterprise located outside the territory of the Party into which temporary entry is sought, during the life of the warranty or directly-related service agreement.

General Service

- Managers, executives, and specialists[1] entering to negotiate specified or defined commercial transactions for an enterprise located in the territory of the other Party.

- Managers, executives, and specialists[1] in the financial services sector (insurers, bankers, or investment brokers) entering to negotiate specified or defined commercial transactions for an enterprise located in the territory of the other Party.

- Public relations and advertising managers, executives, and specialists[1] attending or participating in conventions, or consulting with business associates regarding specified or defined commercial transactions for an enterprise located in the territory of the other Party.

- Tourism personnel (tour and travel agents, tour guides, or tour operators) attending or participating in conventions or conducting a tour that has begun in the territory of the other Party.

- Translators or interpreters performing services as employees of an enterprise located in the territory of the other Party, and for a defined commercial transaction for that enterprise.

APPENDIX 11A.2

PROFESSION

MINIMUM EDUCATION REQUIREMENTS AND ALTERNATIVE CREDENTIALS

Disaster Relief Claims Adjuster Baccalaureate Degree, and successful completion of training in the appropriate areas of insurance adjustment pertaining to disaster relief claims; or three years experience in claims adjustment and successful completion of training in the appropriate areas of insurance adjustment pertaining to disaster relief claims.

Management Consultant

Baccalaureate Degree. If the degree is in a discipline not related to the area of the consulting agreement, then equivalent professional experience as established by statement or professional credential attesting to three years experience in a field or specialty related to the consulting agreement is required.

---

[1] As defined in relation to intra -corporate or company transferees in each Party's Schedule of Commitments to the GATS.

APPENDIX 11A.3

United States

1.   Beginning on the date of entry into force of this Agreement, the United States shall annually approve as many as 5,400 initial applications of business persons of Singapore seeking temporary entry under Section IV of Annex 11A to engage in a business activity at a professional level.

2.   For purposes of paragraph 1, the United States shall not take into account:

(a)   the renewal of a period of temporary entry;

(b)   the entry of a spouse or children accompanying or following to join the principal business person;

(c)   an admission under section 101(a)(15)(H)(i)(b) of the Immigration and Nationality Act, 1952, as it may be amended, including the worldwide numerical limit established by section 214(g)(1)(A) of that Act; or

(d)   an admission under any other provision of section 101(a)(15) of that Act relating to the entry of professionals.

CHAPTER 13: GOVERNMENT PROCUREMENT

ARTICLE 13.1: GENERAL

1.   The Parties reaffirm their rights and obligations under the GPA and their interest in further expanding bilateral trading opportunities in each Party's government procurement market.

2.   The Parties recognize their shared interest in promoting international liberalization of government procurement markets in the context of the rules-based international trading system. The Parties shall continue to cooperate in the review under Article XXIV:7 of the GPA and on procurement matters in APEC and other appropriate international fora. The Parties shall also actively cooperate to implement the WTO Doha Ministerial mandate related to the negotiation of a multilateral agreement on transparency in government procurement.

3.   Nothing in this Chapter shall be construed to derogate from either Party's rights or obligations under the GPA.

4.   The Parties confirm their desire and determination to apply the APEC Non-Binding Principles on Government Procurement, as appropriate, to all their government procurement that is outside the scope of the GPA and this Chapter.

ARTICLE 13.2: SCOPE AND COVERAGE

1.   This Chapter applies to measures adopted or maintained by a Party regarding government procurement.

2.   For purposes of this Chapter, government procurement means a procurement:

    (a)   by an entity specified in a Party's Schedule 1 to Annex 13A;

    (b)   of any combination of goods and services specified in a Party's Schedule 2 to Annex 13A;

    (c)   by any contractual means, including those listed in Article I:2 of the GPA and any build-operate-transfer contract; and

    (d)   in which the contract has a value not less than the relevant threshold set out in Schedule 1 to Annex 13A.

3.   Except as otherwise specified in Annexes 13A and 13B, this Chapter does not cover noncontractual agreements or any form of governmental assistance, including:

    (a)   cooperative agreements;

    (b)   grants;

    (c)   loans;

    (d)   equity infusions;

    (e)   guarantees;

    (f)   fiscal incentives; and

    (g)   governmental provision of goods and services to persons or governmental authorities not specifically covered under the Schedules to Annexes 13A and 13B of this Chapter.

4.   Singapore shall not exercise any control or influence, including through any shares that it owns or controls or its personnel selections to corporate boards or positions, in procurement conducted by government enterprises, as defined in Article 12.8 (Definitions).

5.   In accordance with Article III:3 of the GPA, the provisions of this Chapter do not affect the rights and obligations provided for in Chapters 2 (National Treatment and Market Access for Goods), 8 (Cross-Border Trade in Services), 10 (Financial Services), and 15 (Investment).

6.   (a)   To ensure comprehensive coverage, this Chapter covers government procurement of digital products, as defined in Article 14.4 (Definitions), that are transmitted electronically and are created, produced, contracted for, commissioned, or first made available on commercial terms in the territory of the other Party.

    (b)   For greater certainty, digital products do not include digitized representations of financial instruments. In addition, the obligations on digital products under this Chapter shall not apply to the procurement of broadcasting services.

(c)   For greater certainty, a Party's obligations relating to the government procurement of digital products are addressed only in this Chapter.

ARTICLE 13.3: INCORPORATION OF GPA PROVISIONS

1.   The Parties shall apply the provisions of Articles II, III, IV:1, VI-XV, XVI:1, XVIII, XIX:1-4, XX, the Agreement Notes, and Appendices II-IV of the GPA to all government procurement. To that end, these GPA Articles and Appendices, the notes to the Appendices, Notes to Annexes 1 to 5 of Appendix I,[13-1] Singapore's General Note, and U.S. General Notes 1-4 are incorporated into and made a part of this Chapter, mutatis mutandis. For greater certainty, Article VI is not intended to preclude a Party from preparing, adopting, or applying technical specifications to promote the conservation of natural resources.

2.   For purposes of the incorporation of the GPA under paragraph 1, the term:

(a)   "Agreement" in the GPA means "Chapter;" except that "countries not Parties to this Agreement" means "non-Parties" and "Party to the Agreement" in GPA Article III:2(b) means "Party";

(b)   "Appendix I" in the GPA means "Annex 13A";

(c)   "Annex 1" in the GPA means "Schedule 1.A";

(d)   "Annex 2" in the GPA means "Schedule 1.B";

(e)   "Annex 3" in the GPA means "Schedule 1.C";

(f)   "Annex 4" in the GPA means "Schedule 2.B";

(g)   "Annex 5" in the GPA means "Schedule 2.C";

(h)   "from other Parties" in GPA Article IV:1 means "from the other Party";

(i)   "any other Party" in GPA Article III:1(b) means "a non-Party"; and

(j)   "among suppliers of other Parties or" in GPA Article VIII shall not be incorporated.

3.   If the GPA is amended or is superseded by another agreement, the Parties shall amend this Chapter, as appropriate, after consultations.

ARTICLE 13.4: EXCEPTIONS

1.   Nothing in this Chapter shall be construed to prevent either Party from imposing or enforcing measures:

(a)   necessary to protect public morals, order, or safety;

[13-1] For greater certainty, nothing in this Chapter shall be construed as incorporating U.S. General Note 8.

(b)　　necessary to protect human, animal, or plant life or health;

(c)　　necessary to protect intellectual property; or

(d)　　relating to products or services of handicapped persons, of philanthropic institutions, or of prison labor, provided that such measures are not applied in a manner that would constitute a means of arbitrary or unjustifiable discrimination between countries where the same conditions prevail or a disguised restriction on international trade.

2.　　The Parties understand that paragraph 1(b) includes environmental measures necessary to protect human, animal, or plant life or health.

ARTICLE 13.5: MODIFICATIONS AND RECTIFICATIONS TO COVERAGE

1.　　Where a Party proposes to modify or make minor amendments or technical rectifications of a purely formal nature to its Schedules to Annex 13A, it shall notify the other Party. If the other Party does not object to the proposed modification, minor amendment, or technical rectification within 30 days of the notification, the modification, minor amendment, or technical rectification shall enter into force immediately.

2.　　If a Party objects to the proposed removal of an entity from Annex 13A on the grounds that government control or influence over that entity has not been effectively eliminated, that Party may request further information or consultations with a view to clarifying the nature of such government control or influence, if any, and reaching agreement with the other Party on the entity's status under this Chapter. If the Party removing an entity from Annex 13A reaches agreement with the other Party that government control or influence over the entity has been effectively eliminated, the other Party shall not be entitled to compensatory adjustments.

3.　　A Party may modify its Schedules to Annex 13A for reasons other than the elimination of government control or influence only in exceptional circumstances. In such cases, it shall propose to the other Party appropriate compensatory adjustments in order to maintain a level of coverage comparable to that existing prior to the modification. In considering proposed modifications and any consequential compensatory adjustment, allowance shall be made for the market-opening effects of the removal of government control or influence. The modification shall take effect on agreement by the Parties that the proposed adjustments will maintain a comparable level of coverage.

ARTICLE 13.6: DEFINITIONS

For purposes of this Chapter:

1.　　APEC means Asia Pacific Economic Cooperation;

2.　　broadcasting services means a series of text, video, images, sound recordings and other products scheduled by a content provider for audio and/or visual reception, and for which the content provider has no choice over the scheduling of the series;

3.　　build-operate-transfer contract means any contractual arrangement the primary purpose of which is to provide for the construction or rehabilitation of physical infrastructure, plant, buildings, facilities, or other government-owned works and under which, as consideration for a supplie's execution of a contractual arrangement, an entity grants to the supplier, for a specified period of time, temporary ownership or a right to control and operate, and demand payment for, the use of such works for the duration of the contract; and

4.   GPA means WTO Agreement on Government Procurement.

ANNEX 13A
SCHEDULE 1

COVERED ENTITIES

For the United States:

A.   Central Government Entities

All entities included in United States Appendix I, Annex 1 of the GPA, for procurement covered by that Annex.

      Thresholds:

            for all goods and services (except construction services): US$ 56,190, to be adjusted every two years in accordance with the formula specified in Annex 13B; and

            for construction services: US$ 6,481,000, to be adjusted in accordance with the United States' Appendix I, Annex 1 of the GPA and the procedures set forth in that Agreement, converted into U.S. dollars.

B.   Sub-Central Government Entities

All entities included in United States Appendix I, Annex 2 of the GPA, for procurement covered by that Annex.

      Thresholds:

            for all goods and services (except construction services): US$ 460,000; and

            for construction services: US$ 6,481,000.

      These thresholds are to be adjusted in accordance with the United States' Appendix I, Annex 2 of the GPA and the procedures set forth in that Agreement, converted into U.S. dollars.

C.   All Other Entities

All entities included in the United States' Appendix I, Annex 3 of the GPA, for procurement covered by that Annex.

Thresholds:

for all goods and services (except construction services): the SDR equivalent of US$ 250,000 or US$ 518,000 (400,000 SDRs) in accordance with the respective lists in U.S. Appendix I, Annex 3; and for construction services: US$ 6,481,000.

These thresholds are to be adjusted in accordance with the United States' Appendix I, Annex 3 of the GPA and the procedures set forth in that Agreement, converted into U.S. dollars.

For Singapore:

A.   Central Government Entities

All entities included in Singapore Appendix I, Annex 1 of the GPA, for procurement covered by that Annex.

Thresholds:

for all goods and services (except construction services): S$ 102,710, to be adjusted in accordance with the formula specified in Annex 13B; and

for construction services: S$ 11,376,000, to be adjusted in accordance with adjustment of thresholds under Singapore Appendix I, Annex 1 of the GPA and the procedures set forth in that Agreement, converted into Singapore dollars.

B.   Sub-Central Government Entities

Not applicable for Singapore.

C.   All Other Entities:

All entities included in Singapore Appendix I, Annex 3 of the GPA, for procurement covered by that Annex.

Thresholds:

for all goods and services (except construction services): S$ 910,000; and

for construction services: S$ 11,376,000.

These thresholds are to be adjusted in accordance with adjustment of thresholds under Singapore Appendix I, Annex 3 of the GPA and the procedures set forth in that Agreement, converted into Singapore dollars.

SCHEDULE 2

COVERED GOODS AND SERVICES

For the United States:

A.   Goods

This Chapter applies to all goods covered under the United States Appendix I of the GPA, as well as the products covered by Federal Supply Code 58 (Communications, Detection & Coherent Radiation Equipment), except for the Department of Defense, and subject to the exclusions set out in United States Appendix I for specific entities.

B.   Services (Other than construction services)

This Chapter applies to all services in the Universal List of Services, as contained in document MTN.GNS/W/120 of the WTO, procured by the entities specified in Schedule 1, excluding the following services:

> (1)   all transportation services, including Launching Services (CPC Categories 71, 72, 73, 74, 8859, 8868);

Note: Transportation services, where incidental to a contract for the procurement of supplies, are not subject to this Chapter.

> (2)   dredging;

> (3)   all services purchased in support of military forces overseas;

> (4)   management and operation contracts of certain government or privately owned facilities used for government purposes, including federally funded research and development centers (FFRDCs);

> (5)   public utilities services;

> (6)   basic telecommunications network and services listed in paragraph 2C(a) to (g) of document MTN.GNS/W/120 of the WTO, such as public voice and data services. This exclusion does not include information services, as defined in 47 U.S.C. 153 (20).

> (7)   research and Development; and

> (8)   printing Services (for GPA Annex 2 entities only).

C.   Construction Services

This Chapter applies to government procurement of all services covered under Appendix I, Annex 5 of the GPA.

For Singapore:

A.   Goods

This Chapter applies to all goods covered under Singapore = s Appendix I, Annex I of the GPA.

B.   Services (Other than construction services)

This Chapter applies to all services in the Universal List of Services, as contained in document MTN.GNS/W/120 of the WTO, excluding the following services:

(1)   research and development services;

(2)   police, public order, public safety and security services and compulsory social security services;

(3)   radio and television services, including transmission services;

(4)   exam Services;

(5)   asset management and other financial services procured by MOF (Ministry of Finance) and MAS (Monetary Authority of Singapore) for the purpose of managing official foreign reserves and other foreign assets of the Government of Singapore;

(6)   urban planning and landscape architectural services;

(7)   real estate services (excluding consultancy services, agency services, auction and valuation services);

(8)   supply of potable water for human consumption;

(9)   social services;

(10)   printing of Government legislation and gazette; and

(11)   sale and distribution services for government debt.

C.   Construction Services

This Chapter applies to government procurement of all services covered under Singapore = s Appendix I, Annex 5 of the GPA.

ANNEX 13B
INDEXATION AND CONVERSION OF THRESHOLDS

1.   The calculations referenced in Annex 13A of this Agreement shall be adjusted in accordance with the following formula:

$$T 0 (1 + \delta i) = T 1$$

in which:

T 0 = threshold value on January 1, 2002

ð i = accumulated inflation rate for the ith two-year period

T 1 = new threshold value

and the accumulated inflation rate (ð i) is measured by:

for the United States, the producer price index for finished products published by the U.S. Bureau of Labor Statistics; and

for Singapore, the consumer price index published by the Singapore Department of Statistics.

2.   The first adjustment for inflation, to take effect on January 1, 2004, shall be calculated using the period from November 1, 2001 to October 31, 2003. All subsequent adjustments shall be calculated using two-year periods, each period beginning November 1. The adjustments shall take effect on January 1 of the year immediately following the end of the two-year period.

CHAPTER 15: INVESTMENT

SECTION A – DEFINITIONS

ARTICLE 15.1: DEFINITIONS

For purposes of this Chapter, it is understood that:

1.   central level of government means:

(a)   for the United States, the federal level of government; and

(b)   for Singapore, the national level of government;

2.   Centre means the International Centre for Settlement of Investment Disputes ("ICSID") established by the ICSID Convention;

3.   claimant means an investor of a Party that is a party to an investment dispute with the other Party;

4.   covered investment means, with respect to a Party, an investment in its territory of an investor of the other Party in existence as of the date of entry into force of this Agreement or established, acquired, or expanded thereafter;

5.   disputing parties means the claimant and the respondent;

6.   disputing party means either the claimant or the respondent;

7.   enterprise means any entity constituted or organized under applicable law, whether or not for profit, and whether privately or governmentally owned or controlled, including a corporation, trust, partnership, sole proprietorship, joint venture, association, or similar organization; and a branch of an enterprise;

8.   enterprise of a Party means an enterprise constituted or organized under the law of a Party, and a branch located in the territory of a Party and carrying out business activities there;

9.   freely usable currency means "freely usable currency" as determined by the International Monetary Fund under its Articles of Agreement;

10.   government enterprise means "government enterprise" as defined in Chapter 12 (Anticompetitive Business Conduct, Designated Monopolies, and Government Enterprises);

11.   ICSID Additional Facility Rules means the Rules Governing the Additional Facility for the Administration of Proceedings by the Secretariat of the International Centre for Settlement of Investment Disputes;

12.   ICSID Convention means the Convention on the Settlement of Investment Disputes between States and Nationals of Other States, done at Washington, March 18, 1965;

13.   investment means every asset owned or controlled, directly or indirectly, by an investor, that has the characteristics of an investment.[15-1] Forms that an investment may take include:

   (a)   an enterprise;

   (b)   shares, stock, and other forms of equity participation in an enterprise;

   (c)   bonds, debentures, other debt instruments, and loans;[15-2]

   (d)   futures, options, and other derivatives;

   (e)   turnkey, construction, management, production, concession, revenue-sharing, and other similar contracts;

   (f)   intellectual property rights;

   (g)   licenses, authorizations, permits, and similar rights conferred pursuant to applicable domestic law;[15-3][15-4] and

---

[15-1] Where an asset lacks the characteristics of an investment, that asset is not an investment regardless of the form it may take. The characteristics of an investment include the commitment of capital, the expectation of gain or profit, or the assumption of risk.

[15-2] Some forms of debt, such as bonds, debentures, and long-term notes, are more likely to have the characteristics of an investment, while other forms of debt, such as claims to payment that are immediately due and result from the sale of goods or services, are less likely to have such characteristics.

[15-3] Whether a particular type of license, authorization, permit, or similar instrument (including a concession, to the extent that it has the nature of such an instrument) has the characteristics of an investment depends on such factors as the nature and extent of the rights that the holder has under the domestic law of the Party. Among the licenses, authorizations, permits, and similar instruments that do not have the characteristics of an investment are those that do not create any rights protected under domestic law. For greater certainty, the foregoing is without prejudice to

(h)   other tangible or intangible, movable or immovable property, and related property rights, such as leases, mortgages, liens, and pledges.

14.   investment agreement[15-5] means a written agreement that takes effect on or after the date of entry into force of this Agreement between a national authority[15-6] of a Party and a covered investment or an investor of the other Party (i) that grants rights with respect to natural resources or other assets that a national authority controls, and (ii) that the covered investment or the investor relies on in establishing or acquiring the covered investment;

15.   investment authorization[15-7] means an authorization that the foreign investment authority of a Party grants to a covered investment or an investor of the other Party;

16.   investor of a non-Party means, with respect to a Party, an investor that is seeking to make, is making, or has made an investment in the territory of that Party, that is not an investor of either Party;

17.   investor of a Party means a Party or a national or an enterprise of a Party that is seeking to make, is making, or has made an investment in the territory of the other Party; provided, however, that a natural person who is a dual national shall be deemed to be exclusively a national of the State of his/her dominant and effective nationality;

18.   monopoly means "mo monopoly" as defined in Chapter 12 (Anticompetitive Business Conduct, Designated Monopolies, and Government Enterprises);

19.   New York Convention means the United Nations Convention on the Recognition and Enforcement of Foreign Arbitral Awards, done at New York, June 10, 1958;

20.   non-disputing Party means the Party that is not a party to an investment dispute;

21.   protected information means confidential business information or information that is privileged or otherwise protected from disclosure under a Party's law;

22.   regional level of government means, for the United States, a state of the United States, the District of Columbia, or Puerto Rico. For Singapore, "regional level of government" is not applicable, as Singapore has no government at the regional level;

23.   respondent means the Party that is a party to an investment dispute;

24.   Secretary-General means the Secretary-General of ICSID;

25.   tribunal means an arbitration tribunal established under Article 15.18 or 15.24; and

---

whether any asset associated with the license, authorization, permit, or similar instrument has the characteristics of an investment.

[15-4] The term "investment" does not include an order or judgment entered in a judicial or administrative action.

[15-5] Actions taken by an agency of a Party to enforce laws of general application such as competition law do not come within this definition.

[15-6] For purposes of this definition, "national authority" means (1) for Singapore, a ministry or other government body that is constituted by an Act of Parliament; and (2) for the United States, an authority at the central level of government.

[15-7] Actions taken by an agency of a Party to enforce laws of general application such as competition law do not come within this definition.

26.   UNCITRAL Arbitration Rules means the arbitration rules of the United Nations Commission on International Trade Law.

SECTION B – INVESTMENT

ARTICLE 15.2: SCOPE AND COVERAGE

This Chapter applies to measures adopted or maintained by a Party relating to:

(a)   investors of the other Party;

(b)   covered investments; and

(c)   with respect to Articles 15.8 and 15.10, all investments in the territory of the Party.

ARTICLE 15.3: RELATION TO OTHER CHAPTERS

1.   In the event of any inconsistency between this Chapter and another Chapter, the other Chapter shall prevail to the extent of the inconsistency.

2.   A requirement by a Party that a service provider of the other Party post a bond or other form of financial security as a condition of providing a service into its territory does not of itself make this Chapter applicable to the provision of that cross-border service. This Chapter applies to that Party's treatment of the posted bond or financial security.

3.   This Chapter does not apply to measures adopted or maintained by a Party to the extent that they are covered by Chapter 10 (Financial Services).

ARTICLE 15.4: NATIONAL TREATMENT AND MOST-FAVORED-NATION TREATMENT

1.   Each Party shall accord to investors of the other Party treatment no less favorable than that it accords, in like circumstances, to its own investors with respect to the establishment, acquisition, expansion, management, conduct, operation, and sale or other disposition of investments in its territory. Each Party shall accord to covered investments treatment no less favorable than that it accords, in like circumstances, to investments in its territory of its own investors with respect to the establishment, acquisition, expansion, management, conduct, operation, and sale or other disposition of investments. The treatment each Party shall accord under this paragraph is "national treatment."

2.   The treatment to be accorded by a Party under paragraph 1 means, with respect to a state, territory or possession, treatment no less favorable than the most favorable treatment accorded, in like circumstances, by that state, territory, or possession, to investors, and to investments of investors, of the Party of which it forms a part.

3.   Each Party shall accord to investors of the other Party treatment no less favorable than that it accords, in like circumstances, to investors of any non-Party with respect to the establishment, acquisition, expansion, management, conduct, operation, and sale or other disposition of investments in its territory. Each Party shall accord to covered investments treatment no less favorable than that it accords, in like circumstances, to investments in its

territory of investors of any non-Party with respect to the establishment, acquisition, expansion, management, conduct, operation, and sale or other disposition of investments. The treatment each Party shall accord under this paragraph is "most-favored-nation treatment."

4.   Each Party shall accord to investors of the other Party and to their covered investments the better of national treatment or most-favored-nation treatment.

ARTICLE 15.5: MINIMUM STANDARD OF TREATMENT[15-8]

1.   Each Party shall accord to covered investments treatment in accordance with customary international law, including fair and equitable treatment and full protection and security.

2.   For greater certainty, paragraph 1 prescribes the customary international law minimum standard of treatment of aliens as the minimum standard of treatment to be afforded to covered investments. The concepts of "fair and equitable treatment" and "full protection and security" do not require treatment in addition to or beyond that which is required by that standard, and do not create additional substantive rights.

> (a)   The obligation in paragraph 1 to provide "fair and equitable treatment" includes the obligation not to deny justice in criminal, civil, or administrative adjudicatory proceedings in accordance with the principle of due process embodied in the principal legal systems of the world; and
>
> (b)   The obligation in paragraph 1 to provide "full protection and security" requires each Party to provide the level of police protection required under customary international law.

3.   A determination that there has been a breach of another provision of this Agreement, or of a separate international agreement, does not establish that there has been a breach of this Article.

4.   Without prejudice to paragraph 1 and notwithstanding Article 15.12.5(b), each Party shall accord to investors of the other Party, and to covered investments, non-discriminatory treatment with respect to measures it adopts or maintains relating to losses suffered by investments in its territory owing to armed conflict or civil strife.

5.   Paragraph 4 does not apply to existing measures relating to subsidies or grants that would be inconsistent with Article 15.4.1 and 15.4.2 but for Article 15.12.5(b).

ARTICLE 15.6: EXPROPRIATION[15-9]

1.   Neither Party may expropriate or nationalize a covered investment either directly or indirectly through measures equivalent to expropriation or nationalization ("expropriation"), except:

> (a)   for a public purpose;

[15-8] Article 15.5 is to be interpreted in accordance with the letter exchange on customary international law.

[15-9] Article 15.6 is to be interpreted in accordance with the letter exchange on customary international law and the letter exchange on expropriation, and is subject to the letter exchange on land expropriation.

(b)   in a non-discriminatory manner;

(c)   on payment of prompt, adequate, and effective compensation in accordance with paragraphs 2, 3, and 4; and

(d)   in accordance with due process of law and Article 15.5.1, 15.5.2, and 15.5.3.

2.   Compensation shall:

(a)   be paid without delay;

(b)   be equivalent to the fair market value of the expropriated investment immediately before the expropriatory action was taken ("the date of expropriation");

(c)   be fully realizable and freely transferable; and

(d)   not reflect any change in value occurring because the expropriatory action had become known before the date of expropriation.

3.   If the fair market value is denominated in a freely usable currency, the compensation paid shall be no less than the fair market value on the date of expropriation, plus interest at a commercially reasonable rate for that currency, accrued from the date of expropriation until the date of payment.

4.   If the fair market value is denominated in a currency that is not freely usable, the compensation paid – converted into the currency of payment at the market rate of exchange prevailing on the date of payment – shall be no less than:

(a)   the fair market value on the date of expropriation, converted into a freely usable currency at the market rate of exchange prevailing on that date, plus

(b)   interest, at a commercially reasonable rate for that freely usable currency, accrued from the date of expropriation until the date of payment.

5.   This Article does not apply to the issuance of compulsory licenses granted in relation to intellectual property rights in accordance with the Agreement on Trade-Related Aspects of Intellectual Property Rights ("TRIPS Agreement"), or to the revocation, limitation, or creation of intellectual property rights, to the extent that such issuance, revocation, limitation, or creation is consistent with Chapter 16 (Intellectual Property Rights) of this Agreement.

ARTICLE 15.7: TRANSFERS[15-10]

1.   Each Party shall permit all transfers relating to a covered investment to be made freely and without delay into and out of its territory. Such transfers include:

(a)   contributions to capital;

[15-10] Article 15.7 is subject to Annex 15A.

(b)   profits, dividends, capital gains, and proceeds from the sale of all or any part of the covered investment or from the partial or complete liquidation of the covered investment;

(c)   interest, royalty payments, management fees, and technical assistance and other fees;

(d)   payments made under a contract entered into by the investor, or the covered investment, including payments made pursuant to a loan agreement;

(e)   payments made pursuant to Article 15.6 and Article 15.5.4; and

(f)   payments arising under Section C.

2.   Each Party shall permit transfers relating to a covered investment to be made in a freely usable currency at the market rate of exchange prevailing at the time of transfer.

3.   Each Party shall permit returns in kind relating to a covered investment to be made as authorized or specified in an investment authorization or other written agreement between the Party and a covered investment or an investor of the other Party.

4.   Notwithstanding paragraphs 1, 2, and 3, a Party may prevent a transfer through the equitable, non-discriminatory, and good faith application of its law relating to:

(a)   bankruptcy, insolvency, or the protection of the rights of creditors;

(b)   issuing, trading, or dealing in securities, futures, options, or derivatives;

(c)   financial reporting or record keeping of transfers when necessary to assist law enforcement or financial regulatory authorities;

(d)   criminal or penal offenses; or

(e)   ensuring compliance with orders or judgments in judicial or administrative proceedings.

ARTICLE 15.8: PERFORMANCE REQUIREMENTS[15-11]

1.   Neither Party may impose or enforce any of the following requirements, or enforce any commitment or undertaking, in connection with the establishment, acquisition, expansion, management, conduct, operation, or sale or other disposition of an investment of an investor of a Party or of a non-Party in its territory:

(a)   to export a given level or percentage of goods or services;

(b)   to achieve a given level or percentage of domestic content;

[15-11] Article 15.8 is subject to Annex 15B and Annex 15C.

(c)   to purchase, use, or accord a preference to goods produced in its territory, or to purchase goods from persons in its territory;

(d)   to relate in any way the volume or value of imports to the volume or value of exports or to the amount of foreign exchange inflows associated with such investment;

(e)   to restrict sales of goods or services in its territory that such investment produces or supplies by relating such sales in any way to the volume or value of its exports or foreign exchange earnings;

(f)   to transfer a particular technology, production process, or other proprietary knowledge to a person in its territory; or

(g)   to supply exclusively from the territory of the Party the goods that it produces or the services that it supplies to a specific regional market or to the world market.

2.   Neither Party may condition the receipt or continued receipt of an advantage, in connection with the establishment, acquisition, expansion, management, conduct, operation, or sale or other disposition of an investment in its territory of an investor of a Party or of a non-Party, on compliance with any of the following requirements:

(a)   to achieve a given level or percentage of domestic content;

(b)   to purchase, use, or accord a preference to goods produced in its territory, or to purchase goods from persons in its territory;

(c)   to relate in any way the volume or value of imports to the volume or value of exports or to the amount of foreign exchange inflows associated with such investment; or

(d)   to restrict sales of goods or services in its territory that such investment produces or supplies by relating such sales in any way to the volume or value of its exports or foreign exchange earnings.

3.   (a)   Nothing in paragraph 2 shall be construed to prevent a Party from conditioning the receipt or continued receipt of an advantage, in connection with an investment in its territory of an investor of a Party or of a non-Party, on compliance with a requirement to locate production, supply a service, train or employ workers, construct or expand particular facilities, or carry out research and development, in its territory.

(b)   Paragraph 1(f) does not apply:

(i)   when a Party authorizes use of an intellectual property right in accordance with Article 16.7.6 (Patents), and to measures requiring the disclosure of proprietary information that fall within the scope of, and are consistent with, Article 39 of the TRIPS Agreement; or

(ii)   when the requirement is imposed or the commitment or undertaking is enforced by a court, administrative tribunal, or competition authority to remedy a practice determined after judicial or administrative process to be anticompetitive under the Party's competition laws.

(c)   Paragraphs 1(b), (c), and (f), and 2(a) and (b), shall not be construed to prevent a Party from adopting or maintaining measures, including environmental measures:

(i)   necessary to secure compliance with laws and regulations that are not inconsistent with this Agreement;

(ii)   necessary to protect human, animal, or plant life or health; or

(iii)   related to the conservation of living or non-living exhaustible natural resources;

provided that such measures are not applied in an arbitrary or unjustifiable manner, and provided that such measures do not constitute a disguised restriction on investment or international trade.

(d)   Paragraphs 1(a), (b), and (c), and 2(a) and (b), do not apply to qualification requirements for goods or services with respect to export promotion and foreign aid programs.

(e)   Paragraphs 1(b), (c), (f), and (g), and 2(a) and (b), do not apply to government procurement.

(f)   Paragraphs 2(a) and (b) do not apply to requirements imposed by an importing Party relating to the content of goods necessary to qualify for preferential tariffs or preferential quotas.

4.   For greater certainty, paragraphs 1 and 2 do not apply to any requirement other than the requirements set out in those paragraphs.

ARTICLE 15.9: SENIOR MANAGEMENT AND BOARDS OF DIRECTORS

1.   Neither Party may require that an enterprise of that Party that is a covered investment appoint to senior management positions individuals of any particular nationality.

2.   A Party may require that a majority of the board of directors, or any committee thereof, of an enterprise of that Party that is a covered investment, be of a particular nationality, or resident in the territory of the Party, provided that the requirement does not materially impair the ability of the investor of the other Party to exercise control over its investment.

ARTICLE 15.10: INVESTMENT AND ENVIRONMENT

Nothing in this Chapter shall be construed to prevent a Party from adopting, maintaining, or enforcing any measure otherwise consistent with this Chapter that it considers appropriate to ensure that investment activity in its territory is undertaken in a manner sensitive to environmental concerns.

ARTICLE 15.11: DENIAL OF BENEFITS

A Party may deny the benefits of this Chapter to an investor of the other Party that is an enterprise of such other Party and to investments of that investor if:

(a)   investors of a non-Party own or control the enterprise and the denying Party:

      (i)   does not maintain diplomatic relations with the non-Party; or

      (ii)   adopts or maintains measures with respect to the non-Party or an investor of the non-Party that prohibit transactions with the enterprise or that would be violated or circumvented if the benefits of this Chapter were accorded to the enterprise or to its investments; or

(b)   the enterprise has no substantial business activities in the territory of the other Party, and investors of a non-Party, or of the denying Party, own or control the enterprise.

ARTICLE 15.12: NON-CONFORMING MEASURES

1.   Articles 15.4, 15.8, and 15.9 do not apply to:

(a)   any existing non-conforming measure that is maintained by a Party at:

      (i)   the central level of government, as set out by that Party in its Schedule to Annex 8A,

      (ii)   a regional level of government, as set out by that Party in its Schedule to Annex 8A, or

      (iii)   a local level of government;

(b)   the continuation or prompt renewal of any non-conforming measure referred to in subparagraph (a); or

(c)   an amendment to any non-conforming measure referred to in subparagraph (a) to the extent that the amendment does not decrease the conformity of the measure, as it existed immediately before the amendment, with Articles 15.4, 15.8, and 15.9.

2.   Articles 15.4, 15.8, and 15.9 do not apply to any measure that a Party adopts or maintains with respect to sectors, sub-sectors, or activities, as set out in its Schedule to Annex 8B.

3.   Neither Party may, under any measure adopted after the date of entry into force of this Agreement and covered by its Schedule to Annex 8B, require an investor of the other Party, by reason of its nationality, to sell or otherwise dispose of an investment existing at the time the measure becomes effective.

4.   Article 15.4 does not apply to any measure that is an exception to, or derogation from, the obligations under Article 16.1.3 (General Provisions) as specifically provided for in that Article.

5.   Articles 15.4 and 15.9 do not apply to:

(a)   government procurement; or

(b)   subsidies or grants provided by a Party, including government-supported loans, guarantees, and insurance.

ARTICLE 15.13: SPECIAL FORMALITIES AND INFORMATION REQUIREMENTS

1.   Nothing in Article 15.4.1 and 15.4.2 shall be construed to prevent a Party from adopting or maintaining a measure that prescribes special formalities in connection with covered investments, such as a requirement that investors be residents of the Party or that covered investments be legally constituted under the laws or regulations of the Party, provided that such formalities do not materially impair the protections afforded by a Party to investors of the other Party and covered investments pursuant to this Chapter.

2.   Notwithstanding Article 15.4, a Party may require an investor of the other Party, or a covered investment, to provide information concerning that investment solely for informational or statistical purposes. The Party shall protect such business information that is confidential from any disclosure that would prejudice the competitive position of the investor or the covered investment. Nothing in this paragraph shall be construed to prevent a Party from otherwise obtaining or disclosing information in connection with the equitable and good faith application of its law.

SECTION C – INVESTOR-STATE DISPUTE SETTLEMENT

ARTICLE 15.14: CONSULTATION AND NEGOTIATION

In the event of an investment dispute, the claimant and the respondent should initially seek to resolve the dispute through consultation and negotiation, which may include the use of nonbinding, third-party procedures.

ARTICLE 15.15: SUBMISSION OF A CLAIM TO ARBITRATION[15-12]

1.   In the event that a disputing party considers that an investment dispute cannot be settled by consultation and negotiation:

(a)   the claimant, on its own behalf, may submit to arbitration under this Section a claim:

(i)   that the respondent has breached

(A)   an obligation under Section B,

(B)   an investment authorization, or

(C)   an investment agreement; and

[15-12] Article 15.15 is subject to the letter exchange on land expropriation.

      (ii)   that the claimant has incurred loss or damage by reason of, or arising out of, that breach; and

  (b)   the claimant, on behalf of an enterprise of the respondent that is a juridical person that the claimant owns or controls directly or indirectly, may submit to arbitration under this Section a claim:

      (i)   that the respondent has breached

           (A)   an obligation under Section B,

           (B)   an investment authorization, or

           (C)   an investment agreement; and

      (ii)   that the enterprise has incurred loss or damage by reason of, or arising out of, that breach.

2.   For greater certainty, a claimant may submit to arbitration under this Section a claim that the respondent has breached an obligation under Section B through the actions of a designated monopoly or a government enterprise exercising delegated governmental authority as described in Article 12.3.1(c)(i) and 12.3.2(b) (Designated Monopolies and Government Enterprises), respectively.

3.   Without prejudice to Article 10.1.2 (Scope and Coverage), no claim may be submitted under this Section that alleges a violation of any provision of this Agreement other than an obligation under Section B or the letter exchange on land expropriation.

4.   At least 90 days before submitting any claim to arbitration under this Section, a claimant shall deliver to the respondent a written notice of its intention to submit the claim to arbitration ("notice of intent"). The notice shall specify:

  (a)   the name and address of the claimant and, where a claim is submitted on behalf of an enterprise, the name, address, and place of incorporation of the enterprise;

  (b)   for each claim, the provision of this Agreement, investment authorization, or investment agreement alleged to have been breached and any other relevant provisions;

  (c)   the legal and factual basis for each claim; and

  (d)   the relief sought and the approximate amount of damages claimed.

5.   Provided that six months have elapsed since the events giving rise to the claim, a claimant may submit a claim referred to in paragraph 1:

  (a)   under the ICSID Convention and the ICSID Rules of Procedure for Arbitration Proceedings, provided that both the respondent and the Party of the claimant are parties to the ICSID Convention;

(b)   under the ICSID Additional Facility Rules, provided that either the respondent or the Party of the claimant, but not both, is a party to the ICSID Convention;

(c)   under the UNCITRAL Arbitration Rules; or

(d)   if the claimant and respondent agree, to any other arbitration institution or under any other arbitration rules.

6.   A claim shall be deemed submitted to arbitration under this Section when the claimant's notice of or request for arbitration ("notice of arbitration"):

(a)   referred to in paragraph 1 of Article 36 of the ICSID Convention is received by the Secretary-General;

(b)   referred to in Article 2 of Schedule C of the ICSID Additional Facility Rules is received by the Secretary-General;

(c)   referred to in Article 3 of the UNCITRAL Arbitration Rules, together with the statement of claim referred to in Article 18 of the UNCITRAL Arbitration Rules, are received by the respondent; or

(d)   referred to under any other arbitral institution or arbitral rules selected under paragraph 3(d) is received by the respondent.

7.   The arbitration rules applicable under paragraph 3, and in effect on the date the claim or claims were submitted to arbitration under this Section, shall govern the arbitration except to the extent modified by this Agreement.

8.   The claimant shall provide with the notice of arbitration referred to in paragraph 6:

(a)   the name of the arbitrator that the claimant appoints; or

(b)   the claimant's written consent for the Secretary-General to appoint the claimant's arbitrator.

ARTICLE 15.16: CONSENT OF EACH PARTY TO ARBITRATION

1.   Each Party consents to the submission of a claim to arbitration under this Section in accordance with this Agreement.

2.   The consent under paragraph 1 and the submission of a claim to arbitration under this Section shall satisfy the requirements of:

(a)   Chapter II of the ICSID Convention (Jurisdiction of the Centre) and the ICSID Additional Facility Rules for written consent of the parties to the dispute; and

(b)   Article II of the New York Convention for an "agreement in writing."

ARTICLE 15.17: CONDITIONS AND LIMITATIONS ON CONSENT OF E ACH PARTY

1.   No claim may be submitted to arbitration under this Section if more than three years have elapsed from the date on which the claimant first acquired, or should have first acquired, knowledge of the breach alleged under Article 15.15.1 and knowledge that the claimant (for claims brought under Article 15.15.1(a)) or the enterprise (for claims brought under Article 15.15.1(b)) has incurred loss or damage.

2.   No claim may be submitted to arbitration under this Section unless:

   (a)   the claimant consents in writing to arbitration in accordance with the procedures set out in this Agreement; and

   (b)   the notice of arbitration referred to in Article 15.15.6 is accompanied,

      (i)   for claims submitted to arbitration under Article 15.15.1(a), by the claimant's written waiver; and

      (ii)   for claims submitted to arbitration under Article 15.15.1(b), by the claimant's and the enterprise's written waivers of any right to initiate or continue before any administrative tribunal or court under the law of either Party, or other dispute settlement procedures, any proceeding with respect to any measure alleged to constitute a breach referred to in Article 15.15.

3.   Notwithstanding paragraph 2(b), the claimant (for claims brought under Article 15.15.1(a)) and the claimant or the enterprise (for claims brought under Article 15.15.1(b)) may initiate or continue an action that seeks interim injunctive relief and does not involve the payment of monetary damages before a judicial or administrative tribunal of the respondent, provided that the action is brought for the sole purpose of preserving the claimant's or the enterprise's rights and interests during the pendency of the arbitration.

ARTICLE 15.18: SELECTION OF ARBITRATORS

1.   Unless the disputing parties otherwise agree, the tribunal shall comprise three arbitrators, one arbitrator appointed by each of the disputing parties and the third, who shall be the presiding arbitrator, appointed by agreement of the disputing parties.

2.   The Secretary-General shall serve as appointing authority for an arbitration under this Section.

3.   If a tribunal has not been constituted within 75 days from the date that a claim is submitted to arbitration under this Section, the Secretary-General, on the request of a disputing party, shall appoint, in his or her discretion, the arbitrator or arbitrators not yet appointed.

4.   For purposes of Article 39 of the ICSID Convention and Article 7 of Schedule C to the ICSID Additional Facility Rules, and without prejudice to an objection to an arbitrator on a ground other than nationality:

(a)   the respondent agrees to the appointment of each individual member of a tribunal established under the ICSID Convention or the ICSID Additional Facility Rules;

(b)   a claimant referred to in Article 15.15.1(a) may submit a claim to arbitration under this Section, or continue a claim, under the ICSID Convention or the ICSID Additional Facility Rules, only on condition that the claimant agrees in writing to the appointment of each individual member of the tribunal; and

(c)   a claimant referred to in Article 15.15.1(b) may submit a claim to arbitration under this Section, or continue a claim, under the ICSID Convention or the ICSID Additional Facility Rules, only on condition that the claimant and the enterprise agree in writing to the appointment of each individual member of the tribunal.

ARTICLE 15.19: CONDUCT OF THE ARBITRATION

1.   The disputing parties may agree on the legal place of any arbitration under the arbitral rules applicable under Article 15.15.5(b), (c), or (d). If the disputing parties fail to reach agreement, the tribunal shall determine the place in accordance with the applicable arbitral rules, provided that the place shall be in the territory of either Party or of a third State that is a party to the New York Convention.

2.   The non-disputing Party may make oral and written submissions to the tribunal regarding the interpretation of this Agreement.

3.   The tribunal shall have the authority to accept and consider amicus curiae submissions from any persons and entities in the territories of the Parties and from interested persons and entities outside the territories of the Parties.

4.   Without prejudice to a tribunal's authority to address other objections as a preliminary question, a tribunal shall address and decide as a preliminary question any objection by the respondent that, as a matter of law, a claim submitted is not a claim for which an award in favor of the claimant may be made under Article 15.25.

(a)   Such objection shall be submitted to the tribunal as soon as possible after the tribunal is constituted, and in no event later than the date the tribunal fixes for the respondent to submit its counter-memorial (or, in the case of an amendment to the notice of arbitration referred to in Article 15.15.6, the date the tribunal fixes for the respondent to submit its response to the amendment).

(b)   On receipt of an objection under this paragraph, the tribunal shall suspend any proceedings on the merits, establish a schedule for considering the objection consistent with any schedule it has established for considering any other preliminary question, and issue a decision or award on the objection, stating the grounds therefor.

(c)   In deciding an objection under this paragraph, the tribunal shall assume to be true the claimant's factual allegations in support of any claim in the notice of arbitration (or any amendment thereof) and, in disputes brought under the UNCITRAL Arbitration Rules, the statement of claim referred to in Article 18 of the UNCITRAL Arbitration Rules. The tribunal may also consider any relevant facts not in dispute.

    (d)   The respondent does not waive any objection as to competence or any argument on the merits merely because the respondent did or did not raise an objection under this paragraph or make use of the expedited procedure set out in the following paragraph.

5.   In the event that the respondent so requests within 45 days after the tribunal is constituted, the tribunal shall decide on an expedited basis an objection under paragraph 4 or any objection that the dispute is not within the tribunal's competence. The tribunal shall suspend any proceedings on the merits and issue a decision or award on the objection(s), stating the grounds therefor, no later than 150 days after the date of the request. However, if a disputing party requests a hearing, the tribunal may take an additional 30 days to issue the decision or award. Regardless of whether a hearing is requested, a tribunal may, on a showing of extraordinary cause, delay issuing its decision or award by an additional brief period of time, which may not exceed 30 days.

6.   When it decides a respondent's objection under paragraphs 4 or 5, the tribunal may, if warranted, award to the prevailing disputing party reasonable costs and attorneys' fees incurred in submitting or opposing the objection. In determining whether such an award is warranted, the tribunal shall consider whether either the claimant's claim or the respondent's objection was frivolous, and shall provide the disputing parties a reasonable opportunity to comment.

7.   A respondent may not assert as a defense, counterclaim, right of set-off, or for any other reason that the claimant has received or will receive indemnification or other compensation for all or part of the alleged damages pursuant to an insurance or guarantee contract.

8.   A tribunal may order an interim measure of protection to preserve the rights of a disputing party, or to ensure that the tribunal's jurisdiction is made fully effective, including an order to preserve evidence in the possession or control of a disputing party or to protect the tribunal's jurisdiction. A tribunal may not order attachment or enjoin the application of a measure alleged to constitute a breach referred to in Article 15.15. For purposes of this paragraph, an order includes a recommendation.

9.   (a)   In any arbitration conducted under this Section, at the request of a disputing party, a tribunal shall, before issuing an award on liability, transmit its proposed award to the disputing parties and to the non-disputing Party. Within 60 days after the tribunal transmits its proposed award, the disputing parties may submit written comments to the tribunal concerning any aspect of its proposed award. The tribunal shall consider any such comments and issue its award not later than 45 days after the expiration of the 60-day comment period.

    (b)   Subparagraph (a) shall not apply in any arbitration conducted pursuant to this Section for which an appeal has been made available pursuant to paragraph 10.

10.   If a separate multilateral agreement enters into force as between the Parties that establishes an appellate body for purposes of reviewing awards rendered by tribunals constituted pursuant to international trade or investment arrangements to hear investment disputes, the Parties shall strive to reach an agreement that would have such appellate body review awards

rendered under Article 15.25 of this Section in arbitrations commenced after the appellate body's establishment.

ARTICLE 15.20: TRANSPARENCY OF ARBITRAL PROCEEDINGS

1.   Subject to paragraphs 2 and 4, the respondent shall, after receiving the following documents, promptly transmit them to the non-disputing Party and make them available to the public:

(a)   the notice of intent referred to in Article 15.15.4;

(b)   the notice of arbitration referred to in Article 15.15.6;

(c)   pleadings, memorials, and briefs submitted to the tribunal by a disputing party and any written submissions submitted pursuant to Article 15.19.2 and 15.19.3 and Article 15.24;

(d)   minutes or transcripts of hearings of the tribunal, where available; and

(e)   orders, awards, and decisions of the tribunal.

2.   The tribunal shall conduct hearings open to the public and shall determine, in consultation with the disputing parties, the appropriate logistical arrangements. However, any disputing party that intends to use information designated as protected information in a hearing shall so advise the tribunal. The tribunal shall make appropriate arrangements to protect the information from disclosure.

3.   Nothing in this Section requires a respondent to disclose protected information or to furnish or allow access to information that it may withhold in accordance with Article 21.2 (Essential Security) or Article 21.4 (Disclosure of Information).

4.   Protected information shall, if such information is submitted to the tribunal, be protected from disclosure in accordance with the following procedures:

(a)   Subject to paragraph 4(d), neither the disputing parties nor the tribunal shall disclose to the non-disputing Party or to the public any protected information where the disputing party that provided the information clearly designates it in accordance with paragraph 4(b).

(b)   Any disputing party claiming that certain information constitutes protected information shall clearly designate the information at the time it is submitted to the tribunal.

(c)   A disputing party shall, at the same time that it submits a document containing information claimed to be protected information, submit a redacted version of the document that does not contain the information. Only the redacted version shall be provided to the non-disputing Party and made public in accordance with paragraph 1.

(d)   The tribunal shall decide any objection regarding the designation of information claimed to be protected information. If the tribunal determines that such information was not properly designated, the disputing party that submitted the information may (i) withdraw all or part of its submission containing such information, or (ii) agree to resubmit complete and redacted documents with corrected designations in accordance with the tribunal's determination and paragraph 4(c). In either case, the other disputing party shall, whenever necessary, resubmit complete and redacted documents which either remove the information withdrawn under (i) by the disputing party that first submitted the information or redesignate the information consistent with the designation under (ii) of the disputing party that first submitted the information.

5.   Nothing in this Section authorizes a respondent to withhold from the public information required to be disclosed by its laws.

ARTICLE 15.21: GOVERNING LAW

1.   Subject to paragraph 2, a tribunal shall decide the issues in dispute related to an alleged breach of an obligation in Section B in accordance with this Agreement and applicable rules of international law.

2.   A decision of the Joint Committee declaring its interpretation of a provision of this Agreement under Article 20.1.2 (Joint Committee) shall be binding on a tribunal established under this Section, and any award must be consistent with that decision.

ARTICLE 15.22: INTERPRETATION OF ANNEXES

1.   Where a respondent asserts as a defense that the measure alleged to be a breach is within the scope of a reservation or exception set out in Annex 8A or Annex 8B, the tribunal shall, on request of the respondent, request the interpretation of the Joint Committee on the issue. The Joint Committee shall issue in writing any decision declaring its interpretation under Article 20.1.2 (Joint Committee) to the tribunal within 60 days of delivery of the request.

2.   A decision issued by the Joint Committee under paragraph 1 shall be binding on the tribunal, and any award must be consistent with that decision. If the Joint Committee fails to issue such a decision within 60 days, the tribunal shall decide the issue.

ARTICLE 15.23: EXPERT REPORTS

Without prejudice to the appointment of other kinds of experts where authorized by the applicable arbitration rules, a tribunal, at the request of a disputing party or, unless the disputing parties disapprove, on its own initiative, may appoint one or more experts to report to it in writing on any factual issue concerning environmental, health, safety, or other scientific matters raised by a disputing party in a proceeding, subject to such terms and conditions as the disputing parties may agree.

ARTICLE 15.24: CONSOLIDATION

1.   Where two or more claims have been submitted separately to arbitration under Article 15.15.1 and the claims have a question of law or fact in common and arise out of the same events

or circumstances, any disputing party may seek a consolidation order in accordance with the agreement of all the disputing parties sought to be covered by the order or the terms of paragraphs 2 through 10.

2.   A disputing party that seeks a consolidation order under this Article shall deliver, in writing, a request to the Secretary-General and to all the disputing parties sought to be covered by the order and shall specify in the request:

> (a)   the names and addresses of all the disputing parties sought to be covered by the order;

> (b)   the nature of the order sought; and

> (c)   the grounds on which the order is sought.

3.   Unless the Secretary-General finds within 30 days after receiving a request under paragraph 2 that the request is manifestly unfounded, a tribunal shall be established under this Article.

4.   Unless all the disputing parties sought to be covered by the order otherwise agree, a tribunal established under this Article shall comprise three arbitrators:

> (a)   one arbitrator appointed by agreement of the claimants;

> (b)   one arbitrator appointed by the respondent; and

> (c)   the presiding arbitrator appointed by the Secretary-General, provided, however, that the presiding arbitrator shall not be a national of either Party.

5.   If, within 60 days after the Secretary-General receives a request made under paragraph 2, the respondent fails or the claimants fail to appoint an arbitrator in accordance with paragraph 4, the Secretary-General, on the request of any disputing party sought to be covered by the order, shall appoint the arbitrator or arbitrators not yet appointed. If the respondent fails to appoint an arbitrator, the Secretary-General shall appoint a national of the disputing Party, and if the claimants fail to appoint an arbitrator, the Secretary-General shall appoint a national of the nondisputing Party.

6.   Where a tribunal established under this Article is satisfied that two or more claims that have been submitted to arbitration under Article 15.15.1 have a question of law or fact in common, and arise out of the same events or circumstances, the tribunal may, in the interest of fair and efficient resolution of the claims, and after hearing the disputing parties, by order:

> (a)   assume jurisdiction over, and hear and determine together, all or part of the claims;

> (b)   assume jurisdiction over, and hear and determine one or more of the claims, the determination of which it believes would assist in the resolution of the others; or

(c)   instruct a tribunal previously established under Article 15.18 to assume jurisdiction over, and hear and determine together, all or part of the claims, provided that:

(i)   that tribunal, at the request of any claimant not previously a disputing party before that tribunal, shall be reconstituted with its original members, except that the arbitrator for the claimants shall be appointed pursuant to paragraphs 4(a) and 5; and

(ii)   that tribunal shall decide whether any prior hearing shall be repeated.

7.   Where a tribunal has been established under this Article, a claimant that has submitted a claim to arbitration under Article 15.15.1 and that has not been named in a request made under paragraph 2 may make a written request to the tribunal that it be included in any order made under paragraph 6, and shall specify in the request:

(a)   the name and address of the claimant;

(b)   the nature of the order sought; and

(c)   the grounds on which the order is sought.

The claimant shall deliver a copy of its request to the Secretary-General.

8.   A tribunal established under this Article shall conduct its proceedings in accordance with the UNCITRAL Arbitration Rules, except as modified by this Section.

9.   A tribunal established under Article 15.18 shall not have jurisdiction to decide a claim, or a part of a claim, over which a tribunal established or instructed under this Article has assumed jurisdiction.

10.   On application of a disputing party, a tribunal established under this Article, pending its decision under paragraph 6, may order that the proceedings of a tribunal established under Article 15.18 be stayed, unless the latter tribunal has already adjourned its proceedings.

ARTICLE 15.25: AWARDS

1.   Where a tribunal makes a final award against a respondent, the tribunal may award, separately or in combination, only:

(a)   monetary damages and any applicable interest; and

(b)   restitution of property, in which case the award shall provide that the respondent may pay monetary damages and any applicable interest in lieu of restitution.

A tribunal may also award costs and attorneys' fees in accordance with this Section and the applicable arbitration rules.

2.   Subject to paragraph 1, where a claim is submitted to arbitration under Article 15.15.1(b):

(a)   an award of restitution of property shall provide that restitution be made to the enterprise;

(b)   an award of monetary damages and any applicable interest shall provide that the sum be paid to the enterprise; and

(c)   the award shall provide that it is made without prejudice to any right that any person may have in the relief under applicable domestic law.

3.   A tribunal may not award punitive damages.

4.   An award made by a tribunal shall have no binding force except between the disputing parties and in respect of the particular case.

5.   Subject to paragraph 6 and the applicable review procedure for an interim award, a disputing party shall abide by and comply with an award without delay.

6.   A disputing party may not seek enforcement of a final award until:

(a)   in the case of a final award made under the ICSID Convention,

(i)   120 days have elapsed from the date the award was rendered and no disputing party has requested revision or annulment of the award; or

(ii)   revision or annulment proceedings have been completed; and

(b)   in the case of a final award under the ICSID Additional Facility Rules, the UNCITRAL Arbitration Rules, or the rules selected pursuant to Article 15.15.5(d),

(i)   90 days have elapsed from the date the award was rendered and no disputing party has commenced a proceeding to revise, set aside, or annul the award, or

(ii)   a court has dismissed or allowed an application to revise, set aside, or annul the award and there is no further appeal.

7.   Each Party shall provide for the enforcement of an award in its territory.

8.   If the respondent fails to abide by or comply with a final award, on delivery of a written notification by the non-disputing Party, a panel shall be established under Article 20.4.4(a) (Additional Dispute Settlement Procedures). The requesting Party may seek in such proceedings:

(a)   a determination that the failure to abide by or comply with the final award is inconsistent with the obligations of this Agreement; and

(b)   in accordance with the procedures set forth in Article 20.4.5(b) (Additional Dispute Settlement Procedures), a recommendation that the respondent abide by or comply with the final award.

9.   A disputing party may seek enforcement of an arbitration award under the ICSID Convention or the New York Convention regardless of whether proceedings have been taken under paragraph 8.

10.   A claim that is submitted to arbitration under this Section shall be considered to arise out of a commercial relationship or transaction for purposes of Article I of the New York Convention.

ARTICLE 15.26: STATUS OF LETTER EXCHANGES

The following letters exchanged this day on:

(a)   Customary International Law;

(b)   Expropriation;

(c)   Land Expropriation; and

(d)   Appellate Mechanism shall form an integral part of the Agreement.

ARTICLE 15.27: SERVICE OF DOCUMENTS

Delivery of notices and other documents on a Party shall be made to the place named for that Party in Annex 15D.

ANNEX 15A
TRANSFERS

1.   Where a claimant submits a claim alleging that Singapore has breached an obligation under Section B, other than Article 15.4, that arises from its imposition of restrictive measures with regard to outward payments and transfers, Section C shall apply except as modified below:

(a)   A claimant may submit the claim under Article 15.15 only after one year has elapsed since the measure was adopted.

(b)   If the claim is submitted under Article 15.15.1(b), the claimant may, on behalf of the enterprise, only seek damages with respect to the shares of the enterprise for which the claimant has a beneficial interest.

(c)   Paragraph 1(a) shall not apply to claims that arise from restrictions on:

(i)   payments or transfers on current transactions, including the transfer of profits and dividends of foreign direct investment by investors of the United States;

(ii)   transfers of proceeds of foreign direct investment by investors of the United States, excluding investments designed with the purpose of gaining direct or indirect access to the financial market; or

(iii)   payments pursuant to a loan or bond[15-13] regardless of where it is issued, including inter- and intra-company debt financing between affiliated enterprises, when such payments are made exclusively for the conduct, operation, management, or expansion of such affiliated enterprises, provided that these payments are made in accordance with the maturity date agreed on in the loan or bond agreement.

(d)   Excluding restrictive measures referred to in paragraph 1(c), Singapore shall incur no liability, and shall not be subject to claims, for damages arising from its imposition of restrictive measures with regard to outward payments and transfers that were incurred within one year from the date on which restrictions were imposed, provided that such restrictive measures do not substantially impede transfers.

(e)   Claims arising from Singapore's imposition of restrictive measures with regard to outward payments and transfers shall not be subject to Article 15.24 unless Singapore consents.

2.   The United States may not request the establishment of an arbitral panel under Chapter 20 (Administration and Dispute Settlement) relating to Singapore's imposition of restrictive measures with regard to outward payments and transfers until one year has elapsed since the measure was adopted. In determining whether compensation is owed or benefits should be suspended, or the level of such compensation or suspension, pursuant to Article 20.6 (Non-Implementation), the aggrieved Party and the panel shall consider whether the restrictive measures were implemented at the request of the International Monetary Fund (IMF).

ANNEX 15B
PERFORMANCE REQUIREMENTS

Article 15.8.1 does not preclude enforcement of any commitment, undertaking, or requirement between private parties, where a Party did not impose or require the commitment, undertaking, or requirement. For purposes of this Annex, private parties may include designated monopolies or government enterprises, where such entities are not exercising delegated governmental authority as described in Articles 12.3.1(c)(i) and 12.3.2(b) (Designated Monopolies and Government Enterprises), respectively.

ANNEX 15C
PERFORMANCE REQUIREMENTS

Singapore

With respect to Singapore, Article 15.8.1(f) does not apply with respect to the sale or other disposition of an investment of an investor of a non-Party in its territory.

[15-13] For greater certainty, payments pursuant to a loan or bond shall exclude capital account transactions relating to inter-bank loans, including loans to or from Singapore licensed banks, merchant banks, or finance companies.

ANNEX 15D
SERVICE OF DOCUMENTS ON A PARTY UNDER SECTION C

Singapore

Notices and other documents in disputes under Section C shall be served on Singapore by delivery to:

Director (Trade)
Ministry of Trade and Industry
100 High Street, #09-01
The Treasury
Singapore 179434

United States

Notices and other documents in disputes under Section C shall be served on the United States by delivery to:

Executive Director (L/EX)
Office of the Legal Adviser
Department of State
Washington, DC 20520
United States of America

CHAPTER 16: INTELLECTUAL PROPERTY RIGHTS

ARTICLE 16.1: GENERAL PROVISIONS

1.   Each Party shall, at a minimum, give effect to this Chapter.

2.   (a)   Each Party shall ratify or accede to the following agreements:

        (i)   the Convention Relating to the Distribution of Programme-Carrying Signals Transmitted by Satellite (1974);

        (ii)   the International Convention for the Protection of New Varieties of Plants (1991) (A UPOV Convention @);

        (iii)   the WIPO Copyright Treaty (1996);

        (iv)   the WIPO Performances and Phonograms Treaty (1996); and

        (v)   the Patent Cooperation Treaty (1984).

    (b)   Each Party shall give effect to:

        (i)   Articles 1 through 6 of the Joint Recommendation Concerning Provisions on the Protection of Well-Known Marks (1999), adopted by the Assembly of the Paris Union for the Protection of Industrial Property and the General Assembly of the World Intellectual Property Organization (A WIPO @); and

    (ii)   the Trademark Law Treaty.[16-1]

(c)   Each Party shall make best efforts to ratify or accede to:

    (i)   the Hague Agreement Concerning the International Registration of Industrial Designs (1999); and

    (ii)   the Protocol Relating to the Madrid Agreement Concerning the International Registration of Marks (1989).

3.   In respect of all categories of intellectual property covered in this Chapter, each Party hall accord to nationals[16-2] of the other Party treatment no less favorable than it accords to its own nationals with regard to the protection[16-3] and enjoyment of such intellectual property rights and any benefits derived from such rights.[16-4]

4.   Each Party may derogate from paragraph 3 in relation to its judicial and administrative procedures, including the designation of an address for service or the appointment of an agent within the jurisdiction of a Party, only where such derogations are necessary to secure compliance with laws and regulations that are not inconsistent with this Chapter and where such practices are not applied in a manner that would constitute a disguised restriction on trade.

5.   Paragraphs 3 and 4 do not apply to procedures provided in multilateral agreements concluded under the auspices of WIPO relating to the acquisition or maintenance of intellectual property rights.

6.   Except as otherwise provided in this Chapter:

(a)   this Chapter gives rise to obligations in respect of all subject matter existing at the date of entry into force of this Agreement that is protected on that date in the Party where the protection is claimed and/or that meets or comes subsequently to meet the criteria for protection under the terms of this Chapter;

(b)   a Party shall not be required to restore protection to subject matter that on the date of entry into force of this Agreement has fallen into the public domain in the Party where the protection is claimed.

[16-1] Singapore is not obligated to give effect to Articles 6 and 7 of the Trademark Law Treaty.

[16-2] For purposes of Articles 16.1.3 and 16.5.1, a national of a Party shall also mean, in respect of the relevant right, entities located in such Party that would meet the criteria for eligibility for protection provided for in the agreements listed in Article 16.1.2 and the TRIPS Agreement.

[16-3] For the purposes of paragraphs 3 and 4, "protection" shall include matters affecting the availability, acquisition, scope, maintenance, and enforcement of intellectual property rights as well as matters affecting the use of intellectual property rights specifically covered by this Chapter. For the purposes of paragraphs 3 and 4, "protection" shall also include the prohibition on circumvention of effective technological measures pursuant to paragraph 7 of Article 16.4 and the provision concerning rights management information pursuant to paragraph 8 of Article 16.4.

[16-4] "Benefits derived there from" refers to benefits such as levies on blank tapes.

7.   This Chapter does not give rise to obligations in respect of acts that occurred before the date of entry into force of this Agreement.

ARTICLE 16.2: TRADEMARKS, INCLUDING GEOGRAPHICAL INDICATIONS

1.   Each Party shall provide that trademarks shall include service marks, collective marks, and certification marks,[16-5] and may include geographical indications.[16-6] Neither Party shall require, as a condition of registration, that signs be visually perceptible, but each Party shall make best efforts to register scent marks. Each Party shall afford an opportunity for the registration of a trademark to be opposed.

2.   Each Party shall provide that the owner of a registered trademark shall have the exclusive right to prevent all third parties not having the owner's consent from using in the course of trade identical or similar signs, including geographical indications, for goods or services that are related to those in respect of which the trademark is registered, where such use would result in a likelihood of confusion.

3.   Each Party may provide limited exceptions to the rights conferred by a trademark, such as fair use of descriptive terms, provided that such exceptions take account of the legitimate interests of the owner of the trademark and of third parties.

4.   Article 6bis of the Paris Convention for the Protection of Industrial Property (1967) ("Paris Convention") shall apply, mutatis mutandis, to goods or services that are not similar to those identified by a well-known trademark, whether registered or not, provided that use of that trademark in relation to those goods or services would indicate a connection between those goods or services and the owner of the trademark and provided that the interests of the owner of the trademark are likely to be damaged by such use.

5.   Neither Party shall require recordation of trademark licenses to establish the validity of the license or to assert any rights in a trademark.

6.   Pursuant to Article 20 of the TRIPS Agreement, each Party shall ensure that its provisions mandating the use of a term customary in common language as the common name for a product including, inter alia, requirements concerning the relative size, placement, or style of use of the trademark in relation to the common name, do not impair the use or effectiveness of a trademark used in relation to such products.[16-7]

ARTICLE 16.3: DOMAIN NAMES ON THE INTERNET

1.   Each Party shall participate in the Governmental Advisory Committee of the Internet Corporation for Assigned Names and Numbers (ICANN), which serves to consider and provide advice on the activities of the ICANN as they relate to government concerns, including matters

---

[16-5] Neither Party is obligated to treat certification marks as a separate category in domestic law, provided that such marks are protected.

[16-6] A geographical indication shall be capable of constituting a trademark to the extent that the geographical indication consists of any sign, or any combination of signs, capable of identifying a good or service as originating in the territory of a Party, or a region or locality in that territory, where a given quality, reputation or other characteristic of the good or service is essentially attributable to its geographical origin.

[16-7] This provision is not intended to affect the use of common names of pharmaceutical products in prescribing medicine.

related to intellectual property and the domain name system, as well as to promote responsible country code Top Level Domain (ccTLD) administration, management, and operational practices.

2.   Each Party shall require that registrants of domain names in its ccTLD are subject to a dispute resolution procedure, modeled along the same lines as the principles set forth in ICANN Uniform Domain Name Dispute Resolution Policy (ICANN UDRP), to address and resolve disputes related to the bad-faith registration of domain names in violation of trademarks. Each Party shall also ensure that its corresponding ccTLDs provide public access to a reliable and accurate A WHOIS @ database of domain name registrant contact information.

ARTICLE 16.4: OBLIGATIONS COMMON TO COPYRIGHT AND RELATED RIGHTS

1.   Each Party shall provide that authors, performers, and producers of phonograms and their successors in interest have the right to authorize or prohibit all reproductions, in any manner or form, permanent or temporary (including temporary storage in electronic form).

2.   (a)   Without prejudice to Articles 11(1)(ii), 11bis(1)(i) and (ii), 11ter(1)(ii), 14(1)(ii), and 14bis(1) of the Berne Convention for the Protection of Literary and Artistic Works (1971) ("Berne Convention"), each Party shall provide to authors, performers, producers of phonograms and their successors in interest the exclusive right to authorize or prohibit the communication to the public of their works, performances, or phonograms, by wire or wireless means, including the making available to the public of their works, performances, and phonograms in such a way that members of the public may access them from a place and at a time individually chosen by them. Notwithstanding paragraph 10, a Party may provide limitations or exceptions to this right in the case of performers and producers of phonograms for analog or digital free over-the-air terrestrial broadcasting and, further, a Party may provide limitations with respect to other non-interactive transmissions, in certain special cases provided that such limitations do not conflict with a normal exploitation of performances or phonograms and do not unreasonably prejudice the interests of such right holders.

(b)   Neither Party shall permit the retransmission of television signals (whether terrestrial, cable, or satellite) on the Internet without the authorization of the right holder in the subject matter of the signal.

3.   Each Party shall provide to authors, performers, producers of phonograms, and their successors in interest the exclusive right of authorizing the making available to the public of the original and copies of their works and phonograms through sale or other transfer of ownership.

4.   Each Party shall provide that where the term of protection of a work (including a photographic work), performance, or phonogram is to be calculated:

(a)   on the basis of the life of a natural person, the term shall be not less than the life of the author and 70 years after the author's death; and

(b)   on a basis other than the life of a natural person, the term shall be not less than 70 years from the end of the calendar year of the first authorized publication of the work, performance, or phonogram or, failing such authorized publication within 50 years from the creation of the work, performance, or phonogram, not less than 70 years from the end of the calendar year of the creation of the work, performance, or phonogram.

5.   Each Party shall apply the provisions of Article 18 of the Berne Convention, mutatis mutandis, to the subject matter, rights and obligations in Articles 16.4 and 16.5.

6.   Each Party shall provide that for copyright and related rights, any person acquiring or holding any economic right:

(a)   may freely and separately transfer such right by contract; and

(b)   by virtue of a contract, including contracts of employment underlying the creation of works and phonograms, shall be able to exercise those rights in its own name and enjoy fully the benefits derived from those rights.

7.   (a)   In order to provide adequate legal protection and effective legal remedies against the circumvention of effective technological measures that authors, performers, producers of phonograms, and their successors in interest use in connection with the exercise of their rights and that restrict unauthorized acts in respect of their works, performances, and phonograms, each Party shall provide that any person who:

(i)   knowingly, or having reasonable grounds to know, circumvents without authority any effective technological measure that controls access to a protected work, performance, phonogram, or other subject matter; or

(ii)   manufactures, imports, distributes, offers to the public, provides, or otherwise traffics in devices, products, or components or offers to the public or provides services, which:

(A)   are promoted, advertised, or marketed for the purpose of circumvention of any effective technological measure, or

(B)   have only a limited commercially significant purpose or use other than to circumvent any effective technological measure, or

(C)   are primarily designed, produced, or performed for the purpose of enabling or facilitating the circumvention of any effective technological measure;

shall be liable and subject to the remedies provided for in Article 16.9.5. Each Party shall provide that any person, other than a nonprofit library, archive, educational institution, or public noncommercial broadcasting entity, that is found to have engaged willfully and for purposes of commercial advantage or private financial gain in such activities shall be guilty of a criminal offense.

(b)   For purposes of this paragraph, effective technological measure means any technology, device, or component that, in the normal course of its operation, controls access to a protected work, performance, phonogram, or other subject matter, or protects any copyright or any rights related to copyright.

(c)   Paragraph 7(a) obligates each Party to prohibit circumvention of effective technological measures and does not obligate a Party to require that the design of, or the design and selection of parts and components for, a consumer electronics, telecommunications, or computing product provide for a response to any particular technological measure. The absence of a requirement to respond affirmatively shall not constitute a defense to a claim of violation of that Party's measures implementing paragraph 7(a).

(d)   Each Party shall provide that a violation of the law implementing this paragraph is independent of any infringement that might occur under the Party = s law on copyright and related rights.

(e)   Each Party shall confine exceptions to the prohibition referred to in paragraph 7(a)(ii) on technology, products, services, or devices that circumvent effective technological measures that control access to, and, in the case of clause (i) below, that protect any of the exclusive rights of copyright or related rights in a protected work, to the following activities, provided that they do not impair the adequacy of legal protection or the effectiveness of legal remedies that the Party provides against the circumvention of effective technological measures:

(i)   noninfringing reverse engineering activities with regard to a lawfully obtained copy of a computer program, carried out in good faith with respect to particular elements of that computer program that have not been readily available to the person engaged in such activity, for the sole purpose of achieving interoperability of an independently created computer program with other programs;

(ii)   noninfringing good faith activities, carried out by an appropriately qualified researcher who has lawfully obtained a copy, performance, or display of a work, and who has made a good faith effort to obtain authorization for such activities, to the extent necessary for the sole purpose of identifying and analyzing flaws and vulnerabilities of technologies for scrambling and descrambling of information;

(iii)   the inclusion of a component or part for the sole purpose of preventing the access of minors to inappropriate online content in a technology, product, service, or device provided that such technology, product, service or device itself is not prohibited under the measures implementing paragraph 7(a)(ii); and

(iv)   noninfringing good faith activities that are authorized by the owner of a computer, computer system, or computer network for the sole purpose of testing, investigating, or correcting the security of that computer, computer system, or computer network.

(f)   Each Party shall confine exceptions to the prohibited conduct referred to in paragraph 7(a)(i) to the activities listed in paragraph 7(e) and the following activities, provided that such exceptions do not impair the adequacy of legal protection or the effectiveness of legal remedies the Party provides against the circumvention of effective technological measures:

(i)   access by a nonprofit library, archive, or educational institution to a work not otherwise available to it, for the sole purpose of making acquisition decisions;

(ii)   noninfringing activities for the sole purpose of identifying and disabling a capability to carry out undisclosed collection or dissemination of personally identifying information reflecting the online activities of a natural person in a way that has no other effect on the ability of any person to gain access to any work; and

(iii)   noninfringing uses of a particular class of works when an actual or likely adverse impact on such noninfringing uses with respect to such particular class of works is credibly demonstrated in a legislative or administrative proceeding, provided that any exception adopted in reliance on this clause shall have effect for a period of not more than four years from the date of conclusion of such proceeding.

(g)   Each Party may also provide exceptions to the prohibited conduct referred to in paragraph 7(a) for lawfully authorized activities carried out by government employees, agents, or contractors for the purpose of law enforcement, intelligence, national defense, essential security, or similar government activities.

8.   In order to provide adequate and effective legal remedies to protect rights management information:

(a)   each Party shall provide that any person who without authority, and knowingly, or, with respect to civil remedies, having reasonable grounds to know, that it will induce, enable, facilitate, or conceal an infringement of any copyright or related right,

(i)   knowingly removes or alters any rights management information;

(ii)   distributes or imports for distribution rights management information knowing that the rights management information has been altered without authority; or

(iii)   distributes, imports for distribution, broadcasts, communicates, or makes available to the public copies of works or phonograms, knowing that rights management information has been removed or altered without authority, shall be liable and subject to the remedies in Article 16.9.5. Each Party shall provide that any person, other than a nonprofit library, archive, educational institution, or public noncommercial broadcasting entity, who is found to have engaged willfully and for purposes of commercial advantage or private financial gain in such activities shall be guilty of a criminal offense.

(b)   For purposes of this paragraph, rights management information means information which identifies a work, performance, or phonogram; the author of the work, the performer of the performance, or the producer of the phonogram; or the owner of any right in the work, performance, or phonogram; information about the terms and conditions of the use of the work, performance, or phonogram; and any numbers or codes that represent such information, when any of these items is attached to a copy of the work, performance, or phonogram or appears in conjunction with the communication or making available of a work, performance, or phonogram to the public. Nothing in this paragraph obligates a Party to require the owner of any right in the work, performance, or phonogram to attach rights management information to copies of it or to cause rights management information to appear in connection with a communication of the work, performance, or phonogram to the public.

9.   Each Party shall issue appropriate laws, orders, regulations, administrative, or executive decrees mandating that all government agencies use computer software only as authorized by the right holder. Such measures shall actively regulate the acquisition and management of software for such government use, which may take the form of procedures, such as preparing and maintaining inventories of software present on agency computers, and inventories of existing software licenses.

10.   Each Party shall confine limitations or exceptions to exclusive rights in Articles 16.4 and 16.5 to certain special cases which do not conflict with a normal exploitation of the work, performance, or phonogram, and do not unreasonably prejudice the legitimate interests of the right holder.

ARTICLE 16.5: OBLIGATIONS PERTAINING TO RELATED RIGHTS

1.   Each Party shall accord the rights provided for in this Chapter to performers and producers of phonograms who are nationals of the other Party and to performances or phonograms first published or fixed in the territory of the other Party. A performance or phonogram shall be considered first published in any Party in which it is published within 30 days of its original publication.[16-8]

2.   Each Party shall provide to performers the exclusive right to authorize or prohibit:

(a)   the communication to the public of their unfixed performances, except where the performance is already a broadcast performance, and

(b)   the fixation of their unfixed performances.

3.   With respect to all rights of performers and producers of phonograms, the enjoyment and exercise of the rights provided for in this Chapter shall not be subject to any formality.

4.   For the purposes of this Chapter, the following definitions apply with respect to performers and producers of phonograms:

[16-8] For the application of paragraph 1 of Article 16.5, fixed means the finalization of the master tape or its equivalent.

(a)   performers means actors, singers, musicians, dancers, and other persons who act, sing, deliver, declaim, play in, interpret, or otherwise perform literary or artistic works or expressions of folklore;

(b)   phonogram means the fixation of the sounds of a performance or of other sounds, or of a representation of sounds, other than in the form of a fixation incorporated in a cinematographic or other audiovisual work;[16-9]

(c)   fixation means the embodiment of sounds, or of the representations thereof, from which they can be perceived, reproduced, or communicated through a device;

(d)   producer of a phonogram means the person, or the legal entity, who or which takes the initiative and has the responsibility for the first fixation of the sounds of a performance or other sounds, or the representations of sounds;

(e)   publication of a fixed performance or a phonogram means the offering of copies of the fixed performance or the phonogram to the public, with the consent of the right holder, and provided that copies are offered to the public in reasonable quantity; and

(f)   broadcasting means the transmission by wireless means for public reception of sounds or of images and sounds or of the representations thereof; such transmission by satellite is also broadcasting; transmission of encrypted signals is broadcasting where the means for decrypting are provided to the public by the broadcasting organization or with its consent.

ARTICLE 16.6: PROTECTION OF ENCRYPTED PROGRAM-CARRYING SATELLITE SIGNALS

1.   Each Party shall make it:

(a)   a criminal offense to manufacture, assemble, modify, import, export, sell, lease, or otherwise distribute a tangible or intangible device or system, knowing or having reason to know that the device or system is primarily of assistance in decoding an encrypted program-carrying satellite signal without the authorization of the lawful distributor of such signal;

(b)   a criminal offense willfully to receive or further distribute an encrypted programcarrying satellite signal that has been decoded without the authorization of the lawful distributor of the signal; and

(c)   a civil offense to engage in any activity prohibited under subparagraph (a) or (b).

2.   Each Party shall provide that any civil offense established under subparagraph (c) shall be actionable by any person that holds an interest in the encrypted program-carrying satellite signal or the content thereof.

[16-9] The definition of phonogram provided herein does not suggest that rights in the phonogram are in any way affected through their incorporation into a cinematographic or other audiovisual work.

ARTICLE 16.7: PATENTS

1.   Each Party shall make patents available for any invention, whether a product or a process, in all fields of technology, provided that the invention is new, involves an inventive step, and is capable of industrial application. For purposes of this Article, a Party may treat the terms "inventive step" and "capable of industrial application" as being synonymous with the terms "non-obvious" and "useful", respectively. Each Party may exclude inventions from patentability only as defined in Articles 27.2 and 27.3(a) of the TRIPS Agreement.

2.   Each Party shall provide that patent owners shall also have the right to assign, or transfer by succession, a patent and to conclude licensing contracts. Each Party shall provide a cause of action to prevent or redress the procurement of a patented pharmaceutical product, without the authorization of the patent owner, by a party who knows or has reason to know that such product is or has been distributed in breach of a contract between the right holder and a licensee, regardless of whether such breach occurs in or outside its territory.[16-10] Each Party shall provide that in such a cause of action, notice shall constitute constructive knowledge.

3.   Each Party may provide limited exceptions to the exclusive rights conferred by a patent, provided that such exceptions do not unreasonably conflict with a normal exploitation of the patent and do not unreasonably prejudice the legitimate interests of the patent owner, taking account of the legitimate interests of third parties.

4.   Each Party shall provide that a patent may only be revoked on grounds that would have justified a refusal to grant the patent, or that pertain to the insufficiency of or unauthorized amendments to the patent specification, non-disclosure or misrepresentation of prescribed, material particulars, fraud, and misrepresentation. Where such proceedings include opposition proceedings, a Party may not make such proceedings available prior to the grant of the patent.

5.   If a Party permits the use by a third party of the subject matter of a subsisting patent to support an application for marketing approval of a pharmaceutical product, that Party shall provide that any product produced under such authority shall not be made, used, or sold in the territory of that Party other than for purposes related to meeting requirements for marketing approval, and if the Party permits exportation, the product shall only be exported outside the territory of that Party for purposes of meeting marketing approval requirements of that Party.

6.   Neither Party shall permit the use[16-11] of the subject matter of a patent without the authorization of the right holder except in the following circumstances:

   (a)   to remedy a practice determined after judicial or administrative process to be anticompetitive under the competition laws of the Party;[16-12]

   (b)   in the case of public non-commercial use or in the case of a national emergency or other circumstances of extreme urgency, provided that:

[16-10] A Party may limit such cause of action to cases where the product has been sold or distributed only outside the Party's territory before its procurement inside the Party's territory.

[16-11] A Use" in this provision refers to use other than that allowed in paragraph 3.

[16-12] The Parties recognize that an intellectual property right does not necessarily confer market power upon its owner.

(i)   such use is limited to use by the government or third parties authorized by the government;

(ii)   the patent owner is provided with reasonable and entire compensation for such use and manufacture; and

(iii)   the Party shall not require the patent owner to transfer undisclosed information or technical "know how" related to a patented invention that has been authorized for use without the consent of the patent owner pursuant to this paragraph.

Where a Party's law allows for such use pursuant to subparagraphs (a) and (b), the Party shall respect the provisions of Article 31 of the TRIPS Agreement.

7.   Each Party, at the request of the patent owner, shall extend the term of a patent to compensate for unreasonable delays that occur in granting the patent. For the purposes of this paragraph, an unreasonable delay shall at least include a delay in the issuance of the patent of more than four years from the date of filing of the application with the Party, or two years after a request for examination of the application has been made, whichever is later, provided that periods attributable to actions of the patent applicant need not be included in the determination of such delays.[16-13]

8.   Where a Party provides for the grant of a patent on the basis of an examination of the invention conducted in another country, that Party, at the request of the patent owner, may extend the term of a patent for up to five years to compensate for the unreasonable delay that may occur in the issuance of the patent granted by such other country where that country has extended the term of the patent based on such delay.

ARTICLE 16.8: CERTAIN REGULATED PRODUCTS

1.   If a Party requires the submission of information concerning the safety and efficacy of a pharmaceutical or agricultural chemical product prior to permitting the marketing of such product, the Party shall not permit third parties not having the consent of the party providing the information to market the same or a similar product on the basis of the approval granted to the party submitting such information for a period of at least five years from the date of approval for a pharmaceutical product and ten years from the date of approval for an agricultural chemical product.[16-14]

2.   If a Party provides a means of granting approval to market a product specified in paragraph 1 on the basis of the grant of an approval for marketing of the same or similar product in another country, the Party shall defer the date of any such approval to third parties not having the consent of the party providing the information in the other country for at least five years from the date of approval for a pharmaceutical product and ten years from the date of approval for an

---

[16-13] Periods attributable to actions of the patent applicant shall include such periods of time taken to file prescribed documents relating to the examination as provided in the laws of the Party.

[16-14] Where a Party, on the date of its implementation of the TRIPS Agreement, had in place a system for protecting pharmaceutical or agricultural chemical products not involving new chemical entities from unfair commercial use that conferred a different form or period of protection shorter than that specified in paragraph 1 of Article 16.8, that Party may retain such system notwithstanding the obligations of that paragraph.

agricultural chemical product in the territory of the Party or in the other country, whichever is later.

3.   Where a product is subject to a system of marketing approval pursuant to paragraph 1 or 2 and is also subject to a patent in the territory of that Party, the Party shall not alter the term of protection that it provides pursuant to paragraph 1 or 2 in the event that the patent protection terminates on a date earlier than the end of the term of such protection.

4.   With respect to any pharmaceutical product that is subject to a patent:

(a)   each Party shall make available an extension of the patent term to compensate the patent owner for unreasonable curtailment of the patent term as a result of the marketing approval process;

(b)   the Party shall provide that the patent owner shall be notified of the identity of any third party requesting marketing approval effective during the term of the patent; and

(c)   the Party shall not grant marketing approval to any third party prior to the expiration of the patent term, unless by consent or with the acquiescence of the patent owner.

ARTICLE 16.9: ENFORCEMENT OF INTELLECTUAL PROPERTY RIGHTS

General Obligations

1.   Each Party shall ensure that in judicial and administrative proceedings for the enforcement of intellectual property rights, decisions on the merits of a case, that under the law or practice of the Party are of general application, shall preferably be in writing and shall state the reasons on which the decisions are based.

2.   Each Party shall ensure that its laws and regulations, procedures, final judicial decisions, and administrative rulings of general application pertaining to the enforcement of intellectual property rights shall be published, or where such publication is not practicable, made publicly available, in a national language, in such a manner as to enable the other Party and right holders to become acquainted with them. Nothing in this paragraph shall require a Party to disclose confidential information the disclosure of which would impede law enforcement or otherwise be contrary to the public interest or would prejudice the legitimate commercial interests of particular enterprises, public or private.

3.   Each Party shall inform the public of its efforts to provide effective enforcement of intellectual property rights in its civil, administrative, and criminal system, including any statistical information that the Party may collect for such purposes.

4.   The Parties understand that a decision that a Party makes on the distribution of enforcement resources shall not excuse that Party from complying with this Chapter.

5.   Each Party shall provide for civil remedies against the actions described in paragraphs 7 and 8 of Article 16.4. These shall include at least:

(a)   provisional measures, including seizure of devices and products suspected of being involved in the prohibited activity;

(b)   the opportunity for the right holder to elect between actual damages it suffered (plus any profits attributable to the prohibited activity not taken into account in computing the actual damages) or pre-established damages;

(c)   payment to a prevailing right holder of court costs and fees and reasonable attorney's fees by the party engaged in the prohibited conduct at the conclusion of the civil judicial proceeding; and

(d)   destruction of devices and products found to be involved in the prohibited conduct.

6.   In civil, administrative, and criminal proceedings involving copyright or related rights, each Party shall provide for a presumption that, in the absence of proof to the contrary, the natural person or legal entity whose name is indicated as the author, producer, performer, or publisher of the work, performance, or phonogram in the usual manner, is the designated right holder in such work, performance, or phonogram. Each Party shall also provide for a presumption that, in the absence of proof to the contrary, the copyright or related right subsists in such subject matter.

Civil and Administrative Procedures and Remedies for the Enforcement of Intellectual Property Rights

7.   Each Party shall make available to right holders[16-15] civil judicial procedures concerning the enforcement of any intellectual property right.

8.   Each Party shall provide that in civil judicial proceedings, its judicial authorities shall have the authority, at least with respect to works, phonograms, and performances protected by copyright or related rights, and in cases of trademark infringement, to order the infringer to pay the right holder damages adequate to compensate for the injury the right holder has suffered because of an infringement of that person' s intellectual property right by an infringer engaged in infringing activity, as well as the profits of the infringer that are attributable to the infringement and are not taken into account in computing the actual damages. In addition, in determining injury to the right holder, the judicial authorities shall, inter alia, consider the value of the infringed-upon good or service, according to the suggested retail price of the legitimate good or service.

9.   In civil judicial proceedings, each Party shall, at least with respect to works, phonograms and performances protected by copyright or related rights, and in cases of trademark counterfeiting, establish or maintain pre-established damages that shall be available on the election of the right holder. Each Party shall provide that pre-established damages shall be in an amount sufficiently high to constitute a deterrent to future infringements and with the intent to compensate the right holder for the harm caused by the infringement.

[16-15] For the purpose of Article 16.9 concerning the enforcement of intellectual property rights, the term "right holder" shall include exclusive licensees as well as federations and associations having the legal standing to assert such rights; and the term "exclusive licensee" shall include the exclusive licensee of any one or more of the exclusive rights encompassed in a given intellectual property.

10.   Each Party shall provide that its judicial authorities, except in exceptional circumstances, shall have the authority to order, at the conclusion of the civil judicial proceedings concerning copyright or related rights and trademark counterfeiting, that a prevailing right holder shall be paid court costs or fees and reasonable attorney's fees by the infringing party.

11.   In civil judicial proceedings concerning copyright or related rights infringement and trademark counterfeiting, each Party shall provide that its judicial authorities shall have the authority to order the seizure of suspected infringing goods and any related materials and implements used to accomplish the prohibited activity.

12.   Each Party shall provide that:

(a)   in civil judicial proceedings, at the right holder's request, goods that have been found to be pirated or counterfeit shall be destroyed, except in exceptional cases;

(b)   its judicial authorities have the authority to order that materials and implements which have been used in the creation of the infringing goods be, without compensation of any sort, promptly destroyed or, in exceptional cases, without compensation of any sort, disposed of outside the channels of commerce in such a manner as to minimize the risks of further infringements; and

(c)   in regard to counterfeit trademarked goods, the simple removal of the trademark unlawfully affixed shall not be sufficient to permit the release of goods into the channels of commerce.

13.   Each Party shall provide that in civil judicial proceedings, its judicial authorities shall have the authority to order the infringer to identify third parties that are involved in the production and distribution of the infringing goods or services and their channels of distribution and to provide this information to the right holder. Each Party shall provide that its judicial authorities shall have the authority to fine or imprison, in appropriate cases, persons who fail to abide by valid orders issued by such authorities.

Provisional Measures Concerning the Enforcement of Intellectual Property Rights

14.   Each Party shall provide that requests for relief inaudita altera parte shall be dealt with expeditiously in accordance with the Party's judicial rules.

15.   Each Party shall provide that:

(a)   its judicial authorities have the authority to require the plaintiff to provide any reasonably available evidence in order to satisfy themselves with a sufficient degree of certainty that the plaintiff's right is being infringed or that such infringement is imminent, and to order the plaintiff to provide a reasonable security or equivalent assurance set at a level sufficient to protect the defendant and to prevent abuse, and so as not to unreasonably deter recourse to such procedures.

(b)   in the event that its judicial or other authorities appoint experts, technical or otherwise, that must be paid by the plaintiff, such costs should be closely related, inter alia, to the quantity of work to be performed and should not unreasonably deter recourse to such relief.

Special Requirements Related to Border Measures Concerning the Enforcement of Intellectual Property Rights

16.   Each Party shall provide that any right holder initiating procedures for suspension by the Party's customs authorities of the release of suspected counterfeit trademark or pirated copyright goods[16-16] into free circulation shall be required to provide adequate evidence to satisfy the competent authorities that, under the law of the importing country, there is prima facie an infringement of the right holder's intellectual property right and to supply sufficient information that may reasonably be expected to be within the right holder's knowledge to make the suspected goods reasonably recognizable to the customs authorities.

17.   Each Party shall provide that its competent authorities shall have the authority to require an applicant to provide a reasonable security or equivalent assurance sufficient to protect the defendant and the competent authorities and to prevent abuse. Each Party shall provide that the security or assurance shall not unreasonably deter recourse to these procedures.

18.   Where its competent authorities have made a determination that goods are counterfeit or pirated, the Party shall grant its competent authorities the authority to inform the right holder of the names and addresses of the consignor, the importer, and the consignee, and of the quantity of the goods in question.

19.   Each Party shall provide that its competent authorities may initiate border measures ex officio, without the need for a formal complaint from a private party or right holder. Such measures shall apply to shipments of pirated and counterfeit goods imported into or exported out of a Party's territory, including shipments consigned to a local party. For transshipped goods that are not consigned to a local party, each Party shall, upon request, endeavor to examine such goods. For products transshipped through the territory of a Party destined for the territory of the other Party, the former shall cooperate to provide all available information to the latter Party to enable effective enforcement against shipments of counterfeit or pirated goods. Each Party shall ensure that it has the authority to undertake such cooperation in response to a request by the other Party on counterfeit or pirated goods en route to that other Party.

20.   Each Party shall provide that goods that its competent authorities have determined to be pirated or counterfeit shall be destroyed, except in exceptional cases. In regard to counterfeit trademark goods, the simple removal of the trademark unlawfully affixed shall not be sufficient to permit the release of the goods into the channels of commerce. In no event shall the competent authorities be authorized to permit the export of counterfeit or pirated goods.

[16-16] For the purposes of this Chapter:
(a)   counterfeit trademark goods shall mean any goods, including packaging, bearing without authorization a trademark which is identical to the trademark validly registered in respect of such goods, or which cannot be distinguished in its essential aspects from such a trademark, and which thereby infringes the rights of the owner of the trademark in question under the law of the country of importation; and
(b)   pirated copyright goods shall mean any goods which are copies made without the consent of the right holder or person duly authorized by the right holder in the country of production and which are made directly or indirectly from an article where the making of that copy would have constituted an infringement of a copyright or a related right under the law of the country of importation.

Criminal Procedures and Remedies for the Enforcement of Intellectual Property Rights

21.   Each Party shall provide criminal procedures and penalties to be applied at least in cases of willful trademark counterfeiting or copyright or related rights piracy on a commercial scale. Willful copyright or related rights piracy on a commercial scale includes (i) significant willful infringements of copyright or related rights that have no direct or indirect motivation of financial gain, as well as (ii) willful infringements for purposes of commercial advantage or financial gain.

(a)   Specifically, each Party shall provide:

(i)   remedies that include imprisonment as well as monetary fines sufficiently high to deter future acts of infringement consistent with a policy of removing the monetary incentive of the infringer. Also, each Party shall encourage its judicial authorities to impose such fines at levels sufficient to provide a deterrent to future infringements;

(ii)   that its judicial authorities have the authority to order the seizure of suspected counterfeit or pirated goods, any related materials and implements that have been used in the commission of the offense, any assets traceable to the infringing activity, and documentary evidence relevant to the offense that fall within the scope of such order. Items that are subject to seizure pursuant to such order need not be individually identified so long as they fall within general categories specified in the order;

(iii)   that its judicial authorities shall, except in exceptional cases, order the forfeiture and destruction of all counterfeit or pirated goods, and, at least with respect to willful copyright or related rights piracy, materials and implements that have been used in the creation of the infringing goods. Each Party shall further provide that such forfeiture and destruction shall occur without compensation of any kind to the defendant; and

(iv)   that its authorities may initiate legal action ex officio, without the need for a formal complaint by a private party or right holder.

(b)   Each Party may provide procedures for right holders to initiate private criminal actions. However, these procedures shall not be unduly burdensome or costly for right holders. Each Party shall ensure that non-private criminal actions are the primary means by which it ensures the effective enforcement of its criminal law against willful copyright or related rights piracy. In addition, each Party shall ensure that its competent authorities bring criminal actions, as necessary, to act as a deterrent to further infringements.

Limitations on Liability for Service Providers

22.   Each Party shall provide, consistent with the framework set forth in Article 16.9:

(a)   legal incentives for service providers to cooperate with copyright[16-17]owners in deterring the unauthorized storage and transmission of copyrighted materials; and

(b)   limitations in its law regarding the scope of remedies available against service providers for copyright infringements that they do not control, initiate, or direct, and that take place through systems or networks controlled or operated by them or on their behalf, as set forth in this subparagraph.[16-18]

   (i)   These limitations shall preclude monetary relief and provide reasonable restrictions on court-ordered relief to compel or restrain certain actions for the following functions and shall be confined to those functions:[16-19]

      (A)   transmitting, routing or providing connections for material without modification of its content, or the intermediate and transient storage of such material in the course thereof;

      (B)   caching carried out through an automatic process;

      (C)   storage at the direction of a user of material residing on a system or network controlled or operated by or for the service provider; and

      (D)   referring or linking users to an online location by using information location tools, including hyperlinks and directories.

   (ii)   These limitations shall apply only where the service provider does not initiate the chain of transmission of the material, and does not select the material or its recipients (except to the extent that a function described in clause (i)(D) in itself entails some form of selection).

   (iii)   Qualification by a service provider for the limitations as to each function in clauses (i)(A) through (i)(D) shall be considered separately from qualification for the limitations as to each other function, in accordance with the conditions for qualification set forth in subparagraphs (iv) – (vii).

   (iv)   With respect to functions referred to in clause (i)(B), the limitations shall be conditioned on the service provider:

      (A)   permitting access to cached material in significant part only to users of its system or network who have met conditions on user access to that material;

      (B)   complying with rules concerning the refreshing, reloading, or other updating of the cached material when specified by the person making the material available online in accordance with a generally accepted industry standard data communications

---

[16-17] For purposes of Article 16.9.22, "copyright" shall also include related rights.

[16-18] It is understood that this subparagraph is without prejudice to the availability of defenses to copyright infringement that are of general applicability.

[16-19] Either Party may request consultations with the other Party to consider how to address future functions of a similar nature under this paragraph.

protocol for the system or network through which that person makes the material available;

(C) not interfering with technology consistent with industry standards accepted in the territory of each Party used at the originating site to obtain information about the use of the material, and not modifying its content in transmission to subsequent users; and

(D) expeditiously removing or disabling access, on receipt of an effective notification of claimed infringement, to cached material that has been removed or access to which has been disabled at the originating site.

(v) With respect to functions referred to in clauses (i)(C) and (i)(D), the limitations shall be conditioned on the service provider:

(A) not receiving a financial benefit directly attributable to the infringing activity, in circumstances where it has the right and ability to control such activity;

(B) expeditiously removing or disabling access to the material residing on its system or network on obtaining actual knowledge of the infringement or becoming aware of facts or circumstances from which the infringement was apparent, such as through effective notifications of claimed infringement in accordance with subparagraph (ix) and

(C) publicly designating a representative to receive such notifications.

(vi) Eligibility for the limitations in this subparagraph shall be conditioned on the service provider:

(A) adopting and reasonably implementing a policy that provides for termination in appropriate circumstances of the accounts of repeat infringers; and

(B) accommodating and not interfering with standard technical measures accepted in the territory of each Party that protect and identify copyrighted material, that are developed through an open, voluntary process by a broad consensus of copyright owners and service providers, that are available on reasonable and nondiscriminatory terms, and that do not impose substantial costs on service providers or substantial burdens on their systems or networks.

(vii) Eligibility for the limitations in this subparagraph may not be conditioned on the service provider monitoring its service, or affirmatively seeking facts indicating infringing activity, except to the extent consistent with such technical measures.

(viii)   If the service provider qualifies for the limitations with respect to the functions referred to in clause (i)(A), court-ordered relief to compel or restrain certain actions shall be limited to terminating specified accounts, or to taking reasonable steps to block access to a specific, non-domestic online location. If the service provider qualifies for the limitations with respect to any other function in clause (i), court-ordered relief to compel or restrain certain actions shall be limited to removing or disabling access to the infringing material, terminating specified accounts, and other remedies that a court may find necessary provided that such other remedies are the least burdensome to the service provider among comparably effective forms of relief. Each Party shall provide that any such relief shall be issued with due regard for the relative burden to the service provider and harm to the copyright owner, the technical feasibility and effectiveness of the remedy, and whether less burdensome, comparably effective enforcement methods are available. Except for orders ensuring the preservation of evidence, or other orders having no material adverse effect on the operation of the service provider = s communications network, each Party shall provide that such relief shall be available only where the service provider has received notice of the court order proceedings referred to in this subparagraph and an opportunity to appear before the judicial authority.

(ix)   For purposes of the notice and take down process for the functions referred to in clauses (i)(C) and (D), each Party shall establish appropriate procedures for effective notifications of claimed infringement, and effective counter-notifications by those whose material is removed or disabled through mistake or misidentification. Each Party shall also provide for monetary remedies against any person who makes a knowing material misrepresentation in a notification or counter-notification that causes injury to any interested party as a result of a service provider relying on the misrepresentation.

(x)   If the service provider removes or disables access to material in good faith based on claimed or apparent infringement, each Party shall provide that the service provider shall be exempted from liability for any resulting claims, provided that, in the case of material residing on its system or network, it takes reasonable steps promptly to notify the person making the material available on its system or network that it has done so and, if such person makes an effective counter-notification and is subject to jurisdiction in an infringement suit, to restore the material online unless the person giving the original effective notification seeks judicial relief within a reasonable time.

(xi)   Each Party shall establish an administrative or judicial procedure enabling copyright owners who have given effective notification of claimed infringement to obtain expeditiously from a service provider information in its possession identifying the alleged infringer.

(xii)   For purposes of the functions referred to in clause (i)(A), service provider means a provider of transmission, routing or connections for digital online communications without modification of their content between or among points specified by the user of material of the user = s choosing, and for purposes of the functions referred to in clauses (i)(B) through (i)(D) service provider means a provider or operator of facilities for online services or network access.

ARTICLE 16.10: TRANSITIONAL PROVISIONS

1.   Each Party shall implement the obligations of this Chapter within the following periods:

(a)   Each Party shall ratify or accede to the UPOV Convention and give effect to the obligations in paragraph 4 of Article 16.4 within six months of the date of entry into force of this Agreement or December 31, 2004, whichever date is earlier;

(b)   each Party shall ratify or accede to the agreements listed in paragraph 2(a) of Article 16.1(except for the UPOV Convention) and give effect to Articles 16.4 and 16.5 (except for paragraph 4 of Article 16.4) within one year of the date of entry into force of this Agreement; and

(c)   each Party shall implement each of the other obligations of this Chapter within six months of the date of entry into force of this Agreement.

2.   Except as otherwise provided in this Chapter, the date of entry into force in paragraph 6(b) of Article 16.1 means the date of the expiry of the six-month period commencing on the date this Agreement enters into force.

*

FREE TRADE AGREEMENT BETWEEN THE REPUBLIC OF CHINA AND THE REPUBLIC OF PANAMA*
[excerpts]

The free trade agreement between the Republic of China and the Republic of Panama was signed on 6 May 2003. It entered into force on 1 January 2004.

PART FOUR
INVESTMENT, SERVICES AND RELATED MATTERS

CHAPTER 10
INVESTMENT

Section A - Investment

Article 10.01 Scope and Coverage

1.   This Chapter applies to measures adopted or maintained by a Party relating to:

    (a)   investors of the other Party with respect to all aspects of its investments;

    (b)   investments of investors of the other Party in the territory of the Party; and

    (c)   all investments of the investors of a Party in the territory of the other Party with regard to Article 10.07.

2.   This Chapter does not apply to:

    (a)   measures adopted or maintained by a Party in relation to financial services;

    (b)   measures adopted by a Party to limit the participation of investment of investors of the other Party in its territory for reasons of public order or national security;

    (c)   economic activities reserved by each Party pursuant to its law in force on the date of the signing of this Agreement, as listed in Annex III on economic activities reserved to each Party;

    (d)   government services or functions such as law enforcement, correctional services, income security or unemployment insurance, social security services, social welfare, public education, public training, health, and child care;

---

* *Source*: The Organization of American States (OAS) (2003). "Free Trade Agreement Between the Republic of China and the Republic of Panama", available on the Internet (http://www.sice.oas.org/Trade/PanRC/PANRC_e.asp). [Note added by the editor.]

    (e)   disputes or claims arising before the entry into force of this Agreement or relating to facts that occurred before it entered into force, even if their effects persist thereafter; and

    (f)   government procurement.

3.   This Chapter applies to the entire territory of the Parties and to any level of government regardless of any inconsistent measures that may exist in the law of these government levels.

4.   Notwithstanding the provisions of paragraph 2(d), if a duly authorized investor from a Party provides services or carries out functions such as correctional services, income security or unemployment insurance, social security services, social welfare, public education, public training, health, and child care, the investment of this investor shall be protected by the provisions of this Chapter.

5.   This Chapter shall apply to both investments made prior to and after the entry into force of this Agreement, by investors of a Party in the territory of the other Party.

Article 10.02 National Treatment

1.   Each Party shall accord to investors of the other Party treatment no less favorable than that it accords, in like circumstances, to its own investors with respect to the establishment, acquisition, expansion, management, conduct, operation, and sale or other disposition of investments.

2.   Each Party shall accord to investments of investors of the other Party treatment no less favorable than that it accords, in like circumstances, to investments of its own investors with respect to the establishment, acquisition, expansion, management, conduct, operation, and sale or other disposition of investments.

Article 10.03 Most-Favored-Nation Treatment

1.   Each Party shall accord to investors of the other Party treatment no less favorable than that it accords, in like circumstances, to investors of a non-Party with respect to the establishment, acquisition, expansion, management, conduct, operation, and sale or other disposition of investments.

2.   Each Party shall accord to investments of investors of the other Party treatment no less favorable than that it accords, in like circumstances, to investments of investors of a non-Party with respect to the establishment, acquisition, expansion, management, conduct, operation, and sale or other disposition of investments.

Article 10.04 Fair and Equitable Treatment

Each Party shall accord to investors of the other Party and their investments treatment in accordance with international law, including fair and equitable treatment as well as full protection and security.

Article 10.05 Standard of Treatment

Each Party shall accord to investors of the other Party and to investments of investors of the other Party the better of the treatment required by Articles 10.02, 10.03 and 10.04.

Article 10.06 Compensation for Losses

Each Party shall accord the investors of the other Party whose investments have been adversely affected in its territory due to armed conflict, state of emergency, insurrection, or civil strife, non-discriminatory treatment on any measure adopted or maintained in relation to such losses.

Article 10.07 Performance Requirements

1.   No Party may impose or enforce any of the following requirements, or enforce any commitment or undertaking, in connection with the establishment, acquisition, expansion, management, conduct or operation of an investment of an investor of the other Party in its territory:

    (a)   to export a given level or percentage of goods or services;

    (b)   to achieve a given level or percentage of domestic content;

    (c)   to purchase, use or accord a preference to goods produced or services provided in its territory, or to purchase goods or services from persons in its territory; or

    (d)   to relate in any way the volume or value of imports to the volume or value of exports or to the amount of foreign exchange inflows associated with such investment.

This paragraph does not apply to any requirement other than indicated herein.

2.   No Party may condition the receipt or continued receipt of an advantage, in connection with an investment in its territory of an investor of the other Party, on compliance with any of the following requirements:

    (a)   to achieve a given level or percentage of domestic content;

    (b)   to purchase, use or accord a preference to goods produced in its territory, or to purchase goods from producers in its territory; or

    (c)   to relate in any way the volume or value of imports to the volume or value of exports or to the amount of foreign exchange inflows associated with such investment.

This paragraph does not apply to any requirements other than indicated herein.

3.   The provisions included in:

(a)   paragraph 1(a), (b), and (c) and paragraph 2(a) and (b) do not apply to requirements relating to the qualification of goods and services for programs of export promotion and foreign aid programs;

(b)   paragraph 1(b) and (c) and paragraph 2(a) and (b) do not apply to the procurement by a Party or by a state enterprise; and

(c)   paragraph 2(a) and (b) does not apply to the requirements imposed by an importing Party related to the contents of a good necessary to qualify it for preferential tariffs or quotas.

4.   Nothing in paragraph 2 shall be construed to prevent a Party from conditioning the receipt or continued receipt of an advantage, in connection with an investment in its territory of an investor of the other Party, on compliance with a requirement to locate production, provide a service, train or employ workers, construct or expand particular facilities, or carry out research and development, in its territory.

5.   Provided that these measures are not applied in an arbitrary or unjustified manner or do not constitute a disguised restriction to international trade or investment, nothing in paragraph 1(b) or (c) or 2(a) or (b) shall be construed to prevent a Party from adopting or maintaining measures, including environment measures, necessary to:

(a)   ensure compliance with laws and regulations that are not inconsistent with the provisions of this Agreement;

(b)   protect human, animal or plant life or health; or

(c)   conserve living or non-living exhaustible natural resources.

6.   In the case where, in opinion of a Party, the imposition by the other Party of any of the following requirements shall adversely affect trade flows or constitutes a significant barrier to investment by an investor of a Party, the matter shall be considered by the Commission:

(a)   to restrict sales of goods or services in its territory that such investment produces or provides by relating such sales in any way to the volume or value of its exports or foreign exchange earnings;

(b)   to transfer technology, production process or other proprietary knowledge to a person in its territory, except when the requirement is imposed by a court, administrative tribunal or competition authority to remedy an alleged violation of competition laws or to act in a manner not inconsistent with other provisions of this Agreement; or

(c)   to act as the exclusive supplier of the goods it produces or services it provides to a specific region or world market.

7.   A measure that requires an investment to use a technology to meet generally applicable health, safety or environmental requirements shall not be construed to be inconsistent with paragraph 6(b). For greater certainty, Articles 10.02 and 10.03 apply to the measure.

8.   If the Commission finds that the imposition of any of the above requirements adversely affects the trade flow, or represents a significant barrier to investment by an investor of the other Party, it shall recommend that the practice in question be suspended.

Article 10.08 Senior Management and Boards of Directors

1.   No Party may require that an enterprise of that Party that is an investment of an investor of the other Party appoint to senior management positions individuals of any particular nationality.

2.   A Party may require that a majority of the board of directors, of an enterprise of that Party that is an investment of an investor of the other Party, be of a particular nationality, or resident in the territory of the Party, provided that the requirement does not materially impair the ability of the investor to exercise control over its investment.

Article 10.09 Reservations and Exceptions

1.   Articles 10.02, 10.03, 10.07 and 10.08 do not apply to:

    (a)   any existing non-conforming measure that is maintained by:

        (i)   a Party at the national level, as set out in its Schedule to Annex I or III, or

        (ii)   a local or municipal government;

    (b)   the continuation or prompt renewal of any non-conforming measure referred to in subparagraph (a); or

    (c)   the amendment of any non-conforming measure referred to in subparagraph (a), provided that this amendment does not decrease the conformity of the measure as it existed before its amendment by Articles 10.02, 10.03, 10.07, and 10.08.

2.   Articles 10.02, 10.03, 10.07 and 10.08 shall not apply to any measure adopted or maintained by a Party in relation to sectors, sub-sectors or activities, as are indicated in their Schedule to Annex II.

3.   No Party may, under any measure adopted after the date of entry into force of this Agreement and covered by its Schedule to Annex II, require an investor of the other Party, by reason of its nationality, to sell or otherwise dispose of an investment existing at the time the measure becomes effective.

4.   Article 10.03 does not apply to treatment accorded by a Party under agreements, or with respect to sectors included in its Schedule to Annex IV.

5.   Articles 10.02, 10.03 and 10.08 do not apply to:

    (a)   procurement by a Party or a state enterprise; and

    (b)   subsidies or grants provided by a Party or a state enterprise, including government supported loans, guarantees and insurance.

Article 10.10 Transfers

1.   Each Party shall permit all transfers relating to an investment of an investor of the other Party in the territory of the Party to be made freely and without delay. Such transfers include:

(a)   profits, dividends, interest, capital gains, royalty payments, management fees, technical assistance and other fees, returns in kind and other amounts derived from the investment;

(b)   proceeds from the sale of all or any part of the investment or from the partial or complete liquidation of the investment;

(c)   payments made under a contract entered into by the investor, or its investment, including payments made pursuant to a loan agreement;

(d)   payments made pursuant to Article 10.11; and

(e)   payments arising from the mechanism of dispute settlement under section B of this Chapter.

2.   Each Party shall permit transfers to be made without delay in a freely convertible currency at the market rate of exchange prevailing on the date of transfer.

3.   No Party may require its investors to transfer, or penalize its investors that fail to transfer, the income, earnings, profits or other amounts derived from, or attributable to, investments in the territory of the other Party.

4.   Notwithstanding paragraphs 1 and 2, a Party may prevent a transfer through the equitable, non-discriminatory and good faith application of its laws relating to:

(a)   bankruptcy, insolvency or the protection of the rights of creditors;

(b)   criminal or penal offenses;

(c)   reports of transfers of currency or other monetary instruments;

(d)   ensuring the satisfaction of judgments and arbitral awards in adjudicatory proceedings; or

(e)   issuing, trading or dealing in securities.

5.   Paragraph 3 shall not be construed to prevent a Party from imposing any measure through the equitable, non-discriminatory and good faith application of its laws relating to the matters set out in subparagraphs (a) through (e) of paragraph 4.

Article 10.11 Expropriation and Compensation

1.   No Party may directly or indirectly nationalize or expropriate an investment of an investor of the other Party in its territory or take a measure tantamount to nationalization or expropriation of such an investment ("expropriation"), except:

(a)   for a public purpose, or public order and social interest;

(b)   on a non-discriminatory basis;

(c)   in accordance with due process of law; and

(d)   on payment of compensation in accordance with this Article.

2.   Compensation shall be equivalent to the fair market value of the expropriated investment immediately before the expropriation took place ("date of expropriation"), and shall not reflect any change in value occurring because the intended expropriation had become known earlier. Valuation criteria shall include going concern value, asset value including declared tax value of tangible property, and other criteria, as appropriate, to determine fair market value.

3.   Compensation shall be paid without delay and be fully realizable.

4.   The amount paid as compensation shall be no less than the equivalent amount that would have been paid on that date to the expropriated investor in a currency of free convertibility in the international financial market according to the exchange rate in force on the date in which the fair market price was determined. The compensation shall include the payment of interests computed from the day of dispossession of the expropriated investment until the day of payment, and shall be computed on the basis of a commercially applicable rate for this currency set by the national bank system of the Party where the expropriation occurred.

5.   Upon payment, the compensation shall be freely transferable according to Article 10.10.

6.   This Article does not apply to the issuance of compulsory licenses granted in relation to intellectual property rights, or to the revocation, limitation or creation of intellectual property rights, to the extent that such issuance, revocation, limitation or creation is consistent with TRIPS.

7.   For purposes of this Article and for greater certainty, a non-discriminatory measure of general application shall not be considered a measure tantamount to an expropriation of a debt security or loan covered by this Chapter solely on the ground that the measure imposes costs on the debtor that cause it to default on the debt.

Article 10.12 Special Formalities and Information Requirements

1.   Nothing in Article 10.02 shall be construed to prevent a Party from adopting or maintaining a measure that prescribes special formalities in connection with the establishment of investments by investors of the other Party, such as a requirement that investors be residents of the Party or that investments be legally constituted under the laws or regulations of the Party, provided that such formalities do not materially impair the protections afforded by a Party to investors of the other Party and investments of investors of the other Party pursuant to this Chapter.

2.   Notwithstanding Articles 10.02 and 10.03, a Party may require an investor of the other Party, or its investment in its territory, to provide routine information concerning that investment solely for informational or statistical purposes. The Party shall protect such information that is confidential from any disclosure that would prejudice the competitive position of the investor or

the investment. Nothing in this paragraph shall be construed to prevent a Party from otherwise obtaining or disclosing information in connection with the equitable and good faith application of its law.

Article 10.13 Relation to Other Chapters

1.   In the event of any inconsistency between this Chapter and another Chapter, the latter shall prevail to the extent of the inconsistency.

2.   A requirement by a Party that a service provider of the other Party post a bond or other form of financial security as a condition of providing a service into its territory does not of itself make this Chapter applicable to the provisions of that of cross border service. This Chapter applies to that Party's treatment of the posted bond or financial security.

Article 10.14 Denial of Benefits

Upon notification and consultation done according to Articles 17.04 (Provision of Information) and 19.06 (Consultations), a Party may deny the benefits under this Chapter to an investor of the other Party that is an enterprise of such other Party and to the investment of this investor, if investors of a non Party are owners of or control the enterprise under the terms set out in the definition "investment" of an investor of a Party according to Article 10.39 and the enterprise has no substantial business activities in the territory of the Party under whose law it is constituted or organized.

Article 10.15 Environmental Measures

1.   Nothing in this Chapter shall be construed to prevent a Party from adopting, maintaining or enforcing any measure otherwise consistent with this Chapter that it considers appropriate to ensure that investment activity in its territory is undertaken under its ecological or environmental laws.

2.   The Parties recognize that it is inappropriate to encourage investment by relaxing domestic health, safety or environmental measures. Accordingly, a Party shall not waive or otherwise derogate from, or offer to waive or otherwise derogate from, such measures as an encouragement for the establishment, acquisition, expansion or retention in its territory of an investment of an investor. If a Party considers that the other Party has offered such an encouragement, it may request consultations with the other Party.

Section B-Settlement of Disputes between a Party and an Investor of the other Party

Article 10.16 Purpose

Without prejudice to the rights and obligations of the Parties under Chapter 19 (Dispute Settlement), this Section establishes a mechanism for the settlement of investment disputes arising from the violation of obligations established under Section A of this Chapter that assures both equal treatment among investors of the Parties in accordance with the principle of reciprocity and due process before an impartial tribunal.

Article 10.17 Claim by an Investor of a Party on Its Own Behalf

1.   An investor of a Party may submit to arbitration under this Section a claim on the grounds that the other Party or an enterprise controlled directly or indirectly by the other Party, has breached an obligation under this Chapter if the investor has suffered losses or damages from the violation of this Chapter.

2.   An investor may not make a claim if more than 3 years have elapsed from the date on which the investor first acquired, or should have first acquired, knowledge of the alleged breach and knowledge that the investor has suffered losses or damages.

Article 10.18 Claim by an Investor of a Party on Behalf of an Enterprise

1.   An investor of a Party, on behalf of an enterprise of the other Party that is a juridical person that the investor owns or controls directly or indirectly, may submit to arbitration under this Section a claim that the other Party or an enterprise controlled directly or indirectly by that Party has breached an obligation under this Chapter, whenever the enterprise has suffered losses or damages due to that violation or arising therefrom.

2.   An investor may not make a claim on behalf of an enterprise described in paragraph 1 if more than 3 years have elapsed from the date on which the enterprise first acquired, or should have first acquired, knowledge of the alleged breach and knowledge that the enterprise has suffered losses or damages.

3.   Where an investor makes a claim under this Article and the investor or a noncontrolling investor in the enterprise makes a claim under Article 10.17 arising out of the same events that gave rise to the claim under this Article, and two or more of the claims are submitted to arbitration under Article 10.21, the claims should be heard together by a Tribunal established under Article 10.27, unless the Tribunal finds that the interests of a disputing party would be prejudiced thereby.

4.   An investment may not submit a claim to arbitration under this Section.

Article 10.19 Settlement of a Claim through Consultation and Negotiation

The disputing parties should first attempt to settle a claim through consultation or negotiation.

Article 10.20 Notice of Intent to Submit a Claim to Arbitration

The disputing investor shall deliver to the disputing Party written notice of its intention to submit a claim to arbitration at least ninety (90) days before the claim is submitted, which notice shall specify:

(a)   the name and address of the disputing investor and, where a claim is made under Article 10.18, the name and address and the type of business of the enterprise;

(b)   the provisions of this Chapter alleged to have been breached and any other relevant provisions;

(c)   the issues and the factual basis for the claim; and

(d)   the relief sought and the approximate amount of damages claimed.

Article 10.21 Submission of a Claim to Arbitration

1.   Provided that six months have elapsed since the events giving rise to a claim, a disputing investor may submit the claim to arbitration under:

(a)   the ICSID Convention, provided that both the disputing Party and the Party of the investor are parties to the Convention;

(b)   the Additional Facility Rules of ICSID , provided that either the disputing Party or the Party of the investor, but not both, is a party to the ICSID Convention;

(c)   the UNCITRAL Arbitration Rules; or

(d)   the ICC Arbitration Rules.

2.   The applicable arbitration rules shall govern the arbitration established in this Chapter except to the extent modified by this Section.

Article 10.22 Conditions Precedent to Submission of a Claim to Arbitration

1.   Consent of the disputing parties in the arbitration procedure according to this Chapter shall be considered as a consent to this arbitration that excludes any other procedure.

2.   Each Party may demand the exhaustion of its local administrative remedies as a condition for consenting to the arbitration under this Chapter. Nevertheless, if 6 months have elapsed from the date on which the administrative remedies were lodged and the administrative authorities have not issued a final resolution, the investor may directly appeal to arbitration, according to the provisions of this Section.

3.   A disputing investor may submit a claim under Article 10.17 to arbitration only if:

(a)   the investor consents to arbitration in accordance with the procedures set out in this Section; and

(b)   the investor and, where the claim is for losses or damages to an interest in an enterprise of the other Party that is a juridical person that the investor owns or controls directly or indirectly, the enterprise, waive their right to initiate or continue before any administrative tribunal or court under the law of any Party, or other dispute settlement procedures, any proceedings with respect to the measure of the disputing Party that is alleged to be a breach referred to in Article 10.17, except for proceedings for injunctive, declaratory or other extraordinary relief, not involving the payment of damages, before an administrative tribunal or court under the law of the disputing Party.

4.   A disputing investor may present a claim to the arbitration procedure according to Article 10.18 only if both investor and enterprise:

(a)   consent to submit the claim to arbitration in accordance with the procedures set out in this Section; and

(b)   waive their right to initiate or continue before any administrative tribunal or court under the law of any Party, or other dispute settlement procedures, any proceedings with respect to the measure of the disputing Party that is alleged to be a breach referred to in Article 10.18, except for a proceeding for injunctive, declaratory or other extraordinary relief, not involving the payment of damages, before an administrative tribunal or court under the law of the disputing Party.

5.   The consent and the waiver required by this Article shall be stated in writing, delivered to the disputing Party and included in the submission of the claim to arbitration.

6.   The waiver by the enterprise, under paragraphs 3(b) and 4(b), shall not be required if, and only if, the disputing Party had deprived the disputing investor of the control of an enterprise.

Article 10.23 Consent to Arbitration

1.   Each Party consents to the submission of a claim to arbitration in accordance with the procedures and requirements set out in this Section.

2.   The consent given by paragraph 1 and the submission by a disputing investor of a claim to arbitration shall be deemed as having satisfied the requirement of:

(a)   Chapter II of the ICSID Convention (Jurisdiction of the Centre) and the Additional Facility Rules for written consent of the parties; and

(b)   Article II of the New York Convention for an agreement in writing.

Article 10.24 Number of Arbitrators and Method of Appointment

Except in respect of a Tribunal established under Article 10.27, and unless the disputing parties otherwise agree, the Tribunal shall comprise three arbitrators, one arbitrator appointed by each of the disputing parties and the third, who shall be the presiding arbitrator of the Tribunal, appointed by agreement of the disputing parties.

Article 10.25 Constitution of a Tribunal When a Party Fails to Appoint an Arbitrator or the Disputing Parties Are Unable to Agree on a Presiding Arbitrator

1.   In the event a disputing party does not appoint an arbitrator or an agreement is not reached about the appointment of the presiding arbitrator of the Tribuna l, the arbitrator or the presiding arbitrator of the Tribunal in the arbitration proceeding shall be designated, according to this Section.

2.   Where a Tribunal, not being the one created according to Article 10.27, is not constituted within a period of ninety (90) days from the date on which the claim is submitted to arbitration, the Secretary-General of the ICSID, the Secretary-General of the ICC or an appropriate official at an international organization agreed upon by the disputing parties (hereinafter the Secretary-General), shall appoint the not yet appointed arbitrator or arbitrators, except for the presiding arbitrator of the Tribunal who shall be appointed according to paragraph 3. In any case, the

majority of arbitrators may not be nationals of the disputing Party or the Party of the disputing investor.

3.   The Secretary-General shall appoint the presiding arbitrator of the Tribunal from the roster of arbitrators referred to in paragraph 4, ensuring that the presiding arbitrator of the Tribunal is not a national of the disputing Party or a national of the Party of the disputing investor. In case of not finding in the roster an available arbitrator to head the Tribunal, the Secretary- General shall appoint from the roster of arbitrators of the ICSID the presiding arbitrator of the Tribunal, provided that he or she is of a nationality different from the disputing Party or from the Party of the disputing investor.

4.   On the date of entry into force of this Agreement, the Parties shall establish and maintain a roster of six (6) arbitrators as possible presiding arbitrators of the Tribunal, none of which may be national of a Party, who comply with the rules contemplated in Article 10.21 and have experience in International Law and in investment matters. The members of the roster shall be appointed by mutual agreement, regardless of nationality, for a period of two (2) years that may be extended if the Parties so decide. In case of death or resignation of one member of the roster, the Parties shall appoint by mutual agreement the other person to substitute him or her in its functions for the remaining period to which the former person was appointed.

Article 10.26 Agreement to Appointment of Arbitrators

For purposes of Article 39 of the ICSID Convention and Article 7 of Schedule C to the ICSID Additional Facility Rules, and without prejudice to an objection to an arbitrator based on Article 10.25(3) or on a ground other than nationality:

(a)   the disputing Party agrees to the appointment of each individual member of a Tribunal established under the ICSID Convention or the ICSID Additional Facility Rules;

(b)   a disputing investor referred to in Article 10.17 may submit a claim to arbitration, or continue a claim, under the ICSID Convention or the ICSID Additional Facility Rules, only on condition that the disputing investor agrees in writing to the appointment of each individual member of the Tribunal; and

(c)   a disputing investor referred to in Article 10.18(1) may submit a claim to arbitration, or continue a claim, under the ICSID Convention or the ICSID Additional Facility Rules, only on condition that the disputing investor and the enterprise agree in writing to the appointment of each individual member of the Tribunal.

Article 10.27 Consolidation

1.   A Tribunal established under this Article shall be established under the UNCITRAL Arbitration Rules and shall conduct its proceedings in accordance with those Rules, except as modified by this Section.

2.   Where a Tribunal established under this Article is satisfied that claims have been submitted to arbitration under Article 10.21 that have a question of law or fact in common, the Tribunal may, in the interests of fair and efficient resolution of the claims, and after hearing the disputing parties, by order:

    (a)   assume jurisdiction over, and hear and determine together, all or part of the claims; or

    (b)   assume jurisdiction over, and hear and determine one or more of the claims, the determination of which it believes would assist in the resolution of the others.

3.   A disputing party that seeks an order under paragraph 2 shall request the Secretary-General to establish a Tribunal and shall specify in the request:

    (a)   the name of the disputing Party or disputing investors against which the order is sought;

    (b)   the nature of the order sought; and

    (c)   the grounds on which the order is sought.

4.   The disputing party shall deliver a copy of the request to the disputing Party or disputing investors against which the order is sought.

5.   Within sixty (60) days of receipt of the request, the Secretary-General shall establish a Tribunal comprising three arbitrators. The Secretary-General shall appoint the presiding arbitrator from the roster referred to in Article 10.25(4). In the event that no such presiding arbitrator is available to serve, the Secretary-General shall appoint, from the ICSID Panel of Arbitrators, a presiding arbitrator who is not a national of any of the Parties. The Secretary-General shall appoint the two other members from the roster referred to in Article 10.25(4), and to the extent not available from that roster, from the ICSID Panel of Arbitrators, and to the extent not available from that Panel, in the discretion of the Secretary-General. One member shall be a national of the disputing Party and one member shall be a national of the Party of the disputing investors.

6.   Where a Tribunal has been established under this Article, a disputing investor that has submitted a claim to arbitration under Article 10.17 or 10.18 and that has not been named in a request made under paragraph 3 may make a written request to the Tribunal that it be included in an order made under paragraph 2, and shall specify in the request:

    (a)   the name, address and the type of business of the enterprise of the disputing investor;

    (b)   the nature of the order sought; and

    (c)   the grounds on which the order is sought.

7.   A disputing investor referred to in paragraph 6 shall deliver a copy of its request to the disputing parties named in a request made under paragraph 3.

8.   A Tribunal established under Article 10.21 shall not have jurisdiction to decide a claim, or a part of a claim, over which a Tribunal established under this Article has assumed jurisdiction.

9.   On application of a disputing party, a Tribunal established under this Article, pending its decision under paragraph 2, may order that the proceedings of a Tribunal established under Article 10.21 be stayed, unless the latter Tribunal has already adjourned its proceedings, until there is a decision about the propriety of consolidation.

10.   A disputing Party shall deliver to the Secretariat, within 15 days of receipt by the disputing Party, a copy of:

> (a)   a request for arbitration made under paragraph (1) of Article 36 of the ICSID Convention;

> (b)   a notice of arbitration made under Article 2 of Schedule C of the ICSID Additional Facility Rules;

> (c)   a notice of arbitration given under the UNCITRAL Arbitration Rules; or

> (d)   a request for arbitration made under ICC Arbitration Rules.

11.   A disputing Party shall deliver to the Secretariat a copy of a request made under paragraph 3:

> (a)   within fifteen (15) days of receipt of the request, in the case of a request made by a disputing investor; or

> (b)   within fifteen (15) days of making the request, in the case of a request made by the disputing Party.

12.   A disputing Party shall deliver to the Secretariat a copy of a request made under paragraph 6 within fifteen (15) days of receipt of the request.

13.   The Secretariat shall maintain a public register of the documents referred to in paragraphs 10, 11 and 12.

Article 10.28 Notice

A disputing Party shall deliver to the other Party:

(a)   written notice of a claim that has been submitted to arbitration no later than thirty (30) days after the date that the claim is submitted; and

(b)   copies of all pleadings filed in the arbitration.

Article 10.29 Participation by a Party

On written notice to the disputing parties, a Party may make submissions to a Tribunal on a question of interpretation of this Agreement.

Article 10.30 Documents

1.   A Party shall be entitled, at its own cost, to receive from the disputing Party a copy of:

(a)   the evidence that has been tendered to the Tribunal according to this Section; and

(b)   the written argument of the disputing parties.

2.   A Party receiving information pursuant to paragraph 1 shall treat the confidential information as if it were a disputing Party.

Article 10.31 Venue of Arbitration

Unless the disputing parties agree otherwise, a Tribunal established under this Section shall hold an arbitration in the territory of a party to the New York Convention, selected in accordance with:

(a)   the ICSID Additional Facility Rules if the arbitration is under those Rules, or the ICSID Convention;

(b)   the UNCITRAL Arbitration Rules if the arbitration is under those Rules; or

(c)   the ICC Arbitration Rules if the arbitration is under those Rules.

Article 10.32 Governing Law

1.   A Tribunal established under this Section shall decide the issues in dispute in accordance with this Agreement and applicable rules of international law.

2.   An interpretation by the Commission of a provision of this Agreement shall be binding on a Tribunal established under this Section.

Article 10.33 Interpretation of Annexes

1.   Where a disputing Party asserts as a defense that the measure alleged to be a breach is within the scope of a reservation or exception set out in those Annexes, on request of the disputing Party, the Tribunal shall request the interpretation of the Commission on the issue. The Commission, within sixty (60) days of delivery of the request, shall submit in writing its interpretation to the Tribunal.

2.   Further to Article 10.32(2), a Commission interpretation submitted under paragraph 1 shall be binding on the Tribunal established under this Section. If the Commission fails to submit an interpretation within sixty (60) days, the Tribunal shall decide the issue.

Article 10.34 Expert Reports

Without prejudice to the appointment of other kinds of experts where authorized by the applicable arbitration rules, a Tribunal, at the request of a disputing party or, on its own initiative, may appoint one or more experts to report to it in writing on any factual issue concerning the controversy.

Article 10.35 Interim Measures of Protection

A Tribunal established under this Section may request, or the disputing parties may petition to, in accordance with domestic legislation, national courts for imposing an interim measure of protection to preserve the rights of a disputing party, or to ensure that the Tribunal's jurisdiction is made fully effective. A Tribunal may not order attachment or enjoin the application of the measure alleged to constitute a breach referred to in Article 10.17 or 10.18.

Article 10.36 Final Award

1.   Where a Tribunal established under this Section makes a final award against a Party, the Tribunal may award, only:

 (a)   monetary damages and any applicable interest; or

 (b)   restitution of property, in which case the award shall provide that the disputing Party may pay monetary damages and any applicable interest in lieu of restitution.

A tribunal may also award costs in accordance with the applicable arbitration rules.

2.   Subject to paragraph 1, where a claim is made under Article 10.18(1):

 (a)   an award of restitution of property shall provide that restitution be made to the enterprise; or

 (b)   an award of monetary damages and any applicable interest shall provide that the sum be paid to the enterprise.

3.   The award shall provide that it is made without prejudice to any right that any person may have in the relief under applicable domestic law.

Article 10.37 Finality and Enforcement of an Award

1.   An award made by a Tribunal established under this Section shall have no binding force except between the disputing parties and in respect of the particular case.

2.   Subject to paragraph 3 and the applicable review procedure for an award, a disputing party shall abide by and comply with an award without delay.

3.   A disputing party may not seek enforcement of a final award until:

 (a)   in the case of a final award made under the ICSID Convention

  (i)   120 days have elapsed from the date the award was rendered and no disputing party has requested revision or annulment of the award, or

  (ii)   explanation, revision or annulment proceedings have been completed; and

 (b)   in the case of a final award under the ICSID Additional Facility Rules or the UNCITRAL Arbitration Rules

    (i)   ninety (90) days have elapsed from the date the award was rendered and no disputing party has commenced a proceeding to revise, set aside or annul the award, or

    (ii)   a court has dismissed or allowed an application to revise, set aside or annul the award and there is no further appeal.

4.   Each Party shall provide for the enforcement of an award in its territory.

5.   If a disputing Party fails to abide by or comply with a final award, the Commission, on delivery of a request by a Party whose investor was a party to the arbitration, shall establish a panel under Article 19.09 (Request for an Arbitral Group). The requesting Party may seek in such proceedings:

    (a)   a determination that the failure to abide by or comply with the final award is inconsistent with the obligations of this Agreement; and

    (b)   a recommendation that the Party abide by or comply with the final award.

6.   A disputing investor may seek enforcement of an arbitration award under the New York Convention, or the ICSID Convention, regardless of whether proceedings have been taken under paragraph 5.

7.   A claim that is submitted to arbitration under this Section shall be considered to arise out of a commercial relationship or transaction for purposes of Article I of the New York Convention.

Article 10.38 General Provision

Time when a Claim is Submitted to Arbitration

1.   A claim is submitted to arbitration under this Section when:

    (a)   the request for arbitration under paragraph (1) of Article 36 of the ICSID Convention has been received by the Secretary-General;

    (b)   the notice of arbitration under Article 2 of Schedule C of the ICSID Additional Facility Rules has been received by the Secretary-General;

    (c)   the notice of arbitration given under the UNCITRAL Arbitration Rules is received by the disputing Party; or

    (d)   the request for arbitration under Article 4 of the ICC Arbitration Rules has been received by the Secretariat.

Delivery of Notifications and Other Documents

2.   Delivery of notifications and other documents on a Party shall be made to the place named for that Party in Annex 10.38(2).

Receipts under Insurance or Guarantee Contracts

3.   In an arbitration under this Section, a Party shall not assert, as a defense, counterclaim, right of setoff or otherwise, that the disputing investor has received or will receive, pursuant to an insurance or guarantee contract, indemnification or other compensation for all or part of its alleged damages.

Publication of an Award

4.   The awards shall be published only if there is an agreement in writing by the disputing parties.

Section C - Definitions

Article 10.39 Definitions

For purposes of this Chapter, the following terms shall be understood as:

Additional Facility Rules of ICSID: Additional Facility Rules of ICSID established in 1978;

claim: the claim made by the disputing investor against a Party under Section B of this Chapter;

disputing investor: an investor that makes a claim under Section B of this Chapter;

disputing parties: the disputing investor and the disputing Party;

disputing Party: a Party against which a claim is made under Section B of this Chapter;

disputing party: the disputing investor or the disputing Party;

enterprise: an "enterprise" as defined in Chapter 2 (General Definitions), and a branch of an enterprise;

enterprise of a Party: an enterprise constituted or organized under the law of a Party, and a branch located in the territory of a Party and carrying out business activities there;

ICC: the International Chamber of Commerce;

ICSID: the International Centre for Settlement of Investment Disputes;

ICSID Convention: the Convention on the Settlement of Investment Disputes between States and Nationals of other States, done at Washington, March 18, 1965;

investment: any kind of goods or rights of any nature acquired or used with the purpose of obtaining an economic profit or other business objective, acquired with resources transferred or reinvested by an investor, and including:

(a)   an enterprise, shares in an enterprise, shares in the capital of an enterprise that allow the owner to participate in its income or profits. Debt instruments of an enterprise and loans to an enterprise where:

    (i)   the enterprise is an affiliate of the investor, or

    (ii)   the date of maturity of the debt instrument or loan is at least 3 years,

(b)   a stake in an enterprise that grants to the owner the right to participate in the assets of this enterprise in a liquidation, provided that they do not arise from a debt instrument or a loan excluded under subparagraph (a);

(c)   real estate or other properties, tangible or intangible, including rights in the intellectual property field, as well as any other proprietary right (such as mortgages, liens, usufruct and similar rights), acquired with the expectation of or used with the purpose of obtaining an economic benefit or other business objectives;

(d)   share or benefits arising from the allocation of capital or other resources to the developing of an economic activity in the territory of a Party according, inter alia; to:

    (i)   contracts that involve the presence of the property of an investor in the territory of a Party, including concessions and construction and turnkey contracts, or

    (ii)   contracts where remuneration substantially depends on the production, income or profits of an enterprise, but investment does not include:

(e)   a payment obligation or a credit granted to the State or a state enterprise,

(f)   monetary claims exclusively derived from:

    (i)   commercial contracts for the sale of goods or services by a national or an enterprise in the territory of a Party to an enterprise in the territory of the other Party, or

    (ii)   a credit granted in relation to a commercial transaction, of which expiration date is less than 3 years, such as trade financing, except a loan covered by the provisions of subparagraph (a); or

(g)   any other monetary claim that does not involve the kinds of interests as set out in subparagraphs (a) through (d);

investor of a Party: a Party or a state enterprise of a Party or a national or an enterprise of a Party that makes or has made an investment in the territory of the other Party;

New York Convention: the United Nations Convention on the Recognition and Enforcement of Foreign Arbitral Awards, done at New York, June 10, 1958;

Secretary-General: the Secretary-General of the ICSID, or the ICC;

transfers: remittance and international payments;

Tribunal: an arbitration tribunal established under Article 10.21,and Article 10.27; and

UNCITRAL Arbitration Rules: the arbitration rules of the United Nations Commission on International Trade Law, approved by the United Nations General Assembly on December 15, 1976.

ANNEX 10.38(2)
DELIVERY OF NOTIFICATIONS AND OTHER DOCUMENTS

1.   For purposes of the Article 10.38(2), the place for the delivery of notifications and other documents will be:

(a)   in the case of Panama:
        Ministry of Trade and Industries
        Vice-ministry of Foreign Trade
        Vía Ricardo J. Alfaro, Plaza Edison, Piso #3
        Panamá, República de Panamá

(b)   in the case of the ROC:
        Ministry of Economic Affairs
        No.15 Fu-Chou Street, Taipei
        Taiwan
        The Republic of China

2.   The Parties shall communicate any change of the designated place for the delivery of notifications and other documents.

CHAPTER 11
CROSS-BORDER TRADE IN SERVICES

Article 11.01 Definitions

For purposes of this Chapter, the following terms shall be understood as:

cross-border provision of a service or cross-border trade in services: the provision of a service:

(a)   from the territory of a Party into the territory of the other Party;

(b)   in the territory of a Party to the services consumer of the other Party; or

(c)   by a service provider of a Party, through presence of natural persons of a

Party in the territory of the other Party, but does not include the provision of a service in the territory of a Party by an investment, as defined in Article 10.39 (Definitions), in that territory;

enterprise: an "enterprise" as defined in Chapter 2 (General Definitions);

enterprise of a Party: an enterprise constituted or organized under the law of a Party, and a branch located in the territory of a Party and carrying out business activities there;

quantitative restriction: a non-discriminatory measure that imposes limitations on:

(a)   the number of service providers, whether in the form of a quota, a monopoly or an economic needs test, or by any other quantitative means; or

(b)   the operations of any service provider, whether in the form of a quota or an economic needs test, or by any other quantitative means;

services provided in the performing of government functions: any cross-border service provided by a public institution in non-commercial conditions and without competing with one or more service providers; and.

service provider of a Party: a person of a Party that provides or seeks to provide a cross-border service.

Article 11.02 Scope and Coverage

1.   This Chapter applies to measures adopted or maintained by a Party relating to cross-border trade in services by service providers of the other Party, including measures respecting:

(a)   the production, distribution, marketing, sale and delivery of a service;

(b)   the purchase or use of, or payment for, a cross-border service;

(c)   the access to and use of distribution and transportation systems in connection with the provision of a cross-border service;

(d)   the access to networks and public services of telecommunication and its use;

(e)   the presence in its territory of a cross-border service provider of the other Party; and

(f)   the provision of a bond or other form of financial security as a condition for the provision of a cross-border service.

2.   For purposes of this Chapter, it shall be understood that the measures adopted or maintained by a Party include measures adopted or maintained by non-governmental institutions or bodies in the performance of regulatory, administrative or other functions of a governmental nature delegated to them by the Party.

3.   This Chapter does not apply to:

(a)   subsidies or grants provided by a Party or a state enterprise, including government-supported loans, guarantees and insurance;

(b)   air services, including domestic and international air transportation services, whether scheduled or non-scheduled, and related services in support of air services, other than

(i)   aircraft repair and maintenance services during which an aircraft is withdrawn from service,

(ii)   the selling and marketing of air transport services, and

(iii)   computer reservation system (CRS) services;

(c)   government services or functions such as law enforcement, correctional services, income security or unemployment insurance or social security services, social welfare, public education, public training, health, and child care;

(d)   cross-border financial services; and

(e)   government procurement done by a Party or state enterprise.

4.   Nothing in this Chapter shall be construed to impose any obligation on a Party with respect to a national of the other Party seeking access to its employment market, or employed on a permanent basis in its territory, or to confer any right on that national with respect to that access or employment.

Article 11.03 National Treatment

1.   Each Party shall accord to cross-border services and service providers of the other Party treatment no less favorable than that it accords, in like circumstances, to its own services and service providers.

2.   Specific commitments assumed under this Article shall not be construed to require any Party to compensate for any inherent competitive disadvantages which result from the foreign character of the relevant services or service suppliers.

Article 11.04 Most-Favored-Nation Treatment

Each Party shall accord to cross-border services and service providers of the other Party treatment no less favorable than that it accords, in like circumstances, to services and service providers of any non-Party.

Article 11.05 Standard of Treatment

Each Party shall accord to cross-border services and service providers of the other Party the better of the treatment required by Articles 11.03 and 11.04.

Article 11.06 Local Presence

No Party may require a service provider of the other Party to establish or maintain a representative office or any form of enterprise, or to be resident, in its territory as a condition for the cross-border provision of a service.

Article 11.07 Permission, Authorization, Licensing and Certification

With a view to ensuring that any measure adopted or maintained by a Party relating to the permission, authorization, licensing or certification of nationals of the other Party does not constitute an unnecessary barrier to cross-border trade, each Party shall endeavor to ensure that any such measure:

(a)   is based on objective and transparent criteria, such as competence and the ability to provide a cross-border service;

(b)   is not more burdensome than necessary to ensure the quality of a crossborder service; and

(c)   does not constitute a disguised restriction on the cross-border provision of a service.

Article 11.08 Reservations

1.   Articles 11.03,11.04 and 11.06 do not apply to:

   (a)   any existing non-conforming measure that is maintained by

      (i)   a Party at the national level, as set out in its Schedule to Annex I,

      (ii)   a local or municipal government;

   (b)   the continuation or prompt renewal of any non-conforming measure referred to in subparagraph (a) or

   (c)   an amendment to any non-conforming measure referred to in subparagraph (a) to the extent that the amendment does not decrease the conformity of the measure, as it existed immediately before the amendment, with Articles 11.03,11.04 and 11.06.

2.   Articles 11.03, 11.04 and 11.06 do not apply to any measure that a Party adopts or maintains with respect to sectors, sub-sectors or activities, as set out in its Schedule to Annex II.

Article 11.09 Quantitative Restrictions

1.   Each Party shall set out in its Schedule to Annex V any quantitative restriction that it maintains.

2.   Each Party shall notify the other Party of any quantitative restriction that it adopts, other than at the local government level, after the date of entry into force of this Agreement and shall set out the restriction in its Schedule as referred to in paragraph 1.

3.   Regularly, at least every 2 years, the Parties shall endeavour to negotiate with the aim of liberalizing or eliminating:

   (a)   existing quantitative restrictions maintained by a Party, according to the list referred to in paragraph 1; or

(b)   quantitative restrictions adopted by a Party after the entry into force of this Agreement.

Article 11.10 Denial of Benefits

Subject to prior notification and consultation in accordance with Articles 17.04 (Provision of Information) and 19.06 (Consultations), a Party may deny the benefits of this Chapter to a service provider of the other Party where the Party decides, according to its effective law that the service is being provided by an enterprise that is owned or controlled by persons of a non-Party having no substantial business activities in the territory of the other Party.

Article 11.11 Future Liberalization

The Parties, through future negotiations to be convened by the Commission, shall deepen the liberalization reached in different service sectors, with the aim of eliminating the remaining restrictions listed under Article 11.08(1) and (2).

Article 11.12 Procedures

The Parties shall establish procedures for:

(a)   a Party to notify and include in its relevant Schedule

    (i)   amendments of measures referred to in Article 11.08(1) and (2), and

    (ii)   quantitative restrictions in accordance with Article 11.09; and

(b)   consultations on reservations or quantitative restrictions for further liberalization, if any.

Article 11.13 Disclosure of Confidential Information

No provision in this Chapter may be construed as imposing on the Parties the obligation to provide confidential information of which the disclosure may be an obstacle to the observance of laws or otherwise be damaging to the public interest, or that may injure legitimate trade interests of state and private enterprises.

Article 11.14 Committee on Investment and Cross-border Trade in Services

1.   The Parties hereby establish the Committee on Investment and Cross-border Trade in Services, as set out in Annex 11.14.

2.   The Committee shall hear matters relating to this Chapter and Chapter 10 (Investment) and, without prejudice to the provisions of Article 18.05(2)(Committees), shall have the following functions:

(a)   supervising the implementation and administration of Chapters 10 (Investment) and 11 (Cross-border Trade in Services);

(b)   discussing matters relating to investment and cross-border trade in services presented by a Party;

(c)   analyzing matters that are discussed in other international fora;

(d)   facilitating the exchange of information between the Parties and cooperating in giving advice on investment and cross-border trade in services; and

(e)   establishing working groups or convening panels of experts on matters of interest to the Parties.

3.   The Committee shall meet when necessary or at any other time at the request of either Party. Representatives of other institutions may also take part in its meetings if the relevant authorities deem it appropriate.

ANNEX 11.14
COMMITTEE ON INVESTMENT AND CROSS-BORDER TRADE IN SERVICES

The Committee on Investment and Cross-border Trade in Services set up under Article 11.14 shall be composed of:

(a)   in the case of Panama, the Ministry of Trade and Industries, represented by the Vice-ministry of Foreign Trade or its successor; and

(b)   in the case of the ROC, the Ministry of Economic Affairs, represented by the Bureau of Foreign Trade or its successor.

CHAPTER 12
FINANCIAL SERVICES

Article 12.01 Definitions

For purposes of this Chapter, the following terms shall be understood as:

cross-border provision of financial services or cross-border trade of financial

services: the provision of a financial service:

(a)   from the territory of a Party to the territory of the other Party;

(b)   in the territory of a Party to a consumer of services of the other Party; or

(c)   by a service provider of a Party through the presence of natural persons of a Party in the territory of the other Party;

disputing investor: an investor that submits to arbitration a claim under Article 12.19 and Section B of Chapter 10 (Investment);

enterprise: "enterprise" defined in Chapter 2 (General Definitions);

financial institution: any financial intermediary or other enterprise that is authorized to do financial service business and regulated or supervised as a financial institution under the law of the Party in whose territory it is located;

financial institution of the other Party: a financial institution, including a branch, established under the existing law located in the territory of a Party that is owned or controlled by persons of the other Party;

financial service: a service of a financial nature, including bank, insurance, reinsurance, securities, futures, and a service related or auxiliary to a service of a financial nature;

investment: any kind of goods or rights of any nature acquired or used with the purpose of obtaining an economic profit or other business objective, acquired with resources transferred or reinvested by an investor, and including:

(a)   an enterprise, shares in an enterprise, shares in the capital of an enterprise that allow the owner to participate in its income or profits. Debt instruments of an enterprise and loans to an enterprise where:

>   (i)   the enterprise is an affiliate of the investor, or

>   (ii)   the date of maturity of the debt instrument or loan is at least 3 years;

(b)   a stake in an enterprise that grants to the owner the right to participate in the assets of this enterprise in a liquidation, provided that they do not arise from a debt instrument or a loan excluded under subparagraph (a);

(c)   real estate or other properties, tangible or intangible, including rights in the intellectual property field, as well as any other proprietary right (such as mortgages, liens, usufruct and similar rights), acquired with the expectation of or used with the purpose of obtaining an economic benefit or other business objectives;

(d)   share or benefits arising from the allocation of capital or other resources to the developing of an economic activity in the territory of a Party according, inter alia, to:

>   (i)   contracts that involve the presence of the propriety of an investor in the territory of a Party, including concessions and construction and turnkey contracts, or

>   (ii)   contracts where remuneration substantially depends on the production, income or profits of an enterprise, and

(e)   a loan granted by a provider of cross-border financial services or a debt instrument owned by the provider, except a loan to a financial institution or a debt instrument issued by it, but investment does not include:

(f)   a payment obligation or a credit granted by the State or a state enterprise;

(g)   monetary claims exclusively derived from:

(i) commercial contracts for the sale of goods or services by a national or an enterprise in the territory of a Party to an enterprise in the territory of the other Party, or

(ii) a credit granted in relation to a commercial transaction, of which expiration date is less than 3 years, such as trade financing, except a loan covered by the provisions of subparagraph (a);

(h) any other monetary claim that does not involve the kinds of interests as set out in subparagraphs (a) through (e); or

(i) a loan to a financial institution or a debt instrument issued by a financial institution, except if it is a loan to or a debt instrument issued by a financial institution treated as capital for regulatory purposes by a Party in whose territory the financial institution is located;

investment of an investor of a Party: an investment owned or directly controlled by an investor of the Party. In the case of an enterprise, an investment is property of an investor of a Party if this investor holds more than fifty per cent (50%) of it equity interest. An investment is controlled by an investor of a Party if the investor has the power to:

(a) designate a majority of directors; or

(b) legally manage its operations in any other way;

investor of a Party: a Party or a state enterprise thereof, or a national or enterprise of the Party, that seeks to make, makes or has made an investment in the territory of the other Party. The intention of trying to realize an investment may demonstrate, among other forms, by means of juridical acts tending to materialize the investment, or being in process of compromising the necessary resources to realize it;

new financial service: a financial service not provided in the territory of a Party that is provided within the territory of the other Party, and includes any new form of delivery of a financial service or the sale of a financial product that is not sold in the territory of a Party;

provider of cross-border financial services of a Party: a person authorized by a Party who undertakes the business of providing financial services in its territory and who tries to conduct or conducts cross-border financial services;

provider of financial services of a Party: a person of a Party who undertakes the business of providing some financial service in the territory of the other Party;

public entity: a central bank or monetary authority of a Party, or any financial institution of public nature owned or controlled by a Party, and does not have commercial functions;

regulatory authorities: any governmental body that exercises a supervising authority over providers of financial services or financial institutions; and

self-regulatory organization: any non-governmental body, including any securities or futures exchange or market, clearing agency, or other organization or association, that exercises its own or delegated regulatory or supervisory authority over financial service providers or financial institutions.

Article 12.02 Scope and Coverage

1. This Chapter applies to measures adopted or maintained by a Party relating to:

    (a) financial institutions of the other Party;

    (b) investors of the other Party, and investments of such investors, in financial institutions in the territory of the Party; and

    (c) cross-border trade in financial services.

2. Nothing in this Chapter shall be construed to prevent a Party, or its public entities, from exclusively conducting or providing in its territory:

    (a) activities conducted by the monetary authorities or by any other public institution with the aim of implementing monetary or exchange policies;

    (b) activities or services forming part of a public retirement plan or statutory system of social security; or

    (c) other activities or services for the account or with the guarantee or using the financial resources of the Party, or its public entities.

3. The provisions of this Chapter shall prevail upon those of other Chapters, except where there is an explicit reference to these Chapters.

4. Article 10.11 (Expropriation and Compensation) forms a part of this Chapter.

Article 12.03 Self-regulatory Organizations

Where a Party requires a financial institution or a cross-border financial service provider of the other Party to be a member of, participate in, or have access to, a selfregulatory organization to provide a financial service in or into the territory of that Party, the Party shall ensure observance of the obligations of this Chapter by such selfregulatory organization.

Article 12.04 Right of Establishment

1. The Parties recognize the principle that investors of a Party shall be permitted to establish a financial institution in the territory of the other Party through any forms of establishment and operation that the law of that Party permits.

2. Each Party may impose terms and conditions on establishment of a financial institution that are consistent with Article 12.06.

Article 12.05 Cross-border Trade

1.   No Party may adopt any measure restricting any type of cross-border trade in financial services by cross-border financial service providers of the other Party that the Party permits on the date of entry into force of this Agreement, except to the extent set out in Section B of the Schedule to Annex VI of the Party.

2.   Each Party shall permit persons located in its territory, and its nationals wherever located, to purchase financial services from cross-border financial service providers of the other Party located in the territory of that other Party. This obligation does not require a Party to permit such providers to do business or solicit in its territory. The Parties may define "solicitation" and "doing business" for purposes of this obligation.

3.   Without prejudice to other means of prudential regulation of cross-border trade in financial services, a Party may require the registration of cross-border financial service providers of the other Party and of financial instruments.

Article 12.06 National Treatment

1.   Each Party shall accord to investors of the other Party treatment no less favorable than that it accords to its own investors with respect to the establishment, acquisition, expansion, management, conduct, operation, and sale or other disposition of similar financial institutions and investments in similar financial institutions in its territory.

2.   Each Party shall accord to financial institutions of the other Party and to investments of investors of the other Party in financial institutions treatment no less favorable than that it accords to its own similar financial institutions and to investments of its own investors in similar financial institutions, with respect to the establishment, acquisition, expansion, management, conduct, operation, and sale or other disposition of financial institutions and investments.

3.   Subject to Article 12.05, where a Party permits the cross-border provision of a financial service it shall accord to the cross-border financial service providers of the other Party treatment no less favorable than that it accords to its own similar financial service providers, with respect to the provision of such service.

4.   A Party's treatment of similar financial institutions and similar cross-border financial service providers of the other Party, whether different or identical to that accorded to its own institutions or providers in like circumstances, is consistent with paragraphs 1 through 3 if the treatment affords equal competitive opportunities.

5.   A Party's treatment does not afford equal competitive opportunities if it disadvantages similar financial institutions and similar cross-border financial service providers of the other Party in their ability to provide financial services as compared with the ability of the Party's own financial institutions and similar financial service providers to provide such services.

Article 12.07 Most-Favored-Nation Treatment

Each Party shall accord to investors, financial institutions, investments of investors in financial institutions and cross-border financial service providers of the other Party treatment no less favorable than that it accords in similar circumstances to the investors, financial institutions, investments of investors in financial institutions and cross-border financial service providers of any non-Parties.

Article 12.08 Recognition and Harmonization

1.   Where a Party applies measures included in this Chapter it may recognize the prudential measures of the other Party or of a non-Party. This recognition may be:

(a)   unilaterally granted;

(b)   reached through harmonization or other means; or

(c)   based on an agreement or arrangement with the other Party or with the non-Party.

2.   The Party that grants the recognition of prudential measures according to paragraph 1, shall give the other Party appropriate opportunities to show the existence of circumstances in which there are or shall be equivalent regulations, supervision and implementation of regulations and, as appropriate, procedures to share information between the Parties.

3.   Where a Party grants recognition to the prudential measures according to paragraph 1(c) and the circumstances of paragraph 2 exist, this Party shall give appropriate opportunities to the other Party to negotiate the accession to the agreement or arrangement, or to negotiate a similar agreement or arrangement.

4.   No provision of this Article shall be construed as the application of a mandatory procedure of review of the financial system or the prudential measures of a Party by the other Party.

Article 12.09 Exceptions

1.   Nothing in this Chapter shall be construed to prevent a Party from adopting or maintaining prudential measures such as:

(a)   the protection of fund administrators, investors, depositors, financial market participants, policyholders, policy claimants, or persons to whom a fiduciary duty is owed by a financial institution or cross-border financial service provider;

(b)   the maintenance of the safety, soundness, integrity or financial responsibility of financial institutions or cross-border financial service providers;, and

(c)   ensuring the integrity and stability of the financial system of a Party.

2.   Nothing in this Chapter applies to non-discriminatory measures of general application taken by any public entity in pursuit of monetary and related credit policies or exchange rate policies. This paragraph shall not affect a Party's obligations of Investment Performance Requirements with respect to measures covered by Chapter 10 (Investment) or Article 12.17.

3.   Article 12.06 shall not apply to the granting by a Party to a financial institution of an exclusive right to provide a financial service referred to in Article 12.02 paragraph 2(b).

4.   Notwithstanding Article 12.17(1), (2) and (3), a Party may prevent or limit transfers by a financial institution or cross-border financial service provider to, or for the benefit of, an affiliate of or person related to such institution or service provider, through the equitable, and non-discriminatory application of measures relating to maintenance of the safety, soundness, integrity or financial responsibility of financial institutions or cross-border financial service providers. This paragraph does not prejudice any other provision of this Agreement that permits a Party to restrict transfers.

Article 12.10 Transparency

In addition to the Article 17.03 (Publication), each Party shall undertake the following:

1.   Each Party's regulatory authorities sha ll make available to interested persons all related information for completing applications relating to the provision of financial services.

2.   On the request of an applicant, the regulatory authorities shall inform the applicant of the status of its application. If such authorities require additional information from the applicant, they shall notify the applicant without undue delay.

3.   Each regulatory authority shall make an administrative decision on a completed application of an investor in a fina ncial institution, a financial institution or a cross-border financial service provider of the other Party relating to the provision of a financial service within 120 days. The authority shall promptly notify the applicant of the decision. An application shall not be considered complete until all relevant hearings are held and all necessary information is received. Where it is not practicable for a decision to be made within 120 days, the regulatory authority shall notify the applicant without undue delay and shall endeavor to make the decision within 60 days thereafter.

4.   Nothing in this Chapter requires a Party to disclose or allow access to:

   (a)   information related to the financial affairs and accounts of individual customers of financial institutions or cross-border financial service providers; or

   (b)   any confidential information, the disclosure of which would impede law enforcement or otherwise be contrary to the public interest or prejudice legitimate commercial interests of particular enterprises.

Article 12.11 Committee on Financial Services

1.   The Parties hereby establish the Committee on Financial Services, as set out in Annex 12.11.

2.   The Committee shall hear matters relating to this Chapter and, without prejudice to the provisions of Article 18.05(2) (Committees), shall have the following functions:

   (a)   supervising the implementation of this Chapter and its further elaboration;

   (b)   considering issues regarding financial services that are referred to it by a Party;

(c)   participating in the dispute settlement procedures in accordance with Articles 12.18 and 12.19; and

(d)   facilitating the exchange of information between the supervising authorities, cooperating on advising about prudential regulation and endeavoring to harmonize the normative frameworks for regulations as well as the other policies, if it considers appropriate.

3.   The Committee shall meet as necessary or by request of either Party to assess the implementation of this Chapter.

Article 12.12 Consultations

1.   Without prejudice to Article 19.06 (Consultations), a Party may request consultations with the other Party regarding any matter arising under this Agreement that affects financial services. The other Party shall give sympathetic consideration to the request. The consulting Parties shall report the results of their consultations to the Committee at its meeting.

2.   Consultations under this Article shall include officials of the authorities specified in Annex 12.11.

3.   A Party may request that regulatory authorities of the other Party participate in consultations under this Article regarding measures of general application of that other Party which may affect the operations of financial institutions or cross-border financial service providers in the territory of the requesting Party.

4.   Nothing in this Article shall be construed to require regulatory authorities participating in consultations under paragraph 3 to disclose information or take any action that would interfere with individual regulatory, supervisory, administrative or enforcement matters.

5.   Where a Party requires information for supervisory purposes concerning a financial institution in the territory of the other Party or a cross-border financial service provider in the territory of the other Party, the Party may approach the competent regulatory authority of the other Party to seek the information.

Article 12.13 New Financial Services and Data Processing

1.   Each Party shall allow a financial institution of the other Party to provide any new financial service of a type similar to those that the Party allows to its own financial institutions according to its law. The Party may decide the institutional and juridical forms through which this service shall be offered and may require authorization for the provision of the service. Where an authorization is required, the relevant dispositions shall be issued in a reasonable period of time and may only be denied for prudential reasons, provided that the reasons are not contrary to the law of the Party, and to Articles 12.06 and 12.07.

2.   Each Party shall allow the financial institutions of the other Party to transfer information for processing into or out of the territory of the Party, using any means authorized within it, if this is necessary to conduct regular business activities in these institutions.

3.   Each Party commits itself to respecting the confidentiality of the information processed within its territory and originating in a financial institution located in the other Party.

Article 12.14 Senior Management and Board of Directors

1.   No Party may require financial institutions of the other Party to engage individuals of any particular nationality as senior managerial or other essential personnel.

2.   No Party may require that the board of directors or administrative council of a financial institution of the other Party be composed of nationals of the Party, persons residing in the territory of the Party, or a combination thereof.

Article 12.15 Reservations and Specific Commitments

1.   Articles12.04 through 12.07, 12.13 and 12.14 do not apply to:

    (a)   any existing non-conforming measure that is maintained by a Party at the national level, as set out in Section A of its Schedule to Annex VI;

    (b)   the continuation or prompt renewal of any non-conforming measure refe rred to in subparagraph (a); or

    (c)   an amendment to any non-conforming measure referred to in subparagraph (a) to the extent that the amendment does not decrease the conformity of the measure, as it existed immediately before the amendment, with Articles 12.04 through 12.07, 12.13 and 12.14.

2.   Articles 12.04 through 12.07, 12.13 and 12.14 do not apply to any nonconforming measure that a Party adopts or maintains in accordance with Section B of its Schedule to Annex VI.

3.   Section C of each Party's Schedule to Annex VI sets out certain specific commitments by that Party.

4.   In Chapters 10 (Investment) and 11 (Cross-border Trade in Services) a reservation on matters relating to local presence, national treatment, most-favorednation treatment, senior management and board of directors and administrative council shall be deemed to constitute a reservation from Article 12.04 through 12.07, 12.13 and 12.14, as the case may be, to the extent that the measure, sector, sub-sector or activity set out in the reservation is covered by this Chapter.

Article 12.16 Denial of Benefits

A Party may partially or wholly deny the benefits arising from this Chapter to a provider of financial services of the other Party or to a provider of cross-border financial services of the other Party, upon notification and consultations, according to Articles 12.10 and 12.12, if the Party determines that the service is being provided by an enterprise that does not conduct substantial trade activities in the territory of the other Party and is owned by persons of a non-Party or is under their control.

Article 12.17 Transfers

1.   Each Party shall permit all transfers relating to an investment of an investor of the other Party in the territory of the Party to be made freely and without delay. Such transfers include:

(a)   profits, dividends, interests, capital gains, royalty payments, management fees, technical assistance and other fees, returns in kind and other amounts derived from the investment;

(b)   proceeds from the sale or liquidation of all or part of the investment;

(c)   payments made under a contract entered into by the investor, or its investment, including payments made pursuant to a loan agreement;

(d)   payments made pursuant to Article 10.11 (Expropriation and Compensation); and

(e)   proceeds from a dispute settlement procedure between a Party and an investor of the other Party pursuant to this Chapter and Section B of Chapter 10 (Investment).

2.   Each Party shall permit transfers to be made without delay in a currency of free convertibility at the market rate of exchange prevailing on the date of transfer.

3.   No Party may require its investors to transfer, or penalize its investors that fail to transfer the income, earnings, profits or other amounts derived from, or attributable to, investments in the territory of the other Party.

4.   Notwithstanding paragraphs 1 and 2, a Party may prevent a transfer through the fair and non-discriminatory application of its laws in cases of:

(a)   bankruptcy, insolvency or the protection of the rights of creditors;

(b)   criminal or penal offenses or confirmed administrative resolutions;

(c)   non-compliance with the requirement to report on currency transfers or other monetary instruments;

(d)   ensuring the satisfaction of judgments and awards in adjudicatory proceedings; or

(e)   ensuring the enforcement of laws and regulations on issues, trade and operations of securities.

5.   Paragraph 3 shall not be construed to prevent a Party from imposing any measure through the fair and non-discriminatory application of its laws relating to the matters set out in paragraph 4.

Article 12.18 Dispute Settlement Between the Parties

1.   Chapter 19 (Dispute Settlement) applies as modified by this Article to the settlement of disputes arising under this Chapter.

2.   The Committee on Financial Services shall maintain by consensus a roster of up to eighteen (18) individuals including five (5) individuals of each Party, who are willing and able to serve as arbitrators in disputes related to this Chapte r. The roster members shall meet the quality set out in Chapter 19 (Dispute Settlement) and have broad practicing experience in financial sectors or financial regulation.

3.   For purposes of constituting the arbitral group, the roster referred to in paragraph 2 shall be used, unless the disputing Parties agree that the arbitral group may comprise individuals not included in this roster, provided that they conform to the requirements under paragraph 2. The president shall always be elected from that roster.

4.   In any dispute where the arbitral group finds a measure to be inconsistent with the obligations of this Chapter when a suspension of benefits is processed under Chapter 19 (Dispute Settlement) and the measure affects:

(a)   only the financial services sector, the complaining Party may suspend benefits only in this sector;

(b)   the financial services sector and any other sector, the complaining Party may suspend benefits in the financial services sector that have an effect equivalent to the purpose of the measure in the Party's financial services sector; or

(c)   only a sector other than the financial services sector, the complaining Party may not suspend benefits in the financial services sector.

Article 12.19 Investment Disputes Settlement in Financial Services Between an Investor of a Party and the Other Party

1.   Section B of Chapter 10 (Investment) shall be incorporated into this Chapter and be made as a part of it.

2.   Where an investor of the other Party submits a claim under Article 10.17 (Claim by an Investor of a Party on Its Own Behalf) or 10.18 (Claim by an Investor of a Party on Behalf of an Enterprise) to arbitration under Section B of Chapter 10 (Investment) against a Party and the disputing Party invokes Article 12.09, on request of the disputing Party, the Tribunal shall refer the matter in writing to the Committee for a decision. The Tribunal may not proceed before the receipt of a decision under this Article.

3.   In a referral pursuant to paragraph 2, the Committee shall decide the issue of whether and to what extent Article 12.09 is a valid defense to the claim of the investor. The Committee shall transmit a copy of its decision to the Tribunal and to the Commission. The decision shall be binding on the Tribunal.

4.   Where the Committee has not decided the issue within sixty (60) days of the receipt of the referral under paragraph 2, the disputing Party or the Party of the disputing investor may request the establishment of an arbitral group under Article 19.09 (Request for an Arbitral Group). The arbitral group shall be constituted in accordance with Article 12.18 and shall transmit its final report to the Committee and to the Tribunal. The report shall be binding on the Tribunal.

5.   Where no request for the establishment of an arbitral group pursuant to paragraph 4 has been made within ten (10) days of the expiration of the 60-day period referred to that paragraph, the Tribunal may proceed to decide the matter.

ANNEX 12.11
COMMITTEE ON FINANCIAL SERVICES

The Committee on Financial Services, established under Article 12.11, shall be composed of:

(a)   in the case of Panama, the Ministry of Trade and Industries through the Vice-ministry of Foreign Trade, or its successor, in consultation with the competent authority as appropriate (Superintendence of Banks, Superintendence of Insurance, Reinsurance and National Commission of Securities); and

(b)   in the case of the ROC, the Ministry of Economic Affairs through the Bureau of Foreign Trade, or its successor, in consultation with the competent authorities as appropriate.

CHAPTER 13
TELECOMMUNICATIONS

Article 13.01 Definitions

For purposes of this Chapter, the following terms shall be understood as:

authorized equipment: terminal or other equipment that has been approved for attachment to the public telecommunications transport network in accordance with a Party's conformity assessment procedures;

conformity assessment procedure: "conformity assessment procedure" as defined in Article 9.01 (Definitions), and includes the procedures referred to in Annex 13.01(A);

enhanced or value-added services: those telecommunications services employing computer processing applications that:

(a)   act on the format, content, code, protocol or similar aspects of a customer's transmitted information;

(b)   provide a customer with additional, different or restructured information; or

(c)   involve customer interaction with stored information;

Intra-corporate communications: subject to Annex 13.01(B), telecommunications through which an enterprise communicates:

(a)   internally, with or among its subsidiaries, branches or affiliates, as defined by each Party; or

(b)   on a non-commercial basis with other persons that are fundamental to the economic activity of the company and that have a continuing contractual relationship with it, but does not include telecommunications services provided to persons other than those described herein;

main provider or dominant operator: a provider with the capacity to deeply affect the conditions of participation (from the point of view of prices and supply) of the telecommunication services in a given market due to its control of essential infrastructure or the use of its market position;

monopoly: a body, including a consortium or a governmental body, maintained or designed according to its law, if so allowed, as the exclusive provider of telecommunication networks or public services in any relevant market in the territory of a Party;

network termination point: the final demarcation of the public telecommunications transport network at the customer's premises;

private telecommunications network: subject to Annex 13.01(B), a telecommunications transport network that is used exclusively for intra-corporate communications or between predetermined persons ;

protocol: a set of rules and formats that govern the exchange of information between two peer entities for purposes of transferring signaling or data information;

public telecommunications transport network: public telecommunications infrastructure which permits telecommunications between and among defined network termination points;

public telecommunications transport service: any telecommunications transport service required by a Party, explicitly or in effect, to be offered to the public generally, including telegraph, telephone, telex and data transmission, that typically involves the real-time transmission of customer-supplied information between two or more points without any end-to-end change in the form or content of the customer information;

standards-related measure: a "standards-related measure" as defined in Article 9.01 (Definitions);

telecommunications: any transmission, emission or reception of signs, signals, writings, images, sounds and information of any kind, through a physical line, radioelectricity, optical means or other electromagnetic systems;

telecommunications service: a service supplied by signal transmission and reception through physical lines, radio-electricity, optical means or other electromagnetic systems, but does not mean distribution by cable, radio broadcasting or other kind of electromagnetic distribution of radio and television programmes; and

terminal equipment: any analog or digital device capable of processing, receiving, switching, signaling or transmitting signals by electromagnetic means and that is connected by radio or wire to a public telecommunications transport network at a termination point.

Article 13.02 Scope and Coverage

1.   This Chapter applies to:

(a)   subject to Annex 13.01(A), measures adopted or maintained by a Party relating to access to and use of public telecommunications transport networks or services by persons of the other Party, including prices fixing and access and use by such persons operating private networks for intracorporate communications;

(b)   measures adopted or maintained by a Party relating to the provision of enhanced or value-added services by persons of the other Party in the territory, or across the borders, of a Party; and

(c)   standards-related measures relating to attachment of terminal or other equipment to public telecommunications transport networks.

2.   Except to ensure that persons operating broadcast stations and cable systems have continued access to and use of public telecommunications transport networks and services, this Chapter does not apply to any measure adopted or maintained by a Party relating to cable or broadcast distribution of radio or television programming.

3.   Nothing in this Chapter shall be construed to:

(a)   require a Party to authorize a person of the other Party to establish, construct, acquire, lease, operate or provide telecommunications transport networks or telecommunications transport services;

(b)   require a Party, or require a Party to oblige any person, to establish, construct, acquire, lease, operate or supply telecommunications transport networks or telecommunications transport services not offered to the public generally;

(c)   prevent a Party from prohibiting persons operating private telecommunication networks from using their networks to provide public telecommunications transport networks or services to third persons; or

(d)   require a Party to oblige a person engaged in the cable or broadcast distribution of radio or television programming to make available its cable or broadcast facilities as a public telecommunications transport network.

Article 13.03 Access to and Use of Public Telecommunications Transport Networks and Services

1.   For purposes of this Article, "non-discriminatory" means on terms and conditions no less favorable than those accorded to any other customer or user of like public telecommunications transport networks or services in like circumstances.

2.   Each Party shall ensure that persons of the other Party have access to and use of any public telecommunications transport network or service, including private leased circuits, offered in its territory or across its borders for the conduct of their business, on reasonable and non-discriminatory terms and conditions, including as set out in the rest part of this Article.

3.   Subject to paragraphs 7, 8 and Annex 13.01(B), each Party shall ensure that such persons are permitted to:

(a)   purchase or lease, and attach terminal or other equipment that interfaces with the public telecommunications transport network;

(b)   interconnect private leased or owned circuits with public telecommunications transport networks in the territory, or across the borders, of that Party, including for use in providing dial-up access to and from their customers or users, or with circuits leased or owned by another person on terms and conditions mutually agreed by those persons, according to those set out in Annex 13.01(B);

(c)   perform switching, signaling and processing functions; and

(d)   use operating protocols of their choice, according to the technical plans of each Party.

4.   Without prejudice to its applicable law, each Party shall ensure that the pricing of public telecommunications transport services reflects economic costs directly related to providing the services. Nothing in this paragraph shall be construed to permit a party to establish cross-subsidization between public telecommunications transport services.

5.   Under Annex 13.01(B), each Party shall ensure that persons of the other Party may use public telecommunications transport networks or services for the movement of information in its territory or across its borders, including for Intra-corporate communications, and for access to information contained in data bases or otherwise stored in machine -readable form in the territory of either Party.

6.   Further to Article 20.02 (General Exceptions), nothing in this Chapter shall be construed to prevent a Party from adopting or enforcing any measure necessary to:

(a)   ensure the security and confidentiality of messages; or

(b)   protect the privacy of subscribers to public telecommunications transport networks or services.

7.   Further to Article 13.05, each Party shall ensure that no condition is imposed on access to and use of public telecommunications transport networks or services, other than that necessary to:

(a)   safeguard the public service responsibilities of providers of public telecommunications ransport networks or services, in particular their ability to make their networks or services available to the public generally; or

(b)   protect the technical integrity of public telecommunications transport networks or services.

8.   Provided that conditions for access to and use of public telecommunications transport networks or services satisfy the criteria set out in paragraph 7, such conditions may include:

(a)   a restriction on resale or shared use of such services;

(b)   a requirement to use specified technical interfaces, including interface protocols, for interconnection with such networks or services;

(c)   a restriction on interconnection of private leased or owned circuits with such networks or services or with circuits leased or owned by another person, where the circuits are used in the provision of public telecommunications transport networks or services; and

(d)   a licensing, permit, concession, registration or notification procedure which, if adopted or maintained, is transparent and applications filed thereunder are processed expeditiously.

Article 13.04 Conditions for the Provision of Enhanced or Value-added Services

1.   Each Party shall ensure that:

(a)   any licensing, permit, concession, registration or notification procedure that it adopts or maintains relating to the provision of enhanced or valueadded services is transparent and non-discriminatory, and that applications filed thereunder are processed diligently; and

(b)   information required under such procedures, adjustable under the existing law of the Parties, to demonstrate that the applicant has the financial solvency to begin providing services or to assess conformity of the applicant's terminal or other equipment with the Party's applicable standards or technical regulations.

2.   Without prejudicing the law of either Party, neither Party may require a service provider of enhanced or value-added services to:

(a)   provide those services to the public generally;

(b)   adjust its rates or price on cost base;

(c)   file a tariff or price;

(d)   interconnect its networks with any particular customer or network; or

(e)   conform with any particular standard or technical regulation for interconnection other than for interconnection to a public telecommunications transport network.

3.   Notwithstanding paragraph 2(c), a Party may require the filing of a tariff by:

(a)   such provider to remedy a practice of that provider that the Party has found in a particular case to be anticompetitive under its law; or

(b)   a monopoly, main provider, incumbent carrier to which Article 13.06 applies.

Article 13.05 Standards-Related Measures

1.   Each Party shall ensure that its standards-related measures relating to the attachment of terminal or other equipment to the public telecommunications transport networks, including those measures relating to the use of testing and measuring equipment for conformity assessment procedures, are adopted or maintained only to the extent necessary to:

(a)   prevent technical damage to public telecommunications transport networks;

(b)   prevent technical interference with, or degradation of, public telecommunications transport services;

(c)   prevent electromagnetic interference, and ensure compatibility, with other uses of the electromagnetic spectrum;

(d)   prevent billing equipment malfunction;

(e)   ensure users' safety and access to public telecommunications transport networks or services; or

(f)   ensure electromagnetic spectrum's efficiency.

2.   A Party may require approval for the attachment to the public telecommunications transport network of terminal or other equipment that is not authorized, provided that the criteria for that approval are consistent with paragraph 1.

3.   Each Party shall ensure that the network termination points for its public telecommunications transport networks are defined on a reasonable and transparent basis.

4.   Neither Party may require separate authorization for equipment that is connected on the customer's side of authorized equipment that serves as a protective device fulfilling the criteria of paragraph 1.

5.   Each Party shall:

(a)   ensure that its conformity assessment procedures are transparent and non-discriminatory and that applications filed thereunder are processed expeditiously;

(b)   permit any technically qualified entity to perform the testing required under the Party's conformity assessment procedures for terminal or other equipment to be attached to the public telecommunications transport network, subject to the Party's right to review the accuracy and completeness of the test results; and

(c)   ensure that any measure that it adopts or maintains requiring to be authorized to act as agents for suppliers of telecommunications equipment before the Party's relevant conformity assessment bodies is nondiscriminatory.

6.   When the condition allows it, each Party shall adopt, as part of its conformity assessment procedures, provisions necessary to accept the test results from laboratories or testing facilities in the territory of the other Party for tests performed in accordance with the accepting Party's standards-related measures and procedures.

Article 13.06 Monopolies or Anti-competition Practice

1.   Where a Party maintains or designates a monopoly, or main provider or incumbent carrier, to provide public telecommunications transport networks or services, and the monopoly, directly or through an affiliate, competes in the provision of enhanced or value-added services or other telecommunications-related services or telecommunications-related goods, the Party shall ensure that the monopoly, main provider or incumbent carrier does not use its monopoly position to engage in anticompetitive conduct in those markets, either directly or through its dealings with its affiliates, in such a manner as to affect adversely a person of the other Party. Such conduct may include cross-subsidization, predatory conduct and the discriminatory provision of access to public telecommunications transport networks or services.

2.   To prevent such anticompetitive conduct, each Party shall make efforts to conform with or maintain effective measures as referred to paragraph 1, such as:

(a)   accounting requirements;

(b)   requirements for structural separation;

(c)   rules to ensure that the monopoly, main provider or incumbent carrier accords its competitors access to and use of its public telecommunications transport networks or services on terms and conditions no less favorable than those it accords to itself or its affiliates; or

(d)   rules to ensure the timely disclosure of technical changes to public telecommunications transport networks and their interfaces.

Article 13.07 Transparency

Further to Article 17.03 (Publication), each Party shall make publicly available its measures relating to access to and use of public telecommunications transport networks or services, including measures relating to:

(a)   tariffs, price and other terms and conditions of service;

(b)   specifications of technical interfaces with the networks or services;

(c)   information on bodies responsible for the preparation and adoption of standards-related measures affecting such access and use;

(d)   conditions applying to attachment of terminal or other equipment to the networks; and

(e)   notification, permit, registration, certificate licensing or concession requirements.

Article 13.08 Relation to Other Chapters

In the event of any inconsistency between this Chapter and another Chapter, this Chapter shall prevail to the extent of the inconsistency.

Article 13.09 Relation to Other International Organizations and Agreements

The Parties recognize the importance of international standards for global compatibility and interoperability of telecommunication networks or services and undertake to promote those standards through the work of relevant international bodies, including the International Telecommunication Union and the International Organization for Standardization.

Article 13.10 Technical Cooperation and Other Consultations

1.   To encourage the development of interoperable telecommunications transport services infrastructure, the Parties shall cooperate in the exchange of technical information, the development of government-to-government training programs and other related activities. In implementing this obligation, the Parties shall give special emphasis to existing exchange programs.

2.   The Parties shall consult with a view to determining the feasibility of further liberalizing trade in all telecommunications services, including public telecommunications transport networks and services.

ANNEX 13.01 (A)
CONFORMITY ASSESSMENT PROCEDURE

For purposes of this Chapter, conformity assessment procedures include:

In the case of Panama:

(a)   Act No. 31, February 8, 1996, on the rules governing telecommunications in the Republic of Panama;

(b)   Executive Decree No. 73, April 9, 1997, Telecommunication Rules;

(c)   Resolution JD-119, October 28, 1997, by which the Regulatory Body prohibits the importation into the Republic of Panama of telephonic equipment and wireless intercommunication equipment that do not comply with the National Scheme of Frequency Assignation;

(d)   Resolution JD-952, August 11, 1998, by which the Regulatory Body adopts procedures to test new technology equipment that use frequencies of the radio-electric spectrum; and

(e)   Resolution JD-1785, January 3, 2000, that establishes the procedure for registering and authorizing the introduction in Panamanian territory of wireless intercommunication telephones or equipment.

In the case of the ROC:

(a)   Telecommunications Act, May 21, 2003;

(b)   Compliance Approval Regulations of Telecommunications Terminal Equipment, June 28, 2000;

(c)   Regulations on Inspection and Certification of Controlled Telecommunications Equipment, August 30, 2002;

(d)   Administrative Regulations on Low-Power Radio Waves Radiated Devices, October 23, 2002;

(e)   Administrative Regulations on Controlled Telecommunications Equipment Radio-Frequency Devices, September 14, 2000;

(f)   Rules Governing the Third Generation (3G) Mobile Telecommunications Service, March 6, 2003;

(g)   Administrative Regulations governing 1900Mhz Digital Low-Tier Cordless Telephony Business, March 6, 2003;

(h)   Regulations Governing Fixed Network Telecommunications Businesses, March 6, 2003;

(i)   Administrative Rules on Satellite Communication Services, March 6, 2003;

(j)   Regulations Governing Mobile Telecommunications Businesses, March 6, 2003; and

(k)   Administrative Regulations On Amateur Radios, October 11, 2000.

ANNEX 13.01 (B)
PRIVATE NETWORKS INTERCONNECTION (PRIVATE CIRCUITS)

1.   In the case of both Panama and the ROC, it shall be understood that the private telecommunication networks used in the private communications of a company may not be connected with public telecommunications transport networks nor may be used to provide telecommunication services, even free of charge, to third persons who are not subsidiaries, branch offices or affiliates of a company or that are not owned by it nor are under its control.

2.   The provisions of paragraph 1 shall no longer be effective in Panama or the ROC after its present legal conditions change and it allows the interconnection of the private telecommunication networks used in the internal communications of enterprises to the public telecommunication transport networks and the provision to third persons of services that are key for the economic activities of an enterprise and that maintain a continued contractual relation with it.

CHAPTER 14
TEMPORARY ENTRY FOR BUSINESS PERSONS

Article 14.01 Definitions

1.   For purposes of this Chapter, the following terms shall be understood as:

business activities: legitimate commercial activities undertaken and operated with the purpose of obtaining profits in the market, not including the possibility of obtaining employment, wages or remuneration from a labour source in the territory of a Party;

business person: a national of a Party who is engaged in trade of goods, provision of services or conduct of investment activities;

national: "national" as defined in Chapter 2 (General Definitions), but not including those permanent residents or definitive residents;

labour certification: procedure applied by the competent administrative authority with the purpose of determining if a national of a Party who seeks a temporary entry into the territory of the other Party displaces national workers in the same domestic industry or noticeably harms labour conditions in it;

pattern of practice: a practice repeatedly followed by the immigration authorities of one Party during the representative period immediately before the execution of the same;

temporary entry: entry into the territory of a Party by a business person of the other Party without the intention to establish permanent residence.

2.   For purposes of Annex 14.04:

executive functions: functions assigned in an organization to a person who shall have the following basic responsibilities:

(a)   managing the administration of the organization, or of a relevant component, or function within it;

(b)   establishing the policies and objectives of the organization, component or function; or

(c)   receiving supervision or general direction only from executives in a higher level, the board of directors or the administrative council of the organization or its shareholders.

management functions: functions assigned in an organization to a person who shall have the following basic responsibilities:

(a)   managing the organization or an essential function within it;

(b)   supervising and controlling the work of other professional employees, supervisors or administrators;

(c)   having the authority to engage and dismiss or to recommend these actions, and to undertake other actions related to management of the personnel directly supervised by this person, and to perform senior functions within the organization hierarchy or functions related to his position; or

(d)   performing discretionary actions related to the daily operation of the function over which this person has the authority; and

functions requiring specialized knowledge: functions that require special knowledge of goods, services, research, equipment, techniques, management of an organization or of its interests and their application in international markets, or an advanced level of knowledge or experience in the processes and procedures of the organization.

Article 14.02 General Principles

This Chapter reflects the preferential trading relationship between the Parties, the desirability of facilitating temporary entry on a reciprocal basis and of establishing transparent criteria and procedures for temporary entry, and the necessity to ensure border security and to protect the domestic labor force and permanent employment in their respective territories.

Article 14.03 General Obligations

1.   Each Party shall apply its measures relating to the provisions of this Chapter in accordance with Article 14.02 and, in particular, shall apply expeditiously those measures so as to avoid unduly delaying or impairing trade in goods or services or conduct of investment activities under this Agreement.

2.   The Parties shall endeavor to develop and adopt common criteria, definitions and interpretations for the implementation of this Chapter.

Article 14.04 Grant of Temporary Entry

1.   Each Party shall grant temporary entry to business persons who are otherwise qualified for entry under applicable measures relating to public health and safety and national security, in accordance with this Chapter, including the provision of Annex 14.04 and 14.04(1).

2.   A Party may refuse a temporary entry to a business person where the temporary entry of that person might affect adversely:

   (a)   the settlement of any labor dispute that is in progress at the place or intended place of employment; or

   (b)   the employment of any person who is involved in such dispute.

3.   When a Party refuses a temporary entry in accordance with paragraph 2, the Party shall:

   (a)   inform in writing the business person of the reasons for the refusal; and

   (b)   promptly notify in writing the Party whose business person has been refused entry of the reasons for the refusal.

4.   Each Party shall limit any fees for processing applications for temporary entry of business persons to the approximate cost of services rendered.

5.   An authorization of temporary entry under this Chapter, does not supersede the requirements demanded by the exercise of a profession or activity according to the specific rules in force in the territory of the Party authorizing the temporary entry.

Article 14.05 Provision of Information

1.   Further to Article 17.03 (Publication), each Party shall:

(a)   provide to the other Party such materials as will enable it to become acquainted with its measures relating to this Chapter; and

(b)   no later than one year after the date of entry into force of this Agreement, prepare, publish and make available in its own territory, and in the territory of the other Party, explanatory material in a consolidated document regarding the requirements for temporary entry under this Chapter in such a manner as will enable business persons of the other Party to become acquainted with them.

2.   Each Party shall collect, maintain, and make available to the other Party the information respecting the granting of temporary entry under this Chapter to business persons of the other Party who have been issued immigration documentation, including data specific to each authorized category.

Article 14.06 Dispute Settlement

1.   A Party may not initiate proceedings under Article 19.06 (Consultations) regarding a refusal to grant temporary entry under this Chapter or a particular case arising under Article 14.03 unless:

(a)   the matter involves a pattern of practice; and

(b)   the business person has exhausted the available administrative review regarding the particular matter.

2.   The administrative review referred to in paragraph 1(b) shall be deemed to be exhausted if a final determination in the matter has not been issued by the competent authority within 6 months of the institution of an administrative proceeding, and the failure to issue a determination is not attributable to delay caused by the business person.

Article 14.07 Relation to Other Chapters

Except for this Chapter, Chapters 1 (Initial Provisions), 2 (General Definitions), 18 (Administration of the Agreement) and 21 (Final Provisions) and Articles 17.02 (Information Centre), 17.03 (Publication), 17.04 (Provision of Information) and 17.06 (Administrative Proceedings for Adopting Measures of General Applications), no provision of this Agreement shall impose any obligation on a Party regarding its immigration measures.

ANNEX 14.04
TEMPORARY ENTRY FOR BUSINESS PERSONS

Section A - Business Visitors

1.   Each Party shall grant temporary entry and expedite document verification to a business person seeking to engage in a business activity set out in Appendix 14.04(A)(1), without other

requirements than those established by the existing immigration measures applicable to temporary entry, on presentation of:

(a)   proof of nationality of a Party;

(b)   documentation demonstrating that the business person will be so engaged and describing the purpose of entry, and evidence demonstrating that the proposed business activity is international in scope and that the business person is not seeking to enter the local labor market.

2.   Each Party shall consider that a business person satisfies the requirements of paragraph 1(b) by demonstrating that:

(a)   the primary source of remuneration for the proposed business activity is outside the territory of the Party granting temporary entry; and

(b)   the business person's principal place of business and the actual place of accrual of most of the profits remain outside such territory.

For purpose of this paragraph, a Party that authorizes temporary entry shall normally accept a declaration as to the principal place of business and the actual place of accrual of profits. Where the Party requires further proof, it should be conducted according to its law.

3.   Each Party shall grant temporary entry to a business person seeking to engage in a business activity other than those set out in Appendix 14.04(A)(1), on a basis no less favorable than that provided under the existing provisions of the measures set out in Appendix 14.04(A)(3).

4.   No Party may:

(a)   as a condition for temporary entry under paragraph 1 or 3, require prior approval procedures, petitions, labor certification tests or other procedures of similar effect; or

(b)   impose or maintain any numerical restriction relating to temporary entry inaccordance with paragraph 1 or 3.

5.   Notwithstanding paragraph 4, a Party may require a business person seeking temporary entry under this Section to obtain a visa or its equivalent prior to entry. The Parties shall consider removing their visa or equivalent document requirement.

Section B - Traders and Investors

1.   Each Party shall grant temporary entry and provide documentation verification to a business person, who in a capacity that is supervisory, managerial, executive or requiring specialized knowledge, provided that the business person otherwise complies with existing immigration measures applicable to temporary entry, and seeks to:

(a)   carry on substantial trade in goods or services principally between the territory of the Party of which the business person is a national and the territory of the other Party into which entry is sought; or

(b)   establish, develop, administer or provide advice or key technical services to the operation of an investment to which the business person or the business person's enterprise has committed, or is in the process of committing, a substantial amount of capital,

2.   No Party may:

(a)   as a condition for authorizing temporary entry under paragraph 1, require labor certification tests or other procedures of similar effect; or

(b)   impose or maintain any numerical restriction relating to temporary entry in accordance with paragraph 1.

3.   Notwithstanding paragraph 2, a Party may require a business person seeking temporary entry under this Section to obtain a visa or its equivalent prior to entry. The Parties shall consider avoiding or removing their visa or equivalent document requirement.

Section C - Intra-corporate Transferees

1.   Each Party shall grant temporary entry and provide confirming documentation to a business person employed by an enterprise who seeks to render management, executive or functions requiring specialized knowledge to that enterprise or a subsidiary or affiliate thereof, provided that the business person otherwise complies with effective immigration measures applicable to temporary entry. A Party may require the person to have been employed continuously by the enterprise for 1 year immediately preceding the date of the application for admission.

2.   No Party may:

(a)   as a condition for temporary entry under paragraph 1, require labor certification tests or other procedures of similar effect; or

(b)   impose or maintain any numerical restriction relating to temporary entry under paragraph 1.

3.   Notwithstanding paragraph 2, a Party may require a business person seeking temporary entry under this Section to obtain a visa or its equivalent prior to entry. The Parties shall consider avoiding or removing their visa or equivalent document requirement.

ANNEX 14.04 (1)
SPECIAL PROVISION REGARDING TEMPORARY ENTRY OF BUSINESS PERSONS

For Panama:

1.   It shall be considered that the business persons who enter Panama under any of the categories established in Annex 14.04 carry out activities that are useful or beneficial to the country.

2.   The business persons who enter Panama under any of the categories of Annex 14.04 shall hold a temporary residence permit and may renew this permit for consecutive periods as long as the conditions are maintained. Such persons may not request permanent residence nor change their immigration status, unless they comply with the general provisions of the Migration Law, Decree No. 16, June 30, 1960 and its amendments and of the Decree of the Cabinet No. 363, December 17, 1970.

For the ROC:

1.   The business person shall obtain a visitor or resident visa prior to entry. A visitor visa of which validity no longer than 1 year, multiple entry and 90- day duration of stay may be issued. The business person in possession of a resident visa may stay in the ROC provided the work permit remains valid. The duration of stay may be extendable for consecutive periods as long as the conditions justifying it are maintained. Such a person may not require permanent residence unless satisfying the provisions of the Immigration Law.

2.   If a business person is defined as a resident in the Mainland China area by the Statute Governing the Relations Between the People of the Taiwan Area and the Mainland Area and its Regulations, the person must apply for entry permit according to the said Statute and Regulations.

APPENDIX 14.04(A)(1)
BUSINESS VISITORS

Research and Design

- Technical, scientific and statistical researchers conducting independent research or research for an enterprise established in the territory of the other Party.

Cultivation, Manufacture and Production Purchasing

- Purchasing and production personnel at managerial level conducting commercial operation for an enterprise established in the territory of the other Party.

Marketing

- Market researchers and analysts conducting independent research or analysis, or research or analysis for an enterprise established in the territory of the other Party.

- Trade fair and promotional personnel attending a trade convention.

Sales

- Sales representatives and agents taking orders or negotiating contracts on goods or services for an enterprise established in the territory of the other Party but not delivering goods or providing services.

- Buyers purchasing for an enterprise established in the territory of the other Party.

After-sale Service

- Installation, repair and maintenance personnel, and supervisors, possessing specialized knowledge essential to a seller's contractual obligation, performing services or training workers to perform services, pursuant to a warranty or other service contract incidental to the sale of commercial or industrial equipment or machinery, including computer software, purchased from an enterprise located outside the territory of the Party into which temporary entry is sought, during the life of the warranty or service agreement.

General Service

- Consultants conducting business activities at the level of the provision of crossborder services.

- Management and supervisory personnel engaging in a commercial operation for an enterprise established in the territory of the other Party.

- Financial services personnel engaging in commercial operation for an enterprise established in the territory of the other Party.

- Public relations and advertising personnel consulting with business associates, or attending or participating in conventions.

- Tourism personnel (tour and travel agents, tour guides or tour operators) attending or participating in conventions or conducting a tour that has begun in the territory of the other Party.

APPENDIX 14.04(A)(3)
EXISTING IMMIGRATION MEASURES

In the case of Panama, the Migration Law, Decree No.16, June 30, 1960, and the amendment, published by the Official Gazette 14,167, on July 05, 1960; the Cabinet Decree No.363, December 17, 1970, published by the Official Gazette 16,758,on December 24, 1970.

In the case of the ROC, the Immigration Law, promulgated No. 8800119740 on May 21,1999; the Statute Governing Issuance of ROC Visas on Foreign Passports, promulgated on June 02, 1999, and the Regulations for Issuance of ROC Visas on Foreign Passports, promulgated on May 31, 2000. Employment Service Act, Promulgated on May 8, 1992, amended on January 21, 2002, Enforcement Rules of the Employment Service Act, amended by the Council of Labor Affairs on October 31, 2001.

PART FIVE
COMPETITION POLICY

CHAPTER 15
COMPETITION POLICY, MONOPOLIES AND STATE ENTERPRISES

Section A-Competition Policy

Article 15.01 Objectives

The objectives of the this Chapter consist of assuring that the benefits of the trade liberalization are not reduced by anticompetitive activities and promoting the cooperation and coordination between the authorities of the Parties.

Article 15.02 Cooperation

1.   The Parties recognize the importance of the cooperation and coordination in the application of their enforcement mechanisms, including notification, consultations and mutual exchange of information regarding the enforcement of the competition laws and policies in the area of free trade as long as they do not contravene legal obligations regarding confidentiality.

2.   To such end, each Party shall adopt and maintain measures to prohibit anticompetitive trade practices and shall apply the appropriate enforcement mechanisms under those measures, recognizing that such measures will contribute to the fulfillment of the objectives as set forth in this Agreement.

Section B- Monopolies and State Enterprises

Article 15.03 Monopolies and State Enterprises

1.   Nothing in this Agreement shall prevent a Party from designating or maintaining a monopoly or a state enterprise if and whenever its law permits it.

2.   If a Party's law does permit it, where the Party intends to designate a monopoly or a state enterprise, and the designation may affect the interests of persons of the other Party, the Party shall:

  (a)   wherever possible, provide prior written notification to the other Party of the designation; and

  (b)   endeavor to introduce at the time of designation such conditions on the operation of the monopoly as will minimize or eliminate any nullification or impairment of benefits under this Agreement.

3.   Each Party shall ensure, if designation or maintenance of a monopoly or a state enterprise is permitted by the Party's law, that any monopoly or any state enterprise designated or maintained by the Party:

  (a)   acts in a manner that is not inconsistent with the Party's obligations under this Agreement wherever such a monopoly or a state enterprise exercises any regulatory, administrative or other governmental authority that the Party has delegated to it in connection with the monopolized goods or services such as the power to grant import or export licenses, approve commercial transactions or impose quotas, fees or other charges;

(b)   provides non-discriminatory treatment to investments of investors, to goods and to service providers of the other Party in its purchase or sale of the monopolized goods or services in the relevant market; and

(c)   does not use its monopoly position to engage, either directly or indirectly, in anticompetitive practices that adversely affect an investment of an investor of the other Party.

4.   Paragraph 3 does not apply to procurement by governmental agencies of goods or services for official purposes and not with a view to commercial resale or with a view to use in the production of goods or the provision of services for commercial sale.

PART SIX
INTELLECTUAL PROPERTY RIGHTS

CHAPTER 16
INTELLECTUAL PROPERTY

Section A - General Provisions

Article 16.01 General Provisions

The Parties agree that TRIPS and the following intellectual property (IP) related international conventions shall govern and apply to all intellectual property issues arising from this Agreement:

(a)   the Paris Convention for the Protection of Industrial Property (1967);

(b)   the Bern Convention for the Protection of Literary and Artistic Works (1971);

(c)   the International Convention for the Protection of Performers, Producers of Phonograms and Broadcasting Organizations;

(d)   the Geneva Convention for the Protection of Producers of Phonograms Against Unauthorized Reproduction;

(e)   the Convention of the International Union for the Protection of New Varieties of Plants (UPOV), Act of 1978 or Act of 1991 according to the country;

(f)   the World Intellectual Property Organization (WIPO) Copyright Treaty of 1996; and

(g)   the World Intellectual Property Organization (WIPO) Performances and Phonograms Treaty of 1996.

Section B - Protection of the Intellectual Property Rights

Article 16.02 General Obligations

1.   Each Party shall accord nationals of the other Party appropriate protection and enforcement of intellectual property rights referred to in this Chapter and shall ensure that measures intended for the enforcement of these rights do not create obstacles to legitimate trade.

2.   Each Party may accord in its legislation a broader protection to the intellectual property rights than the protection required in this Chapter, provided that this protection is not inconsistent with the provision of the Chapter.

Article 16.03 Exhaustion of the Copyright and Related Rights

1.   The Parties agree to apply the principle of the copyright and related rights exhaustion, meaning that the holder of the copyright and related rights shall not hinder free trade of legitimate products in a Party, once legally introduced for trade into that Party, by the same right or license holder or by any other authorized third person, provided that these products and the packages that are in immediate contact with them have not suffered any modification or alteration.

2.   The Parties have one year from the entry into force of this Agreement to incorporate this principle into its national legislation.

Article 16.04 Protection of Geographic Indications

1.   Each Party shall recognize and protect the geographical indications of another Party provided for in this Article.

2.   Neither Party shall permit the importation, manufacture or sale of goods using a geographical indication protected by the other Party, unless it is processed and certified in the originating Party according to the applicable legislation governing the geographic indication.

3.   The provisions in paragraphs 1 and 2 shall only be effective with regard to the geographical indications that are protected by the legislation of the Party demanding protection and whose definition agreed upon by section 3 of TRIPS. Likewise, to accede to protection, each Party shall notify the other Party of the geographical indications, which comply with the above-mentioned requirements and shall be included in the scope of protection.

4.   The above mentioned provisions shall be understood without prejudice to the recognition that the Parties may accord to the homonymous geographical indications that may lawfully belong to a non-Party.

Appellation of Origin for Seco

5.   The ROC shall recognize the appellation of origin "Seco" for exclusive use as a kind of spirits made from sugarcane originating in Panama. Consequently it shall not be permitted in the ROC the importation, manufacture or sale of this product, unless it is processed in Panama, according to Panamanian laws, rules, technical regulations and standards applicable to the said product.

6. The provisions of Section C (Enforcement) of this Chapter, as well as those established in Article 23 (1) of TRIPS shall be applicable to the appellation of origin for Seco.

Article 16.05 Protection of Traditional Knowledge

1. Each Party shall protect the collective intellectual property rights and the traditional knowledge of indigenous people on their creations, subject to commercial use, through a special system of registration, promotion and marketing of their rights, aiming at emphasizing the indigenous sociological and cultural values of the indigenous people and the local communities and bring to them social justice.

2. Each Party shall recognize that the customs, traditions, beliefs, spirituality, religiosity, cosmos vision, folklore expressions, artistic manifestations, traditional skills and any other form of traditional expression of the indigenous people and local communities are a part of their cultural heritage.

3. The cultural heritage shall not be subject to any form of exclusivity by unauthorized third parties applying the intellectual property system, unless the request is done by the indigenous people and local communities or by third parties with their authorization.

Article 16.06 Protection of Folklore

Each Party shall ensure the effective protection of all folklore expressions and manifestations and of artistic manifestations of the traditional and popular culture of the indigenous and local communities.

Article 16.07 Relation between Access to Genetic Resources and Intellectual Property

1. Each Party shall protect the access to its genetic resources and the traditional knowledge developed by indigenous people and local communities on the uses of the biological resources containing these genetic resources, against the indiscriminate use of biological diversity, as well as ensuring that the Party will participate in benefits derived from the use of its genetic resources.

2. Each Party shall accord a fair and equitable participation in the benefits derived from the access to its genetic resources and from the uses of its traditional knowledge and folklore expressions.

3. Each Party shall ensure that the protection accorded to the industrial property shall safeguard its biological and genetic heritage. Consequently, the licensing of patents on inventions developed from material obtained from such heritage or traditional knowledge shall be subject to the condition that this material was acquired according to relevant national and international laws and regulations.

Article 16.08 Plant breeders

1. Each Party shall recognize and ensure the so called "breeder's right" through a special system of registration as provided for in the relevant laws and regulations in the territory of each Party, as well as through the mechanism of mutual recognition to be developed as agreed upon by the Parties, with the aim of protecting the rights originating from the use of plant varieties.

2.   The right accorded to the breeder of a plant variety is an intellectual property right which accords to its holder an exclusive right, so that his or her authorization is required to conduct some acts of exploitation of the protected variety.

3.   The breeder's right shall be marketable, transferable and inheritable. The owner of the right may accord to third persons license to exploit the protected varieties.

4.   The breeder's right covers all plant species and genera and shall be applied to any kind of plants and seeds, and to any part thereof that can be used as reproduction or propagation material. The breeder's right shall also be accorded where the variety is new, different, homogeneous and stable.

5.   The right conferred on the breeder shall be granted for twenty (20) years in Panama and for fifteen (15) years in the ROC from the date of concession of the title of protection. In the case of vines, forest trees, fruit trees and ornamental trees, including in each case their rootstocks, the protection shall have a term of twenty five (25) years in Panama and of fifteen (15) years in the ROC. Once the protection term expires, the varieties shall be considered as in the public domain.

Section C - Enforcement

Article 16.09 Applications

1.   The Parties confirm the effective rights and obligations among them with respect to the procedures of observance in accordance with TRIPS.

2.   The Parties recognize that the growing importance of IP protection in traditional knowledge and folklore, genetic resources, geographic indications, plant breeders and other related matters is critical to economic competitiveness in the knowledge-based economy and to sustainable economic development. The Parties, therefore, confirm that either Party which is not party to one or more of the multilateral agreements listed in Article 16.01 shall undertake with the best efforts to pursue affiliation, in due course, to the said agreements.

Article 16.10 Enforcement of Intellectual Property Rights

Each Party shall establish in its legislation administrative, civil and criminal procedures, effective with the objective to reach an adequate and effective protection of the intellectual property rights. Also for all the procedures as mentioned above, the due process as regards the relationship between the plaintiff and the defendant shall be taken into account.

Article 16.11 Enforcement of Border Measures

Each Party shall adopt legislation on measures in border control, to the extent that the customs authorities shall be granted action to inspect or to retain merchandise, with the purposes of suspending or avoiding the free circulation of the merchandise involved to accord the rightholders protection.

Article16.12 Transparency

The Parties shall notify the Committee on Intellectual Property under this Agreement the laws, regulations and the dispositions. In relation to final judicial decisions and administrative rulings of general application, the foregoing shall be published, or where such publication is not practical made publicly available, to enable the governments of each Party and right holders to become acquainted with them.

Article 16.13 Committee on Intellectual Property

1. The Parties hereby establish the Committee on Intellectual Property, as set out in Annex 16.13, to discuss and review all IP related issues arising from this Agreement.

2. An Expert Group of Intellectual Property shall be established under the Committee on Intellectual Property, composed of three IP experts from the Intellectual Property Office in each Party. The Committee or the Expert Group on Intellectual Property shall meet, in principle, once a year or as requested by either Party, subject to mutual agreement. The location of the meeting shall rotate between the Parties.

Article 16.14 Technical Cooperation

The Parties shall establish a system of technical cooperation between the Parties and within the framework of the WTO on matters relating to intellectual property, particularly in areas of newly developed IP -related issues.

ANNEX 16.13
COMMITTEE ON INTELLECTUAL PROPERTY

The Committee on Intellectual Property under Article 16.13 shall be composed of:

(a) in the case of Panama, the Ministry of Trade and Industries through the Vice-ministry of Foreign Trade, or its successor; and

(b) in the case of the ROC, Ministry of Economic Affairs through the Intellectual Property Office, or its successor.

SELECTED UNCTAD PUBLICATIONS ON TRANSNATIONAL CORPORATIONS AND FOREIGN DIRECT INVESTMENT
(For more information, please visit www.unctad.org/en/pub on the web.)

World Investment Report 2003: FDI Policies for Development: National and International Perspectives. 327 p. Sales No. E.03.II.D.8 $49.
http://www.unctad.org/wir/contents/wir02_dl.htm.

World Investment Report 2003: FDI Policies for Development: National and International Perspectives. An Overview. 48 p. UNCTAD/WIR/2003 (Overview). Free of charge.
http://www.unctad.org/wir/contents/wir02_dl.htm.

World Investment Report 2002: Transnational Corporations and Competitiveness. 384 p. Sales No. E.02.II.D.4 $49. http://www.unctad.org/wir/contents/wir02_dl.htm

World Investment Report 2002: Transnational Corporations and Competitiveness. An Overview. 44 p. UNCTAD/WIR/2002 (Overview). Free of charge.
http://www.unctad.org/wir/contents/wir02_dl.htm.

World Investment Report 2001: Promoting Linkages. 356 p. Sales No. E.01.II.D.12 $49.
http://www.unctad.org/wir/contents/wir01content.en.htm

World Investment Report 2001: Promoting Linkages. An Overview. 67 p. UNCTAD/WIR/2001 (Overview). Free of charge. http://www.unctad.org/wir/contents/wir01content.en.htm.

Ten Years of World Investment Reports: The Challenges Ahead. Proceedings of an UNCTAD special event on future challenges in the area of FDI. UNCTAD/ITE/Misc. 45. Free of charge.
http://www.unctad.org/wir/contents/wir_xth.html.

World Investment Report 2000: Cross-border Mergers and Acquisitions and Development. 368 p. Sales No. E.99.II.D.20. $49. http://www.unctad.org/wir/contents/wir00content.en.htm.

World Investment Report 2000: Cross-border Mergers and Acquisitions and Development. An Overview. 75 p. UNCTAD/WIR/2000 (Overview). Free of charge.
http://www.unctad.org/wir/contents/wir00content.en.htm

World Investment Report 1999: Foreign Direct Investment and the Challenge of Development. 543 p. Sales No. E.99.II.D.3. $49. http://www.unctad.org/wir/contents/wir99content.en.htm.

World Investment Report 1999: Foreign Direct Investment and the Challenge of Development. An Overview. 75 p. UNCTAD/WIR/1999 (Overview). Free of charge.
http://www.unctad.org/wir/contents/wir99content.en.htm

World Investment Report 1998: Trends and Determinants. 432 p. Sales No. E.98.II.D.5. $45.
http://www.unctad.org/wir/contents/wir98content.en.htm

World Investment Report 1998: Trends and Determinants. An Overview. 67 p.
UNCTAD/WIR/1998 (Overview). Free of charge.
http://www.unctad.org/wir/contents/wir98content.en.htm

World Investment Report 1997: Transnational Corporations, Market Structure and Competition Policy. 384 p. Sales No. E.97.II.D.10. $45.
http://www.unctad.org/wir/contents/wir97content.en.htm

World Investment Report 1997: Transnational Corporations, Market Structure and Competition Policy. An Overview. 70 p. UNCTAD/ITE/IIT/5 (Overview). Free of charge.
http://www.unctad.org/wir/contents/wir97content.en.htm

World Investment Report 1996: Investment, Trade and International Policy Arrangements. 332 p. Sales No. E.96.II.A.14. $45. http://www.unctad.org/wir/contents/wir96content.en.htm

World Investment Report 1996: Investment, Trade and International Policy Arrangements. An Overview. 51 p. UNCTAD/DTCI/32 (Overview). Free of charge.
http://www.unctad.org/wir/contents/wir96content.en.htm

World Investment Report 1995: Transnational Corporations and Competitiveness. 491 p. Sales No. E.95.II.A.9. $45. http://www.unctad.org/wir/contents/wir95content.en.htm

World Investment Report 1995: Transnational Corporations and Competitiveness. An Overview.
51 p. UNCTAD/DTCI/26 (Overview). Free of charge.
http://www.unctad.org/wir/contents/wir95content.en.htm

World Investment Report 1994: Transnational Corporations, Employment and the Workplace. 482 p. Sales No. E.94.II.A.14. $45. http://www.unctad.org/wir/contents/wir94content.en.htm

World Investment Report 1994: Transnational Corporations, Employment and the Workplace. An Executive Summary. 34 p. UNCTAD/DTCI/10 (Overview). Free of charge.
http://www.unctad.org/wir/contents/wir94content.en.htm

World Investment Report 1993: Transnational Corporations and Integrated International Production. 290 p. Sales No. E.93.II.A.14.
$45.http://www.unctad.org/wir/contents/wir93content.en.htm

World Investment Report 1993: Transnational Corporations and Integrated International Production. An Executive Summary. 31 p. ST/CTC/159 (Executive Summary). Free of charge.
http://www.unctad.org/wir/contents/wir93content.en.htm

World Investment Report 1992: Transnational Corporations as Engines of Growth. 356 p. Sales No. E.92.II.A.19. $45. http://www.unctad.org/wir/contents/wir92content.en.htm

World Investment Report 1992: Transnational Corporations as Engines of Growth. An Executive Summary. 30 p. ST/CTC/143 (Executive Summary). Free of charge.
http://www.unctad.org/wir/contents/wir92content.en.htm

World Investment Report 1991: The Triad in Foreign Direct Investment. 108 p. Sales No.E.91.II.A.12. $25. http://www.unctad.org/wir/contents/wir91content.en.htm

World Investment Directories

World Investment Directory: Vol. VIII: Central and Eastern Europe, 2003. 86 p. (Overview)+CD-Rom (country profiles). Sales No. E.03.II.D.12. $25. http://www.unctad.org/en/docs//iteiit20032_en.pdf(Overview); http://www.unctad.org/en/subsites/dite/fdistats_files/WID2.htm (country profiles).

World Investment Directory, Vol. VII (Parts I and II): Asia and the Pacific, 1999. 332+638 p. Sales No. E.00.II.D.21. $80.

World Investment Directory, Vol. VI: West Asia, 1996. 138 p. Sales No. E.97.II.A.2. $35.

World Investment Directory, Vol. V: Africa, 1996. 461 p. Sales No. E.97.II.A.1. $75.

World Investment Directory, Vol. IV: Latin America and the Caribbean, 1994. 478 p. Sales No. E.94.II.A.10. $65.

World Investment Directory, Vol. III: Developed Countries, 1992. 532 p. Sales No. E.93.II.A.9. $75.

World Investment Directory, Vol. II: Central and Eastern Europe, 1992. 432 p. Sales No. E.93.II.A.1. $65. (Joint publication with the United Nations Economic Commission for Europe.)

World Investment Directory, Vol. I: Asia and the Pacific, 1992. 356 p. Sales No. E.92.II.A.11. $65.

Investment Policy Reviews
http://www.unctad.org/ipr/

***Investment Policy Review of Nepal*.** 95 p. Sales No. E.03.II.D.17. http://www.unctad.org/ipr/nepal.pdf

***Investment Policy Review of Lesotho*.** 93 p. UNCTAD/ITE/IPC/Misc. 25. http://www.unctad.org/en/docs//iteipcmisc25corr1_en.pdf.

***Investment Policy Review of Ghana*.** 93 p. Sales No. E.02.II.D.20. http://www.unctad.org/ipr/ghana.pdf.

***Investment Policy Review of Botswana*.** 107 p. Sales No. E.03.II.D.1. http://www.unctad.org/ipr/botswana.pdf.

***Investment Policy Review of the United Republic of Tanzania*.** 98 p. Sales No. 02.E.II.D.6 $20. http://www.unctad.org/ipr/Tanzania.pdf.

***Investment Policy Review of Ecuador*.** 117 p. Sales No. E.01.II D.31. $25. http://www.unctad.org/ipr/Ecuador.pdf.

***Investment and Innovation Policy Review of Ethiopia*.** 115 p. UNCTAD/ITE/IPC/Misc. 4. Free of charge. http://www.unctad.org/ipr/Ethiopia.pdf.

Investment Policy Review of Mauritius. 84 p. Sales No. E.01.II.D.11. $22.
http://www.unctad.org/ipr/Mauritius.pdf.

Investment Policy Review of Peru. 108 p. Sales No. E.00.II.D.7. $22.
http://www.unctad.org/ipr/Peru.pdf.

Investment Policy Review of Uganda. 75 p. Sales No. E.99.II.D.24. $15.
http://www.unctad.org/ipr/UGANDA.PDF.

Investment Policy Review of Egypt. 113 p. Sales No. E.99.II.D.20. $19.
http://www.unctad.org/ipr/EGYFIN1.PDF.

Investment Policy Review of Uzbekistan. 64 p. UNCTAD/ITE/IIP/Misc.13. Free of charge.
http://www.unctad.org/ipr/Uzbekistan.pdf.

Investment Guides
http://www.unctad.org/en/pub/investguide.en.htm

An Investment Guide to Nepal: Opportunities and Conditions. 88 p.
UNCTAD/ITE/IPC/MISC/2003/1. Free of charge.

An Investment Guide to Mozambique: Opportunities and Conditions. 72 p.
UNCTAD/ITE/IIA/4. Free of charge. http://www.unctad.org/en/docs/poiteiiad4.en.pdf.

An Investment Guide to Uganda: Opportunities and Conditions. 76 p. UNCTAD/ITE/IIT/Misc.
30. Free of charge. http://www.unctad.org/en/docs/poiteiitm30.en.pdf.

An Investment Guide to Bangladesh: Opportunities and Conditions. 66 p.
UNCTAD/ITE/IIT/Misc. 29. Free of charge. http://www.unctad.org/en/docs/poiteiitm29.en.pdf.

An Investment Guide to Mali. 105 p. UNCTAD/ITE/IIT/Misc. 24. Free of charge.
http://www.unctad.org/en/docs/poiteiitm24.en.pdf (joint publication with the International
Chamber of Commerce, in association with PricewaterhouseCoopers).

An Investment Guide to Ethiopia: Opportunities and Conditions. 69 p.
UNCTAD/ITE/IIT/Misc. 19. Free of charge. http://www.unctad.org/en/docs/poiteiitm19.en.pdf
(joint publication with the International Chamber of Commerce, in association with
PricewaterhouseCoopers).

Issues in International Investment Agreements
http://www.unctad.org/en/subsites/dite/iia/IIA_Series/iia_series.htm

Admission and Establishment. 72 p. Sales No. E.99.II.D.10. $12.
http://www.unctad.org/en/subsites/dite/iia/IIA_Series/admission.pdf.

Dispute Settlement (Investor-State). Sales No. E.03.II.D.5. $15.

Dispute Settlement (State-State). Sales No. E.03.II.D.6. $15.

Employment. 69 p. http://www.unctad.org/en/subsites/dite/iia/IIA_Series/employment.pdf.

Environment. 105 p. Sales No. E.01.II.D.3. $15.
http://www.unctad.org/en/subsites/dite/iia/IIA_Series/environment.pdf.

Fair and Equitable Treatment. 64 p. Sales No. E.99.II.D.15. $12.
http://www.unctad.org/en/subsites/dite/iia/IIA_Series/fair.pdf.

Foreign Direct Investment and Development. 88 p. Sales No. E.98.II.D.15. $12.
http://www.unctad.org/en/subsites/dite/iia/IIA_Series/fdi&dev.pdf.

Home Country Measures. 96 p. Sales No.E.01.II.D.19. $12.
http://www.unctad.org/en/subsites/dite/iia/IIA_Series/homecm.pdf.

Host Country Operational Measures. 109 p. Sales No E.01.II.D.18. $15.
http://www.unctad.org/en/subsites/dite/iia/IIA_Series/hostcom.pdf.

Illicit Payments. 108 p. Sales No. E.01.II.D.20. $13.
http://www.unctad.org/en/subsites/dite/iia/IIA_Series/illicitpayments.pdf.

International Investment Agreements: Flexibility for Development. 185 p. Sales No.
E.00.II.D.6. $12. http://www.unctad.org/en/subsites/dite/iia/IIA_Series/flexibilitynew.pdf.

Investment-Related Trade Measures. 64 p. Sales No. E.99.II.D.12. $12.
http://www.unctad.org/en/subsites/dite/iia/IIA_Series/IRTM.pdf.

Lessons from the MAI. 31 p. Sales No. E.99.II.D.26. $12.
http://www.unctad.org/en/subsites/dite/iia/IIA_Series/lessons.pdf.

Most-Favoured-Nation Treatment. 72 p. Sales No. E.99.II.D.11. $12.
http://www.unctad.org/en/subsites/dite/iia/IIA_Series/mfnt.pdf.

National Treatment. 104 p. Sales No. E.99.II.D.16. $12.
http://www.unctad.org/en/subsites/dite/iia/IIA_Series/national.pdf.

Scope and Definition. 96 p. Sales No. E.99.II.D.9. $12.
http://www.unctad.org/en/subsites/dite/iia/IIA_Series/scopedef.pdf.

Social Responsibility. 91 p. Sales No. E.01.II.D.4. $15.
http://www.unctad.org/en/subsites/dite/iia/IIA_Series/socialresp.pdf.

Taking of Property. 83 p. Sales No. E.00.II.D.4. $12.
http://www.unctad.org/en/subsites/dite/iia/IIA_Series/taking.pdf.

Taxation. 111 p. Sales No. E.00.II.D.5. $12.
http://www.unctad.org/en/subsites/dite/iia/IIA_Series/taxation1.pdf.

Transfer of Funds. 68 p. Sales No. E.00.II.D.27. $12.
http://www.unctad.org/en/subsites/dite/iia/IIA_Series/transferoffunds.pdf.

Transfer of Technology. 138p. Sales No. E.01.II.D.33. $18.
http://www.unctad.org/en/subsites/dite/iia/IIA_Series/TRANSFEROFTECH.pdf.

Transfer Pricing. 72 p. Sales No. E.99.II.D.8. $12.

Trends in International Investment Agreements: An Overview. 112 p. Sales No. E.99.II.D.23.
$12. http://www.unctad.org/en/subsites/dite/iia/IIA_Series/trends.pdf.

***Progress Report on Work undertaken within UNCTAD's work programme on international
investment agreements between the 10th Conference of UNCTAD, Bangkok, February 2000
and July 2002***. 90 p. UNCTAD/ITE/IIT/2002. Free of charge.
http://www.unctad.org/en/docs//poiteiit02.en.pdf.

International Investment Instruments

International Investment Instruments: A Compendium. Vol. X. 343 p. Sales No. E.02.II.D.21.
$60. http://www.unctad.org/en/docs//dite3vol10_en.pdf.

International Investment Instruments: A Compendium. Vol. IX. 353 p. Sales No. E.02.II.D.16.
$60. http://www.unctad.org/en/docs/psdited3v9.en.pdf.

International Investment Instruments: A Compendium. Vol. VIII. 335 p. Sales No.
E.02.II.D.15. $60. http://www.unctad.org/en/docs/psdited3v8.en.pdf.

International Investment Instruments: A Compendium. Vol. VII. 339 p. Sales No.
E.02.II.D.14. $60. http://www.unctad.org/en/docs/psdited3v7.en.pdf.

International Investment Instruments: A Compendium. Vol. VI. 568 p. Sales No. E.01.II.D.34.
$60. http://www.unctad.org/en/docs/ps1dited2v6_p1.en.pdf (part one).

International Investment Instruments: A Compendium. Vol. V. 505 p. Sales No. E.00.II.D.14.
$55.

International Investment Instruments: A Compendium. Vol. IV. 319 p. Sales No. E.00.II.D.13.
$55.

International Investment Instruments: A Compendium. Vol. I. 371 p. Sales No. E.96.II.A.9;
Vol. II. 577 p. Sales No. E.96.II.A.10; ***Vol. III***. 389 p. Sales No. E.96.II.A.11; the 3-volume set,
Sales No. E.96.II.A.12. $125.

Bilateral Investment Treaties 1959-1999. 143 p. UNCTAD/ITE/IIA/2, Free of charge. Available
only in electronic version from http://www.unctad.org/en/docs//poiteiiad2.en.pdf.

Bilateral Investment Treaties in the Mid-1990s. 314 p. Sales No. E.98.II.D.8. $46.

ASIT Advisory Studies
http://www.unctad.org/asit/index2.html

No. 17. *The World of Investment Promotion at a Glance: A Survey of Investment Promotion Practices*. UNCTAD/ITE/IPC/3. Free of charge. http://www.unctad.org/en/docs//poiteipcd3.en.pdf.

No. 16. *Tax Incentives and Foreign Direct Investment: A Global Survey*. 180 p. Sales No. E.01.II.D.5. $23. http://www.unctad.org/en/docs//iteipcmisc3_en.pdf.

No. 15. *Investment Regimes in the Arab World: Issues and Policies*. 232 p. Sales No. E/F.00.II.D.32. Summary at: http://www.unctad.org/asit/index2.html.

No. 14. *Handbook on Outward Investment Promotion Agencies and Institutions*. 50 p. Sales No. E.99.II.D.22. $15.

No. 13. *Survey of Best Practices in Investment Promotion*. 71 p. Sales No. E.97.II.D.11. $35. http://www.unctad.org/en/docs//psiteiipd1.en.pdf.

B. Individual Studies

FDI in Least Developed Countries at a Glance: 2002 edition. 150 p. UNCTAD/ITE/IIA/3. Free of charge. http://www.unctad.org/en/subsites/dite/LDCs/fdi_ldcs.htm.

FDI in ACP Economies: Recent Trends and Developments. 36 p. UNCTAD/ITE/IIA/Misc. 2. Free of charge. http://www.unctad.org/en/docs//iteiiamisc2_en.pdf.

Transfer of Technology for Successful Integration into the Global Economy: A Case Study of the Pharmaceutical Industry in India. 58 p. UNCTAD/ITE/IPC/Misc. 22. Free of charge. http://www.unctad.org/en/docs//iteipcmisc22_en.pdf.

Transfer of Technology for Successful Integration into the Global Economy: A Case Study of the South African Automotive Industry. 38 p. UNCTAD/ITE/IPC/Misc. 21. Free of charge. http://www.unctad.org/en/docs//iteipcmisc21_en.pdf.

Transfer of Technology for Successful Integration into the Global Economy: A Case Study of Embraer in Brazil. 64 p. UNCTAD/ITE/IPC/Misc. 20. Free of charge. http://www.unctad.org/en/docs//iteipcmisc20_en.pdf.

Managing the Environment across Borders. 38 p. UNCTAD/ITE/IPC/Misc. 12. Free of charge. http://www.unctad.org/en/docs//iteipcmisc12_en.pdf.

The Tradability of Consulting Services and its implications for developing countries. 189 p. UNCTAD/ITE/IPC/Misc. 8. Free of charge. http://www.unctad.org/en/docs/poiteipcm8.en.pdf.

Compendium of International Arrangements on Transfer of Technology: Selected Instruments. 308 p. Sales No. E.01.II.D.28. $45. http://www.unctad.org/en/docs//psiteipcm5.en.pdf.

Measures of the Transnationalization of Economic Activity. 93 p. Sales No. E.01.II.D.2. $20.

The Competitiveness Challenge: Transnational Corporations and Industrial Restructuring in Developing Countries. 283p. Sales No. E.00.II.D.35. $42.

Integrating International and Financial Performance at the Enterprise Level. 116 p. Sales No. E.00.II.D.28. $18.

FDI Determinants and TNC Strategies: The Case of Brazil. 195 p. Sales No. E.00.II.D.2. $35.

TNC-SME Linkages for Development: Issues-Experiences-Best Practices. *Proceedings of the Special Round Table on TNCs, SMEs and Development, UNCTAD X, 15 February 2000, Bangkok, Thailand.*113 p. UNCTAD/ITE/TEB/1. Free of charge.

Foreign Direct Investment in Africa: Performance and Potential. 89 p. UNCTAD/ITE/IIT/Misc. 15. Free of charge. http://www.unctad.org/en/docs/poiteiitm15.pdf.

The Social Responsibility of Transnational Corporations. 75 p. UNCTAD/ITE/IIT/Misc. 21. Free-of- charge. [Printed version is out of stock.] http://www.unctad.org/en/docs/poiteiitm21.en.pdf.

Handbook on Foreign Direct Investment by Small and Medium-sized Enterprises: Lessons from Asia. 200 p. Sales No. E.98.II.D.4. $48.

Handbook on Foreign Direct Investment by Small and Medium-sized Enterprises: Lessons from Asia. *Executive Summary and Report of the Kunming Conference.* 74 p. Free of charge.

The Financial Crisis in Asia and Foreign Direct Investment: An Assessment. 101 p. Sales No. GV.E.98.0.29. $20. http://www.unctad.org/en/docs//poiteiitd8.en.pdf.

International Investment towards the Year 2002. 166 p. Sales No. GV.E.98.0.15. $29. (Joint publication with Invest in France Mission and Arthur Andersen, in collaboration with DATAR.)

Sharing Asia's Dynamism: Asian Direct Investment in the European Union. 192 p. Sales No. E.97.II.D.1. $26.

Investing in Asia's Dynamism: European Union Direct Investment in Asia. 124 p. ISBN 92-827-7675-1. €14. (Joint publication with the European Commission.)

Electronic materials
Available in electronic version only from the Division's web page at:
http://www.unctad.org/en/subsites/dite/index.html

Prospects for Global and Regional FDI flows: UNCTAD's Worldwide Survey of Investment Promotion Agencies. 15 p. Free of charge. Available at: http://www.unctad.org/en/subsites/dite/docs/rnote031405.pdf.

Outward FDI from Central and Eastern European Countries. 17 p. Free of charge. Available at: http://www.unctad.org/en/subsites/dite/pdfs/CEE_outward_en.pdf.

China: WTO Accession and Growing FDI Flows. 24 p. Free of charge. Available at: http://www.unctad.org/en/subsites/dite/pdfs/PRChina.pdf.

C. Journals

Transnational Corporations Journal (formerly ***The CTC Reporter***). Published three times a year. Annual subscription price: $45; individual issues $20. http://www.unctad.org/en/subsites/dite/1_itncs/1_tncs.htm.

United Nations publications may be obtained from bookstores and distributors throughout the world. Please consult your bookstore or write to:

For Africa and Europe to

Sales Section
United Nations Office at Geneva
Palais des Nations
CH-1211 Geneva 10
Switzerland
Tel: (41-22) 917-1234
Fax: (41-22) 917-0123
E-mail: unpubli@unog.ch

For Asia and the Pacific, the Caribbean, Latin America and North America to:

Sales Section
Room DC2-0853
United Nations Secretariat
New York, NY 10017
United States
Tel: (1-212) 963-8302 or (800) 253-9646
Fax: (1-212) 963-3489
E-mail: publications@un.org

All prices are quoted in United States dollars.

For further information on the work of the Division on Investment, Technology and Enterprise Development, UNCTAD, please address inquiries to:

United Nations Conference on Trade and Development
Division on Investment, Technology and Enterprise Development
Palais des Nations, Room E-10054
CH-1211 Geneva 10, Switzerland
Telephone: (41-22) 907-5534
Fax: (41-22) 907-0498
E-mail: virginie.noblat-pianta@unctad.org
http://www.unctad.org

QUESTIONNAIRE

International Investment Instruments: A Compendium

Volume XI

In order to improve the quality and relevance of the work of the UNCTAD Division on Investment, Technology and Enterprise Development, it would be useful to receive the views of readers on this publication. It would therefore be greatly appreciated if you could complete the following questionnaire and return it to:

Readership Survey
UNCTAD Division on Investment, Technology and Enterprise Development
United Nations Office in Geneva
Palais des Nations
Room E-9123
CH-1211 Geneva 10
Switzerland
Fax: 41-22-907-0194

1. Name and address of respondent (optional):

_____

_____

2. Which of the following best describes your area of work?

Government ☐   Public enterprise ☐

Private enterprise ☐   Academic or research
                           institution ☐

International organization ☐ Media ☐

Not-for-profit organization ☐ Other (specify) _____

3. In which country do you work? _____

4. What is your assessment of the contents of this publication?

Excellent ☐   Adequate ☐

Good ☐   Poor ☐

5. How useful is this publication to your work?

Very useful ☐   Of some use ☐   Irrelevant ☐

6. Please indicate the three things you liked best about this publication:

_____

_____

_____

7. Please indicate the three things you liked least about this publication:

_____

_____

_____

8. Are you a regular recipient of ***Transnational Corporations*** (formerly ***The CTC Reporter***), UNCTAD-DITE's tri-annual refereed journal?

Yes ☐ No ☐

If not, please check here if you would like to receive
a sample copy sent to the name and address you have
given above ☐

*